Writing a Great Movie

KEY TOOLS FOR SUCCESSFUL

SCREENWRITING

Jeff Kitchen

LONE EAGLE PUBLISHING COMPANY™

An imprint of Watson-Guptill Publications/New York

ACKNOWLEDGMENTS
I'd like to thank my wife, Hope Mineo, as well as
Bob Nirkind, Amy Dorta, Leah Lococo, Katherine Happ,
Rita Rosenkranz, Cheri Smith, Steven Dietz,
Bill Kitchen, Irving Fiske, and William Thompson Price.

Executive Editor: Bob Nirkind
Project Editor: Amy Dorta
Designer: Leah Lococo
Production Manager: Katherine Happ

First published in 2006 by Lone Eagle Publishing Company™
Waston-Guptill Publications, Nielsen Business Media, a division of The Nielsen Company
770 Broadway, New York, NY 10003
www.watsonguptill.com

ISBN-13: 978-0-8230-6978-1
ISBN-10: 0-8230-6978-8
Library of Congress Control Number: 2006923457

Printed in the U.S.A.
First printing, 2006
2 3 4 5 6 7 8 9 10

Table of Contents

CHAPTER 3

The 36 Dramatic Situations: Developing and Energizing Your Plot   50

CHAPTER 4

The Enneagram: Creating Deep, Complex, and Distinct Characters   89

CHAPTER 5

Research and Brainstorming: Exploring Possibilities
**   and Opening Up Your Story**

CHAPTER 6

The Central Proposition: Tying Your Plot Together
**   and Cranking Up the Conflict**

CHAPTER 7
**Sequence, Proposition, Plot: Constructing
and Tightening Your Plot** **150**

PART TWO: USING THE KEY TOOLS TO WRITE A GREAT MOVIE

CHAPTER 8

Using Dilemma, Crisis, Decision & Action, and Resolution   **191**

CHAPTER 9
Using Theme

CHAPTER 10
Using the 36 Dramatic Situations

CHAPTER 11
Using the Enneagram

INTRODUCTION

Why do screenwriters go to so much trouble writing a script? It all comes down to one word: audience. It's all about the audience. And for the audience, it's all about two words: GREAT MOVIE! This book is a practical manual on how to write a great movie. It will teach you the craft of the dramatist by focusing on a set of Key Tools for the screenwriter to use within the context of a complete working technique. Part One explains how each tool works and provides a short demonstration to help you understand its function, using a series of successful movies—*Training Day, What Women Want, Minority Report, The Godfather, Tootsie,* and *Blade Runner*—to illustrate. I recommend that you watch those six films carefully before reading this book, because knowing them thoroughly will help you learn and internalize these essential tools and techniques.

Part Two consists of the creation, development, and construction of an actual original screenplay, built from scratch. This will give you a clear picture of how to put the tools to use in your own scripts. Starting with an utterly raw idea, I build it up as demonstrated in Part One, with you watching over my shoulder as I wrestle the script into shape. The process is left as unvarnished as possible in order to show you what you must deal with as a writer—the problems, discoveries, wipeouts, eureka moments, puzzles, and black holes that constitute the daily grunt work of building a script. It is crucial to bridge the gap between understanding these tools and being able to apply them successfully to your own partially developed screenplays. Writers of every skill level can learn this material. My intention is to be as useful and practical as possible so that you can consistently write screenplays that *work*.

Writing a Great Movie focuses on seven Key Tools. These tools come from widely varying sources and are a mixture of classic structural principles and cutting-edge technique. Each tool is explored in one of the seven chapters of Part One, and then demonstrated in the seven chapters of Part Two. The first tool comes from Aristotle's observations about what tends to be common to those dramas that successfully grip an audience—*Dilemma, Crisis, Decision & Action,* and *Resolution.* The next tool, *Theme,* is connected to this first tool because the way in which the central character or protagonist resolves the dilemma expresses the theme of the script. The third is a powerful brainstorming tool known as the *36 Dramatic Situations*, which categorizes story-telling's raw elements—such as madness, disaster, ambition, and sacrifice—and helps trigger story possibilities and enliven your creative process. The *Enneagram* is a highly effective resource for creating and developing dynamic, complex, and realistic characters. This system of personality profiling combines ancient wisdom about human nature with modern psychology; it's great for doing character work. *Research and Brainstorming* are a fifth key part of the complete writing process. The *Central Proposition* adapts the logic of argumentation to dramatic writing, tying the parts of a script together into a coherent whole and enhancing the conflict. Finally, the three-step process called *Sequence, Proposition, Plot* is a remarkable tool for actually constructing the mechanics of the plot. It works with reverse cause and effect to tighten a script and keep it on track, as well as with a sophisticated process of conflict mapping that helps create and structure conflict to keep the audience on the edge of their seats.

Before we get into Part One, I'd like to share some useful insights born of my experience as a writer, script consultant, and dramatic writing teacher for many years. I was classically trained as a playwright in the technique of William Thompson Price, a turn-of-the-century teacher who founded the American School of Playwriting in New York City (the first school of dramatic writing in the history of the world) in 1901. Price took on twenty-eight students—twenty-four of whom went on to have hits on Broadway. I then worked in New York theater as a dramaturg and taught playwriting for several years. When I started teaching the art of screenwriting, I discovered that all the tools from playwriting are perfectly applicable. Good screenwriting is about making a story work dramatically: It has to be actable, and it has to grip the audience. In this book, I teach the craft of the dramatist—the art of dramatic plotting, which works on-screen as well as onstage. And when I talk about drama, I'm referring to all genres, because these tools and techniques work equally well for writing comedy, thriller, action, romantic comedy, horror, science fiction, or what we know as "drama." Whether you're writing a nutball comedy or a bone-crunching thriller, your screenplay has to work dramatically.

IT'S ALL ABOUT THE AUDIENCE

When you go into a movie with major expectations, what *specifically* do you expect? You've heard that this movie will rock your world, and you're excited. But can you put your finger on exactly what you expect from it? Obviously, this will vary with different genres—you expect one thing from an intense drama, something else from a romantic comedy, and yet something else from an action thriller. Examine your expectations as closely as possible. Remember, it's your job as a screenwriter to satisfy audience expectations.

Anyone who has performed live knows intimately that it's all about the audience. Some screenwriters who sit in their rooms concocting wild stories aren't necessarily trained to think in terms of the audience. But that's what this medium is all about: It's a performance medium intended to transform an audience. A movie playing to an empty theater has no power at all—it's just shadows on the wall. The power of the film resides in the response of the audience.

I urge you to make a professional study of the audience—*your* audience. First, pay attention to the buzz about an upcoming film. Why do people want to see it? Are they electrified or just curious? One a scale of 1 to 10, how intense are their expectations? Next, study audiences as you're entering the movie theater. Examine your own expectations as you go in. Gauge the electricity in the air. While the movie plays, feel out the audience response. Are they thrilled? Scared? Let down? Intoxicated? Bored? Exhilarated? Then, when the movie's over, stand outside the theater and watch the audience exit. Study the expressions on their faces. Listen in on their reactions. Be passionately curious about how your fellow moviegoers react to the movie you've just seen together.

When *Star Wars I: The Phantom Menace* came out in 1999, people camped out at Graumann's Chinese Theatre six weeks in advance. On opening night I joined them, specifically in order to study audience expectations. I interviewed the fans, asking, "What are you expecting?" They were pumped! I got answers like, "Oh man, I saw the first *Star Wars* when I was seven and it was the greatest movie ever! I'm expecting a ride to the moon!" When the theater let the first couple hundred people enter, they ran inside screaming, jumping, and whooping it up. Those fans *really* had it—that intense audience expectation—and I wanted to stick my finger in that electric socket. Director Billy Wilder said, "I never overestimate the audience, nor do I underestimate them. I just have a very rational idea as to who we're dealing with, and that we're not making a picture for Harvard Law School, we're making a picture for middle-class people, the people that you see on the subway, or the people that you see in a restaurant. Just normal people."

Study your own reactions. Be your own guinea pig. You're an audience member, too, and you can see right into your own deepest responses. Observe your body chemistry afterward. Are you tripping on adrenaline? Is your gut churning? Are you in a state of shock? Examine your mood. Are you giddy and in love? Do you feel energized, infatuated, distressed, inert, crazed, pissed off, silly, serious, demonic, transfigured? Did the movie match up to your expectations? Think about how you feel when you come out of a truly great film. Consider the various levels of exhilaration, satisfaction, passion, adrenaline, happiness, clarity, fury, energy, or love that you're feeling. As a screenwriter, this is how you want your audience to feel.

The Writer Sculpts the Mood of the Audience

When writing your screenplay, it's essential to ask yourself, "How do I want my audience to feel at the end of my movie?" As the dramatist, you're sculpting the mood in which viewers leave the theater. What mood do you want them to be in? It's like a magic spell or hypnosis, where it all comes together at the end: "When I snap my fingers, you will feel light and refreshed." The more specifically you can pinpoint the mood you intend for the audience, the clearer your focus will be as you write. Bear in mind that it's not an intellectual transformation but an *emotional* one—and there's a huge difference.

I experienced this several years ago after a friend saw the band The Moody Blues. He was in a fabulous mood, and he wanted to pass it on. He told me how phenomenal the show was and how I had to see it the next night. Now, I'd had my fill of that band years before, so I wasn't getting fired up or even pretending very well. My friend became frustrated and said, "No, you're not *getting* it!" He had something inside him that he really wanted me to have. This is what I'm talking about. What do you have in you that you really want to transfer to your audience? What are you trying to do to them? Identify this, and you will see more clearly your intention for the entire movie.

What Do We Hunger For in Movies?

As you walk past the people lined up around the block for a movie, look each one of them in the eye and ask (in your mind), "Why are you here? What do you want from this movie? What are you hungering for? What are your hopes, your dreams, your ambitions, your desires?" Moviegoers are there to get something special. Observe them with the passionate curiosity of a writer, a scientist, a student of human nature, and a fellow moviegoer. Try to get an ever deeper and more complex—but also a clearer and simpler—understanding of the audience. Consider it part of your job, because the audience is who you write for. You're not writing for readers, agents, studio executives, directors, or actors. You're writing for each and every person who enters a theater and wants to see a great movie.

Another good question is, "What's special about a great movie?" Simple enough to ask, but these days it's literally the $64 million question. If everyone knew what was special about a great movie, then each movie you see would be the best movie yet made. Certain movies have a "magic something," and it's your job as a screenwriter to get that magic something into the script. The more you can put your finger on it, the more you'll be able to recognize it when you stumble upon it—or to create it purposefully.

"Why do I love movies?" is yet another good question to ask yourself. Your initial answer may be simple enough, but contemplating it over the years will reveal deeper and deeper levels of understanding. What *are* these bizarre things called "movies"? Why do we love them? What hunger do they satisfy? It's interesting to think about the movies that stay with you, to look back at scenes you'll never forget, and to remember the first time you saw one of your favorite movies. Sit down and make a list of the movies that changed your life, gave you a new outlook, or awakened something in you. Think about why these films had this effect and try to articulate what they did for you.

And then there's the question, "In real life, what transports me?" What sends you over the moon? What puts you in a wildly altered state? To be truly *transported* is an astounding experience. It is to be swept into a different dimension, to be taken to an exalted place, to feel an energetic freedom. Look at the absolute peak experiences in your own life—the ones you can count on one hand, the ones that stand out far above all the others. If you can isolate one of those times, examine the confluence of powerful emotions surrounding it—the intensity, the exhilaration, or the pain. Why will you never forget it? Bring this level of intensity to your writing and it will help you create a great movie. The audience wants your movie to be one of the peak experiences of *their* lives. You're working with the elements of magic and transformation, of rekindling dreams and changing perceptions. Throughout history, the story-teller has traditionally been a bringer of fire, of life, energy, healing, freedom, fun, action, insight, beauty, intensity, focus, and clarity. As a screenwriter, *you* are the storyteller, and you have a wonderful job: bringing powerful transfor-mative energy and a full spectrum of emotions into people's lives.

The Stage and the Altar

Throughout much of history, the stage and the altar were the same thing. The altar *was* a stage, with religious dramas enacted upon it. Generally these dra-mas were about the transformation of the hero and were for the benefit of those gathered there—the audience. From its earliest days drama has served a shamanistic function: to show those watching how to transform themselves. People seek guidance in getting through life's transitions: moving from child-hood into adulthood, entering a marriage or dissolving one, having children, dealing with success or failure, growing old, and facing death, among many others. Think about the great movies that have pointed you in a direction or helped you understand something key about yourself or about the world. At the end of the award-winning film about his life, the character of Gandhi says, "I can show you a way out of hell." It may sound strange to think of movies having a religious function, but transforming an audience certainly can lead to a type of fundamental awakening.

Dr. Martin Luther King, Jr., believed that a powerful emotional experi-ence can be the first step on the road to commitment. Sometimes a great film does just that: It provides an emotional release, an opportunity for conversion or renewal. Comedy can transform an audience as well, and clowns find their ancestry in priests—truth seekers and fountains of creativity. Laughter is very transformative—it clears the air and can open your eyes to new possibilities. Many comedians, knowing how crucial it is to laugh at life, take their jobs very seriously. As Groucho Marx once noted, "They'll never know how necessary our insanity is to their sanity."

Audience Demand

People expect a lot from movies. *Audience demand* is important to understand because it is so powerful, and it's your job as the writer to satisfy it—even if the audience itself is unaware of it. It's like a river that looks lazy on the surface but hides a fierce undercurrent. An excellent way to get in touch with audience demand is to remember the last time someone told you that a particular movie would rock your world and change your life. But when you went to see the movie, you found it really disappointing. Look at your reaction. It wasn't, "Oh, too bad, it was lame." It was more like, "Damn it! I didn't get what I was promised, and I'm mad. I *needed* that!" The mark of a great artist is often that he or she gives the audience what it wants—even if the audience itself doesn't know what it wants. So penetrate into what audiences want and demand—that's your bread and butter. Locating it is like digging below the street, finding the giant electric line that powers the whole city, and tapping into that power. Audiences bring a lot of energy to the theater and if you can tap into it, then it will multiply the power of your movie.

Why does an audience bring such a powerful set of demands to a movie? Because in real life, our demands often go unmet. Notice in your own life the myriad demands that you place on your friends, your spouse, your parents, your children, your neighbors, and your politicians. Look at the demands placed on you in your own life. How many are likely to or can ever be met?

Movies are an arena in which magical things can happen, and that's part of their enchantment—the things that could never happen in real life *can* happen in film and theater, even if only for a few special hours. Many of us have what could be called "chronic avoidance": We tiptoe around tricky or worrisome issues. We agree to unspoken contracts so that certain issues will not be broached. This pressure builds into a tremendous hunger for resolution, and then if someone *does* tackle the issue it may blow up in his or her face, making the problem a thousand times worse—and still leaving it unresolved. The hunger for resolution is still active. People naturally seek closure and meaning in life—sometimes a film can provide this if "real life" cannot.

Another important question to ask yourself is, "How do I intend to penetrate the indifference of the audience?" Today's audiences are very jaded. From their point of view, they've seen it all and they know it all. This isn't true, of course, but the feeling is genuine nonetheless. Plus, anyone entering into a new experience will tend to arrive with a certain degree of insulation. This is natural, but it's something you must overcome to get through to your audience. Compare it to an electrician stripping the rubber coating off a wire to get a live connection.

Drama is often compared to a crucible. In chemistry a crucible is a ceramic pot used to contain a potent chemical, or in steelmaking it's the container that holds the molten steel. Consider the drama as a crucible in which we can experiment with powerful situations, explosive reactions, radical solutions, and forbidden ideas. People often need drastic changes in their lives, but experimenting can be risky. If your marriage is falling apart, you don't just try a radical solution because if it doesn't work, then there goes the rest of your marriage. But you can watch a movie or a play that broaches the subject and thereby get a feel for how it might work for you at home. The movies are a "let's pretend" arena—we can engage in an experiment from a safe distance. We can put out our feelers or perform a taste test to see how it might work in our own life. Some of the best medicines are poisons in the right dosage. In the same way, insights derived from films, when properly used in real life, can liberate people. The healing power of art is continually sought after. It has always been a central part of civilization itself.

Transforming the Audience

A dramatist is a bull in a china shop, going after the sacred cows, going where it's *verboten*. That's part of the fun! The key word in the entertainment industry is *outrageousness*. According to the writer Salman Rushdie, "One of the things a writer is for is to say the unsayable, speak the unspeakable, and ask difficult questions." Your job as a screenwriter is a cross between a bomb maker and a poet: You're blowing up ideas with language. The audience seeks a profound transformative experience, so as a dramatist you're working with elements of great change, cataclysmic transformation, and powerful resolution. It's a chance to really rewire the brains of the audience—to permanently change the way they think—and the audience is up for that. People come to the theater, open their minds, and say, "Come on. Do something, anything. Let's party. I need change."

Catharsis is an emotional release, a fresh start. Aristotle describes it as a cleansing of the undesirable emotions, a purging of the system. Think about how a great movie can make you feel energized or inspired. Sometimes you just need to burn off the normal day-to-day banter rattling around your brain. David Mamet, in *Three Uses of the Knife* (New York: Vintage Books, 1998), says, "The purpose of theater, like magic, like religion—those three harness mates—is to inspire cleansing awe." Catharsis is like an oil change, and it brings up the question, "What do you periodically need to have cleaned out of your system?" Behavioral scientists have proven that people need to change states at least once a day. People come home, have a beer, go jogging, or go to the movies to shift into a different state. The ability to consciously change emotional gears is a vital part of staying sane and happy in a high-pressure world.

This book teaches classic structural technique for the dramatist—the time-tested structures of which most successful plots consist. It's a good thing to have under your belt. You won't want to rely on it for everything, but in my experience it will cover about 85 percent of the scripts you work on. Actor, writer, and director Tim Robbins said in an interview:

> I respect the classical form of film and storytelling. I've done experimental, absurdist and Dadaistic theater and there are ways to incorporate those styles into storytelling, but you've got to go to the classical structure of storytelling. I don't believe in indulgence for the sake of indulgence. I believe in the audience. I think they're central to what we're doing. That's why we're doing it. I'm always aware that an audience will be watching this. I don't want to get too esoteric or intellectual with something I'm doing because it really is entertainment we're doing.

My playwriting teacher, Irving Fiske, who translated *Hamlet* into modern American English in 1946, says in his Introduction, "The profoundest hunger of the modern audience is not for an escape from reality, as is commonly thought, but for an escape *into* reality from much of the meaninglessness of their everyday lives." Certainly, escape from reality is a perfectly valid form of entertainment, but escape into reality is a much more powerful concept. A solid jolt of reality can connect an audience with what really matters to them in their lives.

THE CRAFT OF THE DRAMATIST

A big part of your job as a screenwriter is to dramatize your script. To *dramatize* a story means to make it gripping to an audience by creating continuous, coherent, compelling action. Essentially what we're talking about is turning mere Story into Drama. *Story* means that the material is flat dramatically or is simply information, which doesn't succeed in building the tension to grip an audience.

The following narrative is an example of mere Story: Joey wakes up in the morning, has some orange juice, ties his shoes, and walks his dog. This is merely a succession of events, and isn't compelling to an audience. There's a huge difference between narrative and drama. This book teaches the habits of mind of a trained dramatist, and part of your job as a dramatist is to recognize mere Story when you see it—and to be able to dramatize it. It's much like turning water into wine.

Turning Story into Drama

You want your whole script to be *Drama* and not simply Story. You want each act to be dramatic and not just narrative, engaging and not merely informative. The same goes for each sequence, and for each scene. You never want to revert to mere Story. How do you avoid this? The short answer is: this book. There's no one magic button you can push to turn Story into Drama, but the skilled combination of all the tools and techniques in *Writing a Great Movie* can render every part of your script dramatic.

While a good story is definitely the basis of your script, it is not enough. You need life in your script, but mere life is not enough either. You need character, but mere character is not enough, and you need action, but mere action is not enough. There's an important distinction here: You need storytelling skills as big as you can get them. You need imagination, a sense of adventure and fun, an ability to weave a story together and to spellbind an audience—and you need all these things as big as you can get them. Bear in mind that when applied to bland material, even the most advanced dramatic structure tools simply won't work. Well-structured junk is still just junk. It may run like a Formula One race car, but without great story material, it's still not a movie that anyone will pay to see. To compete as a screenwriter you need a healthy and vigorous imagination. It is hard to stress this enough. But however creative your story is, it still has to be actable and it has to grip an audience if it's going to work in this performance medium.

One of the single biggest misconceptions in the film industry is that a good story automatically makes a good film. There are many excellent novels that don't lend themselves to the movie medium. There's a saying in theater: "It may sound great around a campfire but it's not stageworthy." (Yes, it's a good story, but we can't act it out on stage in a way that will grab an audience.) Your script must be compelling, so that at the high point of suspense, you couldn't pay the audience to leave—they simply must stay and see how it turns out.

Creating Dramatic Action

Your job as a screenwriter is essentially to create *Dramatic Action*. To keep moviegoers on the edge of their seats and engage them emotionally, your script must build intensity, and be alive and gripping. The concept of Dramatic Action is not car chases and shoot-outs, but a state of subjective excitement that a movie creates among the audience. You've probably seen movies in which half the world is being blown up—yet again—and you're nodding off in your seat, while you've seen movies with two people arguing in a living room and you're riveted. Only in the latter are you truly in a state of Dramatic Action.

It's generally acknowledged that 90 to 95 percent of all scripts submitted in both film and theater are atrocious. ("Don't kid yourself," I often hear, "it's 95 percent." Script readers at Hollywood studios tell me it's even 98 percent!) And atrocious is not just a figure of speech: These scripts are unreadable. This means only 2 to 5 percent of all scripts submitted are even worth reading. Is it surprising, then, how many mediocre movies get made? Writing a screenplay is much harder than most people imagine. So what is the problem? Many screenwriters are intelligent and have good stories to tell, but they have yet to grasp the craft of the dramatist. What they're missing may be the riveting power of Dramatic Action.

Creating Unity of Action

Aristotle noticed that those dramas which grip an audience tend to consist of one complete action. He says this in the *Poetics* (New York: Farrar, Strauss and Giroux, LLC, 1961):

> . . . so the plot, being an imitation of an action, must imitate one action and that a whole, the structural union of the parts being such that, if any one of them is displaced or removed, the whole will be disjointed and disturbed. For a thing whose presence or absence makes no visible difference, is not an organic part of the whole.

The ability to locate one main action at the core of a script can help unify it. Look, for instance, at a script as complex as The Godfather. There is one main action at its heart: Michael defeats Don Barzini and saves the Corleone family. Can you find the one main action that constitutes the heart of your script? Aristotle talks about it as the telling of a deed—a hero's deed. Is there one main deed that your hero performs? You've got roughly a two-hour window in which to tell your story, and this length is rather inflexible unless you're successful enough to be allowed a three-hour film. That limit on your time forces you to focus your resources. It's like being in a fight where you only get one punch—you really have to make it count. Find the main action of your script and build everything around it. The tools presented in this book will guide you through doing just that.

Unity of Action is a concept not well understood in either the film or theater industries, but this simple definition has held up well for me over the years:

1. A Single Action
2. A Single Hero
3. A Single Result

You have one main action happening, one central person doing it, and one result springing from it. All the elements of the film serve the one main action, and the script revolves around it. A good example of Unity of Action is a symphony: Each instrument does different things, but they all work together as an orchestra to create one piece of music. In the military and in sports, everyone has their own tasks but they're all working toward the achievement of one goal. In drama, too, we're talking about powerful ideas operating together as a unit to achieve a specific goal—structural unity and coherence. If it's not part of the one main action, then it doesn't belong in the script.

Getting Down to the Core of Your Script

Part of the definition of dramatic writing is that it's a fight to the finish. The old saying goes: Conflict is to drama as sound is to music. Conflict creates suspense, so it is central to what makes a story compelling to an audience. A *fight to the finish* is two people in a knock-down, drag-out fight and only one of them will walk away. It's two dogs fighting over a bone. This is true whether the struggle is over the fate of the world in a thriller or over where to go on the family's Christmas vacation in a romantic comedy.

In the earliest Greek theater, only two characters were onstage—the introduction of a third character by Sophocles was considered a major dramatic innovation. Seeing two main characters in conflict helps you get down to the absolute core of your material. Strip it down to protagonist versus antagonist, and you're at the nucleus of your plot. If this works, then the rest of your script has a good shot at working. If it doesn't, then whatever you add to the plot probably won't help.

Engineering Your Screenplay Before You Write It

William Thompson Price recommends taking all the energy that goes into rewrites and using it to engineer your screenplay properly *before* you write it. Doing the work up front is what *Writing a Great Movie* is all about. This book will show you how to build a script—how to create, develop, and construct a dramatic plot in any genre. It's a lot of work—but so is doing twenty rewrites. Here's what David Mamet has to say on the subject in his book *On Directing Film* (New York: Penguin Books, 1991):

> It's very difficult to shore up something that has been done
> badly. You'd better do your planning up front, when you

have the time. It's like working with glue. When it sets, you've used up your time. When it's almost set, you then have to make quick decisions under pressure. If you design a chair correctly, you can put all the time into designing it correctly and assemble it at your leisure.

Dramatic Writing: An Elusive Art

Dramatic writing is generally considered the most elusive of all the literary disciplines. It's hard to pin down; it's slippery, thorny, and unpredictable. Why does something look good on paper but fail on-screen? Why does a script work most of the way through but then fall apart? How does a movie with big money and all the top people lose a bundle on its opening weekend, while the same basic story shot for a pittance goes on to make a fortune? Even the winners and losers in this scenario may not know. Dramatic writing is mysterious, and it can be a gamble.

Writing a script is much like building a car from scratch: You're literally manufacturing the entire vehicle from the ground up, building tires out of rubber, stretching out your own brake lines, and building your own carburetor. You'll end up with a vehicle, but it may not run. There could be a number of compound, complex problems, and fixing any one of them still doesn't make the damn thing run. Just like this car, a screenplay may never work no matter what you do, and you may never know why.

I urge you to use the Key Tools introduced in Part One as precisely as possible. These tools and techniques cut through the native elusiveness of dramatic writing. They give you a set of talons that will grab on to this slippery thing and make it do what you need it to do. They create certain distinctions that are central to the craft of a dramatist and should not be muddied just because at times they seem inconvenient. As William Thompson Price says in his book *The Philosophy of Dramatic Principle and Method* (New York: W.T. Price Pub., 1912), "In dividing the drama into distinct principles or elements we get at the function of each. By this means we are enabled to make an implement of a principle. We do not confound the uses of each." With *Writing a Great Movie*, you can train yourself in the craft of dramatic writing with the appropriate use of the Key Tools. Adopt the habits of mind of a trained dramatist, and you will learn to think in ways that will help your stories work.

Even as classic structural technique becomes second nature to you, it's important to note that literally *anything* can work. And either it works or it doesn't. A movie is two hours of entertainment—period. It can be someone shouting at a wall for two hours, and if viewers line up around the block for six months to see it, then it works. So learn the craft, but don't limit yourself in how you apply it. And don't worship it. As an artist, you will should become the master of these tools, not their servant. The hammer and saw don't dictate how the house will look—the builder does. Solid skills will help you be consistent as a writer, enabling you to successfully tackle a broad spectrum of plots and genres. Bear in mind, too, that precision of technique doesn't negate the need for deep intuition, heartfelt passion, explosive creativity, and dynamic storytelling. If you combine these crucial elements with substantial craft as a dramatist, then you can assemble the complete package of a solid professional screenwriter—and that is rare indeed.

Principle and Method

This book teaches you to understand first *principle* and then *method*. Certain principles tend to make drama work, and certain methods embody those principles. Essentially, the principle becomes an implement. The more you understand the principle behind a tool, the more you understand its function, and the more you can adapt the tool as needed. In learning how to fly an airplane, it's not enough to know which buttons to push at what time. You must understand the principles of flight, and your understanding will inform your application of method. Then, since you know what happens to the vacuum above the wings, you'll know *why* you're pushing this particular button at this time. In acupuncture, too, there are certain principles—balancing meridians and opening flow—and there are certain methods that abide by those principles—systems of exactly where to put the needles and for how long. In the same way, your understanding of the principles of drama informs your application of the methods. Some of my students understand the underlying principles but can't grasp the actual techniques, and that only gets them so far. Others use the tools well but don't know why, and that's working blindly. You want to know both principle and method, inside and out.

Through teaching these tools for so long and using them hands-on with each student, I've acquired more and more expertise in the complete working process. A friend who is a martial arts teacher says that because teaching has forced him to stick to the basics, it has solidified his foundation as a martial artist in a profound way. He has realized that these basics are first principles for good reason. David Mamet talks about this in *On Directing Film*:

> It's good, as the Stoics tell us, to have tools that are simple
> to understand and of a very limited number—so that we may
> locate and employ them on a moment's notice. I think the
> essential tools in any worthwhile endeavor are incredibly
> simple. And very difficult to master. The task of any artist is
> not to learn many, many techniques but to learn the most
> simple technique perfectly. In doing so, Stanislavski told us,

the difficult will become easy and the easy habitual, so that
the habitual may become beautiful.

It would be easy to flit from one how-to book on screenwriting to another, never putting in the hard work to *really* learn the material, but rather hoping blindly that the next book will magically make it all effortless. This will never happen because writing is always hard, whether you're an absolute beginner or one of the top scriptwriters in the business. However, if you put in the time to gain a substantial mastery of the Key Tools presented in this book, both the principles and the methods, you will emerge with the habits and skills of a trained dramatist—and then your scripts will consistently tend to work.

Storytelling

As a screenwriter, you must pay attention to storytelling—that's the center of the whole process. As a dramatist you must be able to shape the story so that it can by acted in a way that grips the audience, but if the story is lame then the drama will be lame. You can't turn bad grapes into great wine.

Study the best storytellers; steep yourself in them. Read all the time, listen to books on tape, see live theater. Find stories from different cultures and let them all inspire you, light you up, jump-start your imagination, and ignite you with their incredible amperage and magnitude. Refuse to be second-rate. Boil with creative energy. Get crazy. Go wild. Free your mind. Get outside your normal storytelling ruts. Explosive creativity is crucial—tap into it. Don't ever let anybody order you to "stick to what you know" as the sole source for your stories. Astonish audiences. Blow their minds so they'll never think the same way again. Shake up their worlds, shake them awake, shatter their sense of how things are and how they must be. Violate their secure little places as observers. Lift them out of their seats and plunge them into a world of greatness, a world of exuberant passion, exploding adrenaline, ecstatic freedom, untamed savagery, absolute fun, true love, boundless energy, and indomitable spirit.

Think again about how the greatest movies you've ever seen have transfigured you. Reflect upon how you felt as you watched them, how you felt afterward, how you longed for that lift, that energy, that greatness of heart. Remember how you felt walking out of such classics as *The Shawshank Redemption, Braveheart, Raiders of the Lost Ark, Body Heat, Pulp Fiction, The Usual Suspects, The Big Lebowski, Howl's Moving Castle, Blade Runner, Ordinary People, American Beauty, Psycho, Strictly Ballroom, The French Connection, The Lord of the Rings, Gandhi, Rashomon, The Sting, sex, lies, and videotape, The Terminator, Duck Soup, 12 Angry Men, The Bourne Identity, Jerry Maguire, Driving Miss Daisy, L'Age d'Or, One Flew Over the Cuckoo's Nest, The King of Hearts, The Producers, Reds, Lawrence of Arabia, Das Boot, Chinatown, Amadeus,*

Cool Hand Luke, On the Waterfront, The Burmese Harp, M*A*S*H, Back to the Future, Platoon, The Fugitive, Casablanca, Bad Boy Bubby, Regarding Henry, The Seven Samurai, Dances With Wolves, Lethal Weapon, The Hustler, Twelve Monkeys, The Last Emperor, and *In the Heat of the Night*—to name only a handful. Certain films have left an indelible mark on you, on your soul, on your entire life. Do you remember the last time you were absolutely lit up, totally energized, utterly alive? People need that thrill the same way they need oxygen—so many people just limp though life much of the time. The original storytellers were shamans, and their responsibility was freeing people to experience the present fully, awakening people so they could truly *live*. The storytellers of today should strive to do the same.

Ask everybody you know who their favorite writers are, and why, and what those authors do to them. Listen to how your friends talk; watch them as they relive their pleasure, fear, energy, exuberance, adrenaline, and fun. Then go out and read their suggestions. Put a book by your bedside table or on your treadmill. Listen to a book on tape as you drive to work (they're free at the library). Turn off mindless television and work—really work—to be one of the top storytellers in the world, in the history of the world. If you're a screenwriter, then this is your job! People are starving for great stories, and something inside you is screaming to give it to them—otherwise you wouldn't be a writer. If you're going to do it, then be the best. Stun them, stagger them, and transfigure them with your storytelling passion.

Writing a Great Movie is a manual of successful plot creation, development, and construction. I sincerely hope you can add these dependable tools to your screenwriter's toolkit, not displacing other techniques but complementing them and rounding out your abilities as a dramatist. Since this book's primary focus is on structural technique, it does not go into much depth on highly specialized elements such as dialog—a separate topic that would require an entire volume of its own. Remember that to maximize your comprehension of the Key Tools, you should have a real familiarity with the films *Training Day, What Women Want, Minority Report, The Godfather, Tootsie,* and *Blade Runner*, which are explored extensively to illustrate the tools in action. Best of luck with your writing, and please, *knock my socks off at the movies!* That's what it's all about.

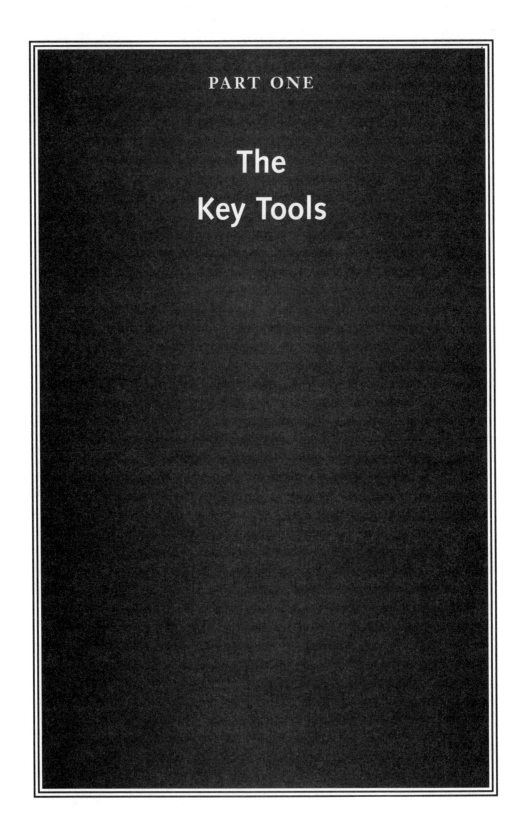

PART ONE

The
Key Tools

Dilemma, Crisis, Decision & Action, and Resolution: Dramatizing a Plot

T wenty-five hundred years ago, the Greek philosopher Aristotle made some astute observations about the nature of drama, using his native Athens as a laboratory. His observations were based on an annual religious theater festival. Each year only one topic would be assigned to all the playwrights. (This would be akin to requiring every filmmaker presenting a new movie at this year's Sundance Film Festival to focus on, say, the Kennedy assassination.) With this one variable intact, Aristotle had the chance to compare and contrast the plays in very specific ways, and he perceived that while some put the audience to sleep, others were thoroughly absorbing. He wondered, "Is there anything in common among those plays that grip an audience?" Studying them, he found that, in fact, they did tend to have in common several elements: Dilemma, Crisis, Decision & Action, and Resolution.

These elements are simply the products of Aristotle's observations, and are neither rules nor dogma nor laws. He was not a dramatist—he never wrote a play that we know of. Sophocles, Euripides, and Aeschylus did not study with him; in truth it was he who studied them.

THE FUNCTION OF DILEMMA IN DRAMATIZING A PLOT

Dilemma may be defined as "a situation with a choice to be made in which neither alternative is acceptable." Two equally unacceptable alternatives—two equally painful choices. The story of someone trapped in a challenging dilemma can be riveting. Let's invent a scenario of two equally bad options. Our character's brother needs a life-or-death operation that costs serious money.

But all the cash our character has is earmarked to finally turn his barely surviving business into a success and to make a down payment on a new home, thus saving his marriage and removing his kids from a dangerous neighborhood. Neither option is good because each is at odds with the other. Forced to choose between sacrificing himself or sacrificing a loved one, our character finds himself paralyzed, unable to make a choice. This is a dilemma to lose sleep over.

Damned If You Do and Damned If You Don't

Two equally unacceptable alternatives. Caught between the devil and the deep blue sea. Kill or be killed. You can't hang on and you can't let go. Trapped between a rock and a hard place. A solid dilemma of this sort can *always* improve the plot. As I've learned from working hands-on with thousands of screenwriters and playwrights over the years, a writer may come in with a well-plotted story, but creating a new dilemma or strengthening an existing one will invariably improve the material.

Essentially, there is either a dilemma inherent in a plot or there is not. If there *is*, then it should be identified, built upon, and complicated in ways that add substantial dimensions to the script. If there *is not*, then we can experiment with the possibility of creating one. We develop a set of intriguing possibilities to heighten Dramatic Action, thereby engaging the audience in the character's fate. A dilemma places the protagonist in a more complex and compelling situation. This in turn makes the actor's role a meatier one, which attracts top actors looking for substance, depth, complexity, and challenge.

An excellent example of a dilemma can be found in the 1956 science-fiction film *Forbidden Planet*. Commander Adams (Leslie Nielsen) has traveled to a shipwrecked space colony to check for survivors and finds only two: the scientist, Morbius (Walter Pidgeon), and his daughter, Altaira (Anne Francis). Morbius has used alien technology found inside the planet to build Robby the Robot, a very sophisticated machine. While demonstrating Robby for Commander Adams, Morbius has Adams give Robby his ray gun. Morbius then orders Robby to point the gun at Commander Adams, who's getting pretty nervous. Morbius orders Robby to fire, but the robot begins to short-circuit instead. Arcing electricity, he's frozen in place. Morbius explains that Robby is caught in a dilemma. On one hand he's been programmed never to disobey Morbius's orders, but on the other hand he's been programmed never to harm a human being. If Morbius leaves Robby in this dilemma he'll melt down, so he releases him from the command. This is a revealing look at how someone acts when they're trapped in a good, strong dilemma.

To create a dilemma, you want your protagonist to "short-circuit" like this—frozen between two terrible choices. Note the important distinction here: Your character is generally not literally hiding at home under the covers, but rather is stuck internally and perhaps limping through life, trapped by the powerful circumstances that you've created.

Trapping a character in a dilemma is much like cornering a wild animal. A cornered animal can be very dangerous, capable of phenomenal acts such as jumping long distances or attacking with astonishing strength. Your characters can do similar things when backed into a tight corner, and this can be spell-binding on-screen. Think about when you've been horribly trapped and remember that desperate, tormented feeling. Notice it the next time it happens and study it as a dramatist.

Look at the characters in your scripts as though they were animals. Animals demonstrate naked behavior. They don't rationalize why they're trying to kill anyone who invades their territory—they just do it. Characters can have similar instincts beneath their complicated social behavior. Look at your protagonist and antagonist as two fierce lions fighting over a carcass, two great apes in combat, or a mother bear protecting her young from a predator. Seek out the core of a character beneath all the human reasoning and clever rationalizations.

A Dilemma of Magnitude

A potent dilemma is important—a dilemma of *magnitude*. Magnitude implies significance. Is it significant to an audience? Look at the difference between the films *The Shawshank Redemption* and *Dumb and Dumber*. This is not a value judgment, because *Dumb and Dumber* was funny as hell, but *The Shawshank Redemption* is a film of more magnitude, more substance. Your goal should be to construct a dilemma of substance. You may have two bad options, but without significance to an audience—for example, it's unacceptable to clean the house and equally unacceptable to wash the car—it has no magnitude. It won't rivet an audience unless it passes the "So what?" test.

The "So what?" test can challenge anything that tries to work its way into your script. Harry Cohn, the founder of Columbia Pictures, ran his development process as follows: He would sit his writers down at a conference table and ask for their ideas. The first writer would lay out his idea and Cohn would respond, "So what?" The next writer would pitch his idea and Cohn would shoot it down the same way. An idea had to pass Cohn's "So what?" test before he was willing to pursue it.

A dilemma of magnitude must pass the "So what?" test. Even in comedy, the protagonist will generally take the dilemma seriously him- or herself, even though it's hilarious to the audience—in fact, the worse it is for him or her, the funnier it is for us. Take Jim Carrey's comedic dilemma in *Bruce Almighty*, where his character temporarily becomes God: It's unacceptable to give up being God because he has all these awesome powers, but it's equally unacceptable to continue being God because he's in over his head. The more things spiral out of control, the more hilarious it is for the audience. Once you get a dilemma up and running, then you should experiment with magnitude. Is your dilemma as significant, as potent as it could be? Does it hit the audience members where it hurts? Does it resonate in each of their own lives? How much more intense could you possibly make this dilemma? Be extremely tough on your own material—everybody else is certainly going to be.

A Sense of Proportion

It's also important to have a sense of proportion in terms of where to use dilemma in your screenplay. A dilemma should kick in after some "set-up time," which enables the audience to get to know and care about the character—about a quarter to a third of the way into a script, when the plot has begun to develop. Once you identify with a character, you are essentially pretending to be that person, so the dilemma will hit you with more force.

The following diagram represents an approximate line of proportion for an entire script:

The first triangle indicates roughly where the Dilemma tends to kick in. The Dilemma will build in intensity until it reaches the make-or-break point of the Crisis (the second triangle). This Crisis requires an immediate Decision & Action (the third triangle), and then the plot is essentially wrapped up by the Resolution (the fourth triangle). Denouement is the last bit of the story after Resolution. It is the aftermath, the epilog, the upshot—also known as the "new equilibrium." It's usually the last minute or two of the film, such as Jake going home in *Training Day* or Michael's men kissing his ring as the door is shut on Kay in *The Godfather.* Bear in mind that this is just an estimated sense of proportion; it does not indicate specific pages where the elements will necessarily be found.

One good, strong dilemma can carry a whole film. Once your protagonist becomes trapped in it, the dilemma can build in intensity until the crisis point forces decision and action. The dilemma is finally resolved at the point of resolution (essentially the film's ending). In other words, one central dilemma can form the *engine* of a drama.

The Use of Dilemma in *Training Day*

In *Training Day* (2001), rookie undercover cop Jake Hoyt (Ethan Hawke) is caught in an intense dilemma when grizzled veteran Alonzo Harris (Denzel Washington) offers him a devil's choice between results and morality. Jake is in awe of Alonzo, a legendary undercover cop. Deeply ambitious, Jake has a shot at joining Alonzo's elite undercover narcotics squad, but Alonzo is dragging him down a slippery ethical slope. Although nothing will make Jake relinquish this incredible opportunity, his dilemma begins in earnest when Alonzo makes him smoke PCP. Alonzo's also got him robbing drug dealers, and being party to murder and armed robbery—all the while explaining that this is the only way an undercover narcotics cop can get real results. In essence, Jake's guru is also his worst enemy. He's damned if he goes along with Alonzo and damned if he doesn't. He can either bend the law to take down the bad guys or go back to being a "patrol fairy" (a regular cop). Jake is trapped, and this trap is what the movie is about. *Training Day*'s dilemma is that while it's unacceptable for Jake to lose this opportunity to be an undercover cop with a heavy hitter like Alonzo, it's equally unacceptable for him to be dragged by Alonzo into tactics of increasingly questionable morality.

Once Jake becomes trapped in his dilemma, he is truly paralyzed by it all the way through to the make-or-break point: when Jake discovers that Alonzo has tried to have him murdered by the Latino gang. Jake goes to arrest Alonzo, and while he is no longer paralyzed by the dilemma, he's still got a tough fight on his hands to fully extricate himself from it. He finally frees himself from the dilemma when he beats Alonzo, takes the money as evidence, and leaves him to his fate. The dilemma carries the film—it's what the movie is all about.

The Use of Dilemma in *What Women Want*

In *What Women Want* (2000), Nick Marshall (Mel Gibson)—a "man's man" at the top of his game in the advertising world—finds himself edged out of his dream job by a woman, Darcy Maguire (Helen Hunt), whom he's determined to drive out by hook or by crook. When he unexpectedly finds he has the ability to hear what the women around him are thinking, he realizes it is the perfect way to get rid of Darcy. He steals her ideas and undermines her by listening in on her thoughts. But Nick discovers that Darcy is not only a true genius in advertising but also an incredible person. The more he sees into her with his mind-reading ability, the more he finds that she is a magnificent creature: talented, sexy, stylish, and totally honest. Although he can't let go of his need for revenge, it's equally hard to "kill her off," so to speak. He hates her but is fascinated by her, and he is falling in love.

The plot is a lot like that of *Amadeus*, which follows the intense love/hate conflict that Antonio Salieri felt for Mozart. Bear in mind that within the context of a romantic comedy, this quest for revenge is given a light touch—but it definitely drives Nick. While his magic skill gives him a way to get rid of

Darcy, it also enables him to see her for who she really is. She's the worst thing that ever happened to him as well as the best. Nick's dilemma is: It's unacceptable not to use this golden opportunity to ruin Darcy for stealing his job, but it's equally unacceptable to destroy her because he's falling in love with her.

The Use of Dilemma in *Minority Report*

The dilemma in *Minority Report* (2002) is complex and tricky to figure out. Rather than merely stating it for you here, it may be more instructive to *demonstrate* my real-time process of getting a handle on it. Bear in mind that there isn't automatically a dilemma in any given film, but it's not difficult to sense the presence of one in *Minority Report*.

Chief John Anderton (Tom Cruise) is the head of Precrime, a police agency that, with the help of new technology, is able to predict murders before they occur. Precrime's three psychics (Precogs) predict that Anderton himself will soon kill a man he's never met, Leo Crow (Mike Binder). Since the Precogs are infallible and the system is perfect, Anderton knows he will be convicted and permanently incarcerated by his own organization. He is forced to run, and on the way out encounters Danny Witwer (Colin Farrell), the Justice Department investigator, who confronts him with evidence of his narcotics use. Anderton's boss, Lamar Burgess (Max von Sydow), has warned him that the Justice Department is trying to take over Precrime, and Anderton believes that Danny is setting him up.

In this future world, when the Precogs tag you, you're guilty. They don't need to catch Anderton in the act of committing murder. When a brown ball pops up with his name on it, they come immediately to lock him away forever. That's the law. No evidence is required, no dead body, no trial, and no appeal. Anderton is guilty because the system is perfect. He totally believes this, and his life's purpose is based on this absolute belief. Precrime is his baby.

One aspect of a possible dilemma is quite obvious: It's unacceptable for John Anderton to be destroyed by Precrime. Not only is his survival at stake, but he's convinced that he's being framed so Danny can break up Precrime. He cannot allow himself to be caught and his life's work to be ruined, so he's fighting for everything he is, has, and believes in.

Now let's look at the opposite side of this proposed dilemma, which is that it would be unacceptable to run. How would John Anderton be divided? What would be powerful enough to counterbalance this burning imperative to escape? Would it be loyalty to Precrime? Would it be his belief in the infallibility of the Precogs—that they must be right and thus he is, in fact, going to kill this Leo Crow? Certainly Anderton must have a nagging doubt, in spite of his powerful belief that Danny is framing him. He's a "priest" and his "religion" or "god" has pointed its finger of doom back at him. Is it unacceptable to stick around, but equally unacceptable to run? Is he damned if he does and damned if he doesn't? But does or doesn't *what*? That's still the puzzle at this point.

Put yourself in John Anderton's shoes. Do you feel frozen, like Robby the Robot in *Forbidden Planet*? As Anderton, you should feel this paralysis, this short-circuiting, this pressure from two sides. But what exactly is it that freezes you up? You can't allow yourself to be destroyed by Precrime so you must run, yet you feel equally compelled to protect Precrime. Is this a "kill or be killed" dilemma? It's clearly unacceptable to be killed by Precrime, but is it *equally* unacceptable to kill Precrime? Although you feel a strong allegiance to Precrime, is it *equal* to your need to escape certain death? This is the main question—if we're barking up the right tree, that is. The dilemma here is not as clear as in *Training Day*. Some dilemmas take much more digging and ferreting out, and this is part of the skill of working with this tool on a wide variety of plots and potential plots.

The clue comes when Anderton questions Precrime's inventor, Iris Hineman (Lois Smith), who tells him there's no escaping the prediction that he'll commit murder. "The Precogs are never wrong," she says, and you can see the defeat in Anderton's face. He's dealing with destiny, with fate. His oracles, the Precogs, have decreed that he will commit murder. While part of him believes something has tampered with the system, he must still believe that what the Precogs saw will, in fact, come true: He, of all people, is "destined" to kill someone he's never met.

But Iris stops him in his tracks when she says that "occasionally they do disagree." Sometimes a Precog will dissent from the other two and generate a minority report—a report that is instantly destroyed to preserve the perception of Precrime's infallibility. Anderton realizes that he may be innocent, and that he may have locked up innocent people.

Now I feel like I'm beginning to get a handle on the dilemma in this film. Is it that he can't stick around and yet he can't leave? The more strongly Anderton is drawn back into Precrime as he runs away from it, the more this dilemma is reinforced. He abducts Agatha (Samantha Morton), the female Precog, who might have his minority report (if it even exists) in her memory—which would give him a way out. Digging deeper, Anderton's dilemma appears to be that it's unacceptable for him to stick around because he will be punished for a future murder, but it's equally unacceptable for him to leave because he has an opportunity to prove his innocence.

In the DVD commentary, Spielberg says, "Is there a flaw in the system or in him? That's what drives Anderton." This takes the dilemma further in an interesting direction; it indicates that the mystery is just too juicy to walk away from. Anderton believes strongly in his own innocence, but he also believes absolutely in the system. He *has* to find out which is broken. His addiction to neuroin (a futuristic drug) and his agony over his missing son and broken marriage expose some self-doubt, but he still cannot believe he will kill this Leo Crow. If he runs away and disappears, then not knowing will drive him crazy. He is utterly compelled to participate, and this strengthens the second half of his dilemma.

Adding layers, dimensions, and complexities to a dilemma makes it richer, deeper, and more riveting. In the end we arrive at the following understanding of this dilemma: It is unacceptable for John Anderton to allow himself to be captured and convicted of a future murder, but it is equally unacceptable for him to disappear before he clears himself. Added to this is the mystery of it all: He must get to the bottom of whether he or the system is flawed.

The Use of Dilemma in *The Godfather*

In *The Godfather* (1972), Michael Corleone (Al Pacino) is caught in a substantial dilemma: He's being drawn into the family business even though he knows it will ruin him. His dilemma is that it's unacceptable to sacrifice his happy and peaceful civilian life by getting involved in the family criminal activities, but it's equally unacceptable to allow the family to be destroyed by his noninvolvement, since it has become increasingly apparent that he's the only one capable of running things properly.

Although Michael has tried to steer well clear of the family business, he gets drawn in by the assassination attempt on his father, Don Vito (Marlon Brando). His brother Sonny (James Caan) is clearly not a good don, and his older brother Fredo (John Cazale) would be much worse. If Michael doesn't step in, the family will fall, but if he does it will cost him his freedom, his happiness, and his soul. He's damned if he does and damned if he doesn't.

The Use of Dilemma in *Tootsie*

In *Tootsie* (1982), Michael Dorsey (Dustin Hoffman), a notoriously difficult actor whom no one will hire, dresses up as a woman and gets cast on a popular soap opera, creating a major dilemma. It's unacceptable to quit being Dorothy Michaels because he's finally got work, a fat paycheck, respect as an actor, and a growing relationship with his costar, Julie (Jessica Lange). It's equally unacceptable to continue being Dorothy because the ruse is proving to be a disaster on many levels. A lecherous actor, John Van Horn (George Gaynes), is French-kissing him and wants more; his friendship that unexpectedly became a romantic relationship with his friend and acting student, Sandy (Teri Garr), is falling apart; and he can only pursue Julie so far because he's dressed as a woman. Even Julie's father, Les (Charles Durning), is trying to get a piece of Dorothy. Michael can't let go and he can't hang on. Becoming Dorothy is simultaneously the best thing that ever happened to him and the worst. It's creating him and destroying him at the same time, and this dilemma is genuinely funny.

The Use of Dilemma in *Blade Runner*

In *Blade Runner* (1982), Rick Deckard (Harrison Ford) is caught in a dilemma over the fate of the replicants (humanoid slave robots). He is told that they are slaughtering people and it is his job to destroy them, but he has also seen how their inventor, Dr. Tyrell (Joe Turkel), treats Rachael (Sean Young). "Rachael is an experiment, nothing more," Tyrell says—she is entirely disposable. But Deckard is moved by Rachael's emotional discovery that she is actually a replicant and not human. His perceptiveness makes him a good detective, and he begins to discover that the replicants are very human, that they have a legitimate grievance, and that killing them is murder.

This is clearer in the original version (not the director's cut) with the voice-over in which Deckard ruminates about why replicants have emotions. He also begins to question his own emotions—blade runners are expected to be detached hunting and killing machines. As he falls in love with Rachael he opens up emotionally, and in the process his fascination with and feelings for the replicants grow. And yet the replicants are still out there killing people, so his internal debate—his dilemma—wavers back and forth. The dilemma is that it's unacceptable to allow the murderous replicants to stay alive, but it's equally unacceptable to kill them because of his feelings for the one who saved his life, and his perception that "retiring" these human-like beings is murder.

BECOMING A STUDENT OF HUMAN DILEMMA

In order to gain expertise in wielding dilemma as a dramatist, you must become a student of human dilemma. Look at those around you who are caught in their own particular dilemmas. Look at specific dilemmas in history and in the news. Dilemma makes headlines because moral dilemmas are newsworthy. Typing *dilemma* at Google (www.google.com) or another search engine will unearth thousands of headlines and stories. One such headline, "Ethical Dilemma Over Stem Cell Donors," discusses where the eggs for stem cell research in California will come from. Critics of collecting the eggs fear long-term health consequences from the fertility drugs used to promote excess egg development, and contend that paying poor women for their eggs essentially encourages them to put their health at risk. And yet the eggs are needed for groundbreaking research. . . . Hence the dilemma.

In an excellent *Hollywood Reporter* article about the television show *Law & Order*, staffer Roz Weinman says, "You can embrace a gigantic array of social, moral, legal, and ethical dilemmas inside this concept. My background in sociology helps in telling stories that raise those kinds of issues. It's a terrific platform for floating unique dilemmas and different points of view." This is clearly someone who understands human dilemma and brings that level of experience to her writing. You can be sure that the writing staff on that show has turned over thousands of dilemmas in their quest for compelling Dramatic Action. That's the kind of work that gets you the gold.

Dilemmas can be found anywhere there is conflict, anywhere people have conflicting needs, ambitions, emotions, imperatives, desires, necessities, or absolutes. So-called "sticky subjects" such as politics, race, class, gender, marriage, children, justice, war, ecology, future planning, the stock market, Pentagon spending, welfare, abortion, taxes, big business, and health insurance are fraught with dilemma. How do people get caught up in these kinds of situations? To use just one example, consider the issue of national security versus privacy. There are serious concerns on both sides: No one wants their country to be vulnerable to attack, nor do people want privacy and personal freedoms stripped away to achieve that end. This dilemma is about the possibility that the cure could be worse than the disease.

Study Dilemma in Your Own Life. Dilemmas are not just something that happens to actors in films. In your own life you are surrounded by hundreds of dilemmas, large and small. They don't have to be earthshaking for them to be real. Your skill as a dramatist will be enhanced considerably if you are able to recognize dilemmas in your own life and understand how prevalent they are. Look at tough choices, both big and small, that have stopped you in your tracks. Are you trapped in a boring job that keeps you from pursuing your art? Do you need to borrow money from a friend, but are hesitant to risk ruining your long-term relationship? Are you staying in a bad marriage because you're afraid of the unknown? What are the most painful dilemmas you've ever faced? Look at areas of meaning and intensity such as loyalty, money, security, betrayal, friendship, politics, career, love, and children. Try to articulate both sides of the dilemma.

It can be easy to avoid dealing with dilemmas in your own life. You may need to call someone for business but know that she's difficult to deal with. Your inner debate goes back and forth: "I want the work, but what should be a two-minute conversation will likely go on for twenty minutes without getting to the point. I need the business, but she'll just drive me crazy." At some point you just opt out of making a decision, thinking, "Oh never mind, I'll think about this tomorrow." Notice the tendency to want to put off even this miniature dilemma, to want to escape because there's no answer in either direction. It's like two magnets pushing away from each other.

Now isolate one of your own dilemmas and observe yourself as you deal with it. State it as: *It's unacceptable for me to _____ but it's equally unacceptable for me to _____.* Study how this dilemma impacts your world. Write about its ramifications, how it paralyzes you, how it makes you feel, the inner debate that rages about it, the sense of frustration, the rage at being trapped in such an impossible choice. Then take it further. Think about how much worse it *could* be. What's the most excruciating form of this dilemma you could possibly imagine? Go off the deep end with it. Find ways to complicate it, add layers to it, dimensionalize it, compound it. Compare it to dilemmas around the world that we can scarcely imagine—a third-world family forced to sell a child into slavery to keep the rest of them alive for a few more months, or people whose farm will be burned down if they don't join a revolution that may get them killed.

Recognize Dilemmas When They Occur. When you see someone caught between two choices, be ready to recognize and describe it in the dramatist's terms: "Wow, you're caught in a classic dilemma." He or she probably never looked at it that way before. While you may not know how to solve the problem, learn to perceive dilemma where another person wouldn't. Compare your budding skill to those special infrared glasses that enable bank robbers to see the red laser beams protecting a bank vault. Recognizing dilemmas when they occur is a crucial skill in screenwriting. If you can't find the dilemma in your script, developing one can add weight and import to your movie. But if it *is* there and you can't see it, then you may be trying to create one while it's already sitting right in front of you, unrecognized.

Connect with the Average Person in the Audience. It's important for the average person in the audience to connect with the dilemma of your protagonist. In other words, are the viewers able to see themselves in it? Does it have significance in their own worlds and their own lives? Hollywood often misses the mark with the average person by assuming that he or she is consumed with the superficial, when actually most people are compelled by something much deeper and more human. Perhaps they are losing sleep because a friend committed suicide or simply because their kids are drifting away. If viewers see a protagonist caught up in something that hits close to home, then they will wonder if this character can find a way out of the dilemma torturing them in their own lives.

The deeper you go, the more universal you get. A movie with a good, strong dilemma about a salmon fisherman in Alaska could impact, for instance, a banker in Tokyo who might say, "Hey, I'm caught in the same dilemma." Or a brickmaker in Argentina might look at the screen and say, "Wow, that's my life up there." Neither individual may know anything about Alaskan fishing, but at a deeper level, this fisherman's dilemma may be about honor and betrayal and duty and survival—all familiar concepts that everyone can grasp.

One question to ask when developing a script is, "Can the guy across the street, who I don't know, relate to the dilemma in this story?" He's your audience after all, and remember, it's all about the audience. Let's say you're writing about a king who must choose between giving up his throne and putting his family in danger. How can you be sure the person across the street relates to that? First ask yourself, "How can *I* relate to this king's dilemma?" You're not a king, but you may know about moving away from family to pursue a career—so yes, kingdom versus family, you can relate to that. And if the king did it *this* way, perhaps you could relate to it even more, and if he did *that* you would *really* feel connected to this character. Start by studying yourself, and you will indirectly be studying the guy across the street. You will be consciously tuning the dilemma of your protagonist to your audience.

Understand the True Meaning of *Dilemma*. The word *dilemma* is often misused and therefore misunderstood. The word has devolved through extensive misuse and is entering popular lexicon so that it is almost becoming correct to say, "I had a dilemma today: I lost my keys." But this is not a dilemma, it's just a situation or a problem. The true definition—"A situation with a choice to be made in which neither alternative is acceptable. Two equally unacceptable alternatives, two equally painful choices"—not only clarifies understanding of Aristotle's observations on drama, but increases the power of a dramatic plot. The more you use it properly, and the more you see dilemma in action all around you, the more you'll be able to fully wield it as a dramatist.

USING DILEMMA AS A WORKING TOOL

The first thing to do is to see if there already *is* a dilemma inherent in your script idea. Is there a situation in which your character is damned if she does and damned if she doesn't? Is your protagonist caught between two choices that trap her, squeeze her, paralyze her? The more you understand dilemma, the more you will recognize its presence. Look for something big and central, not peripheral or minor. Look for a dilemma of magnitude that can carry a whole film, as an engine drives a car. While you can certainly find other motors in a car, such as the ones that work the windshield wipers or the electric windows, they don't power the vehicle.

Make a list of the choices your main character faces. Work up a simple two-column chart, putting yourself in the position of the protagonist and facing your dilemma. Become this character and say, "It's unacceptable for me to _____ and it's equally unacceptable for me to _____" Then assign each unacceptable alternative as a heading to one column and list the active elements on both sides of the dilemma. This allows you to polarize the two sides of the dilemma and to run with each one, exploring its shades of meaning and so the page explodes with all the ramifications of the dilemma. The more angles from which you approach your central character's dilemma, the more clearly and completely you'll understand it. This two-sided chart is a great way to explore the extremes, too, because you can keep stretching the possibilities as you fiddle with the list, twisting the dilemma, trying things on, and breaking out in various directions.

Don't attach too much importance to the statements; just let your mind roam. Remember, no one will ever see this chart. You're just scribbling notes to yourself, so don't worry if you get repetitive or if it sounds stupid or unbelievable. Don't edit yourself to death. Have fun. Let it flow. Trust your instincts. Deliberately stretch the dynamics of your plot, of your characters, and of your whole approach as a screenwriter. Challenge your own creativity and your own storytelling habits. Try to break new ground and to see things from a fresh point of view. (For an example of this in-depth analysis, see the two-column chart for *Training Day* on page 17.)

If you discover there is no dilemma in your story at this point, that's fine, too. Experiment with creating one. Make the plot more powerful by turning a situation into a dilemma. For example, a cop who has to catch the bad guy is a situation, but if he owes his life to the bad guy or the bad guy is his brother, then he's got a much tougher choice. Creating dilemma is about complicating choices—adding alternatives and making them painful. This may sound simple, and in many ways it is, but you will be surprised at how much dramatic horsepower you can add to a script by focusing on the dilemma. Take a good, hard look at the two equally unacceptable alternatives, being as specific as possible. This forces you to pay attention to something you might otherwise overlook. A deep and complex exploration of dilemma can take you on a fascinating journey into the heart of the story and the character in ways that you may never have imagined.

It's important to pay attention to the word *equal* in the phrase "equally unacceptable alternatives." If the alternatives are *equally* unacceptable, you will have the true paralysis that a dilemma creates. If they're not, then there is an easier way out, like being given a choice of whether to jump in the lava or get burned with a match—both choices are unacceptable but not equally unacceptable. The more you pay attention to keeping the alternatives equal, the more you trap the protagonist. As you begin to experiment with the dilemma, playing with story options and exploring extremes, you may intentionally or inadvertently alter one side of the dilemma so it becomes *more* unacceptable than the other. Cure this by keeping careful track of the balancing act, and increasing the power of the choice that has fallen lower on the scale. Electricity will always take the path of least resistance, so to bottle it up both escape routes must be blocked. To keep Robby the Robot short-circuiting—to maintain the paralysis of being caught between two equally painful choices— test and adjust as you go along.

Experiment with Extremes. Once you get a dilemma up and running, start playing with extremes. Take it as far as you possibly can, just to see how far you can go. How excruciating can this dilemma become? There's a great James Bond quote in which the villainous Dr. No says, "Mania is as priceless as genius." Don't play it safe—get crazy. Remember, it's the movies! Cultivate a sense of attack as a storyteller by going after the audience and giving them the ride of their lives. This works in any genre. How nerve-wracking can you make this dilemma? How scary? How funny? How silly? How dangerous? How unpredictable? How disorienting? How beautiful? How disturbing? How moving? How utterly, insanely tweaked?

Take a dilemma to its extreme by imagining it as a torture device. Now think about someone you truly despise, place them in it, and crank the screws so tight that your enemy is screaming. Then take this torture device off, put it on your protagonist, and set the screws *that* tight. As a screenwriter, you probably like your protagonist, so you were treating him too well and letting him off too easily. Torture your protagonist to the point that your *audience* is tortured. You'll have your protagonist really screaming and you'll have your audience on the edge of its seats.

You don't have to keep the dilemma at that ultimate level, but you should know what its limits are. Think about the movies you've seen that didn't go far enough—that had something there but failed to perceive where the story could go, what its potential was. Those movies just chickened out. The process of getting outside the box keeps your material fresh and violates the homogeneity that plagues the film industry.

Make Chaos Your Ally. Exploring the extremes can take you into uncharted waters, but getting outside your safety zone is part of the adventure of screenwriting. This process can plunge you into chaos. Don't be afraid of it—make chaos your ally. Most writers know they aren't doing their job right if they're *not* getting in over their head. The more of the dramatist's craft you conquer, the less afraid you are of chaos. In fact, you will begin to revel in the chaotic process of creation. If it's neat and orderly and simple, then it will often turn out flat, lifeless, uninspiring, and worst of all—boring. Remember, it's the *entertainment* industry. The key word in the entertainment industry is *outrageousness*. Do you want to write the same old movie that everyone is writing, or do you want to create something that blows the lid off everything else?

When you start a script, there may be a point where you feel as if you're getting in over your head. Part of you says, "Uh oh, I'm in trouble here." But another part says, "All right! Now we're getting somewhere." Someone once said that writers are like a show horses: They're not happy unless they're trying to jump over something that might kill them. The best part of the writing process is the point at which anything goes. The story is still wide open and there's a real sense of possibility, adventure, and raw excitement.

Put Yourself in Your Protagonist's Shoes. *Become* the person who is trapped in this dilemma and experience it firsthand. Say to yourself, "Okay, I am this person stuck in this particular dilemma. It's unacceptable to _____ and it's equally unacceptable to _____. I can't move in this direction because of _____, but there's no way I can _____ either. I'm so screwed! How did I get in a position like this? It's an impossible choice. I tried to wriggle out of it, but it won't let me go." Really get in there and live it; thrash it out as though it's happening to you. This will help you to write about it and to understand your character much more fully.

It's also a good exercise to put yourself in the position of your antagonist and look at the protagonist trapped in his dilemma. You're the protagonist's enemy looking at how stuck and vulnerable he is. You see a chink in his armor, maybe even a gaping hole that you can take advantage of. The antagonist doesn't always create the dilemma for the protagonist, but he will always take advantage of it.

Understand the Power of Dilemma. You will find that a dilemma can give you a real handle on your protagonist. A compelling dilemma will pry a character's life wide open, much like the Jaws of Life machine used in car accidents that rips open the wreckage and gets the trapped person out. All of the protagonist's weaknesses will be on display. Or imagine the opposite: a big pair of pliers with each half representing one side of the dilemma. The more you squeeze, the more of a brutal grip you've got on your main character. And because the audience members identify with the protagonist, you've got a brutal grip on them as well.

Dilemma is also a handle with which to grip your plot. Your raw story may have all this energy, yet you may not be quite sure where to channel it. Start with dilemma, then crank it up so that energy is translated directly into the story. *The more powerful your dilemma is, the more powerful your script will be.* There's no hiding from a compelling dilemma, no pretending it isn't happening, and no wishing it away. The power of dilemma can hook good actors, too, who are starving for meatier roles and complex, dangerous, challenging parts. And attracting talent is an important part of getting a film made.

Finally, be sure to examine the ramifications of the dilemma. At first you need a laser focus on the protagonist and her dilemma, but once that's squared away, take a step back and look at the protagonist's entire world. What are the ripple effects? For example, if a Mafia character has to choose between ratting out his brother or doing twenty years of hard time, there are going to be consequences. The choice will impact his relationship with his brother, his ability to think clearly, his relationship with his gang, his ability to sleep, his relationship with his wife and kids, and so on. Understanding these ramifications will help you portray your film's world.

LOOKING DEEPER INTO DILEMMA IN *TRAINING DAY*

Now that you have a solid grasp of dilemma, let's return to *Training Day* to explore Jake's dilemma more deeply. It's unacceptable for Jake to refuse Alonzo's offer to join his undercover narcotics squad, but it's equally unacceptable to join Alonzo because it's contrary to Jake's moral compass. The dilemma is further complicated by Alonzo's torturous ability to counter Jake's misgivings. Everything Alonzo says about having to lie with the snakes to do undercover cop work is absolutely true. After Jake stops the crackheads from raping the schoolgirl, Alonzo says that his squad only goes after "big game": "To protect the sheep you got to catch the wolf, and it takes a wolf to catch a wolf." He also plays on Jake's ego and ambition, saying, "You got the magic eye, Hoyt. You up your street IQ, you gonna do some damage out here, I guarantee. Crime fighter." And after Alonzo shoots the drug dealer, Roger (Scott Glenn), he is able to defuse Jake: "I walk a higher path, son. I can give you the keys to all the doors. . . . You're a leader. You want my job, you got it. You want to lock up poisoners? This is the best place to do it."

This promise is compelling to Jake, who truly wants to make a difference. He knows Alonzo is telling the truth about how things get done in this underworld, but it's still ugly, brutal, and corrupt. Alonzo is very much the devil, seductive and silver-tongued, telling him both what he wants and needs to hear, drawing him deeper into his dilemma. It sounds right and it plays into Jake's ambitions. In the opening scene, Jake tells his wife that if he aces this assignment, he could get his own department division someday: "You should see those guys' houses." Director Antoine Fuqua says in the DVD commentary that Jake's ambition is his fatal flaw. Alonzo is telling Jake not only how to do undercover work, but also how to fulfill his ambitions, how to make detective.

Another aspect distorting Jake's dilemma is that, however questionable Alonzo's methods, the duo *are* making substantial headway in their investigation. David Ayer's screenplay describes Jake as being half impressed, half appalled with Alonzo. Jake is appalled when Alonzo sticks a pen down the throat of the drug dealer, Blue (Snoop Dogg), forcing him to spit out the name of Sandman, a higher-level dealer, but he's impressed when this leads to Alonzo getting the Sandman's address. Then, after Alonzo uses a fake warrant to rob a bundle of cash from Sandman's house, he uses that same money as a bribe to quickly get the valid warrant that gets them into Roger's home. And then, after Alonzo has robbed and killed Roger, even trying to pressure Jake into claiming he was the one who shot Roger, Alonzo shows him how they've just taken a high-end drug dealer off the street. It's appalling, but equally impressive. It's hard to argue with real results—Alonzo says that judges have handed out 15,000 years of incarceration time based on his investigations—and yet do the ends justify the means?

Jake is also constantly being reminded that he has a shot at a "real" job, one with teeth and claws, as opposed to his old job. Having it rubbed in his face that he's a rookie stings, and urges him to succeed even more. In the highwayside scene after the shootout at the Sandman's, Alonzo tells Jake to go back to measuring car wrecks. The camera cuts to a close-up of Jake looking back and forth between Alonzo and a cop helping a stranded motorist change a tire. He is clearly torn.

This illustrates yet another powerful aspect of Jake's dilemma: adventure versus security, a universal dilemma. Adventure is tantalizing and exciting, but it's dangerous and potentially catastrophic. Security can be boring, stagnant, suffocating, and claustrophobic, but at least it is safe and fairly predictable. People stay in bad marriages because the alternative is to face the void. Many feel trapped by this choice; it's a core issue that people face in various ways. It's the devil whispering in your ear, "Go for it. Risk it. What's it all worth if you just chicken out?" and the angel whispering in the other ear, "Wait. Think about how hard you worked to get where you are. Are you going to risk it all on one throw of the dice?" Alonzo represents absolute adventure, but the blade cuts both ways. Jake is forsaking security for adventure—and doing undercover narcotic police work is high-end adventure, to be sure—but as Alonzo's true colors begin to emerge Jake starts to look longingly at the safe harbor he is leaving behind. Neither alternative is any good.

It's easy for the alternatives in a dilemma to get muddled in your brain. Let's look at a handy two-column chart polarizing Jake's alternatives in *Training Day*:

Jake Can't Let Go of his Job	Jake Can't Keep Doing His Job
Damned if he quits	Damned if he doesn't quit
He really wants to be in the squad	Alonzo's morals are corrupt
He's extremely ambitious	He could get arrested or even killed
He's awed by Alonzo	He's appalled by Alonzo
Alonzo is a god in this arena	Alonzo is the devil

This is how to get big results	Must become a criminal to catch criminals
He's totally dedicated	He's being drugged and shot at
He wants to do good	He's an accomplice in theft
He will not quit being a cop	He's violating his vows as a cop
Driven by his career	Headed for jail
Adventure	Destruction
He's making a difference	It's costing him his soul
He's learning the streets	He's becoming corrupt
He's getting results	His moral compass rebels
Freedom	High cost of freedom
Ambition	Danger
Investigation is bearing real fruit	Investigation is costing his integrity
He's joining Alonzo's elite group	Alonzo's making fun of him
Alonzo is his guru	Alonzo is his enemy
Alonzo is persuasive	Alonzo is corrupt
Old job too boring	New job too risky
Power	Loss of soul

An important aspect of this exercise is to let yourself run with it. Don't worry about being repetitive, because you can see fresh aspects of the dilemma by hitting it from different points of view. The columns interplay back and forth, with both sides connecting and opposing, as with "Ambition" on the left and "Danger" on the right. But you can also just run down one side of the page without specific reference to the other side, and then go back and think the other side through.

Another important part of understanding Jake's dilemma is to find ways in which you relate to it personally. In what ways have you been in Jake's shoes? How can you relate to his type of situation? Think about what you want badly and what you'd be willing to sacrifice to get it. Have you ever been caught between achieving results and upholding your ideals? How far have people whom you admire pushed things in order to succeed? And yet, how far is too far? How do you keep your moral compass in the face of conflicting demands? The extent of this dilemma is part of why *Training Day* is so universal and affects people so deeply.

LET'S CREATE A DEMO PLOT WITH A STRONG DILEMMA

Now let's experiment with dilemma by making up a quick demonstration plot and putting it through its paces. Let's start with a detective who is hired by a super-wealthy businessman to protect his wife from unknown assailants. In the process, the detective falls madly in love with her. This is a simple enough idea, but is there any dilemma inherent in the basic premise? Falling in love with the boss's wife is a tough spot to be in, but it can certainly be expanded upon. Let's play around with the plot. Pay attention to possibilities that could thrust our detective into a "damned if he does, damned if he doesn't" situation. Perhaps the wife (let's call her Minky) is wild, feisty, and sexual, and he finds himself immediately attracted to her. She could run with a rich, exotic crowd, which our detective (Zack) finds exhilarating since he's never been around major wealth. But remember that there's substantial danger involved: Somebody is out to kill Minky, and Zack is in the way. To complicate matters further, let's say that there's something about her that makes his sixth sense tingle. In a voice-over we could hear him thinking, "If I had any sense, I'd walk out the door right now. . . ."

Now the plot is expanding with the elements of a strong dilemma. It's unacceptable for Zack to quit this job because it pays well, he's very attracted to Minky, he finds himself in a thrilling world of wealth and power, and someone has pissed him off by trying to hurt him. But it's equally unacceptable to keep the job because it is dangerous and unpredictable, and she is strangely off-kilter—all his instincts are screaming for him to get out while he can.

Let's take our plot further. In one of the attempts on her life, Minky is not only unfazed but even drunkenly defiant, and is actually good in a fight, earning Zack's respect. What if she's too spirited and adventurous—a trouble magnet? What if he's sober, conservative, and industrious, as well as emotionally shutdown and small-minded? What if she reveals that she's attracted to him? What if he can't stop thinking about her? What if she's love-starved and emotionally vulnerable, like a little girl who needs a daddy? But she's also a stimulating woman who challenges him on many fronts. She can be a sexual predator and a reckless troublemaker. Picture Catherine Zeta-Jones as this intoxicating, adventurous bitch-on-wheels who's driving him crazy, but who's also truly audacious, fun, and mesmerizing. Do you see how we're working this in terms of dilemma? We're playing with extremes. How can we make it worse in both directions? How attractive can she be? How dangerous? How unpredictable? How provocative? How resistant can he be? How unprepared? How overwhelmed? We increase the story's pull by complicating the dilemma, by dimensionalizing it, deepening it, and layering it.

Let's take it even further. Minky is a sexual animal who attracts men in droves, many of whom are the wrong kind. What if she intentionally confronts dangerous situations with tough guys—just to make Zack deal with them? What if she taunts him with her desire, dares him to do something about it? He wouldn't be able to sleep—every time he closes his eyes he would see her. She could work to make him jealous, flirting openly and jumping in bed with other men, rubbing it in his face. She could run around the house naked and he would be losing his mind. She's the best thing and the worst thing that's ever happened to him. The more flawed he is, the more susceptible he is to her charms, her perversions, her tweaked energy—but it also makes him more frightened, lost, intimidated, and damaged. She's opening him up emotionally, dragging him out of reclusion and forcing him to really live for the first time. But then the attempts on her life could heat up, and it could get quite touch-and-go. He could be almost killed while protecting her. Her crazy streak could get truly freaky. Now it's a genuinely scary and deeply puzzling mystery. What if she even seems to have a death wish or acts suicidal?

As we play with the possibilities, keep a laser focus on the dilemma. Every idea, every extreme that we try on, it all impacts, improves, and compounds his dilemma. We're turning Story into Drama. This is the process in real time. Our detective's dilemma is really that of a mouse pondering a mousetrap: He knows it's a mousetrap, but the damn cheese is so awesome that he can't walk away from it. Let's look at a two-column chart of his dilemma to clarify things:

Damned If He Keeps the Job	Damned If He Quits the Job
Worst thing that ever happened to him	Best thing that ever happened to him
She's big trouble	She's irresistible
She's got a real enemy	He refuses to be intimidated
She makes him crazy	He's having the time of his life
He's losing control emotionally	He's opening up to life
She's crazy and unpredictable	She's vulnerable and she needs him
He can't sleep	He can't live without her
Danger	Adventure
Death	Fun
Disaster	Freedom
Trouble	Too boring if he quits
Panic	Challenge
She'll cost him his detective license	He's living the high life
He can't trust her	She saves his ass
He could get killed	She could get killed
The mystery is deadly	The mystery is too intriguing
Is he being played for a fool?	The money is too good to quit
He's jealous of her lovers	He won't get to be with her
She's a trouble magnet	She's tough, and good in a fight

This list could go on and on as we explore the material and expand upon it. Now that we can see the dilemma clearly, you should stop and work on this plot yourself. Where can you go with it? How far can you take it? What's the most intense that this dilemma could be? What's the tone of the movie? If it's comic, then how dark is too dark before you puncture the tone? If it's a thriller, how much comic relief strips it of its teeth and claws? It could go in the direction of *The Big Lebowski* or become more like *Body Heat*. This is the process. Work it like a fanatic. Go off the deep end. Fill pages of notes. Turn it inside out and upside down. Change the characters' genders. Attack the audience. What's the scariest you can make it? What's the funniest? What's cliché about it? What's fresh about it? Why do you like it? What bores you about it?

Put yourself in the detective's shoes and live the dilemma. Describe it to yourself from this first person point of view. Think, "I'm this detective and I'm caught in this tough spot." Are you caught in a similar dilemma in your own everyday life? How do the dilemmas in your life match up? Does adventure call to you even though it will cost you your security? Does your buddy want you to drop out of college and travel the world with him? Do you want to quit your job and start a risky but potentially profitable new business? Find a similarity in your own life; it will help you make the connection. The more you can articulate it, the more you'll be able to communicate it. There is no substitute for taking on the role of each of your characters, because it enables you to see their point of view explicitly rather than indirectly and abstractly. Put yourself in the wife's shoes. Or be the killer—how badly do you need to kill this wacko bitch? Even if the killer is totally psychotic, his take on why she deserves to die can be extremely valuable: It can take the story to the next level.

Just exploring in this way can explode your plot into new dimensions. Go back and forth between extreme subjectivity and extreme objectivity. Roll the dilemma around in your subconscious. Brainstorm as hard as you can with it. Do some research on what a bodyguard does. See movies and read novels that play with these concepts; study how masters of the genre handle them. Take plenty of time so the obvious aspects of this type of story become apparent. Twist them, play with them, and tell a great story. Mix your raw storytelling skills with your craft as a dramatist.

Now let's lay out a full statement of the dilemma, including all its aspects, layers, and dimensions. It's unacceptable for Zack to let go of this job because: he's head-over-heels in love with Minky, the pay is incredible, he's having the time of his life, he's being dragged kicking and screaming into really living for the first time, he has a shot at going to bed with her, the mystery is too challenging, he's angry that someone has tried to hurt them both, she needs him, and he's having pure adventurous fun. It's equally unacceptable to keep doing the job because: it's dangerous and he may well get killed, she's all kinds of trouble, he's being dragged out of his emotional safety zone, he's going crazy, he can't trust her, he's afraid he's being set up, she makes him insanely jealous, there's something really odd about her, and all his instincts tell him to run the other way. Remember this dilemma when we pick up our demo plot again (see page 25) and things *really* heat up.

THE FUNCTION OF CRISIS IN DRAMATIZING A PLOT

The second element Aristotle noticed that tends to be common to the most gripping dramas is *Crisis*, the point at which the dilemma comes to a critical juncture: the make-or-break point. Crisis forces the protagonist to react immediately to his dilemma instead of being able to contemplate it from a distance. Figuratively, it's the gun to the head, the moment of truth. While dealing with the dilemma, the protagonist has been worrying, "What am I going to do when I have to make a choice?" Crisis now forces that choice, demanding an *immediate* response.

In submarine terminology, a sub sinking toward the bottom of the ocean will hit what's called "crush depth," where it will implode from the pressure. In a plot, crisis is that moment when the dilemma reaches crush depth. A good, strong dilemma will hold the audience captive with sustained tension, but crisis takes that dilemma and hyper-compresses it, amping the pressure through the roof. The cornered wild animal is now pushed to the limit and ready to pounce. Watch out!

The crisis is the decisive moment, the point of imminent failure. Any number of things in the protagonist's world might be collapsing—his goals, emotions, physical health, romantic connections, sanity, plans, friendships, partnerships, finances, or basic daily operations. Crisis is the crunch point and it generates intense Dramatic Action. Review the line of proportion:

| Dilemma | | Crisis | Decision
& Action | Resolution |

Dilemma has simmered long enough now to reach the boiling point of Crisis, which happens at about the two-thirds or three-quarters point in the script. (Again, this provides just a rough sense of proportion and is not meant to specify page 30, 60, 90, and so on.)

Think about a crisis in your real life. Your spouse is mad at you, the kids are sick, you're late for work, the car won't start, you're on the verge of being fired—and then something *really* bad happens. Crisis is when all the worst possible things happen at the worst possible moment. In your script, it should invite the question, "How many anvils can you drop on your protagonist's head at once?"

The Use of Crisis in *Training Day*

When searching for the crisis in a movie you're watching, you may think you've found it . . . but then discover that things get even worse for the protagonist. Sometimes you can't be sure until after the dust has settled. In studying *Training Day*, it appears at first that Jake's crisis occurs when Alonzo insists that Jake claim he shot Roger. This crisis may seem so obvious that you never question it. But further study reveals that, in fact, the dilemma continues after the shooting when Alonzo manages to chill Jake out in the car. Jake doesn't appear to yield or agree but seems perfectly mellow in the next scene when he follows Alonzo up to the Hillside Gang's house. He's hanging out, playing cards, and apparently trusting Alonzo again (at least to a certain degree), and it's not until Jake discovers that Alonzo left him there to be murdered by Smiley (Cliff Curtis), the gang leader, that he really snaps and goes beyond the point of no return. So in *Training Day*, Jake's actual crisis comes when he's literally staring down the barrel of a gun, and the fullness of who Alonzo really is hits him like a Mack truck.

The Use of Crisis in *What Women Want*

In *What Women Want*, just as Nick's vengeful plan to get rid of Darcy is bearing fruit (he has stolen her idea and landed the Nike account), he finds he has fallen in love with her—and is sweeping her off her feet, too. The crisis point comes as they make out in her new apartment, but then he learns that she's been fired for not doing her job well. It is ironic that just as his revenge is coming to fruition, so is the relationship that reading her mind made possible.

The Use of Crisis in *Minority Report*

In *Minority Report*, John Anderton's crisis occurs when he's in the hotel pointing a gun at Leo Crow, the man it was predicted he would murder—he has learned that Crow abducted and murdered his son—while Agatha screams that he can choose to not fulfill the very murder she predicted. Anderton's whole world is warping and ripping in half at this crisis point, and the rest of his life hangs in the balance.

The Use of Crisis in *The Godfather*

Crisis arises in *The Godfather* following the attempt on Michael's life that kills his Sicilian bride, and the murder of his brother Sonny. The family is in trouble: Barzini (Richard Conte) is muscling in, and Tessio and Clemenza (Abe Vigoda and Richard Castellano), Don Corleone's lieutenants, want to break off. When Don Corleone puts Michael in the hot seat by appointing him head of the family, it propels everything to the next level. Michael is thrust into a leadership crisis.

The Use of Crisis in *Tootsie*

Tootsie displays a good example of multifaceted crisis. Michael's crisis essentially occurs when, dressed as Dorothy, he tries to kiss Julie and she freaks out. Their cozy relationship is over, but he's stuck being a woman because the producer won't let Dorothy out of her contract. But notice how many other catastrophic things happen just when Michael's at his most vulnerable. After he kisses Julie, when he tries to tell her that he's really a man and that he's in love with her, the phone interrupts them—it's her father. Believing Dorothy is a lesbian, Julie now insists that Dorothy go out with Les and let him down easy. Les then proposes marriage, and as Dorothy runs away from him, she is grabbed at home by John Van Horn, who tries to rape her. As soon as John leaves, Sandy is at the door to chew Michael out when he admits he's in love with another woman. All the lies that Michael has been juggling throughout the movie come crashing down on his head all at once.

In the midst of this flurry of breaking points, it's important to put your finger on one key element that ignites the crisis. In *Tootsie* this is when Michael tries to kiss Julie. Everything else complicates the crisis and adds to its crushing weight, but when she blows up at him, he's lost the one thing that was making his life work.

A crisis doesn't have to be that complicated. But in the same way that a complex dilemma can be more sustaining than a simple one, so too can a crisis be most riveting when many systems collapse simultaneously. One useful trick in compounding a crisis is to examine your story around the two-thirds or three-quarters point and pinpoint the elements that are coming unglued. See if you can focus them or make them all gang them up on your protagonist at the crucial moment. While complications aren't necessary, they can certainly enhance the intensity of your crisis.

The Use of Crisis in *Blade Runner*

In *Blade Runner*, Deckard's dilemma about killing the replicants comes to a head when Roy Batty (Rutger Hauer) kills Dr. Tyrell and Sebastian (William Sanderson), the genetic scientist/toymaker. Roy has now killed one of the top industrialists in the solar system on Deckard's watch, and Deckard can no longer debate the fate of the replicants. He is sent to Sebastian's apartment where he runs into Pris (Darryl Hannah), the basic pleasure model replicant, who attacks him and attempts to kill him. His dilemma has reached its crisis point—he must take action.

LET'S ADD A CRISIS TO OUR DEMO PLOT

Now let's experiment with our story about the detective hired to protect the wild, sexy client. We're looking to force his dilemma to a head somewhere around the two-thirds or three-quarters point in the plot. We've got him in a corner—he cannot keep protecting her yet he cannot walk away—and we want to bring all the issues to a crunch point. Let's ask ourselves some questions about bringing the story to a crisis: How bad can it get? What's an entertaining way for this disaster/adventure to come to a head? How risky can she get? How screwed can he get? How close is he to solving her case? What's a humorous way to blow it all up? What's a dangerous way to blow it all up? How can everything get much, much worse? How does the husband factor in? What if Zack finds out Minky's a blackmailer, throwing things into an entirely new light? What if he discovers that it's a much more dangerous game than he ever suspected? What if Minky is truly insane? What if he's been played for a sucker? What if he's now completely in love with her, right at this critical juncture? What if they've finally made love and it was beyond fantastic? What if they've finally made love and she starts acting even crazier? What if the threats to her become extremely dangerous? What if he's losing his mind? What if he discovers she has betrayed him? What if he suspects she has sold him out? Who are the people who are trying to hurt her and what are they really up to?

When working a dilemma such as this to its crisis point, at that critical moment things can be both right on the edge of success as well as courting disaster. For instance, because Zack's dilemma is partially about his inability to leave her, it will amplify the crisis if we really raise the stakes. So we have them finally make love, and now he's totally smitten with her. Adding intensity to that, she also seems to be in love with him, and is perhaps even ready to leave her husband for him. Maybe Minky brings out genuine strength in him, so that he's finally acting like a real man instead of a half-broken guy who can't stand the heat. Maybe he's also very close to finding her attackers. Maybe the husband gives him a huge bonus after a particularly dangerous fight so now he's got some significant savings for the first time in his life. With the addition of all these elements, Zack is now really close to succeeding as well as really close to failing. The crisis will be all the more engrossing.

So here is our crisis in simple form: Right as our detective is closest to discovering who's after the woman he's protecting, they sleep together and fall madly, deeply in love. He's high on life, feeling like he can move mountains, but then learns from her attacker that she's really a blackmailer, and that she's been using him and may have betrayed him. She's seriously on the edge, and his own sanity starts to crack. And right at this juncture, while he's balancing on the edge of the razor where success and failure meet, we'll add that extra weight: They are attacked by her enemy. Our script has reached its crisis.

THE FUNCTION OF DECISION
& ACTION IN DRAMATIZING A PLOT

A crisis forces the protagonist to make an immediate decision and take action. This is the turning point in the script, for good or bad. The word *decision* means "to cut off from"; at this point the protagonist will be forced to cut off the questioning process in which his dilemma has trapped him.

Decision & Action in the face of crisis reveals the true character of the protagonist—the mask is stripped off. A classic example is when the big, strong guy jumps up and runs out screaming while the little guy jumps up and saves the day. Think about how you never know who your real friends are until you've been through a crisis with them. Someone you thought was your friend may desert you when things turn critical, while someone you didn't really know or like may step in and save the day. The audience is fascinated with seeing the mask stripped off. Why? Look at how infrequently we see this kind of naked human emotional reality. Pretence, subterfuge, diplomacy, self-deception, and layer upon conventional layer all cover up reality so that, in fact, it's a rarity to see the true face beneath the mask.

Crisis also offers a crack in reality that can be taken advantage of by the opportune. The Chinese word for crisis is made up of two characters: one for danger and another for opportunity. It is said that great moments are born of great opportunity. Seemingly impossible things can be accomplished in the teeth of a crisis. Scoundrels can overturn a government; adventurers can seize the moment and steer things their own way; desperate people can find strength and courage they never suspected in themselves and use these assets to forge their destinies.

In real life it is people's ability—or inability—to make decisions in critical circumstances that makes them who they are. Those who stand out are good at making decisions in the highest-pressure situations. It's what sets them apart. People rise to positions of leadership based on their ability to handle stress, think clearly, sort through possibilities, and operate using instinct, brains, and character. Great leaders are extremely effective in a crisis. A top compliment among sailors is, "He's a good man in a storm." Conversely, someone who's unable to marshal their forces to get it right, someone who simply cannot work their way through a catastrophic situation, will fail. Decision and action in a crisis is a test of character, and that's why it makes such compelling drama.

Look back over your own life at the crises you've faced and consider those moments when you performed incredibly as well as those in which you fell apart miserably. Many people spend their lives beating themselves up over a failure at a crucial moment. Have you saved someone's life in a tight situation? Have you almost cost someone their life? How do you tend to respond when things become critical? Some people are calm and are effective in a crisis while others panic and come apart at the seams. Who do you know that is best in a tough spot? Who is the worst? How does he or she act? Can you figure out why, and what makes this person tick? Are you surprised at how a seemingly frail person can emerge as a hero, and how a supposed person of power can buckle?

Not only is character revealed in a crisis, but it can actually be formed on the spot. People are capable of phenomenal things when crisis erupts. There are the familiar tales of the little old lady who lifts a car off her grandson, or the laid-back farm boy who snaps in battle and becomes a creature of the jungle. A particular element of character may have been always there, but it never had to reveal itself before.

If Crisis is the make-or-break point at which a paralyzing dilemma reaches its peak, then Decision & Action is the point of no return that finally breaks the stasis. The protagonist has been fundamentally frozen by the escalating dilemma, which becomes more and more pressurized until the point of crisis, when it is hyper-compressed. Something *has* to give. The protagonist is forced by crisis to make a decision and take an action.

Crisis often brings out the best in people, but it can also bring out the worst. In most instances your plot will either end with a *creative resolution* (a happy ending) or a *tragic resolution* (a sad ending). If it's a creative resolution, then at the point of decision and action your protagonist will probably begin to break out of paralysis and kick into high gear. A decision has been made and an action has been taken that launches things toward the conclusion. If the resolution is tragic, then the protagonist may well do the worst possible thing at the most critical moment, beginning the downward spiral to complete failure. You've probably seen this in real life when, at a critical juncture in someone's life, you've tried to convince him or her not to do something obviously wrong, but you simply cannot stop him or her from rushing off into failure. A bad choice at a crucial moment works in a comedy as well. The protagonist, perhaps an Inspector Clouseau type, will get it catastrophically wrong at the decisive moment, making it even more hilarious when he still stumbles into solving the case.

The Use of Decision & Action in *Training Day*
In *Training Day*, when Jake squeaks out of Alonzo's attempt to have him killed, his decision is to take Alonzo down or die trying. His action is to burst in on Alonzo at his girlfriend's apartment, tell him that he's under arrest, and try to seize the $1 million dollars as evidence. Jake has now passed the point of no return and will not stop until Alonzo is in jail or dead.

The Use of Decision & Action in *What Women Want*
In *What Women Want*, Nick's decision is to somehow repair the damage he's done to Darcy. He acts on this by essentially ordering his boss, Dan (Alan

Alda), to rehire Darcy because the whole idea that landed the Nike account was hers. He cannot allow his sabotage to stand unchecked and so he sets out to find Darcy and undo it all, when he gets sidetracked by saving Erin, the suicidal girl. At this point we see Nick for who he really is: a man who is growing and learning, and who cares deeply about Darcy.

The Use of Decision & Action in *Minority Report*

In *Minority Report*, John Anderton's decision is that he will not kill Leo Crow, and his action is to arrest him instead. Things then spin out of control when Crow divulges that the murder prediction was all a set-up and then pulls the trigger, killing himself. Anderton's real character emerges when he refuses to kill Crow.

The Use of Decision & Action in *The Godfather*

In *The Godfather*, Michael's decision is to move the family to Las Vegas, and his action is to essentially declare war on Barzini by going after Barzini's agent, Moe Green (Alex Rocco), the Las Vegas casino owner. This may not be readily apparent, but reviewing the scene shows it's all there: Michael goes after Moe Green to sell his share of their hotel and casino, and Moe explodes at Michael, saying the Corleones are washed up in New York and were chased out of town by Barzini, who can make a deal that allows Moe to keep the hotel and casino. This is not a casual business meeting at all. Michael has thrown down the gauntlet by going after Barzini's guy. This is war. It may seem indirect—Michael and Barzini never go head to head—but the point of no return has definitely been crossed. Michael's action is confirmed by a reaction in the next scene: Don Corleone tells Michael that Barzini will set up a meeting in which someone Michael absolutely trusts will guarantee his safety, and that Michael will be assassinated at the meeting. Bear in mind that Michael is playing it smart—it looks as though he's gotten in over his head and is running away—but it is because everyone underestimates his subtle decision and action that he is able to take them all by surprise in the end.

The Use of Decision & Action in *Tootsie*

Often the protagonist is in more trouble than ever before once he makes his decision and takes action, but he at least is now functioning rather than paralyzed. Once Michael Dorsey in *Tootsie* makes his decision and reveals his true identity on live TV, Julie is furious at him. He has by no means resolved *anything*, but merely gotten out of being Dorothy—at the cost of any connection to Julie. He's out of the frying pan and into the fire. It's not until he makes things right with Les and wins Julie over at the film's conclusion that Michael fully resolves his dilemma. This shows the very real distinction between Decision & Action and the next step, Resolution.

The Use of Decision & Action in *Blade Runner*

In *Blade Runner*, Deckard's decision is to go after the replicants despite his reservations, and his action is to kill Pris (however reluctantly) and then try to shoot Roy, the replicants' leader. He's still trapped in his dilemma, but his hand has been forced and he has to take action. He doesn't like killing Pris—he's still a draftee tormented by an awful job—nor is he happy or eager to go after Roy.

LET'S ADD A DECISION & ACTION TO OUR DEMO PLOT

Back in the demo plot our detective, Zack, is madly in love with his client Minky, but has just learned that she may have betrayed him, and now they're under attack by her enemy. He's clearly got to make a crucial decision and take an action. What's he going to do? His whole world is upside down and he's got to come up with something quickly. Is she the love of his life or is she the worst thing that ever happened to him? Has she really betrayed him or is somebody trying to ruin both of them? Is he even sane enough to deal with these questions now? Can he stave off this deadly attack and somehow survive?

His decision is to break it off with her, and his action is to panic and lash out at her as he fights off the attackers. When she explodes back at him, he realizes that she actually *has* betrayed him. He fights with her, calling her crazy and saying she's ruined his life. He tells her that he knows everything about the blackmail of her assailant, and that he's finished with being her dancing monkey. Our unhappy pair barely escape their attackers and then separate. He hasn't by any means resolved things yet, but he has made a decision under pressure and taken a key action.

THE FUNCTION OF RESOLUTION IN DRAMATIZING A PLOT

Resolution, the fourth of Aristotle's keys to creating riveting drama, occurs when the protagonist actively and conclusively solves the dilemma, for better or worse. The dilemma should be resolved by the protagonist as opposed to someone doing it for her, or to it just happening to fall together. The protagonist should be the one who takes the key actions. If someone else does it for her, it is called *deus ex machina*: a "god in the machine" who appears unexpectedly in order to solve an apparently insoluble problem. Such a scenario is not satisfying to audiences. The cavalry can show up and help John Wayne win the battle, but it shouldn't win the battle for him. A resolution that just happens to come together can be equally ungratifying to audiences.

For a protagonist caught on the horns of a dilemma, things can be resolved several different ways. One way is to choose one of the "horns"—one of the unacceptable alternatives. The other way is to go between the horns. By thinking on her feet, our protagonist is able to come up with a radical third alternative in which she chooses neither of the two equally unacceptable alternatives. When the protagonist devises an unexpected way out, she has found a creative resolution. An excellent example of this is in *The Firm*, when young lawyer Mitch McDeere (Tom Cruise) is trapped between the Mafia law firm he works for and crooked FBI agent Wayne Tarrance (Ed Harris), who tries to muscle him into violating client-attorney privilege to take down the firm. Rather than illegally handing over documents, Mitch comes up with a radical third alternative when he realizes that the firm is systematically over-billing clients through the mail. Mitch presents the FBI with the mail-fraud bust, satisfying the letter of their agreement without violating his client-attorney privilege and being disbarred.

The Use of Resolution in *Training Day*

In *Training Day*, Jake conclusively resolves his dilemma when he beats Alonzo in a fight to the finish and turns in evidence of Alonzo's criminal activity. He destroys Alonzo within the legal world, which is what matters to Jake, as well as within the criminal world. He has finally completed what he set in motion at the point of Decision & Action.

The Use of Resolution in *What Women Want*

In *What Women Want*, Nick chooses one of the horns, conclusively resolving his dilemma by giving up on revenge and instead coming completely clean. He confesses to Darcy that he ripped off her ideas because she "stole" his job, that he feels awful about it, and that he is now totally dazzled by her. He is prepared to lose everything, and fully expects that he's lost her—but she forgives him.

The Use of Resolution in *Minority Report*

The Resolution of *Minority Report* comes when John Anderton finishes off Lamar by broadcasting images of him murdering Anne Lively to the group honoring his retirement from Precrime. Anderton confronts Lamar with the ironic cost of creating a homicide-free society—the murder of Agatha's mother—and demands that Lamar murder him, too, in order to maintain the system. Lamar takes his own life instead.

The Use of Resolution in *The Godfather*

Caught between being a criminal and being a respectable civilian, Michael Corleone resolves his dilemma in *The Godfather* by killing off all his enemies, including the traitors within his organization, to emerge as a soulless crime lord. He achieves total power but loses his connection with the family he set out to save. That's the tragedy of the piece: He resolves the dilemma at the cost of his soul.

The Use of Resolution in *Tootsie*

In *Tootsie*'s Resolution, Michael Dorsey makes up with Les and then reconnects with Julie. He has grown so much as a person that Julie is willing to let him back into her life—this time without the dress.

The Use of Resolution in *Blade Runner*

The resolution in *Blade Runner* comes when Deckard drops out of his trapped situation and runs off with Rachael, one of the replicants he was ordered to "retire." After saving Deckard's life, Roy shows him what it means to really live; Deckard understands and begins living with everything he's got. He finds a radical third alternative in a dead-end dilemma, breaking free of the entire system in which he was trapped.

Maximum Dramatic Reversal

In considering resolution, Aristotle observed maximum *dramatic reversal*, also known as "peripety" (from the Greek *peripeteia*), in those dramas that most grip an audience. A classic example of dramatic reversal is when the hunter becomes the hunted. Other examples include the king becoming a beggar, the master becoming a slave, or the underdog triumphing. Maximum dramatic reversal is about things swinging around to their opposite, and it adds eye-opening intensity and a sense of completion, often through an element of the unexpected. It's part of the kick of a great, satisfying ending.

There are real reversals in each of our six example films. Jake's reversal is apparent by the end of *Training Day*: He is as different as day and night, having gone from a "daisy-fresh rookie" to a streetwise cop. Nick Marshall, too, has clearly undergone a complete reversal: He is open, clearheaded, and the total opposite of the shallow man he was in the beginning. In the beginning of *Minority Report*, Anderton is an absolute believer in Precrime and its ability to shape destiny, but by the end he is totally outside of its universe, a defiant man with free choice. Although he seems unaware of his complete reversal, Michael Corleone starts out as an innocent in *The Godfather* and ends up a cold-blooded Mafia don. In *Tootsie*, Michael Dorsey also undergoes a complete transformation, but in the opposite direction: Instead of neurotic hustler who lies to women and is a pain in the ass to work with, he has become realistic, straightforward, and honest. In *Blade Runner*, Rick Deckard's reversal is substantial, from the emotionally disconnected, passionless person we meet at the beginning of the film (his ex-wife called him Sushi, meaning "cold fish") to the awakened man at the end who drops out of the game and runs off to live his life. Each of these dramatic reversals helps to bring on a resolution that truly grips the audience.

Discovery or Recognition

Aristotle also noted that the most compelling resolutions involve a moment of fundamental *discovery* or *recognition*, often appearing as a revelation, an awakening, or an epiphany. The protagonist may discover that a major blind spot has been causing his problem, or may recognize that he has been part of the problem and, seeing this, can now become part of the solution. In some cases the discovery or recognition is external, with the protagonist learning some crucial piece of information that constitutes a final piece of the puzzle. This kind of realization can set the protagonist free to resolve things conclusively.

Aristotle maintained that recognition and reversal can occur anywhere in a drama, but that clustering them around the resolution will create the most impact. The recognition will open the protagonist's eyes in time for him or her to conclusively resolve the dilemma, and a substantial reversal will enhance the overall dramatic impact. But the resolution should be fixed firmly in finality—that is, it should be irreversible. If the protagonist wins, it should remain a victory; if he loses, it should remain a loss. Audiences tend to be contented by a resolution that doesn't backslide. This is not to say that you should never have an ambiguous ending. If your goal is to irritate or unsettle the audience then, by all means, experiment with ambiguity. But don't give your screenplay an ambiguous ending just because you can't think of a better way to end it.

When Jake Hoyt is beating Alonzo down in *Training Day*, he realizes that he's not like Alonzo—that he has an entirely different way of operating. Nick Marshall has a fundamental awakening in *What Women Want*, and he realizes he's been utterly horrible to Darcy while she has been faultless and magnanimous. In *Minority Report*, John Anderton experiences an external recognition when he makes the crucial discovery that Anne Lively (Jessica Harper) is actually Agatha's mother, and it all clicks: He was framed because he had learned of her existence. In *The Godfather*, Michael Corleone doesn't really experience an internal discovery because he doesn't seem to notice how cold and hard he's become. In spite of his total victory, he's a tragic figure. Instead, his recognition is external—when he gets Carlo to verify that Barzini was behind Sonny's execution at the toll booth. Michael Dorsey's moment of discovery in *Tootsie* is when he tells Julie, "I was a better man with you as a woman than I ever was with a woman as a man, you know what I mean? I just gotta learn to do it without the dress." He finally understands what it means to be in a real relationship, and this helps him pull it all together in the end. In *Blade Runner*, Rick Deckard undergoes a substantial recognition when Roy dies while saving him, showing him what living life to the fullest truly means. This recognition electrifies Deckard, galvanizing him toward his resolution.

LET'S ADD A RESOLUTION
TO OUR DEMO PLOT

Does it seem like our story will have a happy ending for our detective and his wacko client? Will they reunite and live happily ever after? In a romantic comedy caper such as ours, the answer is, probably. But how and why? And on whose terms? Are they happy or crazy at the end, or both? Do they take out the attackers together? How does Zack transform? Does Minky transform as well? What's the secret to all the confusion and hijinks? Did she really betray him or was it a misunderstanding? These are tough questions, especially in a plot so scantily developed. So here is our resolution in simple form: After attempting to leave Minky, Zack inadvertently teams up with her again to eliminate the attackers and remove her from danger. As it turns out, she had only been blackmailing to protect herself from corrupt former business partners who were trying to falsely implicate her. This revelation frees Zack to be with her and he comes to life, transforming into a free-spirited wildman. She has unleashed him from his own inhibitions, and now that they're perfectly matched, she leaves her husband and marries our detective.

Is this a perfect plot? Certainly not, but it demonstrates all the aspects of this tool: the elements of Dilemma, Crisis, Decision & Action, and Resolution. Here it acts simply as a skeletal teaching demonstration, while an actual screenplay could require a good hundred hours to develop it just to this point. To supplement our examination of Aristotle's observations as applied to acknowledged masterpieces such as *Training Day* and *Tootsie*, we're analyzing a plot under construction from the ground up. This practice will help you to consistently create, develop, and structure dramatic plots that work—and they will work, once you have acquired the thought processes and habits of a trained dramatist.

START USING DILEMMA, CRISIS,
DECISION & ACTION, AND RESOLUTION
IN YOUR OWN SCRIPT

Dilemma

1. Does your story have a dilemma or potential dilemma inherent in it? Remember, the main dilemma should happen to your protagonist. Does your central character feel trapped by some hard choices? What are they? Does this pressure build up, as though walls are closing in on him or her? If there is a dilemma inherent in your story, then define it clearly.

2. If a dilemma is missing from your material, then try out possibilities to create one. Look at the difficulty faced by your protagonist and

then create a second, equally painful choice that complicates things for him or her. A dilemma will almost always enhance the dramatic power of your story.

3. Can you frame the dilemma as, *It's unacceptable to* _____ *and it's equally unacceptable to* _____? A dilemma should always put your protagonist between a rock and a hard place.

4. Is the dilemma big enough in scope to carry your entire script? Does it embrace most of the story, or does it get resolved quickly and then vanish? Does the resolution of the dilemma essentially constitute the end of the story?

5. Will your audience care about the protagonist and his or her dilemma? Are viewers going to be riveted by it? Does it pass the "So what?" test? Is it a dilemma of magnitude? If not, why not? What would make it more intense, more significant, more substantial? What's the worst it could be? Does this possibility radically expand your story? Don't try to control the creative process too tightly or be afraid to get in over your head. With an open mind, you may stumble into a bold new dimension.

6. Create a two-column chart polarizing the two equally unacceptable alternatives. This will help you to separate and solidify them. The less abstract the choices, the more easily you can work with them. Get your hands dirty. Don't try to be neat and orderly. Don't fear being repetitive. Use this chart to go hog wild and really play with the dilemma.

7. Have you found yourself in a similar dilemma in your own life, even if it's much smaller in scale? Write about what it's like to be trapped in such a dilemma.

8. Can you gauge how this dilemma might impact strangers? Will the average people in the street care passionately about this type of story and this type of dilemma? Will they identify with it? Will they feel connected to it? Will it move them? Why? The dilemma has to be universal—it has to resonate with real people in the real world, or you will lose your audience.

9. How can you complicate the dilemma and add new layers, aspects, and dimensions to it? You may find that it's much deeper and more complex than you first suspected. Remember that it takes a while for the obvious to become apparent, so you'll continually have new insights about the dilemma as your story develops. But don't forget, all these layers should still constitute one main dilemma, albeit a complex one.

10. Are you limping through the creation process or are you attacking it?

Don't be afraid of chaos. In fact, don't settle for less. Put in the necessary time to generate genuine depth and power, and to tap into the true potential of your story. Give the viewers the ride of their lives.

11. Check periodically to make sure that the two sides of the dilemma are still *equally* unacceptable. Certain plot choices can sometimes undo the dilemma as the two unacceptable alternatives change in relation to each other. Has one side become less painful? If so, then you should beef up the other side to correct the balance. This will ratchet up your story's dramatic power even further.

12. Take some time to write about your protagonist's dilemma. Explore its personality, its flavor, its intricacies, its hidden recesses. Play with the dilemma, try on new things, turn it over in your brain. It's not easy to hold the whole thing in your head. Putting it down on paper enables you to clarify your thinking and to see a complex dilemma more objectively. The more time you spend with the protagonist's dilemma, the more fully and clearly you'll be able to articulate it.

13. Get to know Dilemma inside out by comparing dilemmas in existing films. Compare John Anderton's dilemma in *Minority Report* with Richard Kimble's dilemma in *The Fugitive*. Put yourself in Kimble's shoes so that you feel his dilemma, and then articulate it. Are the two dilemmas similar? How?

14. As you begin to understand your script's dilemma at a deeper level, can you feel it in your bones? Do you carry it with you all the time? Does it deepen your insight into the people around you? Does it add to your plot?

Crisis

1. Does your story come to a crisis—a critical make-or-break point for the protagonist, a point at which a substantial choice must be made—roughly two-thirds to three-quarters of the way through the story? What does the crisis consist of? Articulate it clearly.

2. Does the crisis cause the dilemma to come to a head? Has the dilemma gotten so intense that both halves are at the breaking point? Is your protagonist about to cave in from the pressure? Remember that a crisis may occur when the protagonist is right on the edge of succeeding, so everything crashing down on him or her becomes that much worse.

3. What are the wildest possibilities for your crisis? The scariest? The most unpredictable? The most dangerous? The funniest? (Your response obviously will depend on what type of plot you're writing.)

4. Look at a crisis as the worst possible things happening at the worst possible moment. Could any other awful incidents be heaped onto this moment? These may include events happening nearby in the plot that could be moved to coincide with and complicate the crisis.

5. In your own life, have you been caught in a crisis similar to your protagonist's? Can you remember how it felt, even if it was on a much smaller scale? Writing about it may enhance your understanding and thus your ability to work with the crisis in your script.

6. Think about how the audience will be impacted by this crisis. Is there any way they can dismiss it by saying, "So what?" Can they see their own lives in it? Does it resonate on a universal level?

7. Defining the crisis for your plot can give fresh insight into the dilemma. This is also true of Decision & Action, the point at which a protagonist has to do something decisive about his or her dilemma. Looking back at the dilemma from its crunch point lets you see it form a new point of view. This hindsight can open up entirely new ideas for your plot. Stay flexible and keep your ideas in suspension, allowing new possibilities to work their way into your story.

Decision & Action

1. Does the crisis force your protagonist to make a critical decision? Does he or she take significant action as a result? Can you distinguish between the decision and the action? A decision alone is not enough; drama is the stuff of action.

2. Is the paralysis of the dilemma broken at the point of decision and action? Does your main character make a dynamic change? Does he or she begin either to pull things together or to fall apart at this crucial juncture? Remember, this is not yet the complete transformation that comes with resolution but the solid beginnings of this transformation—for good or bad.

3. Could this decision and action be more intense? What's the most intense it could be? Experiment with extremes. Think of people you know who have been through disastrous situations; think of high-intensity situations you've seen in the news. How does yours compare? Does more intensity improve your movie?

4. Is the true character of your protagonist revealed at this point? What exactly is revealed about him or her? Is something new emerging? Is something clarified? Has something crystallized? How will this affect the audience?

5. Have you been in a similar situation, one in which you had to make a critical decision and action in the face of crisis? How did it feel?

What if the situation had been even more extreme? What if at that point you had done something utterly catastrophic or incredibly heroic? Experiment with the possibilities.

Resolution

1. Does your protagonist actively resolve his or her dilemma? What does your protagonist do to wrap it up? Articulate this clearly. Even in a tragedy, the protagonist should be proactive in completing his or her own destruction.

2. Are you clearly distinguishing between Decision & Action on the one hand and Resolution on the other?

3. Is the resolution fixed in finality so it won't backslide or become undone? If your resolution is ambiguous, is that intentional or did it just somehow end up vague? Consider what will satisfy or disappoint your audience.

4. Is the resolution an ending worthy of a great movie? Is it substantial (even if it's a comedy)? The ending should be the movie's biggest moment. Does it complete the magic spell woven throughout the entire movie?

5. What are some other possible endings? Are you missing an obvious possibility that might better wrap up your story? Have you explored the extremes for your resolution? Try several radically different possible endings just to see if some great possibility is being overlooked. It's a good habit as a storyteller. In the process, you might even stumble onto an entirely different plot for another script.

6. How will the resolution gratify the audience? If it's a tragedy, will it knock the audience down with a powerful emotional experience they'll never forget? If it's a creative upbeat resolution, does the audience's final mood meet your intentions and expectations?

CHAPTER 2

Theme: Developing the Heart of Your Story

The way in which the protagonist resolves the dilemma expresses the *Theme* of the piece. Theme is what the movie is about—its soul, its heart, its animating spirit. Theme is the glue, the essence governing the dramatic material, shaping and binding the complete action of the protagonist into one central, coherent concept. A powerful theme from a great movie will resonate with the audience when the movie is over, and perhaps for the rest of their lives.

THE FUNCTIONS OF THEME

A clear statement of Theme provides a focal point, a unifying thread around which to weave the Dramatic Action. Playwriting teacher William Thompson Price, in *The Analysis of Play Construction and Dramatic Principle* (New York: W.T. Price Pub., 1908), says:

> All great or good plays are based upon Theme. You have only to refer to Shakespeare and Molière to determine the truth for yourself. The ordinary commercial play is one of situations for the sake of situations and not for the sake of Theme. Until we regard Theme of first importance, we shall have few good plays.

A simple example of "situations for the sake of situations" would be a soap opera: The nurse is having sex with the doctor that week for the sake of situation. It's purely about titillation and intrigue, not about thematic depth.

Theme Permeates Your Script

Theme works from the inside out, saturating the plot and the characters with a certain energy. The writer is often not aware at first of the thematic depth in the plot, because the total focus is usually on telling the best story possible. But once the theme is identified, it lends a sense of vision to the piece, gathering the material into one main action and infusing it with resonance and a sense of meaning. This is not to say that you should bombard the audience with it, but the whole script should communicate it at an organic level to the soul of the audience. Price, in *The Philosophy of Dramatic Principle and Method*, says:

> The highest form of plays involves the philosophy of life, so that if the Theme is not worth considering, there is usually little substance in a play. With a Theme your play will be about something . . . Theme does not stand alone. No principle does. Mere Theme will never make a play. But it is a definite something; it furnishes a spiritual atmosphere and the philosophy of the play; it gives the clue to the actual shaping of the play . . . the tone depends on it. It is the largest unit of the play.

Many writers can only clutch abstractly at what they think is the theme of their script. This inability to come to terms with a story's underlying idea can weaken the material. The writer misses the clarifying and strengthening effect that having a grasp of Theme brings to the process. It's important to note that the word *theme*—like *dilemma*—is misused extensively. People will say that the theme of a movie is, say, teen suicide, when that's really just a story element or part of the plot. Focus on the way in which the protagonist resolves the dilemma—this will keep you right on the theme in the truest sense of the word.

Say you're writing a tragedy (a rare type of film these days). Your protagonist, mistakenly thinking he's being brilliant, does something destructive and stupid, such as betraying his best friend to resolve his dilemma, and it gets him killed. If we look at the way in which he resolves his dilemma, we are, in essence, looking at the mechanics of failure. Note that we're not looking at *what* he does, but at *the way in which he does it*—his approach, his method, his thinking. He betrays his friend by way of this messed-up thought process, perhaps telling himself he can outsmart the situation, that he's sharper, faster, and more deserving. In this example, we are looking into the mind of a self-destructive character who is skilled at self-deception and whose thinking is flawed.

Insight on the way a character resolves his or her dilemma can give us as viewers a powerful look at aspects of ourselves—perhaps a brutally unflattering look. It can be a wake-up call. This, then, is the governing idea, what the above story is about thematically: the thought process that lures us into destruction—something we see around us in our daily lives. This theme informs the entire plot and ties it together, sustaining the story, shaping it, animating it, driving it, and setting its tone. It imbues the world of the story with the flavor of loss and failure—even though we in the audience may not recognize it until the trap springs shut on us along with our lead character. The focus is on the mechanics of this guy ruining his life—both his tendency to ruin it and *how* he ruins it. There should be a substantial character arc, a downhill transformation, culminating in his death. But the writer may not wish to overtly telegraph the character's impending failure. If the viewers come to care about him, then his failure will shock them profoundly. The theme will resonate on a deep level because the viewers will see the inescapable truth about their own failures and blind spots. That is the power of a great tragedy.

Theme Focuses Your Material

Your sense of theme will give focus to your story material. Think about your own life experience in relation to the example above. Think of those people you've known with destructive, deceptive, flawed thinking. If you know a psychiatrist, psychologist, or other student of human behavior, talk to him or her about these types of behavior patterns. Perhaps your own thought process has at times failed you in a similar way. Think about your own destructive behavior—how you were utterly compelled to do or say something catastrophic, and how nobody could talk you out of it. Delve to the bottom and really try to understand it at its deepest level. This will give you a clarity and focus that would help immensely if you were to write this script. A substantial comprehension of what's coming across thematically in your developing script will inform your writing, your plotting, your character development, your character's dilemma, your resolution—everything connected with your script. It will inhabit the soul of this script and imbue it with significant power, depth, and resonance.

THE USE OF THEME IN FILMS

Now let's evaluate our six movies to see how each illustrates the tool of Theme. Note that each has particular thematic substance and magnitude.

The Use of Theme in *Training Day*

In *Training Day*, the way in which Jake resolves his dilemma is by sticking to his principles, refusing to be dragged into Alonzo's corrupt system. Jake's moral compass will not follow Alonzo's lead, and he struggles to hold on to his integrity and his life. Thematically, this is what the movie is about: Doing the right thing. He knows what's right and he fights for that with every ounce of strength as his dilemma is resolved. By the end, Jake is blazing with that energy, and the audience is infused with it, too. Screenwriter David Ayer and director Antoine Fuqua both said that this movie asks, "What if one man says no?"—a question that is clearly the underlying idea of the film.

The Use of Theme in *What Women Want*

In *What Women Want*, the way in which Nick Marshall resolves his dilemma is by laying bare his soul to Darcy. He tells her the whole, unvarnished truth, allowing her to see into him just as he saw into her when he was reading her mind. He starts out shallow and closed off—the conventional male, complete with full Las Vegas treatment of women as second-class citizens and mere sex objects. But by seeing what makes Darcy really tick, he is able to transcend his own limitations and begins to experience a full, deep, and sincere relationship. This movie's theme is about opening up to life and opening up to love.

The Use of Theme in *Minority Report*

In *Minority Report*, the way in which John Anderton resolves his dilemma is by cutting through deception, dissolving the smoke and mirrors that hold Precrime together. This is a film about liberation. Anderton frees himself from being hunted, from drug addiction, from guilt, and from a loveless life. He sets free the people wrongly condemned under Precrime, and he liberates the three Precogs from their forced jobs as police psychics. He does all this by finding and fighting for the truth within a paralyzing web of complex, powerful lies. He cuts through the sacrosanct illusions and superstitions that lock everything down in this future world. The film's theme focuses on liberation from deception, from illusion, and from the haze of an enforced status quo.

The Use of Theme in *The Godfather*

In *The Godfather*, the way in which Michael resolves his dilemma is by becoming totally hardened, killing his enemies, and then cutting himself off from his wife and from what he might have been. The movie deals with the cost of power and the loss of the soul. While Michael does achieve total power, it costs him his innocence, his family, his freedom, and his happiness. This brings up a profound thematic question: "How much power do we really need, and what price is it worth?" This theme rings a bell with normal people because even in our everyday lives it is easy to overreach, perhaps taking on two jobs to provide for our families but in the process losing contact with the very family for which we're sacrificing. The famous quote from the Bible says it all: "What profits a man if he gains the whole world but loses his soul?"

The Use of Theme in *Tootsie*

In *Tootsie*, Michael resolves his dilemma when he finally earns Julie's trust and wins her heart. The way in which he does this is by becoming a whole man, honest and solid. Director Sydney Pollack described the theme of *Tootsie* like this: "Becoming a woman made a man out of Michael." This indicates a clear understanding of the soul of the story. Pollack discusses *Tootsie's* theme in

Jon Stevens's book *Actors Turned Directors* (Los Angeles: Silman-James Press, 1997):

> I concentrate very hard on understanding and articulating for myself and everyone else involved what I think the picture's about. By "what it's about" I do not mean story. What a film is about, in my opinion, has nothing to do with story. Quite the opposite. It's everything except the story. It's trying to arrive at a sort of spine, if you will, of the picture—a way of viewing it that directorially instructs you on a way to view each scene.
>
> *Tootsie* was about a man who became a better man for having been a woman. If you start to look at every scene and say, "In what way does this scene illustrate the idea of a man becoming a better man for having been a woman?" you see that, in the beginning, *Tootsie* works very hard to show you that part of him which needs redeeming, because if he's going to be better at something, he has to be worse at it first. The minute I define that as an idea, I can begin to measure every scene against it in some way. That doesn't mean it's going to be a good movie. It just means that I know what it's about, and can communicate that to the actors.

The Use of Theme in *Blade Runner*

In *Blade Runner*, Deckard resolves his dilemma by waking up and taking control of his own life. He grabs Rachael and runs, dropping out of the system that has trapped him. He not only changes the rules, he transcends the entire game. This is a film about humanity, liberty, and freedom—about living life to the fullest. A person on his or her deathbed will tell you, "Live *now* with everything you've got. Don't just be getting ready to live. Do it now!" Roy's intense desire to live electrifies Deckard into action and into life, and this is what the movie is about: living fully.

LET'S EXPLORE THEME
FOR OUR DEMO PLOT

When Zack, our detective from Chapter 1, resolves his dilemma, the way he does so is to release his inhibitions, to embrace life and become totally adventurous. This theme is described in the previous section on Resolution as "he comes to life, transforming into a free-spirited wildman" (see page 33). He was shut down and locked up—virtually trapped in his own life—and when he realizes the true threat to the woman he loves, he breaks free of his bonds and is able to rescue her as he rescues himself. He essentially goes crazy in order to become sane, which psychiatrists will tell you can be a healthy way to liberate yourself from the confines of a restrictive mind. And that's the essence of this movie: a wild path to liberation.

GETTING IN TOUCH WITH YOUR THEME

In his book *On Directing Film*, David Mamet writes that a script properly written communicates the theme clearly and powerfully *once at the end*. He counsels writers to trust in this, explaining that many dramatists are insecure about their ability to create a plot whose theme comes across clearly and powerfully at the script's end. Writers panic and resort to reiterating their theme constantly, he says, concerned that the audience won't get it. They restate it in every other scene and insert it into every tenth line of dialog—to the detriment of the drama. Mamet advises that a scene is just a scene, an event that helps make the plot work, not an opportunity to recapitulate the theme:

> The nail doesn't have to look like a house; it is not a house.
> It is a *nail*. If the house is going to stand, the nail must do
> the work of a nail. To do the work of a nail, it has to *look* like
> a nail.

Jimi Hendrix's comment on music can also be related to theme in this way: "We plan for our sound to go inside the soul of the person actually, and see if they can awaken some kind of thing in their own mind because there are so many sleeping people." If a film awakens something within the viewers, serving as a trigger or catalyst, then the theme can be internalized by them rather than merely impacting them temporarily and then fading away.

You may start out with a theme you feel compelled to communicate and then build a script around it, or you may start out with a killer story idea and gradually discover its thematic depths. Both approaches are valid—although in starting with a theme, beware of coming across as preachy. The most important thing is that you as the dramatist are in touch with your theme.

When Your Theme Takes on a Life of its Own

As you develop a script, your theme may gradually morph into something entirely different from what you set out to communicate. Many times it will end up more profound and more powerful than what you initially had in mind. It is often said that the theme selects the dramatist, so you may find yourself in territory you hadn't anticipated. Here's Price again, from *The Analysis of Play Construction and Dramatic Principle*: ". . . the dramatist begins gathering his material from the moment he selects his Theme—or his Theme selects him, which, perhaps, is the better way." Sometimes a script will drag you into something deeper or insist on a new tack. This is part of the beauty of the writing process: the experience of changing dimensions as you develop your material. If you're too stuck on your original theme, you may not be aware that it has gradually morphed into what might even be the *opposite* of your intention. But while you, the dramatist, are unaware of your theme's transition, your audience may be absorbing the deeper theme by osmosis. Don't miss the boat. If you don't recognize the true theme, you will not be able to work with it, reinforce it, or build upon it, and consequently you will be missing one of the fundamental strengths of your script.

Keep in touch with the theme as it actively emerges in the material by focusing on the way in which your protagonist resolves the dilemma. This will make the difference between seeing what you want to see and seeing what's really there. You may well be surprised and moved by the dynamic new universe you've stumbled into. Conversely, you may say, "No, I see where it has ended up, but I really *do* want my theme to be in line with my original intention." In that case, adjust the way in which the protagonist resolves the dilemma and steer it back toward the theme you prefer. This give-and-take is at the core of the writing process. Either let it take you or steer it yourself, though it's usually a combination of the two. And steering your material may mean hitting it hard with a hammer or feathering it gently—part directing things and part being responsive to whatever comes along.

Your theme shouldn't come across as a platitude, a Sunday school sermon, or a bumper sticker. Bernard Grebanier, in his book *Playwriting* (Thomas Y. Crowell Co., New York, 1961), says:

> Starting one's thinking with a theme is intelligent enough
> but can be somewhat precarious too. It too easily may lead
> the writer into contriving heavily moralistic or propagandis-
> tic demonstrations of an idea, into merely manufacturing
> situation and character for purposes of *illustrating* the theme,
> in which case neither situation nor characters will be dramat-
> ically convincing—so that the play ends by being a kind of
> sermon, which a good play should never be . . . a good theme
> should be an interpretation of life, not a lecture upon it. . . .
> When you have read a story or seen a play, you may not
> be conscious of the theme, but you may "feel" it . . . the
> theme should, rather, be deeply embedded in the action
> and in the nature of the leading characters.

It's a common misconception that the theme of a movie represents a deep answer to one of life's mysteries, or is a pearl of wisdom. This may well be, but the theme also might just be exploring an idea or asking a powerful question. As playwright Eugene Ionesco said, "Why do people always expect authors to answer questions? I am an author because I want to *ask* questions. If I had answers I'd be a politician." A theme doesn't necessarily have to be profound, but some thematic gravity can help any movie. Look for instance at the goofy comedy *Liar, Liar*, which has a resonant theme about integrity.

Starting with a Sense of Theme

As you start to wrestle with understanding your script's theme, you may have only a sense of it. You may not be able to articulate it, but that's okay. Audience members leaving a movie theater may be unable to verbalize its theme, but they can appreciate it at a gut level. As the dramatist, don't be afraid to start at that gut level. Many of us panic when we have only a partial understanding of something—we try to explain it before we really get it. Allow yourself to relax in your partially formed comprehension. Explore your *sense* of theme; dig deeply and develop it from the source.

Consider our example of the tragedy (see page 39)—the protagonist's self-destructive thinking and behavior that destroyed him in the end. While it may be easy to identify this theme, could you have articulated it at first? You *know* what it is, but it can take time to get beyond just *knowing* and *feeling* it. It may not be a conscious thought, but it will be embedded in you. Spend some time contemplating the theme and wrapping your brain around it. Don't feel forced to conceptualize it too early. Free yourself from the compulsion to put words to it prematurely.

Gradually your understanding will gel, and you'll grasp your theme more fully. You'll carry it around and work on it at a subconscious level as it echoes within you. You'll grow antennae for relevant material. You'll pick up things in the world around you, both plot-wise and thematically, and feed them into your subconscious computer. At a certain point in the process, your understanding will crystallize. Then all of a sudden you've got your theme—clearly, cleanly, and completely.

While it's important to state your theme in clear terms, beware of that cute one-line explanation because it can oversimplify the situation. Using a clever little aphorism or adage to sum up your theme can halt the exploring process. Experts in creativity say there are often ten "right" answers to a problem but many people, thinking there's only one, stop looking when they've found the first. If you're satisfied with a surface understanding of your theme, then you won't keep tunneling deeper for more substantial and complete comprehension.

Your theme may seem perfectly obvious once you perceive it, but it can take a great deal of work to achieve that clarity. In *The Philosophy of Dramatic Principle and Method*, Price wrote, "We keep narrowing down from the most general Theme to a specific one; and when it becomes specific it determines the nature of the play." You are really distilling your understanding of theme down to its quintessence, and when you arrive at that point the true identity of your story emerges. What was an unclear mass at first, a coalition of ideas and elements, now coalesces into one entity with a recognizable "personality." This clarity informs the tone, flavor, color, and texture of the script. Have you ever seen a TV weather program showing a hurricane? The eye forms at the center of the storm. The eye is the core of the storm—the clear point at its center around which everything swirls. In screenwriting terms, theme is the living core of your story.

Using Quotations to Explore Theme and Plot

When exploring a new theme, it may help to consult an encyclopedia or book of quotations. There are many, both in print form and on the Internet, but *Bartlett's Familiar Quotations* is probably the best known. Quotations can be useful not only for exploring theme, but also for examining story elements, enlivening characterization, and inspiring possible titles—as well as suggesting great dialog.

Be willing to spend time reflecting on quotes. Be open to unexpected sources; the unexpected can yield surprising freshness, as well as great depth and insight. Think about what you're trying to communicate to your audience with the complete action of your script, and equally important, listen to your material as it takes on a life of its own.

Here are some quotes that connect with the theme and plot of the six films discussed in *Writing a Great Movie*:

Training Day
The grand truth about Nathaniel Hawthorne. He says NO! in thunder;
but the Devil himself cannot make him say yes.
— HERMAN MELVILLE

If a man look sharply and attentively, he shall see Fortune; for though she
is blind, she is not invisible. — FRANCIS BACON

Honor is like an island, rugged and without a beach; once we have left it,
we can never return. — NICOLAS BOILEAU-DESPREAUX

My honor is dearer to me than my life. — MIGUEL DE CERVANTES

Bismarck was a political genius of the highest rank, but he lacked one essen-
tial quality of the constructive statesman: He had no faith in the future.
— A.J.P. TAYLOR

Powerful people never teach powerless people how to take their power
   away from them. — JOHN CLARKE

What Women Want

If we could see the miracle of a single flower clearly, our whole life
   would change. — BUDDHA

Your task is not to seek for love, but merely to seek and find all the
   barriers within yourself that you have built against it. — RUMI

The person who tries to live alone will not succeed as a human being.
   His heart withers if it does not answer another heart. His mind shrinks
   away if he hears only the echoes of his own thoughts and finds no other
   inspiration. — PEARL S. BUCK

It takes a lot of courage to release the familiar and seemingly secure,
   to embrace the new. But there is no real security in what is no longer
   meaningful. There is more security in the adventurous and exciting,
   for in movement there is life, and in change there is power.
                                    — ALAN COHEN

Minority Report

Let justice be done, though the world perish. — KING FERDINAND I

All great truths begin as blasphemies. — GEORGE BERNARD SHAW

Formerly, when religion was strong and science weak, man mistook
   magic for medicine; now, when science is strong and religion weak,
   man mistakes medicine for magic. — THOMAS SZASZ

Reality is that which, when you stop believing in it, doesn't go away.
                                    — PHILIP K. DICK

Among a people generally corrupt, liberty cannot last long.
                                    — EDMUND BURKE

Justice without strength is helpless, strength without justice is
   tyrannical. . . . Unable to make what is just strong, we have
   made what is strong just. — BLAISE PASCAL

Laws are like cobwebs, which may catch small flies, but let wasps
   and hornets break through. — JONATHAN SWIFT

The Godfather
*Power gradually extirpates from the mind every humane
and gentle virtue.*   — EDMUND BURKE

It is a strange desire, to seek power, and to lose liberty.
    — FRANCIS BACON

*You shall have joy, or you shall have power, said God; you shall
not have both.*   — RALPH WALDO EMERSON

*In the struggle for power, there is no middle ground between the highest
elevation and destruction.*   — TACITUS

A partnership with the powerful is never safe.   — PHAEDRUS

Power, like a desolating pestilence, pollutes whatever it touches.
    — PERCY BYSSHE SHELLEY

*Whose game was empires, and whose stakes were thrones; whose table
earth, whose dice were human bones.*   — LORD BYRON

Tootsie
Character is the governing element of life, and is above genius.
    — GEORGE SAUNDERS

I have lost all and found myself.   — JOHN CLARKE

Our experience is composed rather of illusions lost than wisdom gained.
    — JACQUES ROUX

The wise learn many things from their foes.   — ARISTOPHANES

God offers every mind its choice between truth and repose.
    — RALPH WALDO EMERSON

*When first we met we did not guess that Love would prove
so hard a master.*   — ROBERT BRIDGES

*Lay me on an anvil, O God. Beat me and hammer me into a crowbar.
Let me pry loose old walls; let me lift and loosen old foundations.*
    — CARL SANDBURG

Blade Runner
What is life where living is extinct?   — THOMAS HEYWOOD

*Live all you can; it's a mistake not to. It doesn't much matter what
you do in particular so long as you have your life.*   — HENRY JAMES

Study as if you were to live forever. Live as if you were to die tomorrow.

— ISIDORE OF SEVILLE

Dare to be wise: begin! He who postpones the hour of living rightly is like the rustic who waits for the river to run out before he crosses.

— HORACE

Listen to your enemy, for God is talking. — JEWISH PROVERB

Let others lead small lives, but not you. — JIM ROHN

START USING THEME IN YOUR OWN SCRIPT

1. Can you put your finger on the theme of your script? Even if you have trouble articulating it at first, you should be able to sense it. Look at the way in which the protagonist resolves his or her dilemma, and this will take you right to it.

2. Don't be afraid to dwell in a place of partial understanding. If you only have a sense of your theme, explore it; don't feel you have to put it into words right away. An unspoken, unformed thought can be clear enough as a starting point. Meditate on the theme you're sensing. Trust your feelings and instincts, and let your understanding grow naturally.

3. Explore books of quotations. What have other people throughout history said about the theme you're contemplating? What are some of the most pertinent quotes? Do they deepen or clarify your understanding of your theme? Do they also suggest story turns, new characters, intriguing dialog, or possible titles?

4. How has your own understanding of the theme grown and deepened as you spend time contemplating it? Has it taken on a life of its own? Could it be even deeper and more fully developed? How has the theme morphed? Are you happy with where it is now? Do you want to steer it in a certain direction? Tinker with how the protagonist resolves the dilemma and your theme will adjust accordingly.

5. Beware of beginning with a cute, simple, one-line statement of the theme. Instead, explore the theme by writing about it. You may discover that you have a better grasp of it than you suspected.

6. Don't beat the audience to death with the theme. Don't overstate it. It will ring through clearly and powerfully once at the end if you do your job right. Trust that. You want a story that resonates in the hearts and minds of the audience, not a message-laden mechanism.

CHAPTER 3

The 36 Dramatic Situations: Developing & Energizing Your Plot

Storytelling is a fascinating art. Life provides an inexhaustible supply of stories, but we must do the heavy lifting of building them into complete plots that grip and emotionally transform an audience. From conception to construction, the process of plotting a screenplay is equal parts complex technique and child's play. It is a clever combination of the writer's imagination and the resources at the writer's disposal.

One such resource is a book called *Thirty-Six Dramatic Situations*, by Georges Polti (The Editor Co., 1916). The book is founded on thirty-six story elements—such as *Madness, Disaster, Revolt, Ambition*, and *An Enemy Loved*—created in the 1700s by Italian playwright Carlo Gozzi. On the strength of endorsements by eighteenth-century writer-philosophers Johann Wolfgang von Goethe and Friedrich Schiller, the concept hung around for over a century until French classicist Georges Polti began a comprehensive study of Gozzi's work in 1868 and published his book in 1916. Each element presents potential ideas for a story by looking at the situations and playing "What if?" The thirty-six situations suggest story possibilities, trigger unexpected ideas, shake up stale plots, dimensionalize characters, and shatter writer's block. Once you learn how to use them, these situations can serve as a welcome brainstorming tool for those who spend their time spinning and weaving stories.

The *36 Dramatic Situations* are often compared to the periodic table of elements in chemistry. Every material substance that we know can be described quite completely with the 118 elements in the periodic table. Similarly, every plot can be described quite completely with the 36 Dramatic Situations.

Below is the full list of all thirty-six situations. Once you're familiar with them, this list will be all you need most of the time to generate new plot ideas.

1. Supplication
2. Deliverance
3. Crime Pursued by Vengeance
4. Vengeance Taken for Kindred upon Kindred
5. Pursuit
6. Disaster
7. Falling Prey to Cruelty or Misfortune
8. Revolt
9. Daring Enterprise
10. Abduction
11. The Enigma
12. Obtaining
13. Enmity of Kinsmen
14. Rivalry of Kinsmen
15. Murderous Adultery
16. Madness
17. Fatal Imprudence
18. Involuntary Crimes of Love
19. Slaying of a Kinsman Unrecognized
20. Self-sacrifice for an Ideal
21. Self-sacrifice for Kindred
22. All Sacrificed for a Passion
23. Necessity of Sacrificing Loved Ones
24. Rivalry of Superior and Inferior
25. Adultery
26. Crimes of Love
27. Discovery of the Dishonor of a Loved One
28. Obstacles to Love
29. An Enemy Loved
30. Ambition
31. Conflict with a God
32. Mistaken Jealousy
33. Erroneous Judgment
34. Remorse
35. Recovery of a Lost One
36. Loss of Loved Ones

IDENTIFYING AND DEFINING
THE 36 DRAMATIC SITUATIONS

Let's first look at and define the 36 Dramatic Situations, and then focus on how to use them to create and develop plot lines. All thirty-six situations are given simple definitions below to help you understand what they are and how they can vary. Each situation has subheadings, which we will see later (starting on page 74). Bear in mind that the less literally you take these situations, the more you'll be able to make use of them.

1. *Supplication*—Asking or begging for help. There are the obvious forms of this—seeking help, prayer, imploring—but you can also create a situation where a person's negative behavior represents a silent or implied cry for help.

2. *Deliverance*—Rescuing or being rescued. This can be a character saved from something—whether physically, emotionally, or spiritually—or it can be the attempt to save another character or oneself.

3. *Crime Pursued by Vengeance*—This situation is pretty straightforward: A crime has been committed (or merely perceived) and vengeance is sought.

4. *Vengeance Taken for Kindred upon Kindred*—Family infighting. A character getting even with her father because he beat her mother would be vengeance taken for her mom upon her dad. Bear in mind that "kindred" doesn't have to be literal; a character can have a "kinship" with his or her neighbors, friends, or coworkers.

5. *Pursuit*—In pursuit of something or someone, or being pursued. Your character can be in pursuit of something tangible—for example, a wife—or intangible, such as respect.

6. *Disaster*—*Disaster* can be different things to different people. It can be as obvious as a character's house burning down or as seemingly trite as a bad hair day. *Disaster* is entirely context-sensitive: If your character lives in Beverly Hills and somebody dyes her poodle the wrong shade of pink, it may be the end of the universe!

7. *Falling Prey to Cruelty or Misfortune*—A situation in which a character gets into trouble, gets hurt, or is destroyed by another character or by fate. Again, this sense of being "hurt" can be entirely subjective.

8. *Revolt*—Any kind of revolt, from a palace coup to a struggle in a marriage, friendship, or family. Mental, physical, spiritual—this situation covers anything relating to revolt, resistance, or an overturning (or attempted overturning), either literal or metaphoric.

9. *Daring Enterprise*—Doing something bold or adventurous, whether an action or a state of mind.

10. *Abduction*—A situation in which a character is kidnapped or is dragged into something against his or her will. It can also be a psychic abduction: a character drawn into another character's worldview, as in a cult.

11. *The Enigma*—The mystery, the riddle, the whodunit, the quest. This situation involves trying to figure out what to do, how to find something, how to get to the bottom of something. It can be an external riddle or an internal riddle. For example, a character may be seeking an answer about her psyche, her emotions, her pattern of behavior: "How did I get into this? Why do I keep making the same mistake?"

12. *Obtaining*—Trying to acquire or achieve something in any arena—physical, psychological, or spiritual—whether real or imaginary.

13. *Enmity of Kinsmen*—Animosity or hatred between kin (again, not necessarily literal kin). A character hating his brother, co-worker, or neighbors—or his neighbors bearing a grudge against him.

14. *Rivalry of Kinsmen*—A contest, struggle, or show of jealousy between brothers or any form of kin.

15. *Murderous Adultery*—This can involve not only adultery with murder, but also a situation where a character is in a murderous frame of mind due to adultery. Bear in mind that adultery doesn't necessarily have to do with a sexual relationship. If a character is in the Mafia and starts talking to the police, then he's going outside the Mafia relationship, and this can get him whacked.

16. *Madness*—There are many types of *Madness*, from something horrible such as a straitjacketed character in a padded cell to something delightful such as Jim Carrey frantically trying not to tell the truth in *Liar Liar*. *Madness* can be madcap and zany in a totally funny way; the movie *Animal House* comes to mind. This situation may also involve a fear of madness, varying degrees of insanity, or a crazy situation.

17. *Fatal Imprudence*—Doing something so unwise that it can have fatal or near-fatal consequences—although "fatal" is not necessarily literal. In *Tootsie*, when Dorothy tries to kiss Julie, that's *Fatal Imprudence*. No one literally died, but their friendship was dealt a lethal blow.

18. *Involuntary Crimes of Love*—Both this situation and 26. *Crimes of Love* (see page 54) relate to incest. A *Crime of Love* would be a character having sex with his daughter, whereas in an *Involuntary Crime of Love* the character doesn't know it was his daughter but finds out later. Also, consider how *Crimes of Love* can be understood metaphorically: a husband treats his wife poorly, or a parent does

something horrible to a child in the name of love or guidance.

19. *Slaying of a Kinsman Unrecognized*—In the literal sense, this refers to a character killing someone who turns out to be her brother because she didn't recognize him in the dark or after years of absence. But think metaphorically as well, and the situation can become a drunken father verbally abusing his daughter. She can feel "slain" and unrecognized: "Doesn't he know that I'm his little darling?" Or perhaps a boss puts down his most loyal employee so that he feels "slain" and unrecognized.

20. *Self-sacrifice for an Ideal*—Putting oneself on the line for something one believes in. A character can literally sacrifice or be willing to sacrifice his or her life, or can simply give up something he or she loves in order to preserve this ideal.

21. *Self-sacrifice for Kindred*—Sacrificing or being willing to sacrifice oneself for one's kindred (literal or metaphorical). The sacrifice can be material, spiritual, or physical—it need not refer to actual loss of life.

22. *All Sacrificed for a Passion*—Putting everything one is or has on the line for one's passion—throwing caution to the wind for a cause. This can mean either surrender or, conversely, wild excess in the name of some passion. A character can experience a positive transfiguration or lose their kid's college fund in Las Vegas.

23. *Necessity of Sacrificing Loved Ones*—Facing the possibility of having to sacrifice or betray someone a character cares about. This can mean throwing somebody to the wolves, leaving someone behind, or selling someone out.

24. *Rivalry of Superior and Inferior*—This situation is always interesting because it can be entirely subjective: Who is the superior and who is the inferior? The perception of who's on top—who's got the upper hand, who's morally superior, who's in control, who enjoys a higher status—can flicker back and forth from moment to moment. Consider the play *Who's Afraid of Virginia Woolf?*, in which the husband and wife keep one-upping each other with cruelty.

25. *Adultery*—This situation is straightforward, unless you're using it metaphorically in terms of violating a contract or understanding. *Adultery* can be used to play "What if?" in a script that needs an extra complication: What if one of your characters were committing adultery? Cultural responses and consequences will vary within this category, because for some situations the "adultery" is casual while for others it's an offense punishable by death.

26. *Crimes of Love*—Although this situation is primarily sexual in nature,

many types of violation or perceived violation in a love relationship can be viewed as "crimes," such as a wife deceiving a husband or the betrayal of a partner.

27. *Discovery of the Dishonor of a Loved One*—A character learning that he's been betrayed (in any number of ways), or finding out that someone he loves is or has been evil, criminal, or untrustworthy.

28. *Obstacles to Love*—Anything that stands in the way of a relationship, be it a disapproving parent, a jealous husband, a difference in financial or social status, a loved one not feeling love in return, or other forbidding circumstances.

29. *An Enemy Loved*—This situation—a character falling in love with or gaining respect for his or her enemy—can suggest many intriguing possibilities for a plot. Consider *The Silence of the Lambs*: Clarice—along with the audience—is utterly fascinated with and drawn to Hannibal Lecter. In *Blade Runner*, Deckard is drawn to the replicants and feels for them.

30. *Ambition*—The various strivings that a character might have, and the permutations these may undergo as the character and situation change. The whys and wherefores of *Ambition* open up possibilities as well. The *lack* of ambition is also telling—suggestive of a whole different set of possibilities. For instance, one could explore the complete lack of drive in someone who is rich and smart and free, but who fritters his life away.

31. *Conflict with a God*—This situation is almost always used metaphorically or poetically. While there are films in which a character is in actual conflict with a deity, more often in this situation a character confronts the powers that be—say, a weakling versus the neighborhood bully. Any weak entity up against a vastly more powerful force fits this situation; it doesn't require a religious connotation of any kind.

32. *Mistaken Jealousy*—Jealousy becomes a complicated situation when it is mistaken. A character thinks her husband is having an affair when in fact he's secretly working a second job to buy her an awesome anniversary gift. A great example of this is in *Tootsie* when Michael is three hours late for his dinner with Sandy. She waits outside his apartment, sees Dorothy go in, and thinks Dorothy is having an affair with Michael.

33. *Erroneous Judgment*—Any situation in which a bad assessment is made, whether huge or microscopic in scope. This can be a poor choice, jumping to conclusions, muddled thinking, or even just plain stupidity—or it can be the fear of making a bad choice.

34. *Remorse*—A character feeling sorry for an action, a harsh word,

or even a thought—all in varying degrees. There can also be the total *lack* of remorse in a character—think Charles Manson, who believes evil to be his divine calling.

35. *Recovery of a Lost One*—A character may find someone or some object that was lost—even his or her self-esteem or respect. This type of recovery is often getting one's real self back, or reclaiming one's marriage, job, or sense of adventure.

36. *Loss of Loved Ones*—A character may lose someone he or she loves, either through death, moving away, or any other way one can lose someone or something. It doesn't have to be a person that's lost; it can be a career, an object, an emotion, or a state of mind (such as sanity or self-respect). Again, the situation can be crucial, such as losing one's entire family in a fire, or it can be a character's dad missing his or her softball game.

The 36 Dramatic Situations represent one complete spectrum of ideas for storytelling. This tool is an extremely useful resource for writers, but it is by no means the be-all and end-all in creating a story. It is simply a device that comes in handy at certain stages of inventing and developing a story. You'll still need every ounce of creativity and imagination to make a script work. The primary function of the 36 Dramatic Situations is to provoke ideas and stimulate possibilities during plot development. Think of it as a free-association tool. One of the 36 Dramatic Situations may suggest an idea or a stream of ideas for a story already in the works, and that is precisely its job.

The less literally you interpret these dramatic situations, the more actual use you can get out of them. This flexibility can be very useful in triggering numerous alternative ideas for your script. This tool is often mistakenly referred to as the thirty-six dramatic "plots," but *Ambition* is not a plot any more than a piece of wood is a house. It is, rather, simply one element out of which a complex story can blossom.

USING THE 36 DRAMATIC SITUATIONS AS A BRAINSTORMING TOOL

The 36 Dramatic Situations can help you explore the potential in a raw idea, break a hackneyed plot out of cliché, develop multidimensional characters, complicate story lines, and provide unexpected twists in a script. Use this tool as a catalyst for "What if?" For instance, while thinking about your story, look at the situation *Madness* and ask yourself, "What if my character was crazy—completely and utterly off the deep end? Where does that take the story? Does it open up new plot possibilities or complicate things in an interesting way?" Then examine the ramifications of such possibilities: "Okay, if my character is totally nuts, then things would veer off in *this* direction, entirely changing this whole section of the plot. It would complicate everything having to do with this part of the story and completely screw up my ending—but maybe that's just what the script needs."

Follow the possibilities as far along as you can take them, just to see where they go. This is part of the creative process, part of your attack as a storyteller. (The great science-fiction writer Alfred Bester talks about *attack as a storyteller*—the level of energy with which you attack the story and the audience. If you want to see a master at work, read his stunningly creative and deeply resonant books *The Stars My Destination* and *The Demolished Man*. See page 247 for more about this concept.) Having gone out and tried that path, you may then decide either, "Wow, that's perfect! I'm going to use it," or, "I see where that goes, but it's not where I want to take this plot," or, "I want to use only part of it." Brainstorming is very much like trying on shoes: You can try on 200 pairs, but you're not obligated to buy anything.

Free Association

The 36 Dramatic Situations work very well as a free-association tool. One of the situations might prompt ten ideas, each of which can then set off ten more ideas, until your script is exploding with possibilities. Say that you're thinking about your plot and you look at the situation *Disaster*. It may remind you of the tornado that hit your house when you were a kid. You then remember seeing hundreds of family photos spilled onto the front lawn afterward. That in turn might remind you of working on the high school yearbook, when you lost the seniors' photos and the captain of the football team pummeled you in the parking lot. . . . And so on. Remembering how it felt when the football captain broke your tooth may trigger an unexpected idea for an ending that's had you stumped. One of the 36 Dramatic Situations could break the dam and release a flood of ideas, some of which may prove useful in developing your plot. As the flow of free-association ideas cascade, get them all down on paper. If one of the situations takes you on a strange little voyage, then this tool has done its job.

Starting a Story Idea from Scratch

The 36 Dramatic Situations are especially useful when you're just starting out with an idea and are scrambling to get a solid plot up and running. Say you've got a raw idea for a story in which a spy's curious son gets into his dad's hidden espionage equipment and accidentally sparks an international crisis (think *War Games*). You don't yet have a plot or characters or a setting or an ending—just a dynamic idea. Take a quick cruise down the list of the situations. *Supplication* suggests that the kid is in over his head and begging for help. Governments, thinking there's a real emergency, are panicking and looking for help. The father could be pleading for help; the mother, who doesn't know what's really going on, certainly would be. *Deliverance* hints that the kid could end up rescuing his father from a catastrophic situation. Maybe the kid even saves the world, and perhaps this whole adventure saves the family.

Crime Pursued by Vengeance proposes other directions for this story: Has this kid stumbled onto a great crime in the world of espionage or international politics? Are there people after him, perceiving his hijinks as a crime? Does one country retaliate against the other because of what the kid touched off? Does the father flip out on the son? Does the CIA come down on the father—or on the son? *Pursuit* evokes yet more possibilities: People after the kid, people after the father, the kid in pursuit of a solution, or the son seeking respect or attention from his dad. *Vengeance Taken for Kindred upon Kindred* smacks of infighting among the family members, and perhaps turf wars within the CIA. *Disaster* would certainly be very active in a story like this, whether personal disaster, psychological disaster, family disaster, the wrong people getting arrested, the wrong people getting out of jail, people getting killed or almost getting killed, international disaster, new enemies coming into power, possible nuclear disaster, or the end of the world.

Without taking this particular scenario too far, think of how each of the following situations could be active in this script idea: *Falling Prey to Cruelty or Misfortune, Revolt, Daring Enterprise, Abduction, The Enigma, Obtaining, Enmity of Kinsmen, Rivalry of Kinsmen, Madness, Fatal Imprudence, Slaying of a Kinsman Unrecognized, Self-sacrifice for an Ideal, Self-sacrifice for Kindred, All Sacrificed for a Passion, The Necessity of Sacrificing Loved Ones, Rivalry of Superior and Inferior, Discovery of the Dishonor of a Loved One, Obstacles to Love, An Enemy Loved, Ambition, Conflict with a God, Erroneous Judgment, Remorse, Recovery of a Lost One, Loss of Loved Ones.*

Starting with a basic idea—a boy who gets into his dad's spy equipment—and merely thinking about the 36 Dramatic Situations for a few minutes, we have constructed a road map showing many potential routes for a script. You can see how writer's block might cease to be a problem with the cascade of ideas this tool can trigger.

Exploring Plot Possibilities

While in time you might naturally come up with some of the aforementioned ideas, the 36 Dramatic Situations can help you explore a complete spectrum of possibilities more quickly and efficiently. These situations are either already inherent in the material or could be tried out to tweak the plot into new directions and dimensions. At first you may not see how each situation might fit, but as you spend more time with this tool you'll become quite versatile with it. Plus, you may stumble on things that never would have occurred to you in a million years. The important thing is that these thirty-six situations stimulate your mind and activate your imagination. Don't be afraid if you're overwhelmed with possibilities, because that's what true brainstorming really is. The 36 Dramatic Situations are often compared to Pandora's Box: an explosion of possibilities. You may be totally swamped, but it's an embarrassment of riches. Now you've got a full range of ideas to play with. Just take your time and work through the options.

Taking Stock of What You've Already Got

Another function for the 36 Dramatic Situations is to reveal the budding plot elements already present in a raw idea or in a script that needs work. You may be surprised at how your story idea is already seething with possibilities that have gone unnoticed. Seeing the active elements in a raw idea is akin to the astrophysics process known as "spectral analysis." Breaking down the light from a star into colors enables scientists to determine the percentages of iron, hydrogen, and so forth contained in the star. In the same way, you can see that a script idea contains *Remorse, Necessity of Sacrificing Loved Ones, Fatal Imprudence*, etc., before you even start working on it. You may discover that your story is loaded with more potential than you suspected, providing a great platform on which to build.

Maintaining Flexibility

Each of the situations can be applied in varying degrees of intensity, as Polti describes in *Thirty-Six Dramatic Situations*:

> Murder, for instance, may be reduced to a wound, a blow, an attempt, an outrage, an intimidation, a threat, a too-hasty word, an intention not carried out, a temptation, a thought, a wish, an injustice, a destruction of a cherished object, a refusal, a want of pity, an abandonment, a falsehood.

Each situation can be taken literally or in a more figurative sense. There is no one correct way to use the thirty-six situations, and there are no rules. You cannot make a mistake with them, any more than you can with a Lego set or finger paints. If this tool triggers ideas, then it's done its job. And don't be thrown by the slightly antiquated language—you'll get used to it quickly.

Overcoming Blind Spots

The total focus that story building demands can often create tunnel vision, blinding you to potential directions inherent in your material. Or there may be stunningly radical ideas that exist well beyond your normal orbit as a storyteller. In either case, the power of the 36 Dramatic Situations exposes you to a full spectrum of fresh, dynamic story possibilities that you might otherwise miss. For instance, if you feel as though you're forgetting something important but can't quite put your finger on it, then go through the list of thirty-six situations. You might stumble into a new dimension for your story so that your script may no longer inhabit the same universe.

It's important to remember that you are working with the raw elements of plot—the proto-matter of your story—and so the potential is immense for each situation you explore. Experiment. Try on the situations for fun. Play mad scientist and dynamite your ideas into new realms. Magnify parts of the plot, turn them inside out, violate them, and shake it all up. Think of wildly imaginative movies that you've seen and try to write with that adventurous spirit and level of abandon. The 36 Dramatic Situations will take you on many fascinating and fruitful journeys when you learn to use them fully and fearlessly.

THE USE OF THE 36 DRAMATIC SITUATIONS IN FILMS

Now let's look at the 36 Dramatic Situations in each of the six films studied in this book. The primary goal in doing so is to show you the tool in action so that you can familiarize yourself with its function. Once you know how it works, you will be able to develop a raw story idea into a working plot. In other words, the end goal is not this after-the-fact script analysis, but rather constructing a plot of your own. In essence, we're taking a working clock apart to teach you how to build one from scratch.

Each analysis below could go a lot deeper, but that would run too long and complex for our needs in this book. The 36 Dramatic Situations are not an overly complicated tool. Once you understand it fully, then you've got it and you'll be ready to use it. So with that in mind, as you're going through the following analyses, feel free to stop reading and move on once you grasp the process. This section covers all six films, but don't feel as though you have to read them all. Come back to them later if you want to substantiate your knowledge of the 36 Dramatic Situations.

The Use of the 36 Dramatic Situations in *Training Day*

Pretend you are watching *Training Day* again while reviewing the list of thirty-six situations. What's going through your brain? What do you see? Do any of the situations jump out at you in relation to the film? Look down the list (page 51) and select those situations that seem to be active in the nucleus of the story. Can you see: *Revolt, Daring Enterprise, The Enigma, Madness, Rivalry of Kinsmen, Self-sacrifice for an Ideal, Rivalry of Superior and Inferior, Discovery of the Dishonor of a Loved One, An Enemy Loved, Ambition, Conflict with a God, Erroneous Judgment, Slaying of a Kinsman Unrecognized,* and *All Sacrificed for a Passion*? If you don't see how they relate, don't worry. It takes some experience working with the 36 Dramatic Situations to become familiar with them, to see how versatile they are, and to get your sea legs with this tool. Now let's examine each situation, its role, and why it stands out:

Revolt—Jake is in revolt against Alonzo, and he wins. But Alonzo also rebels—against his situation with the Russians as well as against the norms of police work that Jake considers sacred.

Daring Enterprise—Jake is on a brave adventure, dealing with Alonzo and later trying to take him down. Alonzo, too, is involved in *Daring Enterprise*, working the system to hustle and rob and murder his way out of the death sentence that the Russians have hung over his head.

The Enigma—Jake has a life-or-death riddle staring him in the face: He must figure out how to do what Alonzo tells him without losing his soul—or he will lose his place on Alonzo's squad. That's his dilemma, and he's really stuck. In addition, Alonzo clearly has a puzzle on his hands with the high-stakes chess game he's caught up in.

Madness—This is a particularly active element in *Training Day* because Jake's whole world gets turned upside down. He's getting stoned out of his mind on PCP first thing on the job, and Alonzo is utterly unpredictable: scary, intoxicating, loony, wise, deadly, and fatherly all at once. None of Jake's anchors to reality are holding very well. This craziness builds until Alonzo tries to have Jake murdered. Alonzo is caught up in an insane situation as well: His own madness caused him to beat a Russian to death in Las Vegas, so now he owes the Russians $1 million in order to buy his life.

Rivalry of Kinsmen—There's a genuine kinship between Jake and Alonzo—as well as an ongoing rivalry, which escalates to a fight to the death by the end of the film.

Self-sacrifice for an Ideal—This situation is absolutely central to the story because Jake risks everything in his fight for justice, honesty, and his vows as a police officer.

Rivalry of Superior and Inferior—Alonzo appears vastly superior to Jake in virtually every way. If Jake makes a move, Alonzo is there ahead of him; if he wonders about something, Alonzo already has it figured out. It's David versus Goliath. And yet Jake is morally superior to Alonzo, which becomes increasingly apparent as the movie progresses. Ultimately, Jake turns out to be completely superior, as proven when he defeats Alonzo in the film's final struggle.

Discovery of the Dishonor of a Loved One—Jake discovers how deeply and totally crooked Alonzo is, and this knowledge grows as he finds himself sinking deeper and deeper in the mire.

An Enemy Loved—This situation is right at the core of the film: Jake is fascinated with Alonzo. Although it becomes increasingly clear to Jake that Alonzo is his enemy, he has huge respect for him nonetheless. Everything that Alonzo tells him about doing undercover police work is absolutely true, and Jake knows this. On the flip side, Alonzo discovers that he respects Jake for his "magic eye" (Alonzo's term for how Jake sees what other cops miss). Alonzo is reminded of himself when he was young and idealistic.

Ambition—Jake burns with unstoppable ambition. He wants to make Alonzo's squad more than anything. He tells his wife that he wants his own division and wants a house like the division commanders. Jake's ambition is his fatal flaw (see page 16); it drives him into Alonzo's trap. Alonzo has a great deal of ambition as well, not only for the $1 million to pay the Russians, but also for his long-term goals. He would love to be one of the "three wise men" at the restaurant, making high-level decisions and accepting bribes, rather than working the streets.

Conflict with a God—This situation is very much at the nucleus of *Training Day*. Jake is in conflict with Alonzo, who is the god in Jake's new world. Jake is completely in over his head because Alonzo seems infinitely powerful. But then, to Alonzo's surprise, it turns out that Jake is a powerful god in his own right, which he proves by destroying Alonzo.

Erroneous Judgment—Jake vastly underestimates Alonzo in many ways, but Alonzo also underestimates Jake, and it costs him everything.

Slaying of a Kinsman Unrecognized—Jake is feeling "slain"and unrecognized as Alonzo drags his fellow officer deeper into dangerous territory.

All Sacrificed for a Passion—Both Jake and Alonzo are willing to lay everything on the line for what they believe in.

The next step would be to prioritize these situations, because some are more central or pertinent to the story than others. It's helpful to write each one on a 3 x 5 card and then sort them by priority. In computer programming they call this a "bubble sort," in which the best ones float to the top. *Conflict with a God* pops right to the top, followed by *An Enemy Loved, Madness, Ambition, Revolt, Daring Enterprise,* and *The Enigma. Crime Pursued by Vengeance, Rivalry of Superior and Inferior,* and *Self-sacrifice for an Ideal* are all central, too. But *Conflict with a God* is the most central situation for *Training Day,* because Jake is up against such an incredibly powerful foe. He is also fascinated with this foe and has tremendous respect for him, so *An Enemy Loved* is smack at the core of this story as well. *Madness* and *Ambition* are right there, too, because they explain what Jake is experiencing (madness) and who he is (ambition).

The Use of the 36 Dramatic Situations in *What Women Want*

What Women Want is such a sweet love story that right away it's easy to see *Obstacles to Love, An Enemy Loved,* and *Necessity of Sacrificing Loved Ones.* Also quite central are *Deliverance, Ambition, Conflict with a God, Rivalry of Superior and Inferior, Discovery of the Dishonor of a Loved One, Crime Pursued by Vengeance, Madness, The Enigma, Disaster,* and *All Sacrificed for a Passion.*

Obstacles to Love—This situation is central to the story because it concerns the barriers that stand between the growing love of Nick and Darcy: He's hunting her, she's defensive, he's mad at her, and he's reading her mind. The fact that he can hear her thoughts is the biggest obstacle because he's using it to steal her ideas and get her fired. He's a predator—a kinder, gentler predator in this romantic comedy, but a predator just the same. Another impediment is that Darcy got burned by falling in love with her last husband at work, so she's reluctant do that again. Plus, Nick is from old-school Las Vegas where women are second-class citizens, and Darcy is a modern, liberated woman.

An Enemy Loved—Nick has literally fallen in love with his enemy. He's attracted to her on many levels; she's good looking, smart, funny, talented, straightforward, and gregarious. So while he's working to get rid of her, he also has tremendous and growing respect for her—and it grows as he learns more about her. He's fascinated with his enemy. It's the essence of his dilemma.

Necessity of Sacrificing Loved Ones—Nick's mission is to get rid of Darcy, especially once he begins to fall for her. This also describes Darcy's situation: Once she gets to like him, she needs to keep him at arm's length emotionally since she works with him. In the end, too, Darcy has to fire Nick because he stole her idea and got her fired.

Deliverance—Nick's deliverance from his emotionally shutdown state is at the core of this story. He learns how to love, and how to be more connected to the real world, to the people around him, and to his real self.

Ambition—Nick's thwarted ambition is the launching pad of the story: Darcy taking "his" job drives his revenge. Nick gets to work at 10:00 A.M. every day, so he is not overly ambitious, but still he expects to get that corner office. Darcy, on the other hand, is very ambitious—going after big accounts, overhauling an antiquated advertising agency, and working long, hard hours. Nick's ambition grows and changes as the story moves along, and his fall for Darcy mirrors that ambition.

Conflict with a God—Nick is up against a mighty deity in Darcy. She seems to see all and know all, and she is not the pushover that Nick, with his mind-reading ability, expected her to be. But Nick is also a god in his own right since he can hear what women think. With any move she makes, Darcy keeps finding herself a full step behind him.

Rivalry of Superior and Inferior—Nick feels superior to Darcy, and Darcy keeps finding that Nick has beat her to the punch. But conversely, his ability to hear her thoughts reveals that she is, in fact, superior to him in many ways.

Discovery of the Dishonor of a Loved One—Darcy finds out near the end of the movie that Nick has stolen her ideas and robbed her of her job.

Crime Pursued by Vengeance—Nick feels a great injustice has been done when Darcy is hired in his place: She's a woman and she's from outside the firm. Not only is he seeking vengeance, but he's going at it *with* a vengeance. Meanwhile, when Darcy finds out that he's undone her (a crime), she fires him (vengeance). Also, Erin perceives that the whole world is against her—more specifically, the way she's treated at the ad agency is a "crime"—and suicide is her intended vengeance.

Madness—Losing the corner office to Darcy is madness for Nick. But this bizarre ability to read women's minds also drives him crazy. It's madness for Darcy as Nick keeps trumping her best efforts to transform the agency. It's madness for Nick as he falls in love with Darcy while still busy stealing her ideas. Plus, the suicidal Erin is bordering on insanity, and Nick's assistant, Annie, is losing her mind because she isn't getting work commensurate with her abilities.

The Enigma—Nick has to figure out how to get rid of Darcy, an especially demanding challenge since she's so brilliant at her job. He also has to deal with the difficulties of being able to read women's minds and being in love with his sworn enemy. Meanwhile, Darcy has to solve the mystery of Nick outmaneuvering her at each step.

Disaster—It's a disaster when Nick loses his job to Darcy, as well as when he's overwhelmed by hearing the thoughts of all the women around him. It's a disaster for Darcy as Nick keeps mysteriously undermining her. These build to a major disaster when Nick's sabotage gets Darcy fired, and when Darcy learns that he has stolen all her ideas.

All Sacrificed for a Passion—Nick gives up his whole aberrant, chauvinistic persona in the end for his love of Darcy.

The Use of the 36 Dramatic Situations in *Minority Report*

Minority Report presents us with *Madness, Disaster, Pursuit, The Enigma, Conflict with a God, Loss of Loved Ones, Crime Pursued by Vengeance, Rivalry of Superior and Inferior, Falling Prey to Cruelty or Misfortune, Revolt, An Enemy Loved, Daring Enterprise, Supplication, Abduction, Deliverance,* and *Rivalry of Kinsmen*. Let's take a look at how each of these situations is active.

Madness—The Precogs predict that Anderton will kill a man he's never met, his own team is hunting him, he's attacked by venomous plants, he must hide his identity by swapping out his eyes, he kidnaps and goes on the run with a powerful psychic, and he's doubting the very bedrock elements of his entire life—his whole world is upside down. And all this is on top of his grief over his lost son and estranged wife, as well as the madness of his neuroin addiction. The situation is also crazy for the cops in Precrime who are forced to hunt their former boss. Agatha's and the Precog twins' precognitive visions can haunt them. Lamar has used warped logic in committing murder in order to prevent murder, and Lois Hineman, the weird lady in the greenhouse, acts pretty nutty, too. This future world itself is crazed, with all the insanely invasive advertising, the retinal IDs, mechanical police spiders entering your home, and the whole existence of Precrime.

Disaster—Anderton's life falls apart when Precrime fingers for him for the future murder of Leo Crow; his life already was a mess, but Danny coming after him spells disaster. The whole Precrime program hangs on the edge of disaster with the Justice Department trying to take it over. Agatha's life has become a disaster—it took the murder of her mother to get the Precrime program started—and it's a disaster for Lamar when Anderton busts him for that murder.

Pursuit—Anderton is pursued by his own team as he in turn chases down the clues that could free him. Anderton says that "everybody runs," and Agatha keeps yelling, "Run!" Anderton is in pursuit of a solution to the improbable murder prediction, as well as being in pursuit of his old life, his sanity, and his lost family.

The Enigma—Anderton has to figure out whether he or Precrime is flawed. Is he going to kill someone or isn't he? He's attempting to extract the missing minority report from Agatha, if it even exists, while Agatha is trying to uncover the truth about her mother's murder. The Precrime cops are trying to find Anderton as he continues to evade them.

Conflict with a God—Anderton is up against the whole infallible machine of Precrime, as well as Lamar, the man behind the curtain. Anderton's whole universe has disappeared—he's lost his son, his wife, his job, and his sense of which way's up—and he struggles against the world that created him, which grabs at him at every turn. Agatha is in the same boat, trying to resist the weight of the world bearing down on her, crushing the life out of her with never-ending visions of murder.

Loss of Loved Ones—Anderton has lost his connection with Precrime and the people working there, and they've lost him. He's lost his son, his wife, his sense of security, and his confidence—everything that held him together. Agatha has lost her mother and is haunted by it. Lamar is faced with losing Precrime. Leo Crow can't support his family if Anderton doesn't kill him.

Crime Pursued by Vengeance—Danny is going after Anderton with a vengeance for the crime it is foretold he'll commit. Anderton believes he's been framed by Danny for this crime, so he's pursuing exoneration. He's lost his son to a vicious crime, and now seems at war with the whole world. Precrime by definition lashes out at crime, making criminals pay even before crimes are committed. Agatha is searching for an answer to the murder of her mother. Anderton seeks justice and revenge in his attempt to destroy Lamar.

Rivalry of Superior and Inferior—Anderton is hunted by Precrime cops, who outnumber and overpower him in every way, but he continues to come up with resources that give him the upper hand. The Justice Department is attempting to subsume Precrime. Lamar is superior to Anderton in many ways, but Anderton takes him down in the end.

Falling Prey to Cruelty or Misfortune—Anderton's life has been unbearable since his son disappeared and his wife left him. He also falls prey to the prediction that he will commit murder. Agatha is in the same boat: Her mother was murdered and she lives the life of a freak. Anderton is then dragged through hell when he thinks he's found his son's murderer. Lamar suffers when his plan unexpectedly crumbles.

Revolt—Anderton is forced to revolt against Precrime, which is attempting to destroy him. Agatha is fighting to escape her terrible fate as a Precog. The program of Precrime itself is an innovative rebellion against murder. Lamar warns Anderton that the attorney general is out to take over Precrime, so they must rise up and protect themselves and their turf.

An Enemy Loved—Anderton knows and cares for his colleagues in Precrime, who are now hunting him. Lamar, his father figure, has now become his enemy. Lamar loves Anderton but becomes his enemy when he begins inquiring about Anne Lively's murder.

Daring Enterprise—Anderton sticks around to find out if he will really murder Leo Crow, when he should disappear to save himself. He risks having his eyes swapped out, and he breaks into Precrime to steal Agatha. In fact, all his moves are bold once the brown ball drops on him and he goes on the run. Agatha is caught up in it, too, once she's on the outside and helping Anderton. Lamar's murder of Anne Lively in order to keep Agatha for Precrime was an audacious and risky move.

Supplication—Agatha begs Anderton for help in exposing who murdered her mother. Anderton asks for help from Lois Hineman, the greenhouse lady, as well as from Agatha and from Lamar. When Anderton gets away with Agatha, they're both like newborns, flushed out into a new world, lost, in trouble, desperately seeking help from each other.

Abduction—Anderton's son was kidnapped and murdered, supposedly by Leo Crow. Anderton steals Agatha from Precrime. On a more figurative level, Anderton's life has been stolen from him by the loss of his family and by the prediction of his future crime.

Deliverance—Anderton and Agatha rescue each other from their respective fates: Anderton is innocent of murder and is freed from his trap of guilt, fear, addiction, and emotional sterility, and Agatha is released from slavery as a police psychic. Also, the Precogs, Anderton, and Lamar intended to deliver the D.C. area from murder, but in the end America is saved from a national Precrime system. All the haloed prisoners are released, too.

Rivalry of Kinsmen—Anderton is now at war with his former friends and colleagues, the Precrime cops. When Anderton discovers that his father figure, Lamar, is the architect of his arrest, the two go to war.

The Use of the 36 Dramatic Situations in *The Godfather*

In *The Godfather*, it's clear how much *Daring Enterprise* comes into play. Other central situations are *Disaster, Madness, Self-sacrifice for Kindred, Conflict with a God, Rivalry of Superior and Inferior, Revolt, Ambition, Disaster, Pursuit, The Enigma, All Sacrificed for a Passion, Deliverance, Loss of Loved Ones, Discovery of the Dishonor of a Loved One, Crime Pursued by Vengeance,* and *Rivalry of Kinsmen.*

Daring Enterprise—Michael is incredibly bold. This becomes clear when he protects his father from the assassination attempt at the hospital, facing down the brutal police captain, McCluskey. It also pops up when he kills Sollozzo and McCluskey at the restaurant and when he goes after the beautiful Apollonia, in Corleone, Italy. When Apollonia's father feels insulted, Michael explains that he means no offense: He's interested in her, he's in hiding, and he'd like to meet her. He knows exactly what he wants and he goes right after it. At each juncture, Michael displays a bold strategy and daring tactics: going after Moe Green, assassinating the heads of the five families, executing the traitors within his organization, and lying to Kay about all of it. This nerve is a huge part of why Michael is such a fascinating and well-loved character.

Disaster—Michael is on both the receiving and the delivering ends of disaster. It pours down on him: his father is shot, he's drawn into the family business, Sonny is executed, Apollonia is killed in an explosion, and the family struggles with internal divisions. But Michael also doles it out when he gets rid of Sollozzo and McCluskey, the heads of the five families, and Tessio and Carlo.

Madness—Michael is pulled into the madness of the family crime business, drawn into the dark side he had remained apart from previously. His father told him it would ruin his life, and it does; Michael has lost his humanity by the end of the film. There is also a certain madness in the way Barzini secretly betrays the family. The scene is insane when Don Corleone gets shot on the street and Fredo freaks out. Sonny exhibits a form of madness with his hot temper.

Self-sacrifice for Kindred—Once his father gets shot, Michael gives up his happy civilian life in order to try and save the family, which can't survive without him stepping into the driver's seat.

Conflict with a God—Michael is up against Barzini, a powerful warrior who operates behind the scenes. But Barzini must confront both the Godfather and Michael, who also possesses the great powers and abilities of his father—as Barzini discovers by underestimating him.

Rivalry of Superior and Inferior—Barzini feels as though he's well on his way to dominating and eliminating the Corleones, but it's Michael who emerges as the superior warrior. Fredo hates being the older brother who gets left out of the loop. Don Corleone is a master strategist who routinely outthinks his opponents, and Michael is cut from the same cloth.

Revolt—Barzini rebels against the Corleones, and Michael leads a counterrevolution against Barzini to protect his family. There are internal divisions within the Corleone family as well.

Ambition—Michael's original ambition is to live as a legitimate civilian, but that changes with the attempt on his father's life. As things heat up, Michael uses his own ambition to halt the ambitions of his enemies. Almost everyone in the movie is extremely ambitious, hardwired to move a notch up the totem pole whenever possible.

Disaster—The attempts on Don Corleone's life are disastrous to the family, as is Sonny's assassination. So is the attempt on Michael, which kills his Sicilian bride. The family is under attack and showing internal cracks, which portends catastrophe. Michael sows calamity among his enemies, and ends up killing them all. Kay is losing Michael, while Michael loses his soul—a tragedy for them individually and as a couple.

Pursuit—Barzini is out to take down the Corleones, and Michael is looking to destroy him in return. The Corleones are hounded from the outside—the legitimate world, the five families, pressures of the changing business—as well as from the inside.

The Enigma—Michael is challenged by how to protect the family. Once he and his father learn that Barzini is behind it all, they must figure out how to take him down. Barzini searches for the key to destroying the enigmatic Corleones and taking over.

All Sacrificed for a Passion—In the end, Michael gives up everything he used to be, emerging as a soulless crime lord because of his passion to save his family.

Deliverance—Michael rescues the family from danger by killing everyone who could possibly hurt them.

Loss of Loved Ones—Michael loses Sonny, his Sicilian bride, his father, and his happy civilian life with Kay.

Discovery of the Dishonor of a Loved One—The discovery that Tessio is the traitor is a disgrace within the family because he was so close and trusted, and because respect and honor are so valued in the Mafia world.

Crime Pursued by Vengeance—Michael and his family seek a very literal vengeance for the attempts on Don Corleone's life. To Barzini, the Corleones have too much power—a crime that he needs to correct.

Rivalry of Kinsmen—Tessio and Clemenza want to break off from the family. The rivalries between the different families within the Mafia, who should be watching one another's backs, is a rivalry of "kinsmen."

The Use of the 36 Dramatic Situations in *Tootsie*

Obstacles to Love is the situation at the heart of *Tootsie*. This is true of most romantic comedies, since it is what usually provides the tension in these films. The following situations are also central to the plot: *Deliverance, Crime Pursued by Vengeance, Pursuit, Disaster, Revolt, Daring Enterprise, Madness, All Sacrificed for a Passion, Erroneous Judgment, Conflict with a God, The Enigma, Rivalry of Superior and Inferior, Ambition,* and *Recovery of a Lost One.*

Obstacles to Love—We care so much about Michael's love for Julie, but many obstacles stand in the way of their love. Will he escape from his disguise and win her over? Will she discover his secret? Will Michael change as a person—enough to have a shot at winning her? Will Dorothy escape the clutches of John Van Horn or Julie's father? There are also obstacles to Sandy's love for Michael.

Deliverance—By becoming Dorothy, Michael ultimately transforms himself into a new man. He wins Julie and renews his acting career. The lives of all the women on the show are changed—"rescued" by Dorothy.

Crime Pursued by Vengeance—In the beginning, Michael sees how he's treated as an actor as a crime (even though it's his own fault) and seeks vengeance. Dorothy sees how women are being treated and becomes a crusader against this abuse.

Pursuit—Michael is in pursuit of Julie, Sandy is in pursuit of Michael, John Van Horn is in pursuit of Dorothy, and Michael (as Dorothy) is in pursuit of ending the power of the director, Ron Carlisle (Dabney Coleman), over the women on the show, especially Julie.

Disaster—Michael's life is a disaster at the start of the movie. The whole twisted romance with Sandy messes his life up even more. Once he becomes Dorothy, disaster unexpectedly reappears when John Van Horn tongue-kisses Dorothy. Michael's inability to get Julie because he's dressed as a woman is personal disaster, and Dorothy's contract being picked up for another year is a disaster both personal and professional. Then it all really caves in: Dorothy tries to kiss Julie, Les proposes to Dorothy, John Van Horn tries to rape Dorothy, and Sandy explodes when Michael admits he's in love with another woman. Finally, it's a huge blow for both Julie and Les when they discover that Dorothy is really a man. The use of disaster in a comedy accentuates the humor; we laugh most when everything is in shambles.

Revolt—Michael revolts against his stalled career by becoming Dorothy. Then Dorothy leads a revolt of the women against the male-dominated structure of the show.

Daring Enterprise—Michael becoming Dorothy is quite a bold move, and Dorothy herself is an extremely audacious character who inspires courage in the other women on the TV show.

Madness—Michael starts out with real problems that jeopardize his career. But madness is most evident when he becomes Dorothy and everything goes haywire—the whole scheme blows up in his face. Michael's roommate, Jeff, must deal with the comic insanity of Michael being Dorothy, and Sandy's madness is from being left in the dust by Michael for Julie. Things get crazy for Julie when she thinks Dorothy is a lesbian, and again when Dorothy turns out to be a man.

All Sacrificed for a Passion—Michael gives up his manhood to get a much-needed acting role. Michael's passion for Julie ends up burning away all his obnoxious behavior and he emerges as a new man.

Erroneous Judgment—Michael finds that he has seriously misjudged the ramifications of playing a woman on a soap opera—particularly with all the making out that happens on the show.

Conflict with a God—Dorothy clashes with Ron, the director, who finds that he has bitten off more than he can chew. In the beginning of the film, Michael is at odds with the all-powerful entertainment industry, which no longer wants him.

The Enigma—Michael has to solve the conundrum of being on the show and being in love with Julie, all while Sandy chases after him. Sandy is attempting to solve the mystery of what's up with Michael. People on the show are constantly trying to figure out Dorothy.

Rivalry of Superior and Inferior—Ron feels superior to Dorothy at first but quickly finds himself overpowered and unable to recover. The struggle for gender equality also plays out in this 1982 film.

Ambition—Michael is incredibly ambitious to get acting work, but he ruins all his jobs because he must always have things his way. Dorothy is a champion of women's rights, and Michael wants to land Julie. Dorothy inspires Julie with the ambition to break free from Ron's dominance.

Recovery of a Lost One—Michael finally gets Julie back in the end, and Julie gets Dorothy back in essence. Through the whole process of being Dorothy, Michael also gets his true self back.

The Use of the 36 Dramatic Situations in *Blade Runner*

In the original feature release of *Blade Runner*, Deckard and Rachael drive up north to freedom, breaking the story out of the claustrophobic ambiguity of the director's cut ending. The film is about human liberation, and in the original version you truly get the feeling that *Deliverance* is at its core. Other potent situations are *The Enigma, Madness, Supplication, Conflict with a God, An Enemy Loved, Disaster, Revolt, Crime Pursued by Vengeance, Daring Enterprise, Rivalry of Superior and Inferior, Obtaining, Necessity of Sacrificing Loved Ones, Pursuit, Falling Prey to Cruelty or Misfortune, Loss of Loved Ones, Slaying of a Kinsman Unrecognized, Remorse,* and *Obstacles to Love.*

Deliverance—Roy saves Deckard's life and shows him the importance of really living, and Deckard gets it, waking up to escape with Rachael. Deckard and Rachael also save each other from their emotional deadness, essentially making each other human. Their escape to the north delivers them from the dreary, rainy, nightmarish world of 2019. The replicants, too, seek deliverance—from their status as subhuman.

The Enigma—Deckard puzzles over the replicants (much more so in the voice-over version). Why do they collect family photos when they don't have families? Why do they display emotions if they're not human? Why does he care about them? How can he escape the dispiriting job of hunting them?

Madness—The whole world is crazy in *Blade Runner*. It's dismal, dark, twisted, depressing, and abandoned (most people live off-world). The replicants frantically try to extend their four-year life span. As the film builds to climax, the madness all comes to a head: Roy kills Dr. Tyrell and J. F. Sebastian, Deckard stumbles into J. F.'s loony apartment, Roy finds Pris dead, and Deckard faces off with Roy, this unstoppable high-level military replicant who behaves like an insane god.

Supplication—Deckard seeks a way out of his job. Rachael begs him for help once she is discarded by Tyrell and discovers that she's a replicant. The replicants beg for help in extending their life span.

Conflict with a God—Deckard takes on Roy, who is created perfectly superior to everyone. Roy confronts his creator, Dr. Tyrell, demanding the extension of the replicants' life span. Tyrell goes up against Roy, a "god," and loses.

An Enemy Loved—Because he sees them for who they really are—slaves who have been given a raw deal—Deckard feels for the replicants even though they're slaughtering humans. Rachael loves Deckard, whose job it is to kill her. The replicants want to be human despite their rejection and elimination by humans.

Disaster—The entire world is a disaster after a catastrophic world war; radioactivity has forced everyone who can leave to flee to the off-world colonies. A group of renegade replicants have massacred dozens of people and escaped back to earth, where their presence is forbidden. Deckard is drafted back into the Blade Runner unit against his wishes. Rachael makes the shocking discovery that she's not human. The replicants try—and fail—to avoid imminent death by reversing their four-year life span. Dr. Tyrell and J. F. are slain by Roy. Roy finds Pris's dead body.

Revolt—The replicants rebel against their fate as slaves. Deckard revolts against being drafted to hunt replicants.

Crime Pursued by Vengeance—The replicants see their fate as a crime and seek vengeance. Deckard's job is to hunt down the murderous replicants and "retire" them.

Daring Enterprise—Roy is an exceptionally brave leader who strives mightily to save his band of doomed replicants. By the end of the film, Deckard finally learns to live boldly.

Rivalry of Superior and Inferior—Deckard goes up against Roy, who is designed to be "superior in strength and agility, and at least equal in intelligence, to the genetic engineers who created" him. And yet even Roy meets his match when Dr. Tyrell cannot undo his four-year life span and is cruelly indifferent about it.

Obtaining—The replicants are trying to gain longer lives. Deckard ends up acquiring a new, more valuable life, as does Rachael.

Necessity of Sacrificing Loved Ones—Deckard is ordered to kill Rachael, with whom he's falling in love.

Pursuit—Deckard is in pursuit of the replicants, who are in pursuit of more life. Gaff (Edward James Olmos), Deckard's fellow detective, tracks Deckard to keep an eye on things.

Falling Prey to Cruelty or Misfortune—Bad things happen to Deckard, but he sees how truly bad the replicants have it. Rachael is devastated when she discovers that she isn't human. Dr. Tyrell and J. F. get killed, as does Pris. Roy runs out of time and dies.

Loss of Loved Ones—The replicants watch one another die, which is especially painful for Roy and Pris. Rachael loses her "humanity" and learns that her memories are just implants.

Slaying of a Kinsman Unrecognized—Deckard begins to feel a kinship with the replicants, whom he's supposed to "retire." The replicants feel unrecognized by the human race, which uses them as slaves and preordains their death with the built-in four-year life span.

Remorse—Deckard comes to feel remorse for hunting the replicants, and Roy Batty, amazingly, feels remorse in the end as well.

Obstacles to Love—Deckard and Rachael are trapped in a brutal, oppressive world in which Deckard has been ordered to kill Rachael. Roy and Pris face imminent death.

SUBHEADINGS OF
THE 36 DRAMATIC SITUATIONS

All but one of the 36 Dramatic Situations have subheadings, which are useful in suggesting nuance and subtle distinctions to explore within each situation. If you've found one main situation central to your story idea, then its subheadings might offer a deeper and more complex set of story and character possibilities. Below is the complete list of the 36 Dramatic Situations with their subheadings, followed by a brief look at *Training Day* to demonstrate their use. The list is intended as a resource to which you can refer when you're building a plot. The language appears a bit archaic—and some of the subheadings are pretty damn strange—but on the whole you'll find these subheadings lend further value to a remarkably useful tool.

Complete List of Subheadings

1. *Supplication*
   A. Fugitives imploring the powerful for help against their enemies.
      Assistance implored for the performance of a pious duty which has been forbidden.
      Appeals for a refuge in which to die.
   B. Hospitality besought by the shipwrecked.
      Charity entreated by those cast off by their own people, whom they have disgraced.
      Expiation: the seeking of pardon, healing, or deliverance.
      The surrender of a corpse, or of a relic, solicited.
   C. Supplication of the powerful for those dear to the supplicant.
      Supplication to a relative in behalf of another relative.
      Supplication to a mother's lover in her behalf.

2. *Deliverance*
   A. Appearance of a rescuer to the condemned.
   B. A parent replaced upon a throne by his children.
      Rescue by friends, or by strangers grateful for benefits or hospitality.

3. *Crime Pursued by Vengeance*
   A. The avenging of a slain parent or ancestor.
      The avenging of a slain child or descendant.
      Vengeance for a child dishonored.
      The avenging of a slain wife or husband.
      Vengeance for the dishonor, or attempted dishonoring, of a wife.
      Vengeance for a mistress slain.
      Vengeance for a slain or injured friend.

Vengeance for a sister seduced.
  B. Vengeance for intentional injury or spoliation.
      Vengeance for having been despoiled during absence.
      Revenge for an attempted slaying.
      Revenge for a false accusation.
      Vengeance for violation.
      Vengeance for having been robbed of one's own.
      Revenge upon a whole sex for a deception by one.
  C. Professional pursuit of criminals.

4. *Vengeance Taken for Kindred upon Kindred*
  A. A father's death avenged upon a mother.
      A mother's death avenged upon a father.
  B. A brother's death avenged upon a son.
  C. A father's death avenged upon a husband.
  D. A husband's death avenged upon a father.

5. *Pursuit*
  A. Fugitives from justice pursued for brigandage, political
        offenses, etc.
  B. Pursued for a fault of love.
  C. A hero struggling against a power.
  D. A pseudo-madman struggling against an Iago-like alienist.

6. *Disaster*
  A. Defeat suffered.
      A fatherland destroyed.
      The fall of humanity.
      A natural catastrophe.
  B. A monarch overthrown.
  C. Ingratitude suffered.
      The suffering of unjust punishment or enmity.
      An outrage suffered.
  D. Abandonment by a lover or a husband.
      Children lost by their parents.

7. *Falling Prey to Cruelty or Misfortune*
  A. The innocent made the victim of ambitious intrigue.
  B. The innocent despoiled by those who should protect.
  C. The powerful dispossessed and wretched.
      A favorite or an intimate finds himself forgotten.
  D. The unfortunate robbed of their only hope.

8. *Revolt*
 - A. A conspiracy chiefly of one individual.
   A conspiracy of several.
 - B. Revolt of one individual, who influences and involves others.
   A revolt of many.

9. *Daring Enterprise*
 - A. Preparations for war.
 - B. War.
   A combat.
 - C. Carrying off a desired person or object.
   Recapture of a desired object.
 - D. Adventurous expeditions.
   Adventure undertaken for the purpose of obtaining
   a beloved woman.

10. *Abduction*
 - A. Abduction of an unwilling woman.
 - B. Abduction of a consenting woman.
 - C. Recapture of the woman without the slaying of the abductor.
   The same case, with the slaying of the ravisher.
 - D. Rescue of a captive friend.
   Rescue of a child.
   Rescue of a soul in captivity to error.

11. *The Enigma*
 - A. Search for a person who must be found on pain of death.
 - B. A riddle to be solved on pain of death.
   The same case, in which the riddle is proposed by the
   coveted woman.
 - C. Temptations offered with the object of discovering his name.
   Temptations offered with the object of ascertaining the sex.
   Tests for the purpose of ascertaining the mental condition.

12. *Obtaining*
 - A. Efforts to obtain an object by ruse or force.
 - B. Endeavor by means of persuasive eloquence alone.
 - C. Eloquence with an arbitrator.

13. *Enmity of Kinsmen*
 - A. Hatred of brothers—one brother hated by several.
   Reciprocal hatred.
   Hatred between relatives for reasons of self-interest.

B. Hatred of father and son—of the son for the father.
Mutual hatred.
Hatred of daughter for father.
C. Hatred of grandfather for grandson.
D. Hatred of father-in-law for son-in-law.
E. Hatred of mother-in-law for daughter-in-law.
F. Infanticide.

14. *Rivalry of Kinsmen*
A. Malicious rivalry of a brother.
Malicious rivalry of two brothers.
Rivalry of two brothers, with adultery on the part of one.
Rivalry of sisters.
B. Rivalry of father and son, for an unmarried woman.
Rivalry of father and son, for a married woman.
Case similar to the two foregoing, but in which the object
is already the wife of the father.
Rivalry of mother and daughter.
C. Rivalry of cousins.
D. Rivalry of friends.

15. *Murderous Adultery*
A. The slaying of a husband by, or for, a paramour.
The slaying of a trusting lover.
B. Slaying of a wife for a paramour, and in self-interest.

16. *Madness*
A. Kinsmen slain in madness.
Lover slain in madness.
Slaying or injuring of a person not hated.
B. Disgrace brought upon oneself through madness.
C. Loss of loved ones brought about by madness.
D. Madness brought on by fear of hereditary insanity.

17. *Fatal Imprudence*
A. Imprudence the cause of one's own misfortune.
Imprudence the cause of one's own dishonor.
B. Curiosity the cause of one's own misfortune.
Loss of the possession of a loved one, through curiosity.
C. Curiosity the cause of death or misfortune to others.
Imprudence the cause of a relative's death.
Imprudence the cause of a lover's death.
Credulity the cause of kinsmen's deaths.

18. *Involuntary Crimes of Love*

    A. Discovery that one has married one's mother.
        Discovery that one has had a sister as mistress.

    B. Discovery that one has married one's sister.
        The same case, in which the crime has been villainously planned
            by a third person.
        Being upon the point of taking a sister, unknowingly, as mistress.

    C. Being upon the point of violating, unknowingly, a daughter.

    D. Being upon the point of committing an adultery unknowingly.
        Adultery committed unknowingly.

19. *Slaying of a Kinsman Unrecognized*

    A. Being upon the point of slaying a daughter unknowingly,
           by command of a divinity or an oracle.
        The same case through political necessity.
        The same case through a rivalry in love.
        The same case through hatred of the lover of the
           unrecognized daughter.

    B. Being upon the point of killing a son unknowingly.
        The same case, strengthened by Machiavellian instigations.

    C. Being upon the point of slaying a brother unknowingly.

    D. Slaying of a mother unrecognized.

    E. A father slain unknowingly, through Machiavellian advice.

    F. A grandfather slain unknowingly, in vengeance and through
           instigation.

    G. Involuntary killing of a loved woman.
        Being upon the point of killing a lover unrecognized.
        Failure to rescue an unrecognized son.

20. *Self-sacrifice for an Ideal*

    A. Sacrifice of life for the sake of one's word.
        Life sacrificed for the success of one's people.
        Life sacrificed in filial piety.
        Life sacrificed for the sake of one's faith.

    B. Both love and life sacrificed for one's faith, or a cause.
        Love sacrificed to the interests of state.

    C. Sacrifice of well-being to duty.

    D. The ideal of "honor" sacrificed to the ideal of "faith."

21. *Self-sacrifice for Kindred*

    A. Life sacrificed for that of a relative or a loved one.
        Life sacrificed for the happiness of a relative or a loved one.

B. Ambition sacrificed for the happiness of a parent.
   Ambition sacrificed for the life of a parent.
C. Love sacrificed for the sake of a parent's life.
   Love sacrificed for the happiness of one's child.
   The same sacrifice as above, but caused by unjust laws.
D. Life and honor sacrificed for the life of a parent or loved one.
   Modesty sacrificed for the life of a relative or a loved one.

22. *All Sacrificed for a Passion*
   A. Religious vows of chastity broken for a passion.
      Respect for a priest destroyed.
      A future ruined by passion.
      Power ruined by passion.
      Ruin of mind, health, and life.
      Ruin of fortunes, lives, and honors.
   B. Temptations destroying the sense of duty, of pity, etc.
   C. Destruction of honor, fortune, and life by erotic vice.
      The same effect produced by any other vice.

23. *Necessity of Sacrificing Loved Ones*
   A. Necessity for sacrificing a daughter in the public interest.
      Duty of sacrificing her in fulfillment of a vow to God.
      Duty of sacrificing benefactors or loved ones to one's faith.
   B. Duty of sacrificing one's child, unknown to others, under
         the pressure of necessity.
      Duty of sacrificing, under the same circumstances, one's father
         or husband.
      Duty of sacrificing a son-in-law for the public good.
      Duty of contending with a brother-in-law for the public good.
      Duty of contending with a friend.

24. *Rivalry of Superior and Inferior*
   A. Masculine rivalries; of a mortal and an immortal.
      Rivalry of a magician and an ordinary man.
      Rivalry of conqueror and conquered.
      Rivalry of a king and a noble.
      Rivalry of a powerful person and an upstart.
      Rivalry of rich and poor.
      Rivalry of an honored man and a suspected one.
      Rivalry of two who are almost equal.
      Rivalry of the two successive husbands of a divorcée.
   B. Feminine rivalries; of a sorceress and an ordinary woman.

Rivalry of victor and prisoner.
Rivalry of queen and subject.
Rivalry of lady and servant.
Rivalry between memory or an ideal (that of a superior woman)
and a vassal of her own.
C. Double rivalry (A loves B, who loves C, who loves D).

25. *Adultery*
A. A mistress betrayed, for a young woman.
A mistress betrayed, for a young wife.
B. A wife betrayed, for a slave who does not love in return.
A wife betrayed, for debauchery.
A wife betrayed, for a married woman.
A wife betrayed, with the intention of bigamy.
A wife betrayed for a young girl who does not love in return.
A wife envied by a young girl who is in love with her husband.
A wife envied by a courtesan who is in love with her husband.
C. An antagonistic husband sacrificed for a congenial lover.
A husband, believed to be lost, forgotten for a rival.
A commonplace husband sacrificed for a sympathetic lover.
A good husband betrayed for an inferior rival.
A good husband betrayed for a grotesque rival.
A good husband betrayed for a commonplace rival,
by a perverse wife.
A good husband betrayed for a rival less handsome, but useful.
D. Vengeance of a deceived husband.
Jealousy sacrificed for the sake of a cause.
Husband persecuted by a rejected rival.

26. *Crimes of Love*
A. A mother in love with her son.
A daughter in love with her father.
Violation of a daughter by a father.
B. A woman enamored of her stepson.
A woman and her stepson enamored of each other.
A woman being the mistress, at the same time, of a father
and son, both of whom accept the situation.
C. A man becomes the lover of his sister-in-law.
A brother and sister in love with each other.
D. A man enamored of another man, who yields.
E. A woman enamored of a bull.

27. *Discovery of the Dishonor of a Loved One*

    A. Discovery of a mother's shame.
        Discovery of a father's shame.
        Discovery of a daughter's dishonor.
    B. Discovery of dishonor in the family of one's fiancée.
        Discovery that one's wife has been violated before marriage,
            or since the marriage.
        Discovery that one's wife has previously committed a fault.
        Discovery that one's wife has formerly been a prostitute.
        Discovery that one's mistress, formerly a prostitute, has returned
            to her old life.
        Discovery that one's lover is a scoundrel, or that one's mistress is
            a woman of bad character.
        The same discovery concerning one's wife.
    C. Duty of punishing a son who is a traitor to country.
        Duty of punishing a son condemned under a law which the
            father has made.
        Duty of punishing one's mother to avenge one's father.

28. *Obstacles to Love*

    A. Marriage prevented by inequality of rank.
        Inequality of fortune an impediment to marriage.
    B. Marriage prevented by enemies and contingent obstacles.
    C. Marriage forbidden on account of the young woman's previous
            betrothal to another.
    D. A free union impeded by the opposition of relatives.
    E. A free union impeded by the incompatibility of temper
            of the lovers.

29. *An Enemy Loved*

    A. The loved one hated by kinsmen of the lover.
        The lover pursued by the brothers of his beloved.
        The lover hated by the family of his beloved.
        The beloved is an enemy of the party of the woman
            who loves him.
    B. The beloved is the slayer of a kinsman of the woman
            who loves him.

30. *Ambition*

    A. Ambition watched and guarded against by a kinsman,
            or by a person under obligation.
    B. Rebellious ambition.

C. Ambition and covetousness heaping crime upon crime.

31. *Conflict with a God*
A. Struggle against a deity.
   Strife with the believers in a god.
B. Controversy with a deity.
   Punishment for contempt of a god.
   Punishment for pride before a god.

32. *Mistaken Jealousy*
A. The mistake originates in the suspicious mind of the jealous one.
   Mistaken jealousy aroused by fatal chance.
   Mistaken jealousy of a love which is purely platonic.
   Baseless jealousy aroused by malicious rumors.
B. Jealousy suggested by a traitor who is moved by hatred,
      or self-interest.
C. Reciprocal jealousy suggested to husband and wife by a rival.

33. *Erroneous Judgment*
A. False suspicion where faith is necessary.
   False suspicion of a mistress.
   False suspicion aroused by a misunderstood attitude
      of a loved one.
B. False suspicions drawn upon oneself to save a friend.
   They fall upon the innocent.
   The same case as above, but in which the innocent had a guilty
      intention, or believes himself guilty.
   A witness to the crime, in the interest of a loved one, lets
      accusation fall upon the innocent.
C. The accusation is allowed to fall upon an enemy.
   The error is provoked by an enemy.
D. False suspicion thrown by the real culprit upon one
      of his enemies.
   False suspicion thrown by the real culprit upon the second
      victim against whom he has plotted from the beginning.

34. *Remorse*
A. Remorse for an unknown crime.
   Remorse for a parricide.
   Remorse for an assassination.
B. Remorse for a fault of love.
   Remorse for an adultery.

35. *Recovery of a Lost One*
  (There are no subheadings in this situation.)

36. *Loss of Loved Ones*
  A. Witnessing the slaying of kinsmen while powerless to prevent it. Helping to bring misfortune upon one's people through professional secrecy.
  B. Divining the death of a loved one.
  C. Learning of the death of a kinsman or ally.
  D. Relapse into primitive baseness, through despair on learning of the death of a loved one.

Resist the temptation to translate this language literally. For instance, *oracle* could be any warning received in advance; *parricide* becomes any literal or figurative murder of a father figure. Interpret these subheadings with an open mind and a modern sensibility. Allow them to unleash new insights and possibilities for your script.

Working with the Subheadings on the Plot of *Training Day*
Here's a sampling of the subheadings used to take the analysis of *Training Day* to a deeper level. Remember, while what follows is an analytical breakdown of an *existing* screenplay, our primary purpose here is the opposite: exploring a deeper knowledge of the 36 Dramatic Situations to help *build* an original script.

19. *Slaying of a Kinsman Unrecognized*
  Failure to rescue an unrecognized son—Jake sees himself as a kind of son or heir to Alonzo, but Alonzo is willing to sacrifice him. When he fights the crackheads to save the girl from being raped, Alonzo doesn't rescue him even though he's in serious trouble. Alonzo doesn't seem to have much connection to his actual son by Sara (Eva Mendes) either.

20. *Self-sacrifice for an Ideal*
  Sacrifice of life for the sake of one's word—Jake is willing to sacrifice his life for the sake of his word.
  Life sacrificed for the success of one's people—Jake is willing to sacrifice his life so that his daughter might grow up in a world without Alonzo.
  Life sacrificed for the sake of one's faith—Jake is also willing to sacrifice his life for the ideals of honor and justice. He really believes in these things.
  Sacrifice of well-being to duty—Jake is willing to risk his well-being in order to do his duty as a cop.
  The ideal of "honor" sacrificed to the ideal of "faith"—Jake is told that a good undercover cop has to do without a policeman's normal sense of

honor, which has no place in the world of undercover narcotics work, and at first he has faith in what Alonzo is tells him.

22. *All Sacrificed for a Passion*

Religious vows of chastity broken for a passion—Alonzo shows Jake that all his simplistic ideas and noble vows about police work are not only useless but dangerous in undercover work. He gets Jake to do drugs and engage in armed robbery for the sake of achieving his passion: removing drug dealers from the street.

Respect for a priest destroyed—Jake totally loses respect for his "priest," Alonzo.

A future ruined by passion—Alonzo ruins his future because of his various passions, which get him in deep trouble. Jake's passion for justice comes very close to being his undoing.

Power ruined by passion—In the end, Alonzo's power is completely stripped because he has gone too far.

Ruin of mind, health, and life—Jake almost goes down, and Alonzo does.

Ruin of fortunes, lives, and honors—A slight variation of the above.

Temptations destroying the sense of duty, of pity, etc.—The temptations facing Alonzo destroy his sense of duty to the law and to protect Jake, as well as his sense of pity for those whom the police should protect.

Destruction of honor, fortune, and life by vice—Alonzo's industrial-strength vices squeeze the life out of him, first morally and then physically.

24. *Rivalry of Superior and Inferior*

Rivalry of a mortal and an immortal—Alonzo is an "immortal" and Jake is a "mortal."

Rivalry of a magician and an ordinary man—Alonzo is set as the magician and Jake is the ordinary man, but Alonzo learns that Jake is a magician in his own right, and praises his "magic eye." This rivalry is also evident in the gang house when Jake is up against a circle of "magicians" (the gang members playing cards around the table) who all pull the wool over his eyes. On the DVD commentary, Antoine Fuqua describes them as "demons."

Rivalry of conqueror and conquered—Alonzo is the conqueror for much of the script, but in the end it is he who is conquered. This situation also describes Alonzo's relationship with the people on the street, whom he lords over, and who end up helping to destroy him.

Rivalry of a powerful person and an upstart—Jake is clearly the upstart and Alonzo the powerful person.

Rivalry of two who are almost equal—Jake turns out to be a formidable opponent: He's got the magic eye and he stays right with Alonzo the whole way through the ordeals of his training day.

You can see how useful the subheadings are in exploring the subtleties and nuances inherent in each of the thity-six main situations, opening up more and more possibilities with their suggestive nature.

USING THE 36 DRAMATIC SITUATIONS TO JUMP-START A NEW IDEA

This chapter has focused heavily on examining *completed* scripts through the lens of the 36 Dramatic Situations. Now let's take a raw, absolutely undeveloped idea and apply some of these situations to get a script up and running. Remember, we will develop a full plot from scratch in Part Two of this book, so this is just an exercise.

Suppose that a jewel thief finds God and decides he has to return everything he ever stole to make amends. That's it. Nothing else currently exists. This seems like a comedy because it's a funny premise, but it could easily become a drama or thriller. This thief is going to break into homes and put back what he took, or leave a jewel of equal value. It seems obvious that he will get into some trouble and perhaps have some rather strange encounters, especially since he's a radically different person than he used to be. We're going to need a romantic interest, a woman, and also a villain, perhaps a cop who's been after him forever.

So, what's our process? Much of it is pure elbow grease—struggling with lots of possibilities—and the 36 Dramatic Situations are useful for that. So let's take a quick tour through them and see if anything jumps out. At first glance we can see story possibilities arising out of *Supplication, Deliverance, Crime Pursued by Vengeance, Pursuit, Disaster, Revolt, Daring Enterprise, Obtaining, Madness, Fatal Imprudence, All Sacrificed for a Passion, An Enemy Loved, Conflict with a God, Erroneous Judgment, Ambition, Self-sacrifice for an Ideal, Rivalry of Superior and Inferior, Crimes of Love, Remorse,* and *Recovery of a Lost One.* This is by no means intended to be a comprehensive list—we're just playing. Now, which of these situations really stand out in connection to our concept? Which are "radioactive" or evocative? Which suggest deep, dynamic story options? Which situations force you to dig into the possibilities and will not leave you alone? *Disaster* and *Madness* are interesting. *Erroneous Judgment* and *Fatal Imprudence* are intriguing, too, and *Crime Pursued by Vengeance* has promise. Let's try these few out and see where they take us.

Disaster—This situation suggests a lot of unexpected and dangerous (but fun and crazy) episodes happening to the thief. He will obviously stumble onto something that throws his whole world into a tailspin. It goes with the territory: In this type of story, it makes sense that the worst possible things would happen to him. If he's committing break-ins to replace stolen jewels, then he's certainly asking for trouble no matter how great his intentions. People are never grateful for break-ins, even if their jewels are being returned. It's a great way to get yourself shot, which brings up the next situation with the question: Has this guy got a few screws loose?

Madness—Like *Disaster*, this situation seems to fit the story. It implies not only that circumstances are insane, but also that our guy himself might be a bit nuts. Or maybe a lot nuts. Anybody who breaks into homes to return stolen items is probably not all there. Has he always been unhinged or is it a new development? On a scale of 1 to 10, how far gone is he? And how does this impact the story? How does it make it funnier, more unpredictable, goofier, more dangerous? Is he delusional? Neurotic? Flakey? A religious zealot? How intense is his drive to make amends? What is his rationale for all this? Does he get angry when someone tries to stop him returning something? Another strong option related to *Madness* is that our thief could be just plain dumb. Police say that despite the misconception of criminals as misguided geniuses, most are quite stupid—often stunningly so. That can make for some rich plot possibilities, spinning the story in another direction. *Erroneous Judgment* and *Fatal Imprudence* both hint that the jewel thief has gravely misjudged how easy it might be to return stolen items. Does he misread someone whom he encounters? Does he almost get himself killed? Does he stumble onto a scene that isn't what it appears to be? Is he too curious or nosy to walk away from a tricky situation? Does a string of bad judgments get him into more and more trouble? Is he fatalistic about his mission, figuring that he may not survive, but still intent on carrying it out? What if someone is out to destroy him and exploits his new fixation to accomplish it? This suggests an enemy. We haven't talked much about an antagonist yet, but we need one—a potent one. Who might it be? A cop? A fellow thief seeking to thwart him? Or maybe a partner who refuses to return the stuff? Possibly someone who catches him trying to return it?

Crime Pursued by Vengeance—This interesting situation suggests lots of possibilities, potentially steering the plot into an arena we haven't considered yet. If somebody catches the thief trying to restore their jewels, wouldn't they naturally be furious with him for robbing them in the first place? What if he has stolen a fabulous jewel that turns out to be cursed? Perhaps that's what has led to his life falling apart, which led him to find God. What if the original owners don't want the jewel back because of the curse? Maybe their luck changed for the better after it was stolen and it's a hot potato they just don't want. *Crime Pursued by Vengeance* also conjures up a thief racked by guilt—he's been beating himself up for years and now has become the avenger of his own sins. On another, entirely different tack, what if he has been wrongly accused of new robberies that he isn't doing? But by whom is he accused? Why? It might tie in with whoever turns out to be the villain of our story. Also, the cop who's been after the thief for years now has an added opportunity to take him down.

Each of these ideas triggers dozens of other ideas. It is clear how the process of building a story out of a basic idea is dynamically enhanced by exposure to the 36 Dramatic Situations. Many of the options are obvious for a story like this, and you may have stumbled on them without the 36 Dramatic Situations. But this resource is a quick way to consider a large array of directions your story might take. You're not a slave to the tool—it's just a checklist of story prospects.

While exploring these situations, also think about how they affect and are affected by the character's Dilemma. Given his new frame of mind, it's obviously unacceptable for the thief not to return the jewels. But consider what obstacles would make it equally unacceptable to bring the jewels back. Within his own warped take on the world, he must do this in order to square things with his newfound God. The reasoning process that fixes this particular idea in his brain will be crucial to the story, because it drives everything. He should be short-circuiting between the total need to return things and the absolute impossibility of doing so. Exhilaration and panic. Courage and meltdown. A sense of righteousness versus a sense of desperation.

That's going far enough with the 36 Dramatic Situations for this story example. This demonstration should give you a taste of using this tool from the ground up. We'll return to it in Part Two of this book when we use all the Key Tools to develop a real script.

START USING THE 36 DRAMATIC SITUATIONS IN YOUR OWN SCRIPT

1. When starting from scratch with a raw idea, which of the thirty-six main situations trigger promising directions for a movie plot? How many different potential stories do you see in this premise? Allow the 36 Dramatic Situations to help you radically expand your story's potential. If you're not generating a lot of possibilities, then your idea may not be all that strong.
2. Make a set of 3 x 5 index cards with one situation per card, and lay them out on a table. Work with them. Play with them. Sort them for importance to your story; cluster them into combinations. For

instance, see how *Madness* and *Disaster* work together. Throw *Ambition* into that group and watch how all three interact within the world of your protagonist or your antagonist or your story. Feel your way around. Let the situations talk to you. The cards allow you to experiment in a dynamic, movable way.

3. Which situations are the most "radioactive" for your story? Which situations burn themselves into your brain and just won't let go? The most intriguing ones are troublesome, suggestive, and insistent, like a piece of sand in an oyster. Irritate the organism—your story idea—and a pearl may result.

4. Use the situations metaphorically and poetically. If you take them too literally, then you'll miss fully half their value.

5. Let the situations lead you deeper into the heart and soul of the story. Discover what the story is *really* about.

6. Play "free association" with the thirty-six situations and allow them to take you on a journey—one which might not be logical or even sensible, but which leads you into unexpected storytelling realms. Encourage these free-ranging quantum leaps of your imagination.

7. Take thirty-six sheets of blank paper and put one of the situations at the top of each, then write down anything and everything that relates to your plot. See where it takes you.

8. Are you exposed to ideas for plot development that might never have occurred to you without the 36 Dramatic Situations? The process of exploring this tool should open those floodgates.

9. Do the situations take you inside your characters to explore their desires, flaws, transformations, and motivations?

10. Use these situations to shatter cliché in your plot. Let them kick you out of your own storytelling ruts and into drastic new directions or innovative ways of thinking about a story.

11. Keep coming back to the 36 Dramatic Situations at later stages of developing your script. You'll continually see fresh possibilities in the situations as your screenplay evolves.

CHAPTER 4

The Enneagram:
Creating Deep, Complex,
and Distinct Characters

The *Enneagram* (pronounced *ANY-a-gram*) is a remarkable personality profiling system which asserts that there are nine distinct behavioral types. It is a deeply insightful tool that writers can use to create, develop, and dimensionalize characters. Mysterious in origin, the Enneagram is a mixture of ancient wisdom about human nature with cutting-edge modern psychology. Each of the nine types has specific and unique traits, behavior patterns, tendencies, passions, preferences, and motivations. Because screenwriting deals with creating multifaceted, vibrant characters and understanding what makes them tick, the Enneagram is a powerful resource for writers. It can be applied in much the same way as the 36 Dramatic Situations, except that it focuses solely on character work. The Enneagram is also helpful in differentiating your characters so that each has his or her own distinct personality, voice, and traits.

The real power of the Enneagram is that it presents a complex and thorough understanding of how people work and what they're made of, ranging through the full spectrum from their very best to their very worst. It's like having a professional psychiatrist on staff who can provide personality profiles for your characters in the same way that an FBI specialist provides profiles on serial killers. While I present a synopsis of each type in this chapter, there are a number of superb, highly comprehensive books that will take you much deeper into the intricacies of the nine personality types.

THE NINE TYPES OF THE ENNEAGRAM
The word *Enneagram* comes from the nine-pointed star used as a symbol and a working map in this study. There are several schools of the Enneagram,

including Don Riso and Russ Hudson's Enneagram Institute, Helen Palmer, Eli Jaxon-Bear, and Oscar Ichazo—to name just a few. Material presented here is from The Enneagram Institute, whose particular labels for the nine different personality types are: 1, The Reformer; 2, The Helper; 3, The Achiever; 4, The Individualist; 5, The Investigator; 6, The Loyalist; 7, The Enthusiast; 8, The Challenger; and 9, The Peacemaker. In general, the nine types are referred to only as a number, so you would be described as, say, a 1 or a 3. The numbers are value-free and have no connotations; the labels are assigned so that neophytes can get a handle on the system. Below is the nine-pointed Enneagram symbol on which are represented the different personality types:

Each type has three different aspects: *Healthy*, *Average*, and *Unhealthy*. If you're moving toward *integration* (your life is coming together), then you will tend to exhibit Average to Healthy traits. If you're moving toward *disintegration* (your life is falling apart), then you'll tend to exhibit Average to Unhealthy traits. The Unhealthy traits are a fascinating and rich source of character material for a dramatist. They're excellent for flawing, darkening, and deepening characters. It's so easy to like your protagonist, for instance, that you won't necessarily see the negative personality aspects—or if you do, you'll let your protagonist off too easy and end up with a shallower, more predictable character.

Although a person will have traits within him or her from all nine types, one type tends to be dominant or primary. Each type is also described with its *wing*, which indicates shared characteristics with its adjacent type. For instance, a 1 with a 9-wing can mean the person is a Reformer with some aspects of a Peacemaker. For your script, building a persona with this in mind will create a more accurate and believable character. The discipline of the Enneagram is quite sophisticated, providing a wealth of organized and insightful material on how real people behave. Writers can play with and draw from this in creating indelible personalities for screenplays.

The descriptions below of the nine personality types come from The Enneagram Institute's Web site (www.enneagraminstitute.com), a rich source of information that will take you further into the knowledge of human behavior.

1. The Reformer
Enneagram Type One
The Rational, Idealistic Type:
Principled, Purposeful, Self-Controlled, and Perfectionistic

Basic Fear: Of being corrupt/evil, defective
Basic Desire: To be good, to have integrity, to be balanced
Enneagram One with a Nine-Wing: "The Idealist"
Enneagram One with a Two-Wing: "The Advocate"

Profile Summary for the Enneagram Type One
Healthy: Conscientious with strong personal convictions: They have an intense sense of right and wrong, personal religious and moral values. Wish to be rational, reasonable, self-disciplined, mature, moderate in all things. / Extremely principled, always want to be fair, objective, and ethical: truth and justice primary values. Sense of responsibility, personal integrity, and of having a higher purpose often makes them teachers and witnesses to the truth.

At Their Best: Become extraordinarily wise and discerning. By accepting what is, they become transcendentally realistic, knowing the best action to take in each moment. Humane, inspiring, and hopeful: The truth will be heard.

Average: Dissatisfied with reality, they become high-minded idealists, feeling that it is up to them to improve everything: crusaders, advocates, critics. Into "causes" and explaining to others how things "ought" to be. / Afraid of making a mistake: Everything must be consistent with their ideals. Become orderly and well-organized, but impersonal, puritanical, emotionally constricted, rigidly keeping their feelings and impulses in check. Often workaholics—"anal-compulsive," punctual, pedantic, and fastidious. / Highly critical both of self and others: picky, judgmental, perfectionistic. Very opinionated about everything: correcting people and badgering them to "do the right thing"—as they see it. Impatient, never satisfied with anything unless it is done according to their prescriptions. Moralizing, scolding, abrasive, and indignantly angry.

Unhealthy: Can be highly dogmatic, self-righteous, intolerant, and inflexible. Begin dealing in absolutes: They alone know "The Truth." Everyone else is wrong: very severe in judgments, while rationalizing own actions. / Become obsessive about imperfection and the wrong-doing of others, although they may fall into contradictory actions, hypocritically doing the opposite of what they preach. / Become condemnatory toward others, punitive and cruel to rid themselves of "wrong-doers." Severe depressions, nervous breakdowns, and suicide attempts are likely. Generally corresponds to the Obsessive-Compulsive and Depressive personality disorders.

Key Motivations: Want to be right, to strive higher and improve everything, to be consistent with their ideals, to justify themselves, to be beyond criticism so as not to be condemned by anyone.

Examples: Mahatma Gandhi, Hillary Clinton, Al Gore, John Paul II, Sandra Day O'Connor, John Bradshaw, Bill Moyers, Martha Stewart, Ralph Nader, Katherine Hepburn, Harrison Ford, Vanessa Redgrave, Jane Fonda, Meryl Streep, George Harrison, Celine Dion, Joan Baez, George Bernard Shaw, Noam Chomsky, Michael Dukakis, Margaret Thatcher, Rudolph Giuliani, Jerry Brown, Jane Curtin, Gene Siskel, William F. Buckley, Kenneth Starr, The "Church Lady" (*Saturday Night Live*), and "Mr. Spock" (*Star Trek*).

2. The Helper
Enneagram Type Two
The Caring, Interpersonal Type:
Generous, Demonstrative, People-Pleasing, and Possessive

Basic Fear: Of being unwanted, unworthy of being loved
Basic Desire: To feel loved
Enneagram Two with a One-Wing: "Servant"
Enneagram Two with a Three-Wing: "The Host/Hostess"

Profile Summary for the Enneagram Type Two
Healthy: Empathetic, compassionate, feeling for others. Caring and concerned about their needs. Thoughtful, warm-hearted, forgiving, and sincere. / Encouraging and appreciative, able to see the good in others. Service is important, but takes care of self, too: They are nurturing, generous, and giving—a truly loving person.

At Their Best: Become deeply unselfish, humble, and altruistic: giving unconditional love to self and others. Feel it is a privilege to be in the lives of others.

Average: Want to be closer to others, so start "people pleasing," becoming overly friendly, emotionally demonstrative, and full of "good intentions" about everything. Give seductive attention: approval, "strokes," flattery. Love their supreme value, and they talk about it constantly. / Become overly intimate and intrusive: They need to be needed, so they hover, meddle, and control in the name of love. Want others to depend on them: give, but expect a return: send double messages. Enveloping and possessive: the codependent, self-sacrificial person who cannot do enough for others—wearing themselves out for everyone, creating needs for themselves to fulfill./ Increasingly self-important and self-satisfied, feel they are indispensable, although they overrate their efforts in others' behalf. Hypochondria, becoming a "martyr" for others. Overbearing, patronizing, presumptuous.

Unhealthy: Can be manipulative and self-serving, instilling guilt by telling others how much they owe them and make them suffer. Abuse food and medication to "stuff feelings" and get sympathy. Undermine people, making belittling, disparaging remarks. Extremely self-deceptive about their motives and how aggressive and/or selfish their behavior is. / Domineering and coercive: feel entitled to get anything they want from others: the repayment of old debts, money, sexual favors. / Able to excuse and rationalize what they do since they feel abused and victimized by others and are bitterly resentful and angry. Somatization of their aggressions result in chronic health problems as they vindicate themselves by "falling apart" and burdening others. Generally corresponds to the Histrionic and Factitious personality disorders.

Key Motivations: Want to be loved, to express their feelings for others, to be needed and appreciated, to get others to respond to them, to vindicate their claims about themselves.

Examples: Mother Teresa, Barbara Bush, Eleanor Roosevelt, Leo Buscaglia, Monica Lewinsky, Bill Cosby, Barry Manilow, Lionel Richie, Kenny G, Luciano Pavarotti, Lillian Carter, Sammy Davis, Jr., Martin Sheen, Robert Fulghum, Alan Alda, Richard Thomas, Jack Paar, Sally Jessy Raphael, Bishop Desmond Tutu, Ann Landers, "Melanie Hamilton" (*Gone With the Wind*), and "Dr. McCoy" (*Star Trek*).

3. The Achiever
Enneagram Type Three
The Success-Oriented, Pragmatic Type:
Adaptable, Excelling, Driven, and Image-Conscious

Basic Fear: Of being worthless
Basic Desire: To feel valuable and worthwhile
Enneagram Three with a Two-Wing: "The Charmer"
Enneagram Three with a Four-Wing: "The Professional"

Profile Summary for the Enneagram Type Three
Healthy: Self-assured, energetic, and competent with high self-esteem: they believe in themselves and their own value. Adaptable, desirable, charming, and gracious. / Ambitious to improve themselves, to be "the best they can be"—often become outstanding, a human ideal, embodying widely admired cultural qualities. Highly effective: Others are motivated to be like them in some positive way.

At Their Best: Self-accepting, inner-directed, and authentic, everything they seem to be. Modest and charitable, self-deprecatory humor and a fullness of heart emerge. Gentle and benevolent.

Average: Highly concerned with their performance, doing their job well, constantly driving self to achieve goals as if self-worth depends on it. Terrified of failure. Compare self with others in search for status and success. Become careerists, social climbers, invested in exclusivity and being the "best." / Become image-conscious, highly concerned with how they are perceived. Begin to package themselves according to the expectations of others and what they need to do to be successful. Pragmatic and efficient, but also premeditated, losing touch with their own feelings beneath a smooth facade. Problems with intimacy, credibility, and "phoniness" emerge. / Want to impress others with their superiority: constantly promoting themselves, making themselves sound better than they really are. Narcissistic, with grandiose, inflated notions about themselves and their talents. Exhibitionistic and seductive, as if saying, "Look at me!" Arrogance and contempt for others is a defense against feeling jealous of others and their success.

Unhealthy: Fearing failure and humiliation, they can be exploitative and opportunistic, covetous of the success of others, and willing to do "whatever it takes" to preserve the illusion of their superiority. / Devious and deceptive so that their mistakes and wrongdoings will not be exposed. Untrustworthy, maliciously betraying or sabotaging people to triumph over them. Delusionally jealous of others. / Become vindictive, attempting to ruin others' happiness. Relentless, obsessive about destroying whatever reminds them of their own shortcomings and failures. Psychopathic, murder. Generally corresponds to the Narcissistic personality disorder.

Key Motivations: Want to be affirmed, to distinguish themselves from others, to have attention, to be admired, and to impress others.

Examples: Bill Clinton, Oprah Winfrey, Jane Pauley, Michael Landon, Tony Robbins, Tom Cruise, Barbra Streisand, Sharon Stone, Madonna, Shirley MacLaine, Sting, Paul McCartney, Dick Clark, Whitney Houston, Ted Danson, Michael Jordan, Shania Twain, Sylvester Stallone, Arnold Schwarzenegger, Billy Dee Williams, Kathie Lee Gifford, Truman Capote, and O. J. Simpson.

4. The Individualist
Enneagram Type Four
The Sensitive, Withdrawn Type:
Expressive, Dramatic, Self-Absorbed, and Temperamental

Basic Fear: That they have no identity or personal significance
Basic Desire: To find themselves and their significance
(to create an identity)
Enneagram Four with a Three-Wing: "The Aristocrat"
Enneagram Four with a Five-Wing: "The Bohemian"

Profile Summary for the Enneagram Type Four
Healthy: Self-aware, introspective, on the "search for self," aware of feelings and inner impulses. Sensitive and intuitive both to self and others: gentle, tactful, compassionate. / Highly personal, individualistic, "true to self." Self-revealing, emotionally honest, humane. Ironic view of self and life: can be serious and funny, vulnerable and emotionally strong.

At Their Best: Profoundly creative, expressing the personal and the universal, possibly in a work of art. Inspired, self-renewing and regenerating: able to transform all their experiences into something valuable: self-creative.

Average: Take an artistic, romantic orientation to life, creating a beautiful, aesthetic environment to cultivate and prolong personal feelings. Heighten reality through fantasy, passionate feelings, and the imagination. / To stay in touch with feelings, they interiorize everything, taking everything personally, but become self-absorbed and introverted, moody and hypersensitive, shy and self-conscious, unable to be spontaneous or to "get out of themselves." Stay withdrawn to protect their self-image and to buy time to sort out feelings. / Gradually think that they are different from others, and feel that they are exempt from living as everyone else does. They become melancholy dreamers, disdainful, decadent, and sensual, living in a fantasy world. Self-pity and envy of others leads to self-indulgence, and to becoming increasingly impractical, unproductive, effete, and precious.

Unhealthy: When dreams fail, become self-inhibiting and angry at self, depressed and alienated from self and others, blocked and emotionally paralyzed. Ashamed of self, fatigued, and unable to function. / Tormented by delusional self-contempt, self-reproaches, self-hatred, and morbid thoughts: Everything is a source of torment. Blaming others, they drive away anyone who tries to help them. / Despairing, feel hopeless and become self-destructive, possibly abusing alcohol or drugs to escape. In the extreme: Emotional breakdown or suicide is likely. Generally corresponds to the Avoidant, Depressive, and Narcissistic personality disorders.

Key Motivations: Want to express themselves and their individuality, to create and surround themselves with beauty, to maintain certain moods and feelings, to withdraw to protect their self-image, to take care of emotional needs before attending to anything else, to attract a "rescuer."

Examples: Ingmar Bergman, Alan Watts, Sarah McLachlan, Alanis Morissette, Paul Simon, Jeremy Irons, Patrick Stewart, Joseph Fiennes, Martha Graham, Bob Dylan, Miles Davis, Johnny Depp, Anne Rice, Rudolph Nureyev, J. D. Salinger, Anaïs Nin, Marcel Proust, Maria Callas, Tennessee Williams, Edgar Allan Poe, Annie Lennox, Prince, Michael Jackson, Virginia Woolf, Judy Garland, "Blanche DuBois" (*A Streetcar Named Desire*).

5. The Investigator
Enneagram Type Five
The Intense, Cerebral Type:
Perceptive, Innovative, Secretive, and Isolated

Basic Fear: Being useless, helpless, or incapable
Basic Desire: To be capable and competent
Enneagram Five with a Four-Wing: "The Iconoclast"
Enneagram Five with a Six-Wing: "The Problem Solver"

Profile Summary for the Enneagram Type Five

Healthy: Observe everything with extraordinary perceptiveness and insight. Most mentally alert, curious, searching intelligence: Nothing escapes their notice. Foresight and prediction. Able to concentrate: become engrossed in what has caught their attention. / Attain skillful mastery of whatever interests them. Excited by knowledge: Often become expert in some field. Innovative and inventive, producing extremely valuable, original works. Highly independent, idiosyncratic, and whimsical.

At Their Best: Become visionaries, broadly comprehending the world while penetrating it profoundly. Open-minded, take things in whole, in their true context. Make pioneering discoveries and find entirely new ways of doing and perceiving things.

Average: Begin conceptualizing and fine-tuning everything before acting—working things out in their minds: model building, preparing, practicing, and gathering more resources. Studious, acquiring technique. Become specialized, and often "intellectual," often challenging accepted ways of doing things. / Increasingly detached as they become involved with complicated ideas or imaginary worlds. Become preoccupied with their visions and interpretations rather than reality. Are fascinated by off-beat, esoteric subjects, even those involving dark and disturbing elements. Detached from the practical world, a "disembodied mind," although high-strung and intense. / Begin to take an antagonistic stance toward anything which would interfere with their inner world and personal vision. Become provocative and abrasive, with intentionally extreme and radical views. Cynical and argumentative.

Unhealthy: Become reclusive and isolated from reality, eccentric and nihilistic. Highly unstable and fearful of aggressions: They reject and repulse others and all social attachments. / Get obsessed yet frightened by their threatening ideas, becoming horrified, delirious, and prey to gross distortions and phobias. / Seeking oblivion, they may commit suicide or have a psychotic break with reality. Deranged, explosively self-destructive, with schizophrenic overtones. Generally corresponds to the Schizoid Avoidant and Schizotypal personality disorders.

Key Motivations: Want to possess knowledge, to understand the environment, to have everything figured out as a way of defending the self from threats from the environment.

Examples: Albert Einstein, Stephen Hawking, Bill Gates, Georgia O'Keeffe, Stanley Kubrick, John Lennon, Lily Tomlin, Gary Larson, Laurie Anderson, Merce Cunningham, Meredith Monk, James Joyce, Björk, Susan Sontag, Emily Dickinson, Agatha Christie, Ursula K. LeGuin, Jane Goodall, Glenn Gould, John Cage, Bobby Fischer, Tim Burton, David Lynch, Stephen King, Clive Barker, Trent Reznor, Friedrich Nietzsche, Vincent Van Gogh, Kurt Cobain, and "Fox Mulder" (*The X Files*).

6. The Loyalist
Enneagram Type Six
The Committed, Security-Oriented Type:
Engaging, Responsible, Anxious, and Suspicious

Basic Fear: Of being without support and guidance
Basic Desire: To have security and support
Enneagram Six with a Five-Wing: "The Defender"
Enneagram Six with a Seven-Wing: "The Buddy"

Profile Summary for the Enneagram Type Six
Healthy: Able to elicit strong emotional responses from others: very appealing, endearing, lovable, affectionate. Trust important: bonding with others, forming permanent relationships and alliances. / Dedicated to individuals and movements in which they deeply believe. Community builders: responsible, reliable, trustworthy. Hard-working and persevering, sacrificing for others, they create stability and security in their world, bringing a cooperative spirit.

At Their Best: Become self-affirming, trusting of self and others, independent yet symbiotically interdependent and cooperative as an equal. Belief in self leads to true courage, positive thinking, leadership, and rich self-expression.

Average: Start investing their time and energy into whatever they believe will be safe and stable. Organizing and structuring, they look to alliances and authorities for security and continuity. Constantly vigilant, anticipating problems. / To resist having more demands made on them, they react against others passive-aggressively. Become evasive, indecisive, cautious, procrastinating, and ambivalent. Are highly reactive, anxious, and negative, giving contradictory "mixed signals." Internal confusion makes them react unpredictably. / To compensate for insecurities, they become sarcastic and belligerent, blaming others for their problems, taking a tough stance toward "outsiders." Highly reactive and defensive, dividing people into friends and enemies, while looking for threats to their own security. Authoritarian while fearful of authority, highly suspicious yet conspiratorial, and fear-instilling to silence their own fears.

Unhealthy: Fearing that they have ruined their security, they become panicky, volatile, and self-disparaging with acute inferiority feelings. Seeing themselves as defenseless, they seek out a stronger authority or belief to resolve all problems. Highly divisive, disparaging and berating others / Feeling persecuted, that others are "out to get them," they lash out and act irrationally, bringing about what they fear. Fanaticism, violence. / Hysterical, and seeking to escape punishment, they become self-destructive and suicidal. Alcoholism, drug overdoses, "skid row," self-abasing behavior. Generally corresponds to the Passive-Aggressive and Paranoid personality disorders.

Key Motivations: Want to have security, to feel supported by others, to have certitude and reassurance, to test the attitudes of others toward them, to fight against anxiety and insecurity.

Examples: Robert F. Kennedy, Malcolm X, Princess Diana, George H. W. Bush, Tom Hanks, Bruce Springsteen, Candice Bergen, Gilda Radner, Meg Ryan, Helen Hunt, Mel Gibson, Patrick Swayze, Julia Roberts, Phil Donahue, Jay Leno, John Goodman, Diane Keaton, Woody Allen, David Letterman, Andy Rooney, Jessica Lange, Tom Clancy, J. Edgar Hoover, Richard Nixon, and "George Costanza" (*Seinfeld*).

7. The Enthusiast

Enneagram Type Seven

The Busy, Fun-Loving Type:

Spontaneous, Versatile, Acquisitive, and Scattered

Basic Fear: Of being deprived and in pain

Basic Desire: To be satisfied and content—to have their needs fulfilled

Enneagram Seven with a Six-Wing: "The Entertainer"

Enneagram Seven with an Eight-Wing: "The Realist"

Profile Summary for the Enneagram Type Seven

Healthy: Highly responsive, excitable, enthusiastic about sensation and experience. Most extroverted type: stimuli bring immediate responses—they find everything invigorating. Lively, vivacious, eager, spontaneous, resilient, cheerful. / Easily become accomplished achievers, generalists who do many different things well: multi-talented. Practical, productive, usually prolific, cross-fertilizing areas of interest.

At Their Best: Assimilate experiences in depth, making them deeply grateful and appreciative for what they have. Become awed by the simple wonders of life: joyous and ecstatic. Intimations of spiritual reality, of the boundless goodness of life.

Average: As restlessness increases, want to have more options and choices available to them. Become adventurous and "worldly wise," but less focused, constantly seeking new things and experiences: the sophisticate, connoisseur, and consumer. Money, variety, keeping up with the latest trends important. / Unable to discriminate what they really need, become hyperactive, unable to say "no" to themselves, throwing self into constant activity. Uninhibited, doing and saying whatever comes to mind: storytelling, flamboyant exaggerations, witty wisecracking, performing. Fear being bored: in perpetual motion, but do too many things—many ideas but little follow through. / Get into conspicuous consumption and all forms of excess. Self-centered, materialistic, and greedy, never feeling that they have enough. Demanding and pushy, yet unsatisfied and jaded. Addictive, hardened, and insensitive.

Unhealthy: Desperate to quell their anxieties, can be impulsive and infantile: do not know when to stop. Addictions and excess take their toll: debauched, depraved, dissipated escapists, offensive and abusive. / In flight from self, acting out impulses rather than dealing with anxiety or frustrations: go out of control, into erratic mood swings, and compulsive actions (manias). / Finally, their energy and health is completely spent: become claustrophobic and panic-stricken. Often give up on themselves and life: deep depression and despair, self-destructive overdoses, impulsive suicide. Generally corresponds to the Manic-Depressive and Histrionic personality disorders.

Key Motivations: Want to maintain their freedom and happiness, to avoid missing out on worthwhile experiences, to keep themselves excited and occupied, to avoid and discharge pain.

Examples: John F. Kennedy, Benjamin Franklin, Leonard Bernstein, Leonardo DiCaprio, Kate Winslet, Elizabeth Taylor, Wolfgang Amadeus Mozart, Steven Spielberg, Federico Fellini, Richard Feynman, Timothy Leary, Robin Williams, Jim Carrey, Mike Myers, Cameron Diaz, Bette Midler, Chuck Berry, Elton John, Mick Jagger, Gianni Versace, Liza Minnelli, Joan Collins, Malcolm Forbes, Noel Coward, Sarah Ferguson, Larry King, Joan Rivers, Regis Philbin, Howard Stern, John Belushi, and "Auntie Mame" (*Mame*).

8. The Challenger
Enneagram Type Eight
The Powerful, Dominating Type:
Self-Confident, Decisive, Willful, and Confrontational

Basic Fear: Of being harmed or controlled by others
Basic Desire: To protect themselves (to be in control of their own life and destiny)
Enneagram Eight with a Seven-Wing: "The Maverick"
Enneagram Eight with a Nine-Wing: "The Bear"

Profile Summary for the Enneagram Type Eight
Healthy: Self-assertive, self-confident, and strong: have learned to stand up for what they need and want. A resourceful, "can do" attitude and passionate inner drive. / Decisive, authoritative, and commanding: the natural leader others look up to. Take initiative, make things happen: champion people, provider, protective, and honorable, carrying others with their strength.

At Their Best: Become self-restrained and magnanimous, merciful and forbearing, mastering self through their self-surrender to a higher authority. Courageous, willing to put self in serious jeopardy to achieve their vision and have a lasting influence. May achieve true heroism and historical greatness.

Average: Self-sufficiency, financial independence, and having enough resources are important concerns: become enterprising, pragmatic, "rugged individualists," wheeler-dealers. Risk-taking, hardworking, denying own emotional needs. / Begin to dominate their environment, including others: want to feel that others are behind them, supporting their efforts. Swaggering, boastful, forceful, and expansive: the "boss" whose word is law. Proud, egocentric, want to impose their will and vision on everything, not seeing others as equals or treating them with respect. / Become highly combative and intimidating to get their way: confrontational, belligerent, creating adversarial relationships. Everything a test of wills, and they will not back down. Use threats and reprisals to get obedience from others, to keep others off balance and insecure. However, unjust treatment makes others fear and resent them, possibly also band together against them.

Unhealthy: Defying any attempt to control them, become completely ruthless, dictatorial, "might makes right." The criminal and outlaw, renegade, and con artist. Hard-hearted, immoral, and potentially violent. / Develop delusional ideas about their power, invincibility, and ability to prevail: megalomania, feeling omnipotent, invulnerable. Recklessly overextending self. / If they get in danger, they may brutally destroy everything that has not conformed to their will rather than surrender to anyone else. Vengeful, barbaric, murderous. Sociopathic tendencies. Generally corresponds to the Antisocial personality disorder.

Key Motivations: Want to be self-reliant, to prove their strength and resist weakness, to be important in their world, to dominate the environment, and to stay in control of their situation.

Examples: Martin Luther King, Jr., Franklin Roosevelt, Lyndon Johnson, Mikhail Gorbachev, G. I. Gurdjieff, Pablo Picasso, Richard Wagner, Sean Connery, Susan Sarandon, Glenn Close, John Wayne, Charlton Heston, Norman Mailer, Mike Wallace, Barbara Walters, Ann Richards, Toni Morrison, Lee Iacocca, Donald Trump, Frank Sinatra, Bette Davis, Roseanne Barr, James Brown, Chrissie Hynde, Courtney Love, Leona Helmsley, Sigourney Weaver, Fidel Castro, and Saddam Hussein.

9. THE PEACEMAKER

Enneagram Type Nine

The Easygoing, Self-Effacing Type:
Receptive, Reassuring, Agreeable, and Complacent

Basic Fear: Of loss and separation
Basic Desire: To have inner stability "peace of mind"
Enneagram Nine with an Eight-Wing: "The Referee"
Enneagram Nine with a One-Wing: "The Dreamer"

Profile Summary for the Enneagram Type Nine

Healthy: Deeply receptive, accepting, unselfconscious, emotionally stable and serene. Trusting of self and others, at ease with self and life, innocent and simple. Patient, unpretentious, good-natured, genuinely nice people. / Optimistic, reassuring, supportive: have a healing and calming influence—harmonizing groups, bringing people together: a good mediator, synthesizer, and communicator.

At Their Best: Become self-possessed, feeling autonomous and fulfilled: have great equanimity and contentment because they are present to themselves. Paradoxically, at one with self, and thus able to form more profound relationships. Intensely alive, fully connected to self and others.

Average: Fear conflicts, so become self-effacing and accommodating, idealizing others and "going along" with their wishes, saying "yes" to things they do not really want to do. Fall into conventional roles and expectations. Use philosophies and stock sayings to deflect others. / Active, but disengaged, unreflective, and inattentive. Do not want to be affected, so become unresponsive and complacent, walking away from problems and "sweeping them under the rug." Thinking becomes hazy and ruminative, mostly comforting fantasies, as they begin to "tune out" reality, becoming oblivious. Emotionally indolent, unwillingness to exert self or to focus on problems: indifference. / Begin to minimize problems, to appease others and to have "peace at any price." Stubborn, fatalistic, and resigned, as if nothing could be done to change anything. Into wishful thinking and magical solutions. Others frustrated and angry by their procrastination and unresponsiveness.

Unhealthy: Can be highly repressed, undeveloped, and ineffectual. Feel incapable of facing problems: become obstinate, dissociating self from all conflicts. Neglectful and dangerous to others. / Wanting to block out of awareness anything that could affect them, they dissociate so much that they eventually cannot function: numb, depersonalized. / They finally become severely disoriented and catatonic, abandoning themselves, turning into shattered shells. Multiple personalities possible. Generally corresponds to the Schizoid and Dependent personality disorders.

Key Motivations: Want to create harmony in their environment, to avoid conflicts and tension, to preserve things as they are, to resist whatever would upset or disturb them.

Examples: Abraham Lincoln, Joseph Campbell, Carl Jung, Ronald Reagan, Gerald Ford, Queen Elizabeth II, Princess Grace, Walter Cronkite, George Lucas, Walt Disney, John Kennedy, Jr., Sophia Loren, Geena Davis, Lisa Kudrow, Kevin Costner, Keanu Reeves, Woody Harrelson, Ron Howard, Matthew Broderick, Ringo Starr, Whoopi Goldberg, Janet Jackson, Nancy Kerrigan, Jim Hensen, Marc Chagall, Norman Rockwell, "Edith Bunker" (*All In The Family*), and "Marge Simpson" (*The Simpsons*).

USING THE ENNEAGRAM TO ANALYZE CHARACTERS FROM *TRAINING DAY*

Now let's get a look through the lens of the Enneagram at two of the well-known film characters we've been following.

In *Training Day*, Alonzo is an 8, The Challenger. He definitely has good features—that's what's so confusing and beguiling about him. Look at the Healthy traits from this type that match him:

A resourceful, "can do" attitude and passionate inner drive. Decisive, authoritative, and commanding: the natural leader others look up to. Take initiative, make things happen.

But these attributes can go sour:

Enterprising, pragmatic, "rugged individualists," wheeler-dealers . . . dominate their environment, including others: want to feel that others are behind them, supporting their efforts . . . want to impose their will and vision on everything, not seeing others as equals or treating them with respect.

He certainly doesn't show Jake much respect.

> Become highly combative and intimidating to get their way:
> confrontational, belligerent . . . they will not back down.
> Use threats and reprisals to get obedience from others, to keep
> others off balance and insecure. However, unjust treatment
> makes others fear and resent them, possibly also band together
> against them.

This clearly happens with the group living in the Jungle (the dangerous neighborhood where the final showdown takes place). The Unhealthy aspects of an 8, The Challenger certainly describe Alonzo's dark side:

> Defying any attempt to control them, become completely
> ruthless, dictatorial, "might makes right." The criminal and
> outlaw, renegade, and con artist. Hard-hearted, immoral,
> and potentially violent. Develop delusional ideas about their
> power, invincibility, and ability to prevail: megalomania,
> feeling omnipotent, invulnerable.

Alonzo believes his own myth, as when he's charging into gunfire after robbing the Sandman's house for the money:

> Recklessly over-extending self. If they get in danger, they
> may brutally destroy everything that has not conformed to
> their will rather than surrender to anyone else. Vengeful,
> barbaric, murderous. Sociopathic tendencies.

This quick demonstration provides insight into both the good and bad aspects of Alonzo's personality, dissecting his underlying motivations the way a psychiatrist would.

Jake seems like a 3, The Achiever:

> Self-assured, energetic, and competent with high self-esteem:
> They believe in themselves and their own value. . . . Ambitious to improve themselves, to be "the best they can be. . . ."
> Self-accepting, inner-directed, and authentic, everything they
> seem to be.

But valuing hard work and accomplishment can lead a 3 like Jake down a slippery slope:

> Highly concerned with their performance, doing their job
> well, constantly driving self to achieve goals as if self-worth
> depends on it. . . . Become careerists, social climbers, invested

in exclusivity and being the "best." Become image-conscious, highly concerned with how they are perceived.

He's definitely a career climber—we see how ambitious he is. He's also concerned with how he's perceived; when people call him a rookie, that really pushes his buttons. When he refuses the marijuana that Alonzo forces on him, the last thing Alonzo says to get him to smoke it is, "Rookie." Compare his reaction to when someone calls Michael J. Fox's character a chicken in the movie *Back to the Future*.

But Jake also exhibits some traits of a 1, The Reformer, at the end of *Training Day*:

> Conscientious with strong personal convictions: They have an intense sense of right and wrong, personal religious and moral values. Wish to be rational, reasonable, self-disciplined, mature, moderate in all things. Extremely principled, always want to be fair, objective, and ethical: truth and justice primary values. Sense of responsibility, personal integrity, and of having a higher purpose often make them teachers and witnesses to the truth.

Jake refuses to yield to Alonzo's perverse way of doing things, and attacks him to try to lock him away. His sense of justice and fairness is innate, and it informs his decision-making as a cop. It is this strength of character that pulls him through.

Because evaluating someone's Enneagram type can be rather subjective, particularly for those of us who are not experts in the field, we will not analyze the characters from all the six movies studied in this book. The intention here is to expose you to this powerful resource, to give you a solid, working understanding of its function, and to show you how to build a character with it—which we will do next. For a comprehensive guide to the Enneagram in film, check out Thomas Condon's book, *The Enneagram Movie and Video Guide*. It describes the Enneagram types for characters in hundreds of movies. For example, in *Tootsie*, Condon says that Dustin Hoffman (Michael) played an argumentative, hotheaded 6; Bill Murray (Jeff) and Jessica Lange (Julie), both 9ish; Dabney Coleman (Ron), a 3; and Teri Garr (Sandy) and Sydney Pollack (George), both 6s.

LET'S CREATE A CHARACTER WITH THE ENNEAGRAM

Let's build a character who was born into extreme wealth, who because of her money is having a hard time finding love. People are either so awed by her wealth that they defer to her in a worshipful way, or they're so desirous of it that they see only the gold. To complicate things, let's say that she's not very good with people anyway—she's withdrawn and wrapped up in her own world, making it all the harder to find love. So she decides to dress up as a "regular person" in the hopes of learning how "normal" folks live and find love. Looking through the Enneagram list, we discover that a 4, The Individualist, has some characteristics that fit the bill. The overview of this personality style is:

> The Sensitive, Withdrawn Type: Expressive, Dramatic, Self-Absorbed, and Temperamental. Basic Fear: That they have no identity or personal significance. Basic Desire: To find themselves and their significance (to create an identity). . . . On the "search for self."

This all works exceptionally well for the character we've got in mind. The observation about the desire "to create an identity" is particularly stimulating. What kind of person needs to create an identity? Think of a schoolboy busy watching the kids around him and modeling himself on the coolest kids as if it were absolutely crucial to him. Many adults are still searching "to find themselves and their significance."

The Enneagram also says this about Average 4s:

> Heighten reality through fantasy, passionate feelings, and the imagination. . . .They interiorize everything, taking everything personally, but become self-absorbed and introverted, moody and hypersensitive, shy and self-conscious, unable to be spontaneous or to "get out of themselves." Stay withdrawn to protect their self-image and to buy time to sort out feelings. . . .They become melancholy dreamers, disdainful, decadent, and sensual, living in a fantasy world. Self-pity and envy of others.

Focus on that first bit—they "heighten reality through fantasy, passionate feelings, and the imagination"—for a window into this potential character. We're constructing her persona right now, and this is rich building material. She's caught up in her fantasies, her passions, and her imagination—but how? What kind of fantasies? What are her dreams? It says in the description of 4s that they want to "attract a rescuer." Does she dream of a Prince Charming?

The Enneagram also says above that 4s "become self-absorbed and introverted, moody and hypersensitive." That's a fascinating set of personality traits to work with. How would a writer show that? How does someone self-absorbed and hypersensitive navigate the world in disguise? All these questions and insights must be processed by your subconscious computer as you work on her disposition. Shyness would make it hard for her to meet people, but it can also be charming. And remember that she's broken free from her insulated wealthy world to be a "regular Joe," so she's not all that shy—at least she is bashing on the door of her trap. It's intriguing that 4s are described as "melancholy dreamers" and that they can be caught in "self-pity and envy of others." More grist for our mill.

The 4's Unhealthy aspect says:

> When dreams fail, become self-inhibiting and angry at self, depressed and alienated from self and others, blocked and emotionally paralyzed. Ashamed of self, fatigued, and unable to function.

This brings up a darker side of the character's personality, which suggests a more complex, troubled person. Anger, shame, paralysis, depression—these are emotions everybody can identify with. They make her more human, more vulnerable, more real. For even darker possibilities, refer to:

> Despairing, feel hopeless and become self-destructive, possibly abusing alcohol or drugs to escape. In the extreme: emotional breakdown or suicide is likely. Generally corresponds to the Avoidant, Depressive, and Narcissistic personality disorders.

This offers a rather full portrait of someone in trouble and searching for love and a new self. The Key Motivations round out the portrait:

> Want to express themselves and their individuality, to create and surround themselves with beauty, to maintain certain moods and feelings, to withdraw to protect their self-image, to take care of emotional needs before attending to anything else, to attract a "rescuer."

This is all great material with which to form this lonely but complicated person. However, to create a truly full-fledged character it is important to include the positive aspects of a 4. It's too limited and boring to make this character completely flawed, plus she'll need a platform from which to transform herself and find love (assuming this story isn't a tragedy). So here are some of the useful Healthy aspects of a 4:

> Sensitive and intuitive both to self and others: gentle, tactful, compassionate. Highly personal, individualistic, "true to self." Self-revealing, emotionally honest, humane. Ironic view of self and life: can be serious and funny, vulnerable and emotionally strong. . . . Profoundly creative, expressing the

personal and the universal, possibly in a work of art. Inspired,
self-renewing and regenerating: able to transform all their
experiences into something valuable: self-creative.

This is a nice collection of traits for who this character would be when she
turned her life around.

Incorporating some traits of a 2, The Helper, can take us even further in
developing her character. The 2's Basic Fear is "of being unwanted, unworthy
of being loved," and their Basic Desire is "to feel loved." They tend to "want
to be closer to others, so start 'people pleasing,' becoming overly friendly . . . .
Give seductive attention: approval, 'strokes,' flattery." Surely we all know people like that and have been there ourselves, so it rings true and can be thrown
into the mix. Experiment with adding characteristics of a 2 to bring in
another whole dimension. Our goal is not to follow rigorously the study of the
Enneagram, but to create a dynamic personality. Mix and match as needed,
and you'll find that the Enneagram is a remarkably rich resource.

Here's more on the 2:

Become overly intimate and intrusive: They need to be needed, so they hover, meddle, and control in the name of love.
Enveloping and possessive: the codependent, self-sacrificial
person who cannot do enough for others.

Does this help paint the picture of a lonely person? Yes. Does this lonely person sabotage her own efforts by being enveloping and possessive? Certainly.
The Enneagram's scrutiny enhances the complexity of the character, multiply-
ing the potential plot dynamics for this story.

Can be manipulative and self-serving, instilling guilt. . . .
Extremely self-deceptive about their motives and how
aggressive and/or selfish their behavior is. Domineering and
coercive: feel entitled to get anything they want from others.

This is fascinating insight—it's just how a person with a lot of money might
use that sense of entitlement to manipulate someone into being her friend.
She's strengthening our characterization by unconsciously bringing traits
from her wealthy upbringing into the mix. This reveals another part of her
problem, another layer to who she is and what she has to overcome in order
to find love.

Some of the Healthy traits of a 2 are:

Empathetic, compassionate, feeling for others. Caring and
concerned about their needs. Thoughtful, warm-hearted,

forgiving, and sincere. Encouraging and appreciative, able to see the good in others. Service is important, but takes care of self too: They are nurturing, generous, and giving—a truly loving person. . . . Become deeply unselfish, humble, and altruistic: giving unconditional love to self and others. Feel it is a privilege to be in the lives of others.

This fills in the portrait of someone who has really overcome her difficulties and learned how to have a real relationship by the end of the story. This description can also help generate a more complex characterization *before* her transformation, so that while she's troubled, she's much more than that, too—as any real person would be.

By exploring the nine types of the Enneagram with just a general idea of this character in mind, we've unearthed material that substantially enhances any writer's natural process of creating and dimensionalizing a character. We combined the traits from two different personality styles and found unexpected depth, flaws, sympathetic aspects, and color. As we examined the specific traits from the Enneagram, we tried them on for fit and invented behavior for this character based on those traits. We played "What if?" with a powerful resource that offers a plentiful array of spot-on possibilities.

MORE INFORMATION ON THE ENNEAGRAM

To investigate other approaches to the Enneagram, seek out the many books on the subject with comprehensive chapters on each of the nine personality types. These books explore childhood patterns, the self-preservation instinct, the social and sexual instinct, and so much more. The Enneagram will help you dig deeply into human nature, offering a gold mine of material for in-depth character study. For further reference, check out *The Wisdom of the Enneagram* and *Discovering Your Personality Type*, by Don Riso and Russ Hudson, Helen Palmer's *The Enneagram: Understanding Yourself and the Others In Your Life*, or Eli Jaxon-Bear's *The Enneagram of Liberation: From Fixation to Freedom*. Most bookstores will have a section on the Enneagram.

START USING THE ENNEAGRAM
IN YOUR OWN SCRIPT

1. Which of the nine personality types of the Enneagram resonate with each of your characters? Don't feel as though you must pick one right away. Explore them all. Play with them. Use both positive and negative aspects of the type to expand upon your initial impression of the character.

2. Think about real people you know who fit certain Enneagram types and use that to get a handle on some of your characters' attributes. If you know someone well and can see the underlying mechanics of their personality through the lens of the Enneagram, this can give you a lot of insight into developing a character with similar traits.

3. Do any of the types represent personality attributes you'd like your characters to have? Rather than merely identify them, you can actively mold characters to an Enneagram type. Assemble and build extraordinary characters from the wealth of traits, preferences, instincts, and tendencies at your disposal.

4. Use the nine personality types to make your characters different from one another. Give each of them a distinct voice. Heighten conflict by reinforcing character types that contrast. Make sure that your characters don't just reflect your own personality.

5. Create flaws in your characters with the Average and Unhealthy aspects from their type. This makes them more human and recognizable, as well as giving them room to grow and change as the plot develops.

6. Does understanding the characters in your script open up new avenues in your plot? Knowing that a certain type of character tends to act in a certain way can suggest new scenes or plot twists.

7. Get a book on the Enneagram and study the character types in more depth. This will expose you to a comprehensive knowledge of your characters that will open many doors and answer many questions. The better you know your characters, the more they'll talk to you and take you places.

8. The Enneagram Institute's Web site (www.enneagraminstitute.com) has an inexpensive test that you can take to determine your personality type. Take it while pretending to be your protagonist and answering all the questions in character.

9. Examine several different "schools" of the Enneagram to see how they present slightly different takes on the nine personality types. This will supplement your knowledge of the Enneagram, giving you even more facility in developing characters for your screenplays.

CHAPTER 5

Research and Brainstorming: Exploring Possibilities and Opening Up Your Story

The old saying, "Good material can meet you halfway," is often true. It usually happens in unexpected ways. As you research and explore material relevant to your story, you may happen on surprising information that unlocks story possibilities and lifts your ideas to another level. The material can yield ready-made story elements that mesh magically with the plot you've been developing and help tie it together. This discovery process is a large part of the fun of writing, because you often find yourself stumbling into an exciting new dimension. *Research* can bring fresh air to a project that's going stale, can grease the wheels when you're stuck, and can inject a dose of realism into a script with too much imagination and not enough substance. Once you've got some solid research under your belt, the process of *Brainstorming* can really take off. You've got great material upon which to build and you're loaded with genuine options for your plot and characters. Now you can really break loose in a creative explosion, based on great research.

USING RESEARCH TO EXPLORE STORY POTENTIAL AND BUILD PLOT

Research involves exploring anything and everything connected with your plot: experts, books, legends, mythology, current events, history, movies. Research can populate your plot with fresh concepts, factual knowledge, understanding of a specialized world, insight into character types, and so on. It's the material out of which you construct your plot—the cloth from which the suit is cut. Truth is often stranger than fiction, and research will dig up things you couldn't have imagined.

The ability to do quality research constitutes an entire discipline within the craft of screenwriting. Tracking down the diverse material that both grounds your story in fact and opens up bold new horizons can be truly stimulating. You become part detective, part librarian, and part amateur aficionado on your subject. There is no substitute for immersing yourself in authentic material. The closer you come to the real people who live it, or to world-class experts in that arena, the more well-informed your script will be and the better off you are.

Go to the Source

Make every effort to talk to a real-life expert on a topic, or to see the real place where your story happened. Firsthand research is the best kind, and will often take you well beyond what you'd been envisioning. Let's say you're writing a script about a crooked cop who is forced by circumstances to become honest. One of the first things to do is to talk to real cops. That's usually not too hard—especially in L.A., they can be even quite responsive to screenwriters. But how do you find a crooked cop? No cop is going to admit to being dishonest, but perhaps you could interview a former cop in prison. Now that's hardcore research. That's not just plugged in; that's sticking your finger right into the electric socket.

A former cop might tell you about a major turning point in his life: Where did things go so catastrophically wrong? Where did he begin to question his criminal ways and look at life with new eyes? The cop's true experiences will almost certainly dwarf your imagined ideas, opening a floodgate of possibilities for your script. A firsthand source can deepen, clarify, and even radically alter your perception of a character's dilemma, crisis, decision and action, and resolution. The material is meeting you halfway, providing unexpected story potential. Compare your research efforts to a long, dangerous trek through the wilderness; the source is someone who meets you at the midpoint with specialized equipment for the journey ahead—maps, supplies, and guidance. And there are so many people out there who might act as that source. Sometimes things come together with amazing coincidence or synchronicity. People and events show up in your life that relate to your story in some way, and the research you expected would be difficult instead unfolds naturally and in fascinating ways.

One example of terrific research is an electrifying HBO documentary called *Unchained Memories: Readings from the Slave Narratives.* Toward the end of the 1930s, about 100,000 former slaves were still alive; writers from the WPA (Work Projects Administration) interviewed more than 2,000 of them. The documentary presents these firsthand accounts of slave life through readings by today's top black actors, along with archival material from that period, making that heartbreaking world stunningly real. You couldn't even begin to write about that era in a realistic manner without exposure to source material of this quality.

Use Great Resources

If it's not possible to get the story straight from the horse's mouth, then reading books and scouring the Internet are obvious choices. There are books now that focus on Internet research, such as *Facts in a Flash: A Research Guide for Writers*, by Ellen Metter. But bear in mind that for all its convenience, the Internet can still be a limited resource. It's still just sections of certain materials that cannot begin to stack up against a specialized book on a given topic. Learn how to use a library, and ask a librarian to help you. Remember, a librarian has astonishing amounts of information at his or her fingertips. If you need to own the books, buying them used on Amazon (www.amazon.com) or other book sites can save you a fortune. There are also research experts and information retrieval firms which can fulfill highly specific requests.

Seeing other movies is a great form of research. Studying everything within your genre can help you begin to "speak the language" of that type of movie. *Video Hound's Golden Movie Retriever* is a great resource for finding movies on a particular topic. Movies are sorted into categories with headings such as (in the Rs) Roaring '20s, Robots/Androids, Rock Stars on Film, Rodeos, Role Reversal, and so on. If you're writing, say, a spy story and want to see other films in the genre, the book list hundreds of them, and even indicate those considered to be the best.

Focus Your Research

Do some work with the 36 Dramatic Situations, Dilemma, Crisis, Decision & Action, Resolution, and Theme before getting into serious Research. Then you'll have more of a sense of what you're up to as a storyteller, allowing you to target the research rather than taking a scattershot approach. This is not only time-efficient but also more focused. William Thompson Price said, "The Theme points like a finger post to the Material, to the field from which you are to supplement your experience and philosophy."

Hold Your Story Ideas in Suspension

One of a trained dramatist's habits of mind is to be plastic and flexible, always on the lookout for something that might enhance, complete, or crystallize a story. Think of the possibilities that might fall in your lap as you explore your material. Pouring the story's structure in concrete too soon can cut you off from unforeseen and vibrant alternatives. Price's words on this topic provide excellent guidance. Here he discusses research in *The Philosophy of Dramatic Principle and Method*:

Sound your Theme and Material to the bottom before deter-
mining upon your play. If you gain the idea for it, hold it in
reserve, awaiting the possible chance for something better.
The idea will inevitably be modified or improved in some
manner. There may be hundreds of plays in that Material so
why take the first thing that occurs to you? You may get a
great drama instead of a superficial one by questioning and
cross-questioning everything. At least you will get substance
rather than shadow . . . nothing in details, or absolutely in
outline can be fixed until you have taken all your bearings
and sounded all the possibilities. . . . The deeper you go, the
more suggestive the facts.

This wise advice speaks to holding all in suspension as you develop a script by
trying on various combinations and configurations. You're not married to any
one path until you've tried them all and found what truly works for your plot.

In his book *The Analysis of Play Construction and Dramatic Principle*, Price
gives the following advice on gathering together your research material:

The real dramatist goes to real life. He will find everything
there waiting for him; he does not create everything, he
adapts it. . . . Go back, then, to nature for your Material, and
trust to your art to make use of it. The minerals in the mines
have to be delved for. No miner can manufacture gold, and
no dramatist can create human nature. Your play must have
substance. . . . What a trivial vanity it is that some authors
have that they must "create" everything, spin it out of their
brains without recourse to the facts of the world. . . . Cease
mere dreaming and empty imaginings and reach out your
hand for the Material that lies about you in abundance. . . .
The trained dramatic mind is occupied much longer in gathering the Material and in constructing the play, shaping his
material, than in the actual writing. How long or short it
requires to "write" a play is immaterial, but if we assume that
a year is given to it, three fourths of that time had best be
applied to the preliminary research and thought.

Price isn't saying you ought to spend nine months out of that year researching, but that you can spend this much time working out, planning, developing, and structuring a script. Part of that time includes research. He empha-
sizes that you can take all the time that normally goes into rewrites and put it
into engineering your script properly *before* you write it.

Know When to Stop

Research can be utterly crucial to developing a story, but don't fall into the trap of endless research, which can become a means of avoiding the writing itself. You may love your material so much that you don't want to stop steeping yourself in it. You may even establish lifelong fascinations through research on subjects in which you previously had no interest—that's another exciting thing about writing. But sometimes you just have to wrest yourself out of the research stage and get on with building your script. You can always go back to reading later on.

Bear in mind that some stories require little or no research. Stephen King says he often needs just enough information to lie colorfully. Gather information if you need it, but don't get too caught up in it. You're the creator, so do whatever you want—bend or twist anything you need. It's just a movie. Remember the great old saying, "Never let the facts get in the way of a good story."

Don't Limit Yourself to "Write What You Know"

Good research also leads you away from the fallacy that you should write only what you know. Such thinking is a cruel trap. We write because we want to *create*. Don't let some writing teacher steer you back to your own closed loop for story material. You may have lived an interesting life, but don't get stuck rehashing it. You can learn virtually anything you want or need for writing outside your personal experience, especially now that information is more readily available than ever before. If you want to write about building rockets and you don't know the first thing about it, then go out and *learn*. Read for months if that's what it takes. Peruse the Internet. Talk to experts. If you can, go to a lab that builds rockets. Make it into an adventure. This is not being stuck with the same old stuff or breathing the same old air—it's the ecstatic freedom of creating.

Be passionate about refusing these limits, as is the author of the following article on this very subject. One of my former students, a vice president at a Hollywood film studio, thought this article should be reprinted every month in *Variety* to remind the industry of its point. It's called "Doom Eager: Writing What We Need to Know," by Seattle-based director and playwright Steven Dietz.

> PETEY (broken): Stan, don't let them tell you what to do!
> —Harold Pinter, *The Birthday Party* (1958)

"Write about what you know." The words echo down from above us with the authority of soldiers. The words sit on our laps as we stare at our typewriters. They fester inside us like a computer virus left over from a well-meaning mentor. "Write about what you know." A cunning phrase, which takes a moment to utter and can take a lifetime to overcome.

Obviously, every playwright writes out of personal experience in either a direct or oblique manner, whether consciously or unconsciously. At its most innocent, the "stick to what you know" admonition provides a sort of creative comfort. It is a way of saying, "Yes, there are interesting, important things about your life that you can relate to others. Trust that and tell your stories." I am not worried about the harmless, cheerleading use of this phrase. But I hear it used in the theatre with increasing regularity for a different purpose. I hear it used to censor playwrights.

If you've been present at discussions of new plays, or involved in the developmental process in any way, you have heard statements not unlike the following: "Who are you, a heterosexual man, to write about the love between two women?" "Who are you, a black woman, to write about the patriarchal Native American culture?" "Who are you, a well-to-do kid from Seattle, to write about the struggles of immigrants in the Rio Grande valley?" "Who are you, an aging white man, to write about the experiences of inner-city black youth?" Stick to *your own life* is the implication. Your life is the sole palette from which you may draw your material. So learn that. Learn to stay on your side of the creative yellow line. In our bohemian smugness, it never occurs to us that this is, in any way, censorship. Far from it. In fact, we've become experts at making this attitude a virtue. Instead of censorship, it is called "sensitivity." It is called "multicultural awareness." Most frighteningly, it is called "politically correct." And, as often as not, these who-are-you-to-be-writing-that comments are not coming from audience members who find something unpleasing or offensive about the given play—these words are coming from workers in the profession, from directors, dramaturges, actors and incredibly, other playwrights. I believe that uttering these words to a playwright is tantamount to becoming the small-minded, censor-happy goons that we so vocally abhor.

We cannot have the ethics of our creativity both ways. We cannot on one hand support and pursue the long overdue call for nontraditional casting, and on the other hand tell playwrights that their sex, age, race, creed, sexual preference and physical condition determines the kind of plays they can write. We cannot, belatedly, rail against the politics of the National Endowment for the Arts, and in the same breath tell a writer that a given topic is the exclusive province of someone else. We cannot wear Rushdie on our sleeve and Helms in our heart. That is not "awareness." That is fear. What we fear is that we may be surprised by what we find buried in the unfamiliar; that our cherished and entrenched beliefs may be put in danger; or, perhaps, that we may discover, in others, similarities to ourselves. We must remember that the theatre only shines when it pries at the locked door, when in dares to look fear in the face.

What better way to begin to close the distance between our various communities (ethnic, religious, political, sexual) than by opening doors and venturing in? Where is the long overdue call for nontraditional playwriting? What value is there in taking refuge in the idea that "I'll never know how a woman/man thinks. I'll never know how a black/white/Hispanic/Asian person thinks. I'll never know how a gay/straight/lesbian/bisexual person thinks. I'll never know what it's like to be a veteran, or a Native American, or a mother, or a white supremacist, or a brain surgeon, or a spy, or an Olympic athlete, or a communist, or a dock worker, or an anti-abortion activist, or Jewish/Catholic/Muslim, or a disabled person, or a southerner, or an orphan, or a high-fashion model, or an eighteenth-century poet, or a feminist, or a foreign visitor, or the Amish, or a Republican, or a person with a terminal illness, or a father, or the homeless." No, perhaps you won't. But be advised that you have chosen a profession in which it is your *mandate* to be an explorer, not a curator, of your society. A profession which is to be questioned, as Brecht said, "not about whether it manages to interest the spectator in buying a ticket, but about whether it manages to interest him in the world."

Our integrity, not merely as artists but as citizens of the world, centers on engaging in dialogue with the "out there," probing the parts of our world that are foreign to us. Only through this sort of active engagement will we begin to approach "awareness." Only through dialogue, and not entrenchment, will we arrive at a truly "multicultural" art form. We will get nowhere by waiting for others to address our burning questions, with the cunning rationalization that the topic is better served by someone else. That doesn't wash. Never did, never will. We learn only when we lean into, not away from, our questions.

The signal we must send is this: Yes, certainly, "write about what you know," but, should the spirit move you, be brave enough to "write about *what you need to know*." Write about cultures that mystify you, write absolutely everything you think about the opposite sex, write about strangers who intrigue you, write with gusto about the people you will never meet, write with abandon about anything outside of your experience that fascinates, frightens, inspires, angers or seduces you. "But how do I know what they're thinking?" You're a *writer*. You *guess*. You *invent* their lives and action with as much truth and passion as you can summon. You make your case and you await the verdict of the audience, of critics, of your peers. *At that point* is when they should have their say about the value of your attempt, and not before. *At that point* they should have every opportunity to question, praise, denounce, inform, trash, prize, badmouth, bless, boycott, emulate or burn your work. *At that point* you may bask in the realization that you have broadened your horizons and those of your community. Or you may find out that you were just dead wrong. And that, too, will teach you something. Attempts, not results, are the only sacred things in the theatre.

So be "doom eager." Wrestle with what is uncertain to you. Venture into those places that the world tells you belong to someone else. Did you get into theatre to think *small?* Did you become a writer so other people could *tell you what to do?* Do not let *anyone*, no matter their title or position, no matter their notoriety, no matter the cause or people they are championing, tell you what you are allowed to write. We risk the greatest loss when we allow our questions to be made smaller.

"Nothing can stop progress in the American theatre except the workers themselves," Robert Edmund Jones wrote in 1941. Nearly fifty years later, those words shine like a beacon.

It's so easy these days to allow yourself to be told what you can or cannot do to succeed, and the film industry is full of people eager to do both. Take the time to get in touch with your own voice as a writer and then stick to it—a distinct voice is highly prized in screenwriters. Skill and confidence make for an unbeatable army. Figure out what you *really* want in the world—many people are frightened to acknowledge their deepest desires—and go for it with all your energy. Find the stories that you're moved to tell and don't let anybody steer you away from them, no matter what. And remember: There's no better research than a life lived fully.

USING BRAINSTORMING TO EXPLORE POSSIBILITIES AND SHATTER STORY LIMITS

At the end of your research you should feel super-saturated, as though you're loaded with great material and you've really covered the territory. This is a good time to get into *Brainstorming*. Brainstorming is the vigorous and explosive exploration of all the various possibilities in a plot. While in some ways you're brainstorming at any given point in the development of a story, once you've acquired a specialized knowledge your brainstorming can really take off. How can you brainstorm about a rocket-building story without any concept of what's involved?

Stretch the envelope as far as you can. Explore each idea in every possible direction, no matter how farfetched it may seem. Experts in creativity say that people who solve age-old problems often try out a crazy idea that works unexpectedly. Other people may have had the idea before but never went all the way with it. As a writer, you should have a healthy imagination. Give it free reign. Remember, the key word in the entertainment industry is *outrageousness*.

The trick to brainstorming is to let your brain explode like popcorn. Does certain music kindle your inner fire? Do certain writers inspire you? Does watching a favorite movie set your mind racing? Whatever gets you going, light that rocket and let it run rampant. Don't edit yourself to death, but let it flow, let it erupt. If you force it to come out clean and organized, then you're slowing that creativity down to a trickle. Just get it all down on paper—you can sort it out later. The emphasis is on freedom, inventiveness, spontaneity. Let new ideas and untried possibilities bubble up, even if they don't make sense. It can be like surfing a giant wave. Just get on it and ride. If you're lucky, you may have ten ideas per second pouring out of your brain for hours on end.

Why not go out dancing to live music when you've got a new story in your head. The movement and physical violence of wild dancing stokes your energy and charges your spirit. It can bring both you and your story to life so that your story becomes alive, breathing, challenging, moving, ecstatic. It's so rare to be roaring wild in this modern, domesticated world! (I write to hardcore punk music, and it pumps me up in a way that nothing else even comes close to.) Music and movement can make you see things in a whole new way. It's the total opposite of sitting in a chair and trying to *think* wild. Some people say they can't create unless they move—they have to dance an idea into existence.

INCUBATING IDEAS AND LETTING YOUR SUBCONSCIOUS PERCOLATE

At a certain point in brainstorming, you burn out. This signals a good time to give your brain a rest. Let the ideas settle in your mind. Escaping from the intensity of your work, both mentally and physically, is an important part of the creative process. Get away from your desk and take a bike ride or a walk on the beach. Use your body and rest your mind, and solutions will simmer and steep until ready. The conscious mind can be like a radio voice that just yammers on endlessly. Switch it off and let things incubate.

Your subconscious mind is a powerful creative entity, and when it gets some computing time to itself it can offer up amazing poetic results. Give your subconscious a chance to think. Ideas can bubble up that you might never have thought of consciously. For this to happen, you must be able to get out of your own way, so to speak. Because you've focused so much attention on your story, the lyrical genius of your subconscious knows what you're trying to create. Given a chance, it will feed you ideas. You may have a dream, a random thought percolating up from nowhere, an auditory hallucination, or coincidental things appearing before you in print. This is your subconscious providing you with solutions. Learn to relax and open up to it. Being receptive is essential to developing a creative vision.

DOUBLE-CHECKING WHAT YOU'VE CREATED SO FAR

After using all the tools mentioned so far in this book, step by step, your script has probably come light-years from where it started. But as a story grows, evolves, and morphs, it's critical to reevaluate and make adjustments, or to entirely revise your plot as needed.

Revisiting the 36 Dramatic Situations

This is a good time to go back and review the 36 Dramatic Situations. Even just taking a quick cruise through the list on page 51, you may find fresh ideas jumping out at you now that you've picked up a novel approach while researching and brainstorming. After some development, a script will often be entirely different from what it was when you were starting out. By going back to it, you'll no doubt see many innovative possibilities. You're wrestling with new plot problems, trying to nail down your ending, and struggling to understand your characters more completely. The 36 Dramatic Situations are a resource that you can keep coming back to as needed.

Restating Dilemma, Crisis, Decision & Action, and Resolution

Now go back and look at your dilemma again. It may have grown and changed as you developed the script and made certain plot choices. Articulate the dilemma as it now stands by stating it as two equally unacceptable alternatives. Are they still equal? It may no longer be a true dilemma if one of the alternatives has become less unacceptable. Remember, you want two *equally* painful choices. You'll also find that so much time spent thinking about your character's dilemma means you'll now be able to state it more fully and completely. You may have started out with a rather tentative statement—"She's damned if she does and damned if she doesn't"—that helped you get a handle on your dilemma, but now you can come back and articulate it with all its ramifications, layers, and dimensions.

Next revisit your crisis, because it may have grown and changed, too. Now that some time has passed and you have acquired more knowledge and insight through research and brainstorming, you may have enhanced the crisis. Stop and state it clearly now. Nail it down again in much the same way that you might check your roof rack on a cross-country trip to make sure it's still tied down tightly.

Decision and action is a crucial turning point in the script, so it's important to check it again. Does your earlier take on it still hold up? Can you revamp it for stronger effect? Do you understand your character's decision and action more clearly now that you've spent a lot of time thinking about it?

Your resolution completes the transformation of your protagonist as it brings your audience's ride to an end. You can keep tinkering with it because, since this *is* the end, it doesn't generally send ripples of change through the rest of the script. Think about the mood you want for your audience when the movie is over, and ensure that your resolution produces that mood.

Check in on your theme as well. Look at the resolution and the way in which the protagonist resolves the dilemma. The theme almost always grows as the plot does, so it may no longer be what it used to be. If it's transformed into something else, are you satisfied with it now? Can you articulate it clearly?

START USING RESEARCH AND BRAINSTORMING IN YOUR OWN SCRIPT

1. Identify some good sources for research on the story you're developing. What's the best possible source? How can you get to it?
2. Do you know any experts in the field? Do you know someone who knows someone? Remember, there's a difference between classroom expertise and someone who's really lived it. Both can be useful, but a soldier who fought in Vietnam will have real-world experience that

a professor with a background in military history will not. At the same time, a professor will definitely have insights the soldier won't. Consider these slants when choosing and interviewing a source.

3. Dig deep into your research to unearth dynamic story options that you never expected. Allow yourself to be lured down unfamiliar and unpredictable story avenues. If you don't try to control everything, you could stumble into untouched worlds. You may even discover an entirely separate screenplay or two lurking in the material. Remember that you're a storyteller by trade, so always be on the lookout for a hot lead.

4. Are you open to your material or are you already locked into the first conception of your plot? Keep coming back to the living energy of your original idea, but stay flexible about how you execute the plot possibilities.

5. Details are important to a convincing representation of reality, but don't get trapped in perpetual research. Bear in mind that strict accuracy is rarely necessary, and some stories require no research whatsoever.

6. In order to brainstorm you must allow your imagination to explode with possibilities. Don't be afraid of chaos. As a storyteller it's part of your business. Don't be afraid to get in trouble with your story. If you're not in over your head, then you're probably not doing your job right. Screenwriting is an adventure into the unknown, and too much control can stifle your imagination.

7. Do you end up with the same old stuff everyone else is writing? Do you go to the movies and rant about all the lousy films being made, and then go home and work on a predictable, anemic screenplay? If so, then find ways to shatter your approach to your story or to storytelling in general. Research using deeper and more obscure sources than ever before. Brainstorm with abandon.

8. Learn how to occasionally turn off your conscious mind—the yammering brain—and allow yourself to drift. Observe your dreams, your visions, your poetic impulses. Get away from your desk and take a walk. Work your body and rest your mind. Give your subconscious a chance to do some thinking without you. Leave your notes at home and forget your story, then sit down somewhere new with a blank piece of paper and see what pops up for your story. Unexpected solutions often appear seemingly from nowhere.

The Central Proposition:
Tying Your Plot Together and
Cranking Up the Conflict

The *Central Proposition* is a uniquely potent tool that will give you a crystal-clear focus on your script by forcing you to strip it down to its absolute bare bones: the central and compelling action of the plot. It uses the power of logic to help bring order to the chaotic creative process so necessary to the development of a dynamic story. In fact, the structural power of the proposition enables you to go even further creatively than you might otherwise. It has a power as irresistible as that of a lever, helping to pull what might be a collection of clever story components together into a coherent plot. The Central Proposition burrows to the core of the script's plot. It strips the complete action down to its essentials, providing you with a valuable degree of objectivity, much like an x-ray of your story.

The Central Proposition was created by William Thompson Price (see page xiv), who reminds us that we can have all the things that Aristotle talked about (dilemma, crisis, etc.) but still not necessarily have a functional drama. In order to have a great race car, you need a good strong engine, a solid transmission, and so on. However, while you may *have* an engine, it may be sitting on a workbench; you may have a transmission, but it's on the garage floor. You've got all these components, but they're not yet functioning as something you can actually drive. What Price did was to create a tool that ties all the parts of a script together into a coherent whole.

Price was a highly educated, world-traveled lawyer who largely gave up his legal practice to devote himself to his true passion—the theater. He worked for some of the top producers of the day and read thousands of plays, many of them poorly written. He began to despair, wondering what was tripping up these playwrights. They weren't stupid and they often had good stories to tell, but they just didn't possess solid craft as dramatists. Price tried to create a tool that would help them make their scripts work.

As a lawyer, Price was trained to use logic to strip a complex argument down to a clear statement of the facts, so he brought this kind of thinking to dramatic structure. He went back to the syllogism of formal logic. A *syllogism* is a logical argument consisting of three sentences—two premises leading to a conclusion: A and B, therefore C. The most famous is:

> All men are mortal.
> Socrates is a man.
> Therefore, Socrates is mortal.

This argument is demonstrably true—it's irrefutable. Price said that a plot has its own logic, and one ought to be able to state the complete action of the plot with this level of simplicity and clarity. A lawyer goes through the same process in preparing a case for presentation in court. A proposition is a type of syllogism. A lawyer putting forth a proposition or a proposal to the court: "You say my client stole this car. I can prove he wasn't in town that day. Therefore my client is innocent."

The ability to structure a solid, logical argument can be very useful in constructing a dramatic plot because argument, in the form of conflict, lies at the core of a movie. It is said that conflict is to drama as sound is to music.

ADAPTING THE PROPOSITION OF LOGIC TO DRAMA

So Price adapted the proposition of formal logic to drama, and it's called the Central Proposition. We can use it to strip the plot down to a simple statement of the facts, focusing on the central conflict of the script. Conflict is clearly context-sensitive, because it will play out quite differently in a romantic comedy than in an action-thriller. But there should be some kind of conflict or opposition in every screenplay in order to create suspense.

The Introduction to this book mentions that in the earliest Greek theater there were only two characters in a play. Stripping your plot down to just protagonist and antagonist takes you right to its nucleus—and making it work at that level will impact everything else. That's exactly what we're doing here with the proposition: stating the action of the entire plot in three steps, focusing on the conflict. We set up a fight, touch it off, and then bring it to a conclusion.

A bar fight starts off as a shoving match and then erupts into a knock-down, drag-out fight. It's over when one of the combatants walks away. In a screenplay we're doing much the same. We establish a potential fight between the protagonist and the antagonist fairly early in the script, and the audience can sense that these two are going to go at it later in the story. Then, at around the two-thirds or three-quarters point of the script, we touch off a fight to the finish, which only one can win. This brings the viewers to the edge of their seats, wondering if their protagonist can pull it off. However, rather than just state the conclusion, Price adapted this tool to focus on the fact that the audience is caught up in wondering how the fight will turn out. This gets at what's dramatic about the conflict.

So the Central Proposition consists of three sentences in which we (1) Set up a potential fight, (2) Touch off a fight to the finish, and (3) Leave it hanging in the form of a question in the minds of the audience. We'll get into the details of the adapted third step soon, but for now let's get a firm understanding of the first two steps.

Set Up the Potential Fight

Let's say that we're developing a plot in which two gold miners fight over a claim. Our hero struggles to keep a claim jumper from stealing his hard-earned mine with phony paperwork and pure thievery. We'll call our protagonist Tasker, and our villain will be Sharp. If, fairly early in the plot, Sharp brings in a fake sheriff and a trumped-up charge to force Tasker off his claim, then the two combatants would fight and Tasker could drive Sharp away. They have essentially crossed swords, but it's not a showdown—yet—and the viewers are compelled to see where this conflict is headed.

Touch Off the Fight to the Finish

Later in the film, if Sharp returns with reinforcements to take out our miner, then Tasker would launch an all-out attack to try to vanquish the predator for good. Now the *fight to the finish* has begun. This is war. It's the inevitable knock-down, drag-out conflict toward which the whole movie's been building. Only one of them will own that mine when it's over, and thus starts the most gripping section of the film: from this declaration of war to the ending.

It's important to have a sense of proportion when using this tool. Below is a diagram to give a general understanding of this proportion:

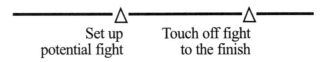

The first triangle is roughly where the set-up often occurs, and the second triangle shows where the touch-off is usually triggered. Bear in mind that this is very approximate and is intended only to convey a general sense of proportion.

When the fight to the finish has only just started, people come up on the edge of their seats, wondering how it's going to turn out. We've created Dramatic Action—that state of subjective excitement in which you hope to put the audience (see page xxi). At this point of high suspense, if we could wave a magic wand and freeze the audience, then we could go out and get a closer look at their reactions. Let's focus on one member of this frozen audience. We want to know how riveted is this person? Is her pulse racing? Is she white-knuckled? Do we have her or don't we? If we don't, then the plot we've set up and touched off isn't working well dramatically. And if it's not working, can we put our finger on why not, and can we correct it?

Price said that part of our job as dramatists is to engage the audience in an unresolved situation—and the fact that they're on the edge of their seats is what's truly dramatic about the plot. This is an important point. Think about how the best movies catch you up in an uncertain story: The degree to which you need to know how it ends is a measure of how dramatic the plot is. If you don't care, then it's dramatically flat.

The Central Dramatic Question: Leaving the Audience Hanging

At this point, when the fight to the finish has only just started, a question appears in the minds of the audience, something roughly like: How is it going to turn out? This is called the *Central Dramatic Question*. It exists only in the minds of the audience—not on-screen, not in dialog. In our gold miner's story, the Central Dramatic Question is, *Will Tasker defeat Sharp and keep his mine?*

The question in their minds will be highly specific because the audience is watching a highly specific set of events. It will not be general or generic, such as, *Will the good guy win?* It will relate exactly to what they're watching and to the way in which it is currently unresolved. As the screenwriter, you must be absolutely in touch with the audience at this point of your script. If this question in their minds is weak, then it indicates that you're proposing an ineffective drama. If the question is strong, it's an indication that the plot is riveting.

If the Central Dramatic Question does turn out to be weak, then we can experiment with strengthening it. By altering the set-up or the touch-off, we can adjust the power of the question and the audience response. What we're really experimenting with is a working model of the plot. Before engineers build a $50 million bridge, they construct a wooden model, subjecting it to crush tests and shear tests to determine how it holds up. If the model crushes too easily, then they might double the uprights or make other adjustments. Once the model performs well, they build the full-scale bridge. The process is similar with the Central Proposition. Once you've set up the conflict and touched it off in your script, then you try to gauge how engrossed the audience is. Do you have them or not? On a scale of 1 to 10, to what degree do you have them in your grip? If it scores low, then what element of the set-up or the touch-off can you modify to intensify the Dramatic Action?

Understand that the question in the minds of the audience is going to be rather simple and straightforward, not overcomplicated or intellectualized. They're caught up in the immediacy of a powerful emotional experience. Keep it simple and clear when you're trying to isolate the question in the minds of the audience, and you'll generally be right on track.

One of the necessary skills in using this tool is to be extremely objective regarding the Central Dramatic Question. It's very much a mind-reading trick. Imagine a magic camera that can take a picture of the question in the viewers' minds. Or try a trick that I developed from using this tool over the years: When the fight to the finish has just ignited, pretend you are out sitting with the audience and ask, "What's the question in our collective mind right now?" *Become* the audience at this high point of suspense. Feel out what "we're" thinking, what exactly has us on the edge of our seats. Not what it *should be*, or what you insist it *must be*, or what it *would be* if the audience weren't clueless—but what that question *actually is* in cold, hard fact.

Take our chief example: In *Training Day*, the potential clash is set up early in the script when Jake challenges Alonzo about ripping off the Sandman's cash with the fake search warrant. They square off about the reality of under-cover work, and Alonzo insists that Jake either play it his way or go back to boring conventional police work. With this background well established, Jake then sparks the fight to the finish late in the movie when he tries to arrest Alonzo and seize his $1 million as evidence. Alonzo distracts Jake for a split second, flicks a cigarette in his eyes, grabs a hidden shotgun, and comes up shooting. They're no longer just preparing to fight and they're no longer simply skirmishing. This is war. Now, what is the question in the minds of the audience? You can sense it quite easily—it just becomes a matter of articulating it. Isn't it something like, *Will Jake defeat Alonzo?* Or even, *Can Jake possibly defeat Alonzo?* But bear in mind that Jake is trying to jail Alonzo for cor-ruption, so wouldn't the question be something more like, *Can Jake take Alonzo down?* That's pretty much it. It's not complicated or intellectual, just a gut reaction—the audience is riveted and wondering how things will turn out. If this was your script and you were mapping out the plot, you'd get a sense of its power fairly early in the development process by gauging the strength of this Central Dramatic Question.

When trying to measure this question's potency, it's crucial to take into account the context of the whole story. It's one thing to isolate the wording of the question at this high point of suspense; it's quite another to measure that question's true impact. For instance, in our example of the gold miners, we said that the Central Dramatic Question would be, *Will Tasker defeat Sharp and keep his mine?* But how much does the audience really care? How much do they like this miner and care about his fate?

Perhaps audience sympathy hasn't been stoked very well and reaction is lukewarm. This would make the Central Dramatic Question weak. But maybe the audience has seen Tasker lose his new bride in a fire that he barely survived, involving viewers much more in his fate. What if Sharp set the fire? Now they loathe him and care even more about the outcome of the miners' fight. What if Tasker has just discovered that his mine is incredibly rich and he's trying to keep that a secret until his brothers arrive to help him defend it? Each time we play with the variables in this way, the stakes go up and the viewers are gripped more intensely. The question itself never changes, but we come to care about it *so* much more. There are many more factors in assessing audience tension than just the specific language of the question. It's very important to read the minds of the audience and articulate the question, but in order to judge how powerfully that question really impacts the audience it's equally important to evaluate it within the context of the story.

As you work with the Central Proposition, recall that you're dealing only with the main action. Bernard Grebanier says it well in his book *Playwriting*: "Proposition is an analysis of the *main action* only [emphasis by Grebanier]. It has reference *only to action*, not to motives, psychological states, moral issues or theme, for plot is entirely a matter of action." Aristotle says something quite similar in the *Poetics*:

> Most important of all is the structure of the incidents.
> For Tragedy is an imitation, not of men but of an action
> and of life . . . it is by their actions that men are happy
> or the reverse. Dramatic action, therefore is not with a view
> to the representation of character; character comes in as a
> subsidiary to the actions.

To locate the Central Proposition, we're cooking down the entire story to its essence and focusing on the conflict. We're stripping the plot to its absolute core, in which two main actions lead up to a pivotal question for the audience. However, since there are hundreds of actions in a screenplay, how do you distinguish which of them sets up the conflict and touches it off?

CONSTRUCTING
THE CENTRAL PROPOSITION

The three components of the Central Proposition are isolated with a five-step process using deductive logic, starting at the end of the film and working in reverse. Some aspects of the proposition are slippery, so working backward helps pin them down. First, we look at the fight to the finish. Second, we ask about the question in the minds of the audience: How will this fight turn out? Third, we pinpoint the action that touches off the fight to the finish. Fourth, we reason in reverse to determine what earlier action sets up the potential fight. Finally, the fifth step identifies the element linking the set-up and the touch-off. To assemble the three-sentence Central Proposition—(1) Setting up the potential fight, (2) Touching off the fight to the finish, and (3) Stating the dramatic question that arises in the minds of the audience—we will need these five pieces in hand. We'll keep *Training Day* at the forefront as we study this process, so that next we can use its five components to determine the Central Proposition.

Step 1: Visualize the Fight to the Finish

First, we must *Visualize the fight to the finish*. Can you see it—literally see the fight to the finish—in your mind, as though you're watching a movie? In *Training Day* we see Jake and Alonzo fighting it out in that rough neighborhood, and in *Blade Runner* Deckard and Roy have a showdown on the roof. Remember, conflict is of a different nature in a romantic comedy than it is in an action adventure. Pay attention to the context when you apply it to your own script.

To really emphasize opposition or conflict, you want to have two real people actually going at each other. Keep in mind that you're writing for live actors. A character's struggle with addiction or a fight against an unjust law won't play well unless an actual human being personifies the addiction or the law. Imagine one boxer trying to fight in a ring and this point will become quite clear. Always remember that your script has to be actable. So the question here is, does the level of conflict in your script build to a fight to the finish, one that you can really envision?

Step 2: What is the Central Dramatic Question?

Next we ask, *What's the question in the mind of the audience once the fight to the finish has only just started and they don't know how it's going to turn out?* We start with the fight to the finish and the Central Dramatic Question because it's easiest to find this high point of suspense in your script. The beginning of the fight to the finish is the point of no return, and the audience genuinely doesn't know how it's going to turn out. The Central Dramatic Question in *Training Day* is, *Can Jake take Alonzo down?* In your own script, get down to the real question in the viewers' minds, not what you hope it is. Be brutally honest with yourself—self-deception is useless in analyzing your own material. If you use it properly, this tool offers a real x-ray of your material's deep structure.

Step 3: What Action by the Protagonist Touches Off the Fight to the Finish?

Now we ask, *What action by the protagonist touches off the fight to the finish, giving rise to the Central Dramatic Question?* Concentrate on the action of the protagonist, because that's where the audience's focal point will be. Bear in mind that there might not be a touch-off in your plot so far. Conflict isn't necessarily inherent in a story; often, it needs to be developed. You may not notice how underdeveloped your conflict is until you apply the proposition to your script. And if it does exist, you may well be surprised by how weak your protagonist's attack is when viewed under the harsh light of this tool. Once you notice this, then you can experiment with beefing it up—sometimes to a great degree—which empowers the whole script.

In *Training Day*, Jake touches off the fight to the finish when he goes into Alonzo's girlfriend's apartment, tells Alonzo he's under arrest, and tries to take the $1 million for evidence. From this point on it's war, and only one of them can win.

Step 4: What Earlier Action by the Protagonist Sets Up the Potential Fight?

Next we ask, *What earlier action by the protagonist sets up the potential fight?* This time we're moving backward a giant step in the story. In our proportion diagram for the overall script, the fight to the finish tends to start late, but setting up the potential fight happens earlier, perhaps a third or a quarter of the way into the story (although it's flexible according to the demands of the specific material).

Set up
potential fight

The first triangle indicates roughly where the potential fight is often set up. Remember, we're trying to incorporate the proportion of the entire script with this tool—trying to encompass the complete action. Essentially, we're setting up the conflict. This set-up is a point at which the protagonist and the antagonist "cross swords" or have a run-in, like a shoving match that will burst into a fight later. Bear in mind that quite often there may be no protagonist-antagonist conflict early on in the story as you've developed it so far. The Central Proposition will make this apparent so you can construct a scene that does set up a potential fight. And this, too, will boost your story's power, sometimes immensely since you're making your protagonist so much more proactive.

In *Training Day*, this scene occurs when Alonzo robs the Sandman and Jake challenges him about the stolen money, saying that Alonzo almost got them killed or put in prison. Alonzo tells Jake to forget working undercover with him, so Jake finally relents—for now. But they do go at it, setting up the audience expectation that the conflict between these two will clash later on. The set-up scene creates Dramatic Action, engaging the audience. Jake and Alonzo are at each other's throats, and it stays that way at varying levels until their fight turns deadly.

Step 5: Do the Set-up and the Touch-off Have Anything in Common that Can Bind Them Together?

The last step in generating our dramatic proposition is to ask, *Do the set-up and the touch-off have anything in common that can bind them together?* What does this mean? All we're trying to do is link the set-up and the touch-off of the fight because it helps tie the script together, helping to unify the plot. To understand it, we go back to the syllogism from which Price derived the Central Proposition, paying attention to the part of it that's known as the "common term" (seen in italics below):

> All *men* are mortal.
> Socrates is a *man*.
> Therefore Socrates is mortal.

In formal logic, two premises that lead to a conclusion should be connected by a common term—in this case, the word "man." This creates a valid chain of logic between them and is part of the reason why the above argument is irrefutable. We want this power as dramatists because a solid connection between the set-up and the touch-off will help make our script coherent and solid. In essence, we're talking about a connecting rod—something that links them. Various elements in a story can serve as the common term, but whatever it is, if we can bind the set-up and the touch-off together in some way then it helps unify the plot.

As shown above in *Training Day*, a potential fight is set up when Jake challenges Alonzo about robbing the Sandman, and the fight to the finish is touched off when Jake tries to arrest Alonzo and take the $1 million as evidence of Alonzo's crime. In order to isolate the common term in this proposition, we ask, *Is there anything similar or common between the point when Jake challenges Alonzo, and the point when he tries to arrest him?* In both situations Jake is really shocked at Alonzo's blatant corruption. Jake will not stand for this and the intensity of his refusal grows as he discovers the depth of Alonzo's treachery. So, we could say that the common thing between the set-up and the touch-off of the fight is that Jake cannot allow this blatantly corrupt activity to go unchallenged.

The Use of the Central Proposition for *Training Day*

Now let's assemble the three-sentence proposition from its component parts (the common term is underlined):

Set up the potential fight
Jake is <u>unable to remain silent after Alonzo robs the Sandman</u>, and
he challenges Alonzo on his conduct.

Touch off the fight to the finish
Now fully aware that Alonzo is a murdering thief, <u>Jake refuses to let
him go free</u>, and tries to arrest him and seize the $1 million as evi-
dence of his corruption.

The Central Dramatic Question
Can Jake take Alonzo down?

Putting More Detail into the Proposition. We have stripped the plot to its
skeleton—right down to its chassis and engine. This important process should
help you see the most basic plot without any padding whatsoever. However,
Price did emphasize that once the plot is laid bare, it's good to let a little bit
of information back into the proposition so that a stranger to the story can
make sense of it. For instance, who the heck is Jake? From the scant information in the three-sentence Central Proposition, he could be a used car sales-
man in Cincinnati for all we know.

The Complete Proposition for *Training Day*. Adding a few phrases into
the mix can give a clearer picture of the movie. Imagine this as a short pitch
to a Hollywood studio executive.

Set up the potential fight
Jake Hoyt, an ambitious rookie policeman on his first day as an
undercover narcotics cop, finds himself under the supervision of
Alonzo Harris, a wild, unconventional, street-smart veteran who
shakes up Jake's entire view of police work. When Alonzo robs a
drug dealer, Jake cannot allow this corruption to go unchecked
and so challenges Alonzo on his conduct.

Touch off the fight to the finish
Jake is drawn deeper into the questionable world of Alonzo and his
crazy, criminal mode of policing. Things escalate when Alonzo and
his crew of rogue undercover cops rob and murder a high-level drug
dealer, and then order Jake to claim he was the one who pulled the
trigger. When Jake will not be part of it, Alonzo almost has him
murdered but Jake escapes. Now fully aware that Alonzo is a murdering thief, Jake finds him, tells him he's under arrest, and tries to
take the $1 million that will prove Alonzo is a dirty cop.

The Central Dramatic Question
Can Jake take Alonzo down?

A WORD ABOUT THE ANTAGONIST

Since we're dealing specifically with the protagonist-antagonist conflict in this chapter, let's focus on the antagonist for a minute. Alfred Hitchcock said that the more powerful your antagonist is, the more complex and dangerous the situation is, the more formidable your protagonist must be to overcome it, and therefore the more powerful the movie is. Think of the saying, "The movie is only as good as its villain." If you ratchet up the intensity of your antagonist, the whole energy of the script rises. Sometimes you'll find that there's plenty of room to pump up the antagonist because you haven't paid much attention to that character. But in almost any case you can get a little more out of even a well-defined antagonist. Stack your antagonist against the all-time greats. How does he or she compare to Keyser Soze? Hannibal Lecter? Matty Walker from *Body Heat*? Darth Vader? Gordon Gekko from *Wall Street*? HAL 9000? Alex Forrest from *Fatal Attraction*? The Terminator? Noah Cross from *Chinatown*? Annie Wilkes from *Misery*? Sergeant Barnes from *Platoon*? Or any of the other all-time great villains?

THE USE OF THE CENTRAL PROPOSITION FOR FILMS

Now that we've done *Training Day*, let's apply the Central Proposition to the rest of the movies we're working with. You'll see how versatile it is as we encounter different genres and styles.

The Use of the Central Proposition for *What Women Want*

The conflict in *What Women Want* is intriguing because there's very little overt resistance from Darcy. The opposition is there because Nick and Darcy are definitely competing at certain levels, but she has no idea she's being taken advantage of. Nick is obviously very active in his secret war against Darcy.

The fight to the finish is about his attempt to win Darcy back, but it takes some unexpected turns. He actually starts the fight by demanding that Dan, their boss, rehire her. Then Nick must struggle through all the problems he caused in trying to get rid of her. On his way to find Darcy he hears that Erin (the suicidal girl) didn't come to work, so he goes to her and tries to straighten out the mess he's made by treating the firm's women so badly that they're falling apart. After he rescues Erin, he learns that his daughter is freaking out at the prom, so he tries to be a real father for the first time in his life. After setting that right, he admits to Darcy the truth about what he did to her. Nick is running the gauntlet, confronting his screwed-up behavior pattern and undoing all his messes so that he can become someone who really deserves

Darcy. He's fighting for his life—his emotional life—and for the love of the most amazing woman he's ever met.

Let's work our way back through the five steps to construct the proposition for *What Women Want*.

Step 1: Visualize the Fight to the Finish
Nick is fighting to win Darcy back. To do so, he must dig himself out from under a lifetime of mistreating women—in an attempt to set everything right and become the man Darcy fell in love with.

Step 2: What is the Central Dramatic Question?
Will Nick somehow manage to win Darcy back?

Step 3: What Action by the Protagonist Touches Off the Fight to the Finish?
Nick demands that Dan rehire Darcy and then fights through all the things that separate him from her.

Step 4: What Earlier Action by the Protagonist Sets Up the Potential Fight?
Nick gets into a skirmish with Darcy when Dan asks their opinions about some artwork. Nick reads Darcy's mind and steals her idea, taking credit for it with Dan. Darcy plans a rebuttal in her mind, but Nick hears her thoughts and shuts her down, making himself look good and making her look bad.

Step 5: Do the Set-up and the Touch-off Have Anything in Common that Can Bind Them Together?
In both the set-up and the touch-off scenes, Nick is attracted to Darcy. In the set-up, he can't help noticing how beautiful and open she is, and he gets into a real conversation with her about his daughter and the prom. By the time he starts the fight to the finish, hoping to win her back, he's fully in love with her—and she with him.

Here's the stripped-down assembly of the three-sentence proposition (again, the common term is underlined):

Set up the potential fight
Nick, <u>attracted to Darcy in spite of himself</u>, reads her mind and steals her idea, making himself look good and her look bad when Dan asks their opinion on some artwork.

Touch off the fight to the finish
<u>Now fully in love with Darcy</u>, Nick demands that Dan hire her back, and then struggles to undo all the damage he's done.

The Central Dramatic Question
Will Nick manage to win Darcy back?

Now let's fill out the proposition with some clarifying detail so that it makes sense to someone who doesn't know the story:

Set up the potential fight
Nick Marshall, a chauvinistic lady's man, is an advertising executive who gets passed over for creative director when Darcy Maguire, a woman from outside the company, gets the job. He vows to get rid of her, and when he mysteriously acquires the ability to read women's minds, he begins using it to unseat her. When their boss asks about some artwork, Nick, beginning to fall for Darcy in spite of himself, telepathically steals her idea and makes her look bad.

Touch off the fight to the finish
As Nick succeeds more and more in his effort to undermine Darcy, he also finds that he's falling in love with this truly incredible woman. Even though his resolve is wavering, he steals a major idea of hers, lands a huge new client, and ends up with all the credit. Upon learning that she's been fired, and now completely realizing he's in love with her, he goes to the boss and demands her rehire, and then starts fighting his way through all the things that separate him from her.

The Central Dramatic Question
Will Nick manage to win Darcy back?

The Use of the Central Proposition for *Minority Report*
The conflict in *Minority Report*, as with most action and adventure films, is much more apparent because there's little ambiguity in a life-or-death situation. The central struggle is clear and literal. Let's work through the five steps to construct the proposition for this film.

Step 1: Visualize the Fight to the Finish
Anderton is fighting to get out of his conviction for a future murder.

Step 2: What is the Central Dramatic Question?
Will Anderton succeed in escaping the frame-up?

Step 3: What Action by the Protagonist Touches Off the Fight to the Finish?

When Anderton refuses his predicted future—to kill Leo Crow—he really starts to fight against Lamar's plan. He doesn't know yet that Lamar is behind everything, but this action throws a monkey wrench into the gears of Lamar's plan, and it's Anderton's first major move in the endgame to extract himself from the trap.

Step 4: What Earlier Action by the Protagonist Sets up the Potential Fight?

Anderton fights to escape Danny Witwer and the Precrime cops once he's been flagged for a future murder he knows he wouldn't commit.

Step 5: Do the Set-up and the Touch-off Have Anything in Common that Can Bind Them Together?

Anderton knows that something is off or suspicious about the prediction. Just before his fight with Danny, he suspects that he's been framed; then just before he refuses to kill Crow, Agatha screams at him that he can choose not to follow it.

Here's the bare-bones version:

Set up the potential fight
Anderton, <u>certain that the prediction is all wrong</u>, fights his own Precrime cops and Danny in a desperate attempt to escape.

Touch off the fight to the finish
Hearing the psychic Agatha's cries that <u>he can choose not to fulfill the prediction</u>, Anderton refuses to kill Leo Crow and resolves to figure out who set him up and why.

The Central Dramatic Question
Will Anderton succeed in escaping the frame-up?

Now let's add more detail to flesh out the proposition.

Set up the potential fight
John Anderton, head of the D.C. Precrime police unit that prevents murder through the use of psychics known as "Precogs," learns of a prediction that he will kill a man named Leo Crow, whom he's never met. Determined to prove that something is totally wrong with the prediction, Anderton goes on the run to escape his own squad of cops as well as Danny Witwer, an investigator who may be trying to frame him.

Touch off the fight to the finish
Now in hiding, Anderton struggles to solve this murder prediction
and learns that one of the Precogs may have proof that the future
murder is not a certainty. He abducts the Precog, Agatha, and they
find Leo Crow, the man they learn had kidnapped and murdered
Anderton's son. Anderton is about to execute Crow, but when Agatha
screams that Anderton can choose, he becomes convinced that something is wrong and refuses to shoot Crow. Discovering that this was
a setup to trick him into killing Crow, Anderton starts digging to
find out who framed him.

The Central Dramatic Question
Will Anderton succeed in escaping the frame-up?

The Use of the Central Proposition for *The Godfather*

Some additional explanation is required to locate the central conflict in *The
Godfather*, as it is somewhat subterranean. The fight to the finish—the war on
Barzini—is largely hidden, because Michael never goes directly head-to-head
with Barzini, who operates entirely behind the scenes through his agents
Sollozzo, Moe Green, Carlo, and Tessio. But when Michael and Moe Green
argue over the Las Vegas hotel and casino that they co-own, Moe threatens to
deal with Barzini, who has chased the Corleones out of New York. In the next
scene, Don Corleone warns Michael that Barzini will call a meeting at which
his safety will supposedly be guaranteed, but that he'll by assassinated there.
The point of no return has been crossed. We are left with the Central
Dramatic Question: Can Michael defeat Barzini and save the family?

What set up this potential fight was Michael's execution of Sollozzo,
Barzini's agent in a power play to overthrow the Corleones. It's as if the leader
of the Crips sends a messenger to the leader of the Bloods and they kill the
messenger—you know there's going to be a fight. The common term has to
do with Michael being thrust into a position of power—both when Sollozzo
requests a meeting with him and when Don Corleone puts him in charge of
the family—and he takes control in both situations

Now let's lay out the five steps needed to determine the Central
Proposition for *The Godfather*.

Step 1: Visualize the Fight to the Finish
Michael is involved in an indirect fight with Don Barzini.

Step 2: What is the Central Dramatic Question?
Will Michael defeat Barzini and save the family?

Step 3: What Action by the Protagonist Touches Off the Fight to the Finish?
Michael declares war on Barzini by throwing down the gauntlet at Barzini's agent, Moe Green.

Step 4: What Earlier Action by the Protagonist Sets up the Potential Fight?
Michael executes Barzini's agent, Sollozzo.

Step 5: Do the Set-up and the Touch-off Have Anything in Common that Can Bind Them Together?
Michael finds himself thrust into a position of power and takes control of the situation.

Here's the three-sentence proposition:

Set up the potential fight
Michael, <u>finding himself thrust into a position of power, takes control of the situation</u> and executes Barzini's agent, Sollozzo.

Touch off the fight to the finish
Michael, <u>now put in charge of the family by his father, takes control</u> and declares war on Barzini by throwing down the gauntlet at Barzini's agent, Moe Green.

The Central Dramatic Question
Will Michael defeat Barzini and save the family?

Now let's review the proposition again with a little more detail.

Set up the potential fight
Michael Corleone, son of a Mafia don in the 1940s, does not want to enter the family business, but an attempt on his father's life changes all that. When the would-be assassin, Sollozzo, asks for a meeting with him, Michael finds himself in the driver's seat and, taking control of the situation, executes Sollozzo and his bodyguard, McCluskey.

Touch off the fight to the finish
Having been made head of the family operation by his ailing father, Michael takes control and launches a surreptitious attack on Barzini,

the don behind it all, pretending to run from New York and then throwing down the gauntlet at Barzini's agent, Moe Green, by threatening to take over the hotel and casino that they co-own.

The Central Dramatic Question
Will Michael destroy Barzini and save the family?

The Use of the Central Proposition for *Tootsie*

Tootsie is very challenging to break down to the basics because it has a more complex structure. It's essentially a play within a play: Dorothy's drama inside Michael's drama. To find the central action, ask yourself, "What is the high point of suspense?" At first it seems that Dorothy and Ron (two guys fighting over a girl) support most of the conflict throughout the script. That holds up—to a degree. Their fight comes to a head when Julie is about to break up with Ron, and Dorothy tells him that she knows him a lot better than he thinks. But that's the play within the play—and it doesn't give rise to the Central Dramatic Question of the script as a whole.

But ask yourself: When were you most on the edge of your seat? It's actually when Dorothy is unveiling on live television, coming down the stairs telling this gigantic lie as she tries to reveal that her character is really a man. This seems to be the point of no return, where both audiences are hanging on every word and wondering how it's going to turn out. In terms of conflict, it brings up an interesting angle—the clash between Michael and Julie. This has been brewing since Michael propositioned Julie with her own pick-up line and got a drink thrown in his face. They're definitely in conflict until he finally wins her over at the end of the movie. In romantic comedies the lovers are often at odds, and that's certainly the case here.

Let's look at it in the following terms:

Step 1: Visualize the Fight to the Finish
Michael is struggling to land Julie now that he infuriated her by unveiling as a man.

Step 2: What is the Central Dramatic Question?
Will Michael be able to win Julie back?

Step 3: What Action by the Protagonist Touches Off the Fight to the Finish?
Michael unveils on live TV, revealing that Dorothy is really a man who's been substantially deceiving Julie and her father, Les.

Step 4: What Earlier Action by the Protagonist Sets Up the Potential Fight?
Michael tries on Julie the very pick-up line that she recommended to Dorothy, which she finds insulting, and he gets a drink thrown in his face.

Step 5: Do the Set-up and the Touch-off Have Anything in Common that Can Bind Them Together?
Michael is trapped as Dorothy but is utterly desperate to get Julie.

We can assemble the basic three-sentence proposition as follows:

Set up the potential fight
Michael, <u>trapped as Dorothy but desperate for Julie</u>, tries a pick-up line on Julie that she herself suggested.

Touch off the fight to the finish
<u>Stuck as Dorothy and now madly in love with Julie</u>, Michael pulls off his wig on live TV to reveal that Dorothy is really a man.

The Central Dramatic Question
Will Michael somehow manage to win Julie back?

Now let's assemble the proposition again, this time with enough detail so that a stranger to the story can make sense of it.

Set up the potential fight
Michael Dorsey, a "difficult" actor whom no one will hire, disguises himself as a woman to land a role on a soap opera, where he falls in love with Julie, a beautiful woman trapped in a powerless relationship with the show's director, Ron. They become good friends as Dorothy inspires Julie to free herself from Ron, and when Michael, desperate to win Julie, tries on her the pick-up line that she suggested to Dorothy, he gets a drink thrown in his face.

Touch off the fight to the finish
Michael falls more in love with Julie, but he is trapped in his role as Dorothy when her contract on the show gets extended. At Dorothy's prompting, Julie breaks up with Ron, and Michael (dressed as Dorothy) tries to kiss her but she freaks out and ends their friendship. Michael, now more desperate than ever to land Julie but completely trapped as Dorothy, reveals on live TV that Dorothy is really a man.

The Central Dramatic Question
Will Michael somehow manage to win Julie back?

The Use of the Central Proposition for *Blade Runner*

Finally we take a look at *Blade Runner*, isolating the separate parts of the proposition. As usual we begin by locating the high point of suspense.

Step 1: Visualize the Fight to the Finish
Deckard and Roy Batty are fighting it out on the roof.

Step 2: What is the Central Dramatic Question?
Can Deckard possibly defeat Roy?

Step 3: What Action by the Protagonist Touches Off the Fight to the Finish?
Deckard kills Pris and tries to kill Roy.

Step 4: What Earlier Action by the Protagonist Sets Up the Potential Fight?
Deckard follows clues to Zhora, the snake lady, and kills her. He's now starting to take out the replicants.

Step 5: Do the Set-up and the Touch-off Have Anything in Common that Can Bind Them Together?
The common element is that Deckard feels for the replicants, making him reluctant to kill them.

Stripped-down proposition:

Set up the potential fight
Deckard, <u>although feeling for the replicants and reluctant to kill them</u>, follows clues to Zhora, the snake lady, and kills her.

Touch off the fight to the finish
<u>Now in love with Rachael and even more sympathetic to the replicants</u>, Deckard is forced to kill Pris and face off with Roy, who has killed Dr. Tyrell and J. F. Sebastian.

The Central Dramatic Question
Can Deckard possibly defeat Roy?

Filled-out proposition:

Set up the potential fight
Rick Deckard, a retired bounty hunter in a dystopian future,

is drafted back into the police to destroy four dangerous genetically engineered slaves known as "replicants." After meeting their cruel creator, Dr. Tyrell, he begins to see things from the replicants' point of view, feeling for them and becoming reluctant to "retire" them, yet he finds Zhora, the snake lady, and kills her.

Touch off the fight to the finish
Although Deckard has fallen in love with Rachael, a replicant who saved his life, and now feels more sympathy for the replicants and is less willing to retire them, he's forced to kill Pris and face off with the unstoppable combat model Roy, who has killed Dr. Tyrell, the replicants' creator.

The Central Dramatic Question
Can Deckard possibly defeat Roy?

THE NUCLEUS OF YOUR PLOT

As you plan and revise your own script, be mindful of the simple way that one of Price's students, Arthur Edwin Krows, sums up the Central Proposition in his book *Playwriting for Profit* (New York: Longmans, Green and Co., 1928):

> . . . Price's formulation is primarily a matter of stating succinctly: first, the circumstances out of which the action proper grows; second, the precipitating act which compels a fight to the finish; and finally, the objective of the play as a whole, expressed in alternatives—one in favor of one side at issue, the other in favor of the other.

The Central Proposition can be a tricky tool to master, but once you get the hang of it, it will be extremely useful in tying together a plot that is under construction. The proposition can unite a collection of story elements into one coherent plot. It forces you to get right down to the nucleus of the plot and state it clearly, cleanly, and completely as a logical argument.

When it comes time to apply the proposition to your own plot, part of you may rebel against having to get that clear. You've become used to chaotic brainstorming, fuzzy logic, and an unfettered creative process. Now it comes time to put a bridle and saddle on this wild horse, and you resist. Remind yourself that the clarity and power of this tool will bring you a new level of control over the material. It often helps build, develop, or outright create conflict where it might have been weak, ineffective, or even nonexistent. The Central Proposition locates the gaps and suggests solutions, and can help pin down the mysterious missing *something* that really makes the script click.

Getting Some Distance from Your Work

It's very easy to be hypnotized by your own material. You say to yourself, "How can it not be great? There's so much great stuff in it!" The proposition can objectify your plot, giving expression to its fundamental elements and allowing you to see it from a distance in order to evaluate it. You may find that stripping your plot down this far leads you to think, "Wow, I didn't know my plot was that solid." Conversely, you may find yourself asking, "Is that all I've got?" If it's not working, this is a good time to notice. You don't want to find out that your Central Dramatic Question is weak on the opening night of your $30 million movie, when it will be painfully obvious. You don't want the audience members to be falling asleep right when you expect them to be the most spellbound. The discovery that your plot is dramatically flat while it's still in your workshop is an extremely valuable one.

Conflict or opposition comes in many forms. Whatever form you've got, you should set it up and then touch it off—and the dramatic question in the minds of the audience will give you a measure of its power. If it isn't working, then tweak it as needed, either in a big way or just a bit. Set up several possible propositions in parallel and observe which ones grab you more than others. Play with them. Try things on. Mess things up. Stir the pot and experiment with the shape of the whole plot. You're not trapped by details yet, since at this point you're dealing with the deep structure of your story. You're flexible and free in a way that you won't be later in the development process when your plot solidifies. That's what this tool is all about—you get the core structure *right* before you actually start writing or even outlining the screenplay.

Pulling All the Elements Together

The proposition is the true starting point for plot construction. Prior to this, we've been collecting good "parts" with which to build a movie. Dilemma, Crisis, Decision & Action, and Resolution are all solid components, but they don't automatically make a plot function. The 36 Dramatic Situations and the Enneagram are good elements, too, but are still only a piece of the pie. Even Research and Brainstorming and all the hard work that goes into creating a plot don't automatically pull it all together. The Central Proposition is a tool that can take you from the point where you're done gathering your wits to the point where you're ready to begin constructing your plot.

You can try different propositions as you experiment and shape your plot. The thing to remember is that it's truly a proposal for a movie—a pitch—and either it works or it doesn't. You can say, "Okay, what if I try the plot this way? Hmmm, not bad. What if I try it *that* way? Interesting. What about *this?* Weak. How about this version? Wow! That really kicks. Now I'm onto something hot."

The Genetic Identity of Your Story

The Central Proposition displays the most compact rendering of the complete action of your plot—your whole story reduced to a single-celled organism. Once you find a proposition that works, the genetic identity of the plot is in many ways determined, just as before *you* were conceived, there was only a sperm and an egg—but once they combined, your genetic identity was determined. All the cell division and growth thereafter carry that same identity. Here you get to shape your script at its nucleus, and that is a big part of the power of the proposition.

Price reflects on this in his book, *The Philosophy of Dramatic Principle and Method*:

> One main proposition is the essence of unity; it is unity, and
> unity can be procured in no other way. It is impossible that
> two main ideas exist in the same play. The house will be di-
> vided against itself. Two bodies cannot occupy the same space
> at the same time. The play itself, that which is developed from
> the one idea, is about many things; but the discerning eye
> of the author should penetrate to the heart of things. True
> dramatic instinct (which is largely the product of training)
> usually does this with unerring promptness, for that one idea
> is naturally the largest idea. . . . A proposition involves the
> whole play. It must have a certain magnitude and the play
> must be commensurate with it. It suggests action, for the last
> clause requires that a problem be worked out. Doubt is
> expressed. The facts are given. Opposition is encountered.

It is from this kernel of action that your script blossoms, from this skeleton that you can flesh our your story.

When I started learning to write, I spent three years reading two books: Price's *The Analysis of Play Construction and Dramatic Principle* and Krows's *Playwriting for Profit*. After that, I decided to see what other playwriting books had to say about Price. I didn't find many references, but one book—the aforementioned book, *Playwriting*—had lots of them. I looked it over and read the following quote to my playwriting teacher, Irving Fiske:

> Eventually Price was able to formulate his law of plot, the
> proposition—which, we are quite willing to agree, is the one
> significant contribution to the science of playwriting since
> Aristotle's *Poetics*. This was the judgment of many of his stu-
> dents, among whom were the most successful American
> dramatists of their generation. It is a large remark, but as we

say, we do not dispute it—even though Price's very name seems unknown to the public or to the scholars these days. If we ourselves were asked to whom we were indebted for the basis of our ideas about playwriting, we should have to answer, "Aristotle and Price."

Irving said, "Wow, he really understands Price. Who wrote that?" I turned the book over and read the name off the cover: Bernard Grebanier. Irving jumped and exclaimed, "He was my teacher!" It turns out that he had studied playwriting with Grebanier in Brooklyn years before, and the textbook for that class was *Playwriting for Profit*. This is how I found out that I was the fifth generation in this school of playwriting, something I never would have known that if I hadn't stumbled over that quote.

USING THE CENTRAL PROPOSITION IN A DEMO PLOT

Let's use the gold miner's claim-jumping story that we worked with earlier (starting on page 126) to practice the five-step process and then lay out the three-sentence proposition. Remember that Tasker is our protagonist and Sharp is the villain. In order to visualize the fight to the finish, think through what we'd be seeing on the actual movie screen. We said earlier that Sharp returns to the mine with reinforcements and tries to eliminate Tasker, who then goes on an all-out attack to finish off Sharp. What would this fight actually look like? Wouldn't it be a kind of mountainside shootout, with some dynamite thrown in for good measure? Perhaps Tasker has prepared the ground with booby traps like landslides and cave-ins. Now can you see it?

Step 1: Visualize the Fight to the Finish
Tasker and a heavily reinforced Sharp fight it out on a mountainside for control of Tasker's gold mine.

Step 2: What is the Central Dramatic Question?
Can Tasker fight off Sharp and keep his mine?

Step 3: What Action by the Protagonist Touches Off the Fight to the Finish?
Tasker launches his attack on Sharp's raiders by detonating twin dynamite explosions in a canyon, killing half of Sharp's men in one move.

Step 4: What Earlier Action by the Protagonist Sets up the Potential Fight?
Tasker drives off Sharp and his fake sheriff when they try to force him from his claim.

Step 5: Do the Set-up and the Touch-off Have Anything in Common that Can Bind Them Together?
Tasker is determined to hang on to his mine.

Here's the stripped-down, three-sentence proposition:

Set up the potential fight
Tasker, <u>determined to hang on to his mine</u>, chases away Sharp and his fake sheriff when they try to drive him off his claim with fake documents.

Touch off the fight to the finish
Having unexpectedly found a massive vein of silver and now <u>totally desperate to hold his mine</u> until his brothers arrive, Tasker launches an all-out attack on Sharp and his band of mercenaries.

The Central Dramatic Question
Can Tasker fight off Sharp and keep his mine?

Again, let's assemble the full proposition, with a little more information included:

Set up the potential fight
Tasker, a gold miner in 1880s Nevada who has found a vein on his claim, is being watched by Sharp, an unscrupulous claim jumper who preys on solitary miners. Seeing Tasker's success, Sharp shows up with a friend disguised as a sheriff and presents some forged paper work purporting that the claim actually belongs to Sharp. Tasker refuses to be bullied and chases them away, firing his shotgun above their heads.

Touch off the fight to the finish
Sharp is not scared off so easily, and as he rounds up some hired guns to try again, Tasker discovers a stunning vein of silver in his gold mine. Keeping it quiet, he telegraphs his brothers come out as partners, urging them to rush as things are becoming dangerous. Sharp brings his group of killers up Tasker's mountain to ambush him, but Tasker has prepared the ground beforehand with dynamite booby traps and landslide triggers. He launches an out-and-out attack by detonating twin dynamite explosions in a canyon, decimating half of Sharp's men at once.

The Central Dramatic Question
Can Tasker fight off Sharp and keep his mine?

This has been a look at using the Central Proposition to frame up and reinforce the conflict in a script that doesn't exist yet. As you saw, the exact same five-step process works to construct a script or take one apart for analysis. Practice it by dismantling some of your favorite films. Bear in mind that while it can take some time to master this tool, it's definitely worth the work.

START USING THE CENTRAL PROPOSITION IN YOUR OWN SCRIPT

1. Make sure you're thinking in terms of the full scope of your script—a sense of proportion is a skill crucial to gaining a mastery of the Central Proposition. Set up the potential fight somewhere around the one-quarter to one-third point. Touch off the fight to the finish near the two-thirds or three-quarters point in the story.
2. Have you developed conflict in your story? If you haven't, the Central Proposition will point this out very quickly. This tool will suggest the generation of conflict or opposition, creating the suspense required to push the audience members to the edge of their seats.
3. Can you distill your script down to two central characters in conflict? Remember that the oldest Greek theater had only two characters in the whole play. Try to envision your plot *that* stripped down. It forces you to be very objective and very clear.
4. Does the conflict between the two central characters break out into a final showdown near the end? Can you visualize that "fight to the finish"—really *see* it—as though you were watching the end of your movie in your head?
5. Think about what touches off the fight to the finish. This is the onset of a war (entirely within the context of your material—whether an action film, a romantic comedy, a period drama, or whatever). Now let your imagination take you into the audience at this high point of suspense. Get a feel for the question in their collective mind as to how things will turn out for the protagonist. This is the Central Dramatic Question. Keep the question simple and direct because it's usually a gut question for the audience.
6. Is the Central Dramatic Question powerful enough? How intense is the Dramatic Action it creates? Could it be more powerful or are you surprised by its strength already?
7. What action by your protagonist sparks the fight to the finish? It should be a powerful action touched off by your main character,

because we tend to want our protagonist to be proactive, a prime mover.

8. Step back to an earlier point in the plot. What action by your protagonist sets up a potential fight? This set-up tends to occur around the one-quarter or one-third point in the plot, so reason backward from the touch-off of the fight to the finish. Bear in mind that you should incorporate the proportion of the entire story. Is there some substantial conflict that starts to build the pressure early on?

9. Opposition comes in many forms. Don't get too bent out of shape about the conflict aspect of this tool. All you're really trying to do is to set up an action and then touch it off so that the audience is left hanging at the point of high suspense. If the viewers are really on the edge of their seats, then you've creating effective Dramatic Action.

10. Is there anything in common between the set-up and the touch-off of the fight to the finish that can bind them together? Some kind of valid, logical connection between the two will help unite the entire script into a coherent whole. Don't get too hung up on this connecting element—it can be something simple, as long as it ties them together in some way.

11. Now stand back from the proposition and evaluate it. Does the core action of your script grab you as much as you hoped it would? Is it powerful? Is it pathetic? Is it somewhere in between? What are you going to do about it?

12. If your Central Proposition is weak, then play with either the set-up or the touch-off, or both, to invigorate the plot. Stoke up one fire or the other to increase audience sympathy and interest. Look at everything in the story that contributes to its dramatic power; alter the various factors one by one and observe what makes the proposition more powerful.

13. Configure the proposition several different ways. This is the right time in your development process to experiment with radically diverse possibilities. Measure various propositions in parallel so you can compare different takes on the material—perhaps wildly different takes.

CHAPTER 7

Sequence, Proposition, Plot: Constructing and Tightening Your Plot

Sequence, Proposition, Plot is a three-step process that helps screenwriters to build a sound plot. Academy Award-winning writer William Goldman (*Butch Cassidy and the Sundance Kid, Marathon Man*) likens screenwriting to carpentry: "The single most important thing contributed by the screenwriter is the structure." You must assemble all the parts discussed in this book so far into a coherent sequence of events that moves along well and grips your audience. Plot construction is both an art and a science. If you take the time to properly engineer your story structure before you actually write the script, then much of the misery of extensive rewrites can be avoided.

In order to construct a plot, you must think it through first. Most writers prepare an outline before they start, sketching out the basics of the story—the big picture—and then filling in the details as needed, weaving them in gradually, fleshing out the plot, working from general to the specific. As Aristotle says in the *Poetics*, in constructing the plot, the writer "should first sketch its general outline, and then fill in the episodes and amplify in detail."

SEQUENCE, PROPOSITION, PLOT: A THREE-STEP PROCESS

Sequence, Proposition, Plot is an innovative outlining tool with several powerful features that strengthen and dramatize a script. It knits the incidents of your story together into a tight progression of cause and effect, such that the first event causes the second event (the effect), which then causes the third, and so on in a continuous chain. Sequence, Proposition, Plot also utilizes a more sophisticated form of the Central Proposition (from Chapter 6) in order to introduce conflict throughout all the different sections of the screenplay. The overall script should demonstrate good momentum and compelling conflict; each act, each sequence, and each scene should do the same. In this way, you can build continuous Dramatic Action into your script as you construct it from these building blocks. This can be much harder than it sounds. But Sequence, Proposition, Plot is so good at unifying and driving a script that the Hollywood studio creative executives who've learned it from me consistently say that it's the most advanced development tool in the film industry. So now let's see what comprises each of these three steps.

Step 1: Sequence

Sequence is the series of incidents that constitutes your script—the order of events that make up the forward flow of your story. These incidents should be connected by cause and effect such that, as we've said, the first event causes the second, which causes the third, and so on, through to the end of the story. This keeps the story moving forward smoothly and eliminates dead spots where you can lose the audience.

This book's Introduction talked about the difference between Story and Drama (see page xxi). One of the symptoms of mere Story is that it's *episodic*—a succession of unconnected episodes that don't really go anywhere and don't build much tension. Here's how Aristotle defines it in the *Poetics*: "Of all plots and actions the episodic are the worst. I call a plot 'episodic' in which the episodes or acts succeed one another without probable or necessary sequence." To create this tight chain of cause and effect, start from the ending and work backward, building from each effect back to its cause. It works like a charm, and once you get the hang of it you'll wonder how you ever did without it.

To construct this reverse sequence, start by asking, *What is the Object of the script?* The *Object* is a simple, clear statement of where you want the story to end up—the point on the horizon toward which you're moving. The ability to state the objective of any exercise can be clarifying and is crucial to obtaining results. If you go into a lawyer's, a doctor's, or a policeman's office with bits and pieces of fact and emotions all over the place, you will hear, "Wait a minute. What's the *point*?" When you succinctly reply, "Oh, I need *this*," the lawyer/doctor/police officer will say, "Okay, now we can talk."

In *Training Day*, the *Object* of the script is that Jake defeats Alonzo, completes his training, and emerges anew as a powerful man. This is the writer's objective, not the protagonist's. An actor might think in terms of his or her objective as a character, but this *Object* is where you, the writer, want the script to end up, and it might be diametrically opposed to what the protagonist intends. In *The Godfather*, Michael Corleone's goal is not to become a soulless crime lord, but that was the objective of the writers.

Once we know the *Object* of the script, then we want to know, *What is the Final Effect that demonstrates this Object on-screen with real actors?* If the *Object* is *what* we want to achieve, then the *Final Effect* is how we actually stage it with action demonstrated by real actors. The *Object* can be abstract, but the *Final Effect* should be real and actable. The *Final Effect* in *Training Day* is that Alonzo is executed by the Russians and Jake goes home. This shows that Alonzo has been defeated, and Jake will move forward with his integrity and sense of self intact as a good cop.

Next we want to know: *What is the Immediate Cause of the Final Effect?* More specifically in this case, what is the *Immediate Cause* of Alonzo being executed? Jake takes Alonzo's $1 million to use as evidence against him, so Alonzo can't pay off the Russians. We use the word "immediate" here to make you seek the cause from among the events just prior to the ending, and not from some distant cause or abstract idea.

Now we ask: *What's the cause of Jake being able to take the money?* Jake defeats Alonzo in the fight with some help from the neighborhood locals. We then continue reasoning backward from each effect to its direct cause. The cause of Jake defeating Alonzo is that he drops onto Alonzo's car, and Alonzo gets stunned from smashing the car around to shake Jake off. The cause of Jake dropping onto the car is that Alonzo beats the stuffing out of him and attempts to leave him behind. The cause of Alonzo beating up Jake is that Jake tries to arrest Alonzo and seize the $1 million as evidence. Follow a straight line from each effect back to what caused it and you will build an unbroken chain of events that comprise the spine of your story. Jake tries to arrest Alonzo and seize the money, which causes Alonzo to beat the daylights out of him and take off to pay the Russians, which causes Jake to drop onto Alonzo's car in a desperate attempt to stop him, which causes Alonzo to get stunned when he smashes his car around trying to knock Jake off it, which causes Jake to punch Alonzo out and be able to take the money, which causes the locals to see that the loathsome Alonzo is weakened, which causes them to help Jake defeat Alonzo, which causes Jake to be able to leave with the money as evidence that Alonzo robbed and murdered Roger, which causes Alonzo to be killed by the Russians when he shows up without it, which causes Jake to be able to go home free, his training completed—now a powerful, honest cop.

Separating the Necessary from the Unnecessary. When building backward, notice that in each instance we ask what is the *cause* of each effect, not *what comes before it.* This is the major distinction that makes this tool work, and it helps separate the Necessary from the Unnecessary. The ability to separate the Necessary from the Unnecessary is a crucial skill for the dramatist because the screenplay is an extremely lean literary form that demands total economy.

You can really experience this if you're turning a 400-page novel into a 110-page script. A lot of material simply cannot make its way into the script, and it's your job to decide what's Necessary and what's not. Bernard Grebanier (in his book *Playwriting*) says, "Drama has a tendency to be stripped of matters unessential to the plot. . . . In the best plays everything counts. There is no place for tangential material or merely graceful ornamentation."

The trick for separating the Necessary from the Unnecessary is to locate the true cause of a given effect, and not simply what comes before it. Any number of things can come before, but only one thing actually *caused* it. You are looking for the spine of the plot, unencumbered by unnecessary detail, to ensure that the action is continuous.

William Thompson Price said that the work of the amateur is characterized by the Unnecessary. Dialog and descriptions are overdone, scenes tend to be overwritten, acts are bloated, and so on. Price recognized that whole scenes may be unnecessary, or perhaps even an entire act. For that matter, your entire script may be unnecessary. This may sound humorous or harsh, but if you've ever worked as a studio script reader, you'll know it's no joke. Good cause and effect is important; it moves the material forward smoothly and solidly without going off on tangents that slow the story down. When you set up a cause you create an expectation in the audience, and when you deliver on it, then you've got them hooked. If you wander off into something else, then you've got a dead spot—a section that's dramatically flat.

So the trick is to ask, *What is the cause of something?*, and not *what came before it*. Suppose your sister orders you to buy a lottery ticket because she had a dream, and you do so, winning a ton of money. A number of things might happen *before* you win the money—you lose your car keys, buy some cigarettes, get a parking ticket—but the *cause* of your winning is that your sister made you buy a ticket, and the cause of that was her dream. Reasoning backward through a story in this way helps you find the main building blocks of the plot. It keeps you from being blinded by a blizzard of unnecessary detail.

This freedom from a profusion of unnecessary detail enables you to escape the trap of not being able to see the forest for the trees. It's easy to get caught up in your story, and it's difficult to achieve genuine objectivity. *Reverse cause and effect* allows you to strip your plot in the same way that radically pruning a tree exposes the major branches. Working this way helps you to get at the essentials and make them function. Many screenwriters have a beautifully written scene in a script that doesn't work, which is much like having an ornately furnished room in a house that's falling down. There may be oak trim, gold leaf, and carved marble, but the house itself is caving in. If the big picture doesn't work, then the particulars *do not* matter. Getting caught up in too much detail can make that hard to do.

When you're building a skyscraper, the steelwork comes first—the girders and beams. If one of your workers came rushing up in a panic and said, "Hey boss, what about the wallpaper in the bathroom on the tenth floor?" you'd say, "We'll deal with that when it becomes necessary." You'd just be gumming up the works by worrying about wallpaper at that point. You've got to get the girders and beams up first to establish the shape of the building, the superstructure. Once that's completed, then it becomes necessary to put in floors and walls; next comes the plumbing and wiring, and then the sheetrock and painting. Finally it's time for the wallpaper in the bathroom on the tenth floor. You execute each step as it becomes necessary. Getting caught up in details before they're required only clogs things up. This understanding is all part of a trained dramatist's habits of mind. We're thinking systematically about deep structure, getting the macro up and running. We'll gradually work our way down from the general to the specific, weaving in more and more detail at the appropriate time.

Reverse Cause and Effect for *Training Day*. Let's look at our Sequence for *Training Day* at this macro level and demonstrate the process of building backward by reviewing a section of the film. Remember, we're analyzing here, but primarily to learn how to construct an original screenplay.

Object: Jake defeats Alonzo, completes his training, and emerges anew as a powerful man.

Final Effect: Alonzo is executed by the Russians and Jake goes home.

Immediate Cause: Jake takes Alonzo's $1 million as evidence, so Alonzo is unable to pay the Russians.

Cause: Jake defeats Alonzo in the fight with some help from the neighborhood locals.

Cause: Jake drops onto Alonzo's car, and Alonzo gets stunned from smashing the car around to shake him off.

Cause: Alonzo beats the stuffing out of Jake and attempts to leave with the money.

Cause: Jake tries to arrest Alonzo and a gunfight erupts.

Cause: Jake goes to the home of Alonzo's girlfriend to arrest him and seize the money as evidence.

Cause: Smiley lets Jake go.

Cause: Jake says he found the wallet when he saved a girl from rape, and she verifies it on the phone.

Cause: The gang members jump Jake and are about to kill him when they find the wallet that belongs to Smiley's niece.

Cause: Alonzo drops Jake off at Hillside Gang with payment to kill him.

This Sequence continues on back to the beginning of the plot, as you'll see (starting on page 162).

Developing Just a Little More Detail. Having sketched in the big picture using reverse cause and effect, you will repeat the process when you divide the script into acts. Fleshing out each act by chaining backward, you weave in a little more detail as you go. Then when you divide each act into sequences, you reason backward through each sequence, amplifying the particulars yet a bit more. (There is an overlap in terminology here because we're applying a tool called Sequence to a section of an act known as a *sequence*. There are two to five sequences in an act, and two to five scenes in a sequence. In a bank robbery movie, for instance, an act might consist of the *planning sequence*, the *robbery sequence*, and the *getaway sequence*.) Lastly, you divide each sequence into scenes, expanding the detail a little further with reverse cause and effect, and now you're down to the full specifics of the scene. You've added to the weave on each pass, gradually filling it in. This progression is shown in the diagram below:

Say you're developing a hard-boiled *noir* thriller and in one of the plot points needed to make your story work, your ex-cop-turned-undertaker finds the mob boss's accountant and extracts some financial records. You've only got a rough idea of how it all works at this point, but all you need for now is *the big picture* (Diagram A)—it's hard enough trying to make the whole script work. Too much detail would only clog things up and make your job more complicated than it already is. However at the *act level* (Diagram B), it does become necessary to think it through a little more, so you create some specifics as you chain backward. Maybe this ex-cop/undertaker is out to avenge the murder of a neighbor that he hated. Just because the guy was a foulmouthed drunk who played his music too loud doesn't mean he deserved to get his head blown off in front of his kids for refusing to pay protection money to a mob boss. So our ex-cop follows some leads to the hit man and uses his undertaker skills to extract the whereabouts of the mob boss's accountant. Then he uses similar techniques to torture the financial records out of the accountant.

Then at the *sequence level* (Diagram C) it becomes necessary to figure out even more of the particulars. Let's say the ex-cop asks around, gets a description of the hit man, and follows his trail to the race track. Then he takes the hit man back to his funeral home and threatens to cremate him if he doesn't talk. He gets the information he wants about the mob boss's accountant, snatches the bean counter, and brings him back to the funeral home where he terrorizes him into revealing information about the mob boss's hidden accounts.

At the *scene level* (Diagram D) you'd develop final detail by visualizing everything a little more completely. Let's say that when the ex-cop finds the hit man at the race track, he's out behind a kennel about to poison one of his dogs that's too old to race anymore. The ex-cop pistol-whips the guy and forces him back to the funeral home at gunpoint, bringing along the friendly greyhound as a pet. In the basement, he makes the hit man get into a steel casket that's in front of a cremation furnace, and threatens to burn him up if he doesn't spill about where to find the boss's accountant. When he gets that information, he locks the guy in the casket and goes for the accountant. He grabs the accountant coming out of church and takes him back to the funeral home in the hearse, then takes him downstairs where the hit man is still locked in the steel coffin, yelling his head off about how he's going to kill *everybody*. The ex-cop tells the accountant that it's the boss's hit man in the coffin and demands the boss's offshore accounts and passwords. When the accountant won't budge, he pushes the button that slides the coffin into the furnace. The hit man is cremated alive while the horrified accountant listens to his screams. Now the accountant offers so much information that our guy has to make him talk slower so he can write it all down.

Notice how we worked our way from the general to the specific, at first just needing our guy to find an accountant and get information out of him but gradually expanding the particulars, working systematically on each successive pass to flesh it out a little more until we had enough detail to write the scenes. We've followed Aristotle's incredibly astute recommendation to a T: "first sketch in its general outline, and then fill in the episodes and amplify in detail."

A Note About Scene. It's important to know that a scene is not merely a camera set-up; a scene is a complete unit of action. Imagine a comic mugging scene in which the victim is not at all intimidated. The mugger grabs the victim in the subway and demands all her money, but she laughs in his face and throws him down the stairs. The mugger races after her and accosts her again on the street. It's a new location and a new camera set-up, but it's still part of the same scene. He pretends to have a gun in his pocket but she just breaks his finger. She climbs in a taxicab and the mugger leaps in after her with a knife, but she disarms him with karate, steals his wallet, and throws him out of the cab. The scene ends with the woman finding a huge wad of loot in his wallet and asking the cabbie to stop at an expensive shoe store. Even though it took place in several locations, all of this was the mugging scene. It's one complete action.

Step 2: Proposition

Next we'll perform a second procedure on the story material that you just stitched together with reverse cause and effect (Sequence). Now we're going to use the second step of this tool: Proposition. It's like doing several different processes to one piece of raw wool. First you groom it, then you dye it, and then you weave it into cloth. We're doing the same thing here.

The next step is to take this tight sequence of cause and effect and frame it as a conflict using a more advanced form of the Central Proposition from Chapter 6. We're still setting up a potential fight and touching off a fight to the finish, causing the Central Dramatic Question to arise in the minds of the audience. But here we're working with a two-sided proposition in which both the protagonist and the antagonist put forth their own argument. What we call an "argument" actually consists of two separate lines of reasoning. If we're having an argument, then you have your position and I have mine. There are literally two opposing arguments, as you can see here:

Protagonist	Antagonist
Setting up a potential fight	Setting up a potential fight
Touching off a fight to the finish	Touching off a fight to the finish

Central Dramatic
Question

In formal logic this is called *a double proposition* or *parallel syllogisms*. Before we see Proposition in its final form, there's one more thing to take into account: *audience sympathy*. Part of your job as a dramatist is to capture audience sympathy for the protagonist and keep it. The audience must side with the protagonist's argument. If our hero starts doing something despicable, we usually stop rooting for him. You must both secure and maintain audience sympathy, because if we're not interested in the fate of the protagonist, then the movie isn't compelling.

Directing Audience Sympathy. One way to gain the audience's sympathy for the protagonist is for the antagonist to strike first. This is known as the *Initial Act of Aggression*, and it's part of setting up the potential fight. It's the evil land-grabber coming in and saying, "We're taking over your ranch and there's nothing you can do about it." Once you become aware of this, you'll see it in films all the time. In *Training Day*, the *Initial Act of Aggression* is when Alonzo almost gets Jake killed when they rob the Sandman's house. This opens up the active conflict and allows the protagonist to retaliate while maintaining the sympathy of the audience, which is called *Justified Retaliation*. In *Training Day*, Jake answers the *Initial Act of Aggression* by angrily challenging Alonzo about committing the robbery.

Next, in order to advance the conflict toward the point of open warfare while still keeping audience sympathy for the protagonist, we can have the antagonist exacerbate the situation, which we call the *Aggravation of the Issue*. In *Training Day*, this is when Alonzo tries to have Jake murdered by the Hillside Gang. It's in response to this escalation by the antagonist that the protagonist can throw the first punch—the *Precipitating Act* that literally starts the fight to the finish. To *precipitate* means to make something happen before it's ready to happen naturally. You precipitate rain by seeding the clouds, you precipitate a psychosis by pushing somebody's buttons, and you precipitate a fight by jumping in on someone, taking the fight to them. An audience wants its protagonist to be proactive, the maker of events—the one who takes the offensive rather than the one who merely reacts.

This can be a subtle distinction, because the protagonist is obviously reacting to the antagonist in various ways, but the *Precipitating Act* involves going on the offensive—taking the conflict to a whole new level. An excellent example of someone precipitating a fight is in *Tootsie*, when Dorothy shows up for the first time and Ron, the director, tells her she's not right for the part, not tough enough. She explodes on him: "How about if I knee your balls through the roof of your mouth? Is that tough enough for you?" She's not merely reacting to him—she jumps right down his throat, suddenly escalating the fight. She acts precipitously. In *Training Day*, the *Precipitating Act* comes when Jake touches off the fight to the finish by trying to arrest Alonzo and seize the $1 million as evidence.

Proposition for *Training Day*. Essentially what we've described here is the big picture—a map of the conflict for the whole story:

Protagonist	**Antagonist**
	Initial Act of Aggression
	Alonzo robs the Sandman with
	a fake warrant and risks getting
	Jake killed or arrested.
Justified Retaliation	
Jake challenges Alonzo,	
saying he stole that money.	
	Aggravation of the Issue
	Alonzo tries to have Jake
	murdered by the Hillside Gang.
Precipitating Act	
Jake comes after Alonzo, and	
tries to arrest him and seize	
the $1 million as evidence.	

Central Dramatic Question
Will Jake take down Alonzo or will Alonzo destroy him?

In the top two blocks of action we've set up the potential fight, then in the next two blocks we've touched off the fight to the finish, giving rise to the Central Dramatic Question in the minds of the audience. The question is two-sided now because the Proposition is two-sided. The Proposition also directs the audience's sympathy by making the antagonist the aggressor.

Step 3: Plot

The third part of the Sequence, Proposition, Plot process answers the Central Dramatic Question and completes the action, essentially wrapping up the plot. Within the context of Sequence, Proposition, Plot, the term *Plot* has a special-ized definition. With Sequence we reason backward, tying the story together with cause and effect, and with Proposition we set up a two-sided conflict and touch it off, leaving it hanging in the form of a question. With Plot we answer the question and complete the action. This is distinct from what we normally refer to as the plot of a movie—the incidents that comprise a story.

The fight to the finish is touched off at the two-thirds or three-quarters point, and now we're continuing on from the Central Dramatic Question to the end. We've already established the ending because we've done reverse cause and effect. As defined by Price in *The Analysis of Play Construction and Dramatic Principle*, Plot is "the steps necessarily taken to get from the central dramatic question to the pre-established ending."

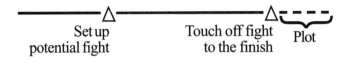

In this diagram, the first triangle sets up the potential fight (*Initial Act of Aggression* and *Justified Retaliation*) and the second triangle touches off the fight to the finish (*Aggravation of the Issue* and *Precipitating Act*). The section after the fight to the finish starts, indicated by the dashes, is Plot.

Rather than just listing the steps that answer the question and complete the action, let's continue on in the two-sided format we've been using for the Proposition. This helps map out the rest of the conflict through to the ending with what is known as *balanced opposition*—an even mix of the back-and-forth between the protagonist (on the left) and the antagonist (on the right). The section below the Central Dramatic Question is Plot.

Central Dramatic Question
Will Jake take down Alonzo
or will Alonzo destroy him?

Alonzo fights back,
almost kills Jake, and is leaving.

Jake attacks again, roughs up
Alonzo badly, and takes the money.

Alonzo tries to intimidate Jake
into quitting, and the locals
into killing Jake.

Jake beats Alonzo and gets away
with the money as evidence,
finishing him off.

Plot is really a continuation of the two-sided argument from the Proposition stage, with the Central Dramatic Question as the pivotal point. Mirroring how Proposition builds opposing arguments toward the fight to the finish, Plot is the back-and-forth between the protagonist and antagonist once the fight to the finish has started.

THE FULL APPLICATION OF
SEQUENCE, PROPOSITION, PLOT

So that explains the individual parts of this tool. Now let's see how the whole system of Sequence, Proposition, Plot works, because that's where the real magic kicks in. You use it first to sketch in the general outline of the story, rendering it both tight and dramatic. Then you break the script into acts and apply Sequence, Proposition, Plot to each act. You start with the first act, saying, "What's the *Object* of this act?" and "What's the *Final Effect* that demonstrates that *Object* on-screen with real actors?" and so on. Next you frame the conflict for that act in the form of the double Proposition, either mapping out the conflict that's inherent in the act or creating it if it isn't there. Then you answer the Central Dramatic Question and wrap it up with the third step, Plot. You do this for all the acts, making each one tight and dramatic, and then you divide the acts up into sequences.

As you do Sequence, Proposition, Plot for each of the sequences, you're fleshing out the mechanics of your story, further amplifying the detail as it becomes necessary. If you've got three or four acts and each one consists of two to five sequences, then we're talking about doing this three-step process perhaps another fifteen or more times. If each sequence has good forward momentum and grips the audience, then you are creating continuous Dramatic Action. You never want to revert to mere Story, in which the material goes flat dramatically. This is a lot of work, make no mistake about it, but to properly develop and structure an effective screenplay takes this kind of labor-intensive effort. You've got to do the work somewhere—and it's much easier putting in the hours here, where you have control over the shape of the story, rather than slugging it out through endless rewrites, where the script can easily get away from you or lose its original energy. Take another look at David Mamet's quote about taking the time to design the chair properly before you glue it together (see page xxiii).

Once you've gone through all your sequences, you then break them down into scenes. Now you do Sequence, Proposition, Plot for the first scene, which gives you a fully detailed outline, and then you write the dialog. Then you do Sequence, Proposition, Plot for the next scene and write it out, and you're on a roll—based on all the hard work you've put into building the structural underpinnings of the story. In Part Two of this book, I'll create and construct a real screenplay using this process to demonstrate it in action.

The following diagram shows a hierarchical pyramid structure of Sequence, Proposition, Plot applied to the whole script, then to each act, to each sequence, and each scene:

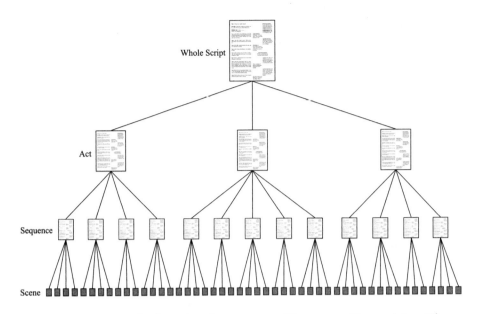

Constructing your script by using the process of Sequence, Proposition, Plot creates Unity of Action. Each scene is its own coherent dramatic unit but is also part of a sequence, which is in and of itself coherent and compelling. Each sequence moves the plot forward and is part of an act, which itself is tightly knit and dramatically sound. In turn, each act is a working part of the whole script, which itself is logical, consistent, flowing, and dramatic. Continuous, coherent, compelling Dramatic Action is the name of the game. In *The Analysis of Play Construction and Dramatic Principle*, Price puts it this way:

> You must have perceived by this time that a law of Unity runs through a play, each principle in a play and each part of a play being distinct in itself, but with relations to the other principles and parts. At the very outset the Theme demanded Unity. You considered the Proposition and saw that it must be ONE thing, one definite thing, so that when asked what your play is about you could reply briefly and would not wander off into a multitude of Details. You saw that each act was about one thing, each scene about one thing, and that each step was a development toward one given end. Following this out, you have seen that a play is a Unit made up of other Units.

Examples from *Training Day* follow to make all this more tangible. Recall the increasingly tight weave in the diagrams on page 155 as you review Sequence, Proposition, Plot for the overall script, an act, a sequence, and a scene.

Sequence, Proposition, Plot for Overall Script of Training Day

First, we look at the script as a whole using Sequence (reverse cause and effect).

Object: Jake defeats Alonzo, completes his training, and emerges anew as a powerful man.

Final Effect: Alonzo is executed by the Russians and Jake goes home.

Immediate Cause: Jake takes Alonzo's $1 million as evidence, so Alonzo is unable to pay the Russians.

Cause: Jake defeats Alonzo in the fight with some help from the neighborhood locals.

Cause: Jake drops onto Alonzo's car and Alonzo gets stunned from smashing the car around to shake him off.

Cause: Alonzo beats the stuffing out of Jake and attempts to leave with the money.

Cause: Jake tries to arrest Alonzo and a gunfight erupts.

Cause: Jake goes to the home of Alonzo's girlfriend to confront Alonzo.

Cause: Smiley lets Jake go.

Cause: Jake says he found the wallet when he saved a girl from getting raped, and she verifies it on the phone.

Cause: Smiley and his crew jump Jake and are about to kill him when they find the wallet that belongs to Smiley's niece.

Cause: Alonzo drops Jake off at Hillside Gang with payment to kill him.

Cause: Jake will not be a member of Alonzo's team or play his twisted game.

Cause: Alonzo tries to talk Jake into seeing things his way.

Cause: Jake refuses to claim that he shot Roger, and Alonzo manages to get his own men and Jake to calm down.

Cause: Jake takes the gun away from Alonzo and turns it on him.

Cause: Alonzo shoots Roger and tries to force Jake to claim he did it.

Cause: Alonzo and his crew raid Roger's house and rob him of $1 million.

Cause: Alonzo bribes the three wise men to let him "tax" Roger for the $1 million dollars to pay off the Russians, and "buys" a real warrant.

Cause: Alonzo robs $40,000 from the Sandman's house with a fake warrant.

Cause: Alonzo forces information out of Blue, the drug dealer, by sticking a pen down his throat.

Cause: Alonzo fires Jake up about being a wolf and then sics him on Blue.

Cause: Jake is angry that Alonzo let the crackhead rapists go.

Cause: Jake stops the rape but Alonzo lets them go.

Cause: Jake is stoned, but when he spots a rape in action he makes Alonzo stop to break it up.

Cause: Alonzo forces Jake at gunpoint and the threat of expulsion to smoke marijuana laced with PCP.

Cause: Alonzo takes the dope and the pipe off the college kids.

Cause: Alonzo and Jake start their day's work by staking out a dealer and pulling over some college kids who just scored.

Cause: Jake shows up, extremely ambitious, and says he'll do anything Alonzo wants him to.

Cause: Jake wakes up ready to roll for his first day of work as an undercover narcotics cop.

By working our way backward through each of the major plot points in the film, we have laid bare the spine of the script—the Sequence. The conflict map below charts Proposition and Plot for the overall script of *Training Day*. Note that the Central Dramatic Question marks the point at which Proposition ends and Plot begins.

Protagonist	**Antagonist**
	Initial Act of Aggression
	Alonzo robs the Sandman with
	a fake warrant and risks getting
Justified Retaliation	Jake arrested or killed.
Jake challenges Alonzo,	
saying he stole that money.	
	Aggravation of the Issue
	Alonzo tries to have Jake
Precipitating Act	murdered by the Hillside Gang.
Jake comes after Alonzo, and	
tries to arrest him and seize the	
$1 million for evidence.	

Central Dramatic Question
Will Jake take down Alonzo or will Alonzo destroy him?

	Alonzo fights back, almost
	kills Jake, and is leaving.
Jake attacks again, roughs up	
Alonzo badly, and takes his money.	
	Alonzo tries to intimidate Jake into
	quitting, and the locals into killing Jake.
Jake beats Alonzo and gets away	
with the money as evidence, finishing	
him off.	

So that's Sequence, Proposition, Plot for the overall script of *Training Day*. We're dealing with a sketch of the general outline, so the reverse cause and effect doesn't encompass much detail at all. In analyzing a script, this is very useful because it provides an objective look at the big picture, and can help you find major holes in the cause and effect that might adversely affect the storyline.

When you're constructing an original screenplay, this process will help you stitch together all the story parts, scenes, and elements from your notes into one solid chain of events. If you're working backward and discover a point at which there is no cause for a given effect, then you can create one on the spot and thereby fill a hole in the plot. You would say to yourself, "Well, what *would* cause that to happen?" There may be any number of possibilities and you can pick the one that works best. Or there might not be any obvious causes that occur to you, forcing you to really wrack your brain. The worst-case scenario would be that a cause *cannot* be invented under any circumstances, revealing that you have an insoluble hole in your script. But the good news is that you're discovering it in your outlining process, rather than fifty pages into your script—which happens *a lot* to writers who don't structure their stories first—they call it "hitting the brick wall."

Proposition and Plot cover the entire proportion of the story, and as we said, the set-up of the fight tends to occur about one-quarter to one-third of the way into the story, with the touch-off coming out around the two-thirds or three-quarters mark. It helps to maintain that sense of proportion when using Proposition, Plot because the Central Dramatic Question in our two-column argument above appears to be at the mid-point of the script, which can be misleading, especially to a novice.

Sequence, Proposition, Plot for Act III of *Training Day*

Here is this tool applied to Act III (the final act) of *Training Day*. Notice that the Sequence stage here at the act level includes a little more detail than at the overall script level, especially to a novice:

Object: Jake defeats Alonzo, completes his training, and emerges anew as a powerful man.

Final Effect: Jake arrives home as a voiceover plays of the reported news of Alonzo's death while serving a high-risk warrant.

Immediate Cause: Alonzo drives to his rendezvous without the money and is executed by the Russians.

Cause: The neighborhood locals keep Alonzo from going after Jake, and Alonzo's power fades to nothing.

Cause: Jake walks off with the money.

Cause: The locals have Jake's back and they let him leave.

Cause: Jake strips Alonzo's badge off him.

Cause: Jake and Alonzo face off, and Alonzo doubts Jake has the balls to shoot him.

Cause: Jake punches out Alonzo and takes the bag of money.

Cause: Alonzo tries to get rid of Jake and gets stunned badly from smashing the car around to shake him off it.

Cause: Jake drops down on Alonzo's car as he's getting away.

Cause: Alonzo pummels Jake, leaves him badly beaten, and is getting away with the money.

Cause: Jake hunts Alonzo on the roof, and Alonzo jumps him.

Cause: Alonzo's son gets in the middle of the gunfight, giving Alonzo time to climb out the window.

Cause: Alonzo flicks a cigarette in Jake's eyes, grabs his shotgun, and they have a gunfight.

Cause: Jake bursts in on Alonzo, his gun drawn, and tries to arrest him and seize the money as evidence.

Cause: Jake gets Alonzo's son to let him in the house.

Cause: Jake goes to the dangerous neighborhood to hunt down Alonzo.

Cause: Smiley lets Jake go.

Cause: Smiley's cousin verifies Jake's story.

Cause: Smiley doesn't believe Jake saved his cousin, so he calls her.

Cause: Jake says he found the wallet after he saved a girl from getting raped.

Cause: The guys find the pink wallet that belongs to Smiley's cousin.

Cause: The gang members are about to shoot Jake in the bathtub.

Cause: The guys subdue Jake.

Cause: Jake attacks the gang.

Cause: It's obvious the gang is about to kill Jake.

Cause: Jake sees that Alonzo has left him, and the gang members show Jake the money Alonzo gave them.

Cause: The gang members cajole Jake's gun away from him and take his ammunition clip.

Cause: Alonzo leaves Jake with the gang members, and saying he's going to the bathroom.

Cause: Alonzo takes Jake to the Hillside Gang with presents and cash.

And now on to Proposition and Plot for Act III of *Training Day*:

Protagonist	**Antagonist**
	Initial Act of Aggression Alonzo drops Jake off at the gang house to be killed.
Justified Retaliation Jake goes to Alonzo's place and tries to arrest him to take the money as evidence.	
	Aggravation of the Issue Alonzo pummels Jake and is getting away with the money.
Precipitating Act Jake drops down on the car hood and goes on the attack.	

Central Dramatic Question
Will Jake be able to defeat Alonzo, or will Alonzo kill him?

	Alonzo smashes his car into everything, trying to kill Jake or shake him off.
Jake pounds Alonzo when he's stunned and grabs the bag of money.	
	Alonzo tries to intimidate Jake and then goes for the gun.
Jake shoots Alonzo in the ass and leaves with the money as evidence, finishing him off.	

You can see that in the reverse cause and effect, the entire third act is retraced (we went through it once already for the overall script), but now more detail is being included. You use this same process when you're building a script—doing repeated passes through increasingly smaller units of the plot (script, act, sequence, scene), amplifying the particulars as you figure out that section of the story in a little more detail.

One trick to working this way is to develop the skill of knowing *how much* is just a little more detail. You just want a bit more, one more layer to weave in to what you've already got. There's a great example of this in a science fiction short story that I read once. A guy asks a computer for information on a battleship and the computer asks how much detail he wants. It says that it can give it to him in a paragraph, in 10 pages, 200 pages, or 4,000 pages. As you work with this tool, you'll get a feel for how much detail is just a little more.

What we've done above is to map out the conflict within Act III using the Proposition and Plot aspects of our tool. Notice that it was the same process for the script as a whole, but now we're applying it to the next smaller unit within the story. The same proportion holds for the act as it did for the whole script: The touch-off of the fight occurs at about the two-thirds or three-quarters point. Know where you are at each step proportionately, and bear in mind roughly where the conflict sets up and touches off.

Sequence, Proposition, Plot for Act III, Sequence 1 of *Training Day*

Now review Sequence, Proposition, Plot for a sequence within Act III of *Training Day*—the Hillside Gang sequence, in which Jake is almost executed. Notice that we're including even more detail in the reverse cause and effect.

Object: Smiley lets Jake go.

Final Effect: Smiley thanks Jake for protecting his cousin and says that taking the job to kill him was just business.

Immediate Cause: Smiley puts the gun down and pulls Jake out of the tub.

Cause: Smiley's cousin verifies what Jake said about saving her.

Cause: Smiley forces his cousin to tell the truth.

Cause: Smiley's cousin is lying.

Cause: Smiley calls his cousin to check on Jake's story.

Cause Jake says he found the wallet after he saved the girl from getting raped.

Cause: One guy takes his wallet and notices that it belongs to Smiley's cousin.

Cause: The guys are about to shoot Jake but want his money first.

Cause: The guys put Jake in the tub and get ready to shoot him.

Cause: The gang drags Jake into the bathroom.

Cause: The gang beats up Jake.

Cause: Jake attacks the gang and decks Smiley.

Cause: Smiley intimates that Alonzo paid him to kill Jake and reveals that Alonzo has to pay $1 million to buy his way out of having killed a Russian.

Cause: Smiley tells Jake that Alonzo has left him, and the mood turns dark in the room.

Cause: One guy points Jake's gun at him, and Jake says he's got to leave.

Cause: The gang cajoles Jake's gun away from him and Smiley takes the ammo clip out.

Cause: The guys goof around and get Jake off guard.

Cause: Alonzo drops Jake off while he "goes to the bathroom."

Now look at the structure of the conflict within this sequence.

Protagonist	**Antagonist**
	Initial Act of Aggression The guys cajole Jake's gun away, take his bullets, and point his gun at him.
Justified Retaliation Jake says he's got to leave.	
	Aggravation of the Issue It becomes obvious that the gang is going to kill Jake.
Precipitating Act Jake attacks the guys and slugs Smiley while trying to get away.	

Central Dramatic Question
Will Jake get out of there or will they kill him?

	The guys beat Jake up, drag him into the bathtub, and get ready to kill him.
When the guys find the wallet, Jake claims that he saved the girl from getting raped.	
	Smiley thinks Jake's lying and did something to his cousin. He calls her.
Jake's story checks out and he is let go.	

Notice how much the detail has expanded. Think about the section in all these passes that describe Jake's gun getting pointed at him in the gang house. The first pass for the overall script pass doesn't even mention the gun because it's too small a detail. It says: *Smiley and his crew jump Jake and are about to kill him.* In the Act III section it gets expanded to: *The gang members cajole Jake's gun away from him and take his ammo clip.* Then in the section we just looked at, it has become three separate causes: (1) *The guys goof around and get Jake off guard, (2) The gang cajoles Jake's gun away from him and Smiley takes the ammo clip out, (3) One guy points Jake's gun at him, and Jake says he's got to leave.*

Look at how the Proposition, Plot conflict map perfectly represents what happens in this sequence. It's the classic shoving match that turns into a knock-down, drag-out fight. Notice how the *Initial Act of Aggression* is the guys tricking Jake into handing over his gun. Jake clearly precipitates the fight to the finish when he jumps Smiley. He's going for the knock-out punch and everybody in the audience came up on the edge of their seat, wondering if he can somehow make it out of that room.

Sequence, Proposition, Plot for Act III, Sequence 2, Scene 3 of *Training Day*

It's crucial that each scene works dramatically because the scenes are the only part of the film the audience is truly aware of. Remember the Michelin Tires commercial explaining how that little square of rubber is the only contact your car actually has with the road, so you should buy the best tires available? Well, the scene is the only part of the movie that the audience actually interacts with. Movies basically consist of one scene after another, and the audience is not saying, "Wow, did you check out the second act structure?" They don't see the underlying deep composition, any more than you see the steel girders inside a finished skyscraper.

Look at how detailed this reverse cause and effect becomes. You can practically hear the dialog. Try reading from the bottom up, and see how well the action flows.

Object: Jake walks off with the money and leaves Alonzo powerless.

Final Effect: Alonzo rages at the locals, but he's got no power anymore.

Immediate Cause: Jake walks off with the money as Alonzo yells at him.

Cause: One of the locals picks up a gun and covers Jake so he can leave.

Cause: Jake rips Alonzo's badge off and says he doesn't deserve it.

Cause: Alonzo says he wants to go home, and Jake lowers his gun.

Cause: Jake says he's taking the money as evidence and asks Alonzo if he wants to go to jail or go home.
Cause: Alonzo freaks out at Jake, raging that he *has* to have that money.

Cause: Jake will not back down—he's taking the money from Alonzo as evidence that he robbed and murdered Roger.

Cause: Alonzo's mind is blown that Jake shot him in the ass, and he shows real fear.

Cause: Jake shoots Alonzo.

Cause: Alonzo goes for the gun.

Cause: Alonzo says Jake doesn't have the balls to shoot a cop in the back, and he threatens to grab the gun.

Cause: One of the locals puts a gun down near Alonzo.

Cause: Alonzo offers to make anyone rich who puts a bullet in Jake's head.

Cause: Jake points a gun at Alonzo.

Cause: Jake slugs Alonzo and takes the money.

Cause: Alonzo slams the car around trying to get Jake off, and gets stunned.

Cause: Jake drops on the car's hood as Alonzo drives off with the money.

Now let's look at the structure of the conflict for this scene:

Protagonist	Antagonist
	Initial Act of Aggression Alonzo says he'll make anybody rich who puts a bullet in Jake's head.
Justified Retaliation Jake says the locals are not like Alonzo, just as he's learned that he's not like him.	
	Aggravation of the Issue Alonzo challenges Jake, saying that he doesn't have the balls to shoot a cop. He says Jake will get the gas chamber and then he goes for the gun.
Precipitating Act Jake shoots Alonzo in the ass.	

Central Dramatic Question

Will Jake stop Alonzo, or will Alonzo somehow still pull this off?

	Alonzo rages at Jake to give him the money.
Jake takes Alonzo's badge, saying he doesn't deserve it. Jake gets back-up from two locals, who let him leave.	
	Alonzo screams at Jake to stop and tries to power trip the locals.
Jake walks off, getting out with the money as evidence.	

Again, notice the proportion. Late in the scene when Jake shoots Alonzo in the ass, it touches off a fight to the finish within the scene itself. There's so much detail at the scene level that we're paraphrasing the dialog. Writing a scene is simple with this kind of in-depth structural map to work from.

You'll see a lot of Sequence, Proposition, Plot in Part Two of this book as I develop and construct an original screenplay. I'll guide you through my entire thought process as I wrestle the story into shape, doing exactly what we just did here—but I'll be building a plot, not just analyzing one. I'll take Sequence, Proposition, Plot all the way from the overall story level down to the scene level—and then I'll write the actual scenes. I want you to get as much practical working experience as possible with this master tool so that you can use it properly, and consistently make your scripts work.

A Quick Review of What We've Done with *Training Day*

Let's get an overview of what we've done applying Sequence, Proposition, Plot to *Training Day*. The following diagrams showing our work from this chapter, printed small and basically unreadable, are intended for instructional purposes. Bear in mind that for simplicity, they only show the first page of the reverse cause and effect (see expanded versions starting on page162). First, we see the whole script on the left and Act III on the right:

Next we have Act III, Sequence 1 on the left, and Act III, Sequence 2, Scene 3 on the right:

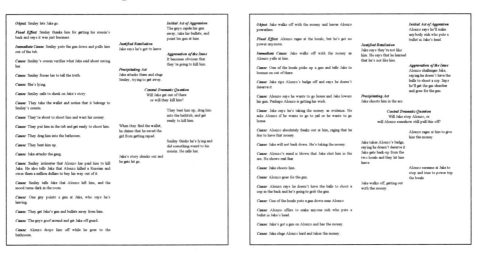

Act III, Sequence 1

Object: Smiley lets Jake go.

Final Effect: Smiley thanks him for getting his cousin's back and says it was just business.

Immediate Cause: Smiley puts the gun down and pulls him out of the tub.

Cause: Smiley's cousin verifies what Jake said about saving her.

Cause: Smiley forces her to tell the truth.

Cause: She's lying.

Cause: Smiley calls to check on Jake's story.

Cause: They take the wallet and notice that it belongs to Smiley's cousin.

Cause: They're about to shoot him and want his money.

Cause: They put him in the tub and get ready to shoot him.

Cause: They drag him into the bathroom.

Cause: They beat him up.

Cause: Smiley attacks the gang.

Cause: Smiley intimates that Alonzo has paid him to kill Jake. He also tells Jake that Alonzo killed a Russian and owes them a million dollars to buy his way out of it.

Cause: Smiley tells Jake that Alonzo left him, and the mood turns dark in the room.

Cause: One guy points a gun at Jake, who says he's leaving.

Cause: They get Jake's gun and bullets away from him.

Cause: The guys goof around and get Jake off guard.

Cause: Alonzo drops him off while he goes to the bathroom.

Initial Act of Aggression
The guys cajole his gun away, take his bullets, and point his gun at him.

Justified Retaliation
Jake says he's got to leave.

Aggravation of the Issue
It becomes obvious that they're going to kill him.

Precipitating Act
Jake attacks them and slugs Smiley, trying to get away.

Central Dramatic Question
Will Jake get out of there or will they kill him?

They beat him up, drag him into the bathtub, and get ready to kill him.

When they find the wallet, he claims that he saved the girl from getting raped.

Smiley thinks he's lying and did something weird to his cousin. He calls her.

Jake's story checks out and he gets let go.

Act III, Sequence 2, Scene 3

Object: Jake walks off with the money and leaves Alonzo powerless.

Final Effect: Alonzo rages at the locals, but he's got no power anymore.

Immediate Cause: Jake walks off with the money as Alonzo yells at him.

Cause: One of the locals picks up a gun and tells Jake to bounce on out of there.

Cause: Jake rips Alonzo's badge off and says he doesn't deserve it.

Cause: Alonzo says he wants to go home and Jake lowers his gun. Perhaps Alonzo is getting his wish.

Cause: Jake says he's taking the money as evidence. He asks Alonzo if he wants to go to jail or he wants to go home.

Cause: Alonzo absolutely freaks out at him, raging that he has to have that money.

Cause: Jake will not back down. He's taking the money.

Cause: Alonzo's mind is blown that Jake shot him in the ass. He shows real fear.

Cause: Jake shoots him.

Cause: Alonzo goes for the gun.

Cause: Jake says he doesn't have the balls to shoot a cop in the back and he's going to grab the gun.

Cause: One of the locals puts a gun down near Alonzo.

Cause: Alonzo offers to make anyone rich who puts a bullet in Jake's head.

Cause: Jake's got a gun on Alonzo and has the money.

Cause: Jake slugs Alonzo hard and takes the money.

Initial Act of Aggression
Alonzo says he'll make anybody rich who puts a bullet in Jake's head.

Justified Retaliation
Jake says they're not like him. He says that he learned that he's not like him.

Aggravation of the Issue
Alonzo challenges Jake, saying he doesn't have the balls to shoot a cop. Says he'll get the gun chamber and goes for the gun.

Precipitating Act
Jake shoots him in the ass.

Central Dramatic Question
Will Jake stop Alonzo, or will Alonzo somehow still pull this off?

Alonzo rages at him to give him the money.

Alonzo screams at Jake to stop and tries to power trip the locals.

Jake walks off, leaving out with the money.

These diagrams should help you see the big picture and give you a better grasp of what we've just done.

CONSTRUCTING A STORY WITH SEQUENCE, PROPOSITION, PLOT

Rather than analyzing an existing plot as we've just done, in most instances you'll be using Sequence, Proposition, Plot to construct a plot for your own screenplay. To demonstrate this I've prepared the following example: Imagine that we're writing a script in one section of which our protagonist, a thief, must ditch a crooked detective who's so hot on his trail that he can't do business. In laying out reverse cause and effect for the whole script, it would take only one line to say that the thief gets rid of the detective by framing him. It's simple and presented with no detail, which is the proper way to treat it on the first pass. In going over the material again at the *act level*, however, we would create more detail, adding that the thief pretends to make a huge score using counterfeit money, knowing that the detective is watching. When the detective swoops in and relieves the thief of the cash, he's promptly busted for the counterfeit money by the Secret Service, who the thief had tipped off—so the detective is now out of the way.

Reverse Cause and Effect for a Sequence

Now let's outline Sequence, Proposition, Plot for the actual sequence in which our thief frames the detective. This sequence is just one unit of the act, and the frame-up is just one key action in the entire plot, but our job is to make it function as a gripping, actable segment of the script. So we're going to flesh out the framing of this crooked detective. To do so, must think through the particulars of how it would happen in more detail. This raises a lot of questions. How does the thief get the counterfeit money? Why wouldn't the detective suspect anything? Where would the fake robbery take place? How does the thief get word to the Secret Service that this detective will have the funny money? How does the thief make sure that the charges will really stick? What's to prevent the detective from saying the counterfeit money was part of an investigation? There are many other potential questions and pitfalls to be addressed by firming up the details. These may even be notes to yourself to inform your writing, not actual details that make it into the script. We want to keep it simple, unencumbered, and clear. Remember, this is for just one sequence within one act, and we'll already be dealing with a fair amount of detail. Let's call the thief Mitchell and the detective, Kepler.

> *What's the Object of the sequence?* Mitchell gets Kepler arrested and sent to jail, freeing him to pursue his line of work.

> *What's the Final Effect that demonstrates the Object on-screen with real actors?* Secret Service agents arrest Kepler for possession of counterfeit money, and then find hidden in his house the plates for the fake bills, which Mitchell had planted to make the charges stick.

> *What's the Immediate Cause of the Secret Service arresting Kepler?* The Secret Service picks Kepler up and finds the phony money on him.

> *What's the cause of the Secret Service finding the money on him?* Kepler grabs Mitchell after the heist and takes all the money.

> *What's the cause of Kepler grabbing Mitchell?* Mitchell comes out of a mansion loaded with cash, and Kepler is waiting in ambush.

> *What's the cause of Mitchell coming out of the mansion with the money?* Mitchell pulls off a fake robbery.

> *What's the cause of Mitchell doing the robbery?* Mitchell gets word to the Secret Service that Kepler has bogus money.

> *What's the cause of Mitchell alerting the Secret Service?* Mitchell acquires the counterfeit money.

> *What's the cause of Mitchell getting the counterfeit money?* Mitchell goes to a counterfeiter seeking help to get rid of the corrupt detective, and convinces her to let him use her phony bills for the job.

> *What's the cause of Mitchell going to the counterfeiter?* Kepler tells Mitchell that he wants a cut of the action or there'll be no getting rid of him, and Mitchell won't be able to commit any more robberies.

See how we've expanded upon the detail by thinking it through one more time? We've answered some questions and raised still more, which we'll answer when we use Sequence, Proposition, Plot at the scene level.

Developing the Proposition, Plot for a Sequence

Now we move on to Proposition and Plot. When working with this tool, look at the conflict you've already got as well as what you're missing, and then build from there. At this point some of the elements don't exist yet, and that's okay. Remember, here we're actually *creating* the conflict. Or more specifically, we're mapping out the opposition that we've imagined so far, seeing where the gaps are, and then filling in those gaps, thereby fleshing out the full conflict. This is different from the analytical work we were doing with *Training Day*— here, it's a work in progress. We're *building* a plot using this tool.

Protagonist	**Antagonist**
	Initial Act of Aggression
	Kepler tells Mitchell to cut him in on the action or he'll stop him from committing any more heists.
Justified Retaliation	
Mitchell tells Kepler that he won't go along. He then acquires some counterfeit money and sets a plan in motion to take Kepler down.	
	Aggravation of the Issue
	(No action here by Kepler yet that advances the conflict.)
Precipitating Act	
(No action here by Mitchell that touches off the fight to the finish.)	

Central Dramatic Question
(Question is unknown at this point.)

	(No action here by Kepler yet.)
Mitchell commits the fake robbery.	
	Kepler grabs Mitchell and takes the money.
Mitchell signals the Secret Service agents, who capture Kepler with all the counterfeit money as well as the plates planted by Mitchell.	

An X-Ray of the Action

By mapping out the conflict as it stands so far, we've discovered that Kepler is not all that proactive as of yet, and that Mitchell takes no action to start the fight to the finish. Like an x-ray, Proposition gets beneath the doughy flesh of narrative to the script's skeleton form. It shows us what actions we've already got in terms of conflict, as well as what we're missing. It also indirectly suggests possibilities for key actions in order to *create* conflict. While we've set up the potential fight, the script is still lacking when it comes to touching off the fight to the finish. Time to get creative.

First, we're looking to give Kepler an *Aggravation of the Issue*—an action that aggravates the situation—so let's have him beat up Mitchell when he says he's not going to play along. Now we're propelling the conflict forward while keeping audience sympathy for our protagonist. But we also want to create a *Precipitating Act*—an action by Mitchell that touches off the fight to the finish. It should be a strong attack, something with a chance to finish off the antagonist. One route would be for Mitchell to hook up a chain from the rear axle of Kepler's car to a tree. Then, when Mitchell speeds off in his car and Kepler races after him, the rear axle would rip out. That's a fitting choice: Mitchell actually *wants* Kepler to catch him with the counterfeit money, and this should send Kepler charging to intercept the fake robbery. This gives rise to a more intriguing Central Dramatic Question, because we're supposed to want Kepler to catch him, but we're also enjoying watching Mitchell yank his chain (so to speak). The question might be something like, "Will Mitchell pull off his deception or will Kepler not to fall for it?"

Next we need an action by the detective in response to this attack—the act that constitutes the first step in Plot for this sequence—and we've got it. Wouldn't he come flying after Mitchell in a rage and catch up in time to see the supposed robbery? That sounds right. So now we've added all the elements suggested by this tool, which has helped flesh out the conflict and dramatize this sequence. Sequence makes it tight, while Proposition and Plot make it dramatic. On the next page, let's map out what we've built, tested, thought through, and revised:

Protagonist	Antagonist
	Initial Act of Aggression
	Kepler tells Mitchell to cut him in on the action or he'll stop Mitchell from committing any more heists.
Justified Retaliation	
Mitchell tells Kepler that he won't go along. He then acquires some counterfeit money and sets a plan in motion to take Kepler down.	
	Aggravation of the Issue
	Kepler beats up Mitchell, warning him to get used to his new partner in crime.
Precipitating Act	
Mitchell chains Kepler's car to a tree and races off, causing Kepler's axle to rip out when he follows at high speed.	

Central Dramatic Question
Will Mitchell pull off his deception, or will Kepler not fall for it?

	Kepler commandeers a car and races after Mitchell, arriving in time to see where he commits the "robbery."
Mitchell commites the fake robbery.	
	Kepler grabs Mitchell and takes the money.
Mitchell signals the Secret Service agents, who capture Kepler with all the counterfeit money as well as the plates planted by Mitchell.	

This chart gives us a good look at the real process of building portions of a script using Sequence, Proposition, Plot. We've filled in the gaps so this sequence works dramatically, and these details flesh out more and more of our script.

Creating a Scene with Sequence, Proposition, Plot

Now let's divide our sequence into scenes and apply Sequence, Proposition, Plot to develop a scene. First, review the reverse cause and effect we already generated (see page 174) and look for natural divisions. It appears that four scenes occur in this sequence: (1) Kepler tells Mitchell that he wants a cut, (2) Mitchell convinces the counterfeiter to provide the fake money, (3) Mitchell commits the fake robbery and Kepler grabs the money, and (4) The Secret Service agents arrest Kepler and search his house. However for proper use of this tool, it't necessary to look not just at the reverse Sequence, but also at the Proposition, Plot (see page 177), because we created a new scene with the fight and the chaining of Kepler's axle. Looking at both Sequence and Proposition, Plot before moving down to the next level is part of using this tool properly, because together, they tell the whole story. We'll explore Sequence, Proposition, Plot for Scene 2.

Because we're working at scene level, we're looking to add final detail—a level of detail that will allow us to write the scene directly after structuring it. To start with, who is this counterfeiter? Why not make her a female? Let's call her Melika. Are she and Mitchell old friends? Enemies? Mitchell could steal the bad bills from Melika, but a conversation between them could be more interesting, giving us a look at Mitchell using whatever charm, muscle, brains, or chutzpah he's got to work his friend or enemy or ally. Exactly how much money are we talking about? How convincing are the bills? Will Detective Kepler suspect their legitimacy? Why would Melika fork them over? Is Mitchell buying them? Begging for them? Trading for them? Does Melika need to get rid of the bills? Are they too hot to move? Is the market saturated with them? Is the law after Melika? Does this fake heist put her at risk? Does it divert suspicion away from her? Is there any kind of sexual tension between Mitchell and Melika? Do they have a history as lovers? What's in it for her? Is he blackmailing her?

These and many more questions naturally arise while we think this scene through. We must figure out what we want the scene to look like. We need entertainment value, and we need the scene to achieve its *Object* (see below), but beyond that we can go in many possible directions—as long as the scene is not boring. We must create Dramatic Action so that we're not just present-ing information. It has to be actable, and it should reveal more of what Mitchell is made of, how he thinks, and how he works. If this is a thriller, then should we stay with that tone or use this scene as a breather, as comic relief? These decisions are all part of the process.

Reverse Cause and Effect for a Scene

So let's develop the scene using reverse cause and effect:

Object: Mitchell convinces Melika to let him use the funny money to frame Kepler.

Final Effect: Melika agrees and gives Mitchell a duffel bag full of counterfeit money.

Immediate Cause: Mitchell says he'll cut Melika in on the take of a future robbery.

Cause: Melika will not give Mitchell any of the counterfeit money.

Cause: Mitchell argues that with this fake money, they can take down Kepler once and for all.

Cause: Melika doesn't care if she can't move the money now—she'll just wait it out.

Cause: Mitchell says that the money's too hot now anyway, since there's too much of it in circulation and the Secret Service is on to it.

Cause: Melika says that she doesn't want anything to do with Mitchell's plan—or with him.

Cause: Mitchell tells Melika that he's got a chance to take down Kepler if she's willing to hand over a bunch of her world-class phony Benjamins. He tries his sexual charm on her.

What we're doing here is to think our way through one possible take for this scene. Notice that as we map reverse cause and effect for this scene, we're actually writing out more detail into each cause, answering the questions raised on page 178. In many instances, we're even paraphrasing dialog.

Consider another possible direction for this scene: Mitchell could just as easily have to fight for his life, killing Melika in self-defense, and still end up with the fake bills. Remember that with this sophisticated outlining tool, any framework can be scrapped and redone. It provides an easy way to sketch out some possibilities and then revise things as much as is needed.

Now let's do Proposition and Plot for this scene to make sure that the conflict and Dramatic Action really pop. One of my main questions for this scene is, what's the fight? Is there a conflict that the whole scene builds toward? If so, then our job is to set it up and touch it off. If not, then we should seriously consider creating some opposition in this scene in order to make it more substantial for the actors and more gripping to the audience.

Developing Proposition, Plot for a Scene

Proposition is intended as a proposal for the conflict between the protagonist and the antagonist. Here is just one possible way to shape this scene:

Protagonist	Antagonist
	Initial Act of Aggression Melika says she doesn't want anything to do with Mitchell or his idiotic plan.
Justified Retaliation Mitchell tries to control his temper and tells Melika to get real—the money's too hot for her to use for quite a while anyway.	
	Aggravation of the Issue Melika says it's her damn paper and she'll sit on it if she wants to, or burn it before she gives it to him.
Precipitating Act Mitchell becomes furious and insists that her anger for him shouldn't stop a golden chance to stick it to Kepler, whom they both hate.	

Central Dramatic Question
Will Mitchell get the money from Melika,
or will she refuse?

Protagonist	Antagonist
	Melika says nobody tells her what to do, and besides, why should she risk getting in trouble for him?
Mitchell is desperate, says he's got a big job coming up, and offers her 25 percent of the take, which would be $1.5 million.	
	Melika demands 50 percent, but says she'll throw in the counterfeit plates, which will get Kepler royally screwed.
Mitchell's mad about the 50 percent but takes the deal, and loves getting the plates.	

Do you see how we escalated the conflict between them? The Proposition solidifies the conflict and the dramatic power of the scene. Obviously, Melika doesn't want to hand over her fake dough, but we worked to develop the scene with some personal animosity between them, heightening the intensity and making the interaction less dull, less cut-and-dry. In using a tool like this, you're bringing everything in your arsenal to bear—not just mechanically filling in the outline. While this process may appear mechanical, you're acutally creating on the spot—literally bringing the script to life as you go along, filling in the flesh as you construct the skeleton—based on the structural outline you've already put together.

Writing Dialog Based on the Structure We've Developed

Let's continue introducing innovative detail: It's time to write the dialog for this scene. The Sequence, Proposition, Plot above is really just a guide to the dialog, similar to the way jazz musicians know they're going to play A, B#, D but improvise all around that. We will be following the basic form, but playing with it as well. While writing a scene it's imperative to be looking at the layouts for Sequence and for Proposition and Plot. Taken together, these represent the complete blueprint to the scene.

When writing dialog, bear in mind that there's a huge difference between real conversation and great dialog. Real conversation can ramble forever, say nothing, and be extremely boring. In a scene you've generally got to achieve an objective in a limited amount of time. But the conversation also has to live and breathe and have room to wander a bit. Dialog must be interesting, and it also needs to be immediately comprehensible because the words are flying at the audience. They have to understand what's happening right as it happens.

All the characters should sound distinct from one another, such that you could remove their names from above the written dialog on the page and still know who's speaking. They each need their own speech patterns, vocabulary, flavor, personality, color, rhythm, cadence, and diction—and these should all change as their emotional states vary. People often don't speak in full sentences, and they cut each other off in mid sentence. You don't want "on the nose" dialog, in which characters simply tell us what they're doing ("I'm leaving now" as they walk out the door) or what they're obviously feeling ("I'm furious with you") because it's boring, redundant, and amateurish—think third-grade theater. Things are often said in subtext, in which what's really being said is camouflaged or being delivered indirectly, so that the words spoken might even be the opposite of what is meant. If you're angry with your spouse, but are having difficulty addressing the subject directly, your conversation about might be about, say, yard work, but you both know exactly what's being communicated in disguise, beneath your words.

Daily speech is peppered with humor, sexual innuendo, anger, affection, danger, love, desperation, seduction, outrage, silliness, and the thousand other things that flow out of us on a constant basis. Listen to real people in your daily life and acquire an ear for dialog. The best test for how your own written dialog sounds is to hear it. Organize a reading, preferably with actors who perform the various roles, and tape it. Then you can, for instance, listen to your entire first act while driving to work. Some writers act out the parts to get in character, and many writers say that their characters start talking to them after a while.

INT. DENTIST'S OFFICE - DAY
MITCHELL sits in the dentist's chair, his mouth pried open, as MELIKA, 36, a female dentist with long, red hair cascading down her back, stares into his open maw.

> MELIKA
> Spit it out . . . then get out.

> MITCHELL
> Yeah, yeah. Great to see you too, babe. Look, I need a little favor, you know?

> MELIKA
> *(as she pokes him with an instrument)*
> How little?

> MITCHELL
> OW! Damn it. I need a hundred pounds of your Benjamins.

> MELIKA
> MY Benjamins?
> *(jabbing him again)*
> You get dropped on your head?

> MITCHELL
> OUCH! Don't friggin' *do* that! Look, I got a chance to set up Kepler and put him in the slammer, big time.

> MELIKA
> With *my* money . . . what's wrong with your money?

> MITCHELL
> Well, I ain't doing so hot right now and—

> MELIKA
> Precisely.

MITCHELL

And mine ain't counterfeit.
(as he makes eyes at her)
Plus, you make the best in the west.

MELIKA

I don't fall for your pick-up lines . . . anymore. So it's
no to both questions . . . and especially to *you*.

MITCHELL

Look babe, you're gonna have to sit on it for years
before things cool down enough to move any more,
and you know it.
(she jabs him again)
OW! Christ! Come on! He's out to sink me! I ain't
kiddin', all right?

MELIKA

(grabbing a drill and revving it up)
I'll burn it before I let you waltz out of here with my
artwork, you lousy, two-timing piece of. . . .

She leans in with the shrieking drill and he grabs her arm in a death grip.

MITCHELL

She didn't mean nothing! Damn you! Just gimme the
paper! You hate Kepler as bad as I do, and you know
it! *COME ON!* I need this!

He shoves her away and leaps out of the chair, but she rams him back into it.

MELIKA

You want to talk Benjies, you stay in the chair.
Rules are rules.

MITCHELL

Okay, okay. But keep that crap outta my face!

MELIKA

Everybody hates that crooked dick, but nobody tells
me what to do with my greenbacks, you read me?
(he nods, swallowing his anger)
Besides, what's in it for me? I stick my neck out and
I'm the one who gets the guillotine.

MITCHELL

All right, all right. Listen, I got this job on New
Year's worth a bundle . . . I. . . .
(hating to say the words)
I could cut you in for a . . . a quarter. Be worth a
million five.

MELIKA

Now you're talking, stud, but I'm gonna need half—

Mitchell surges out of his chair, but she holds a finger to her lips and he stops.

MELIKA

Half, because I got one Special Agent Dykstra of the
Secret Service scouring the entire Southwest for the
purveyor of these picture-perfect hundreds.

MITCHELL

He onto you?

MELIKA

Hell no. You think he's gonna look twice at a whole-
some little dentist who drives a Honda?

MITCHELL

Okay, okay . . . fifty percent. Goddamn you.

MELIKA

And I'll throw in the plates.

Mitchell stares at her in utter disbelief, a smile blooming on his face.

MELIKA

They're blown anyway. This batch is too hot, like
you said. You plant the plates in Kepler's house and
we make sure Special Agent Dykstra knows where
to look.
(laughing raucously)
Kepler'll be pulling Social Security before he sees the
real world again.

MITCHELL

I swear to god I could kiss you.

MELIKA

Well, damn boy, don't let a little thing like me

busting your jaw for sleeping with that cheap-ass skank stop you.

He kisses her and she kisses him back, pinning him to the dentist chair.

As you can see, Sequence, Proposition, Plot for this scene provided a great platform from which to build. But it still allowed us to create a cool, fun scene based on that structure by improvising along the way. No need to be a slave to the structure or to robotically fill in the dialog and details. Let it breathe. Just like weaving live plants into an arched garden trellis, you get the basic shape of the trellis, but it's filled with a living organism. You've established the basic shape of the script—and then filled it with life and breath.

A Quick Review of What We've Done with this Demo Story

Let's get a brief overview of what we've done by applying Sequence, Proposition, Plot to the sequence and to the scene in this demo story. The sequence is shown on the left and the scene on the right:

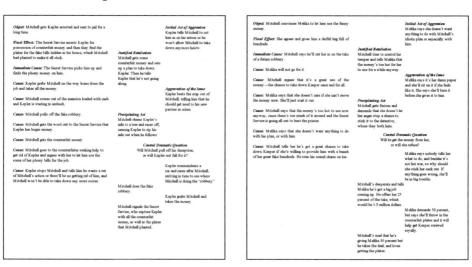

So that's how to use Sequence, Proposition, Plot to construct a script, working from the general to the specific. You'll see a lot more of this tool in Part Two of this book. You saw that when it came time to actually write in the dialog, a solid structure already existed to work from—and yet still we created more detail, the true final detail. The scene achieves its *Object*: for Mitchell to obtain the counterfeit money. It also fits into the larger sequence, which achieves its objective: for Mitchell to successfully frame Kepler. Presumably, taking Kepler out of the picture helps achieve the objective of the act in which the sequence resides, and that act helps achieve the objective of the whole script. This is Unity of Action—a structurally integrated plot—which means that each unit contributes to its constituent larger unit, all of which contributes to the whole (see Aristotle's quote on page xxii). That's exactly what Price means when he says that "a play is a Unit made up of other Units" (see page 162). Sequence, Proposition, Plot is a unique, innovative, and powerful tool for plot construction that will help you engineer your script properly before you write it.

START USING SEQUENCE, PROPOSITION, PLOT IN YOUR OWN SCRIPT

1. Use this tool once your story is pretty well in hand. Start by stating the *Object* of your script simply and clearly. The *Object* is the mark you're shooting for, the point on the horizon that your script is trying to reach. Do the same for each act, focusing on the point the plot should reach by the end of the act, and again for each sequence and each scene.

2. What's the *Final Effect* that demonstrates the *Object* on-screen, with actions exhibited by real actors? The *Object* is what you want to achieve; now you have to create a real event.

3. What's the *Immediate Cause* of the *Final Effect*? This is not merely the incident that comes just before it, but instead the one action that actually *causes* it. When you're doing reverse cause and effect for the overall story—make sure you're not getting into too much detail. The first pass through the material is just a scouting trip; you're laying down trail markers, so keep it simple and travel light.
    Free yourself from the profusion of unnecessary detail, as though you're wearing snowshoes in very deep snow, enabling you to walk along the surface, instead of sinking up to your hip with each step.

4. Keep working backward through your script, only seeking the *cause* of a given effect, thereby separating the Necessary from the Unnecessary. This will make your script lean and mean. You'll be surprised at the things that *don't* make it into your first pass. True, they may be picked up on successive passes, but even when you're done there will still be story elements that never become necessary and can be left out of the script. After all, when you're done making a suit, there's always cloth left on the floor.

5. As you map out reverse cause and effect for the acts, then the sequences, and then the scenes, add in *only a little more* detail as it becomes necessary. You're gradually weaving detail into the telling of the story, work-

ing from the general to the specific with each successive pass.

6. When doing Proposition, remember our proportion diagram. The antagonist's *Initial Act of Aggression*—the set-up of the potential fight—generally comes one-quarter or one-third of the way into the script, not at the very beginning. It can certainly come earlier, but allow some exposition before the conflict gets rolling.

7. Does your protagonist retaliate? *Justified Retaliation* helps create a proactive character who garners audience sympathy. If this element of the conflict isn't there, the Proposition will indirectly suggest it. Then you can introduce or develop it to enhance the Dramatic Action whether at the overall script, act, sequence, or scene level.

8. Remember that the *Aggravation of the Issue* tends to occur at roughly the two-thirds or three-quarters point. Again, this is true for the overall script, and also for each act, sequence, and scene. This sense of proportion is crucial in working with Sequence, Proposition, Plot.

9. The *Precipitating Act* should be a strong action by the protagonist that really touches off the fight to the finish. It will get the audience members on the edge of their seats, and will help turn mere Story into true Drama.

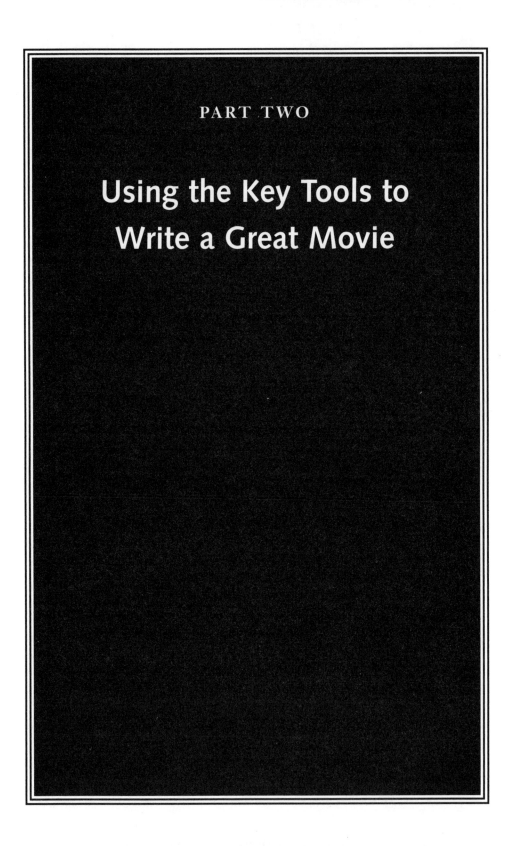

PART TWO

Using the Key Tools to Write a Great Movie

Part Two of this book is markedly different from Part One. It will plunge you into an intense experiential learning process, giving you the real experience of using the Key Tools covered in Part One rather than merely discussing them. All the tools will be demonstrated by inventing and structuring an original screenplay—a script I'm actually writing as a commercially salable project—and developing it from the ground up. In my classes, I work hands-on with each student on his or her own script; here we will get as close as possible to that process by building a script as you watch over my shoulder. I want to take you from an intellectual understanding of the Key Tools to the firsthand familiarity of seeing them in action as we apply them to a real screenplay.

This depth of process means that Part Two of this book is as different from Part One as working in an emergency room is from studying in medical school. It's real, it's messy, and it's immediate. Now that we're constructing an actual screenplay, it's much harder to compartmentalize the use of the Key Tools. They can't necessarily be used sequentially, since the story creation process is chaotic, wild, and free-flowing. Part Two will be a living, breathing, growing creature within a similar chapter framework to Part One, but with more wiggle room. Compare it to wrestling a bear in the wilderness versus studying one at the zoo.

For the plot, I've chosen to build a comedic thriller that should make the learning experience fun. It's hard work to internalize and master this material, so I've done my best to make it engaging. Keep in mind that you're seeing only the first pass in the development of this story, which would normally be followed by rewrites and polishing touches. Regardless of the story's merits, for someone who wants to learn sound screenwriting practices, this is the real deal. Although we'll start with nothing but a raw idea—a single sentence—you'll witness as the entire plot comes into existence. I will breathe life into every aspect of the story, describing in full the technique as we progress. Part Two of this book is an instructional documentary which shows the working process of a professional screenwriter.

While I'll be using the Key Tools from Part One of the book to bootstrap the story into existence, there is a catch-22 involved. A tool can give you some traction to get a story up and running, but you can't *fully* use the tool until you've added more story material upon which to implement it. Once you can sense the main character's Dilemma, you can get a handle on the plot, which then allows you to do more work with Dilemma. But you also need to utilize the 36 Dramatic Situations to break out the story, to awaken it and expand on the plot possibilities. Plus, you need to use the Enneagram to create and dimensionalize the characters, all while doing ongoing Research and Brainstorming as a central part of the start-up process. In fact, I must warn you that you will be sent on one detour, steering you from a discussion on utilizing dilemma to the chapters on the 36 Dramatic Situations, the Enneagram, and Research and Brainstorming. Once I've developed the story further with these three tools, then you'll be sent back to complete the chapter on Dilemma. This detour is quite manageable, but I'm letting you know about it beforehand so that it's less disorienting. The point is that I have to use several tools at once in order to even begin to lay the foundation of a working plot. It's hard work to invent a story and get it off the launch pad. As you start a script, there are truly neither plot nor characters nor setting—nothing to hang your hat on. It's as if you're sitting at the bottom of an abyss, trying to carve a few handholds so that there's something to grab on to and pull your way out.

The battlefield of this growing story is strewn with partially completed ideas, the beginnings of structures, flights of fancy, developing characters, tunnel vision and night blindness, exploding possibilities, the obvious that has yet to be noticed, abandoned storylines, and leaps of imagination. Giving birth is neither neat nor painless. The process is definitely chaotic, but it does have a certain logic to it. In expert hands, essentially it's loosely controlled pandemonium with lots of give-and-take. It's part method and part madness, kind of like steering an explosion. Ride along with me and experience the fun, the pain, the exuberance, the frustration, the anarchy and pure bedlam, the excitement of cascading ideas, the hits, the near misses and total misses, the burnout, the determination, the research, the brainstorming, and the joining of various puzzle pieces—the whole building process from A to Z that constitutes the construction of a script. It's a white-water ride with an experienced guide, and it represents the very real process that you will go through in putting together your own screenplay.

An unusual feature in Part Two is an inside look at my Writer's Notebook. This is distinct from the process of applying the tools to the developing plot, because the notebook section displays my notes for the actual thinking, inventing, spit-balling, and seat-of-the-pants scrambling that happens as I figure out the story itself. This story development process is an ongoing progression, and the application of each successive tool raises fresh questions about the plot. In most instances I'm developing the plot in conjunction with the use of one of the tools, and so that creation process is included with the section on that tool. But occasionally I have to just stop everything and figure things out—to develop a solution or add a new layer to the plot or mull over possibilities. In these instances, having nothing to do with any specific tools, I change over to my Writer's Notebook. This is distinguished from the rest of the text by a different font, which you'll first encounter in Chapter 10. In this way, the full scope of my creative process is completely transparent to you without being confusing. So strap yourself in and have fun!

CHAPTER 8

Using Dilemma, Crisis, Decision & Action, and Resolution

N ow let's get started building this screenplay from square one. It will take some time to spin up a story from a raw premise, but I'll be using Dilemma from the very beginning to help bootstrap the story into existence. I'll also be using the 36 Dramatic Situations, the Enneagram, and Research and Brainstorming early in the process to bring it to life.

FOCUSING ON DILEMMA
WHILE CREATING A STORY

I want to create a perfect crime plot with the promise of great wealth for the protagonist, but also with the threat of significant danger. Bear in mind that as I write this, I have nothing at all beyond what you see here. I'm literally building the script as you watch. There are no details of any kind—no title, no setting, no characters, and no ending. The script is entirely unformed. I played with some possibilities and came up with the following idea: *A reformed pathological liar and kleptomaniac with two strikes against him gets blackmailed into a revenge-oriented "perfect" crime by his demented former cellmate, to whom he owes his life.* I envision this story told in the style of Elmore Leonard (author of *Out of Sight* and *Get Shorty*, both adapted to successful screenplays)—a rollicking thriller that's both wacky and dangerous.

Beginning with the Raw Idea

This is obviously just a raw idea that still needs *everything* in order to become a screenplay. At this point, I have no idea what this "perfect" crime might be, as literally no story elements exist yet except the above premise. A *premise* is the simple explanation of a movie idea, such as, "Three nuns accidentally rob a bank, get stuck hiding out in the criminal underground, and end up inadvertently taking down a mighty crime lord." All I've got now is an intriguing premise, but a bad premise will not make a good movie, so at least I'm starting off right. Always be on the lookout for that rare *great* premise—one that a producer would kill for.

Developing the Story

So we're looking at someone who used to be a pathological liar and a kleptomaniac. Let's call him Cutter, and let's say he's the best liar anyone can imagine, as well as a thief *par excellence*. He's got two strikes against him, so a third conviction will send him back to the pen for life. Since he's reformed, let's create a wife, Margarita, to whom he's vowed he'll never lie or steal again. Thus far, he has kept his word. But into his nice little world comes his former cellmate, a colorful, dangerous rogue who once saved Cutter's life in prison—let's call him Apollo. (I found this name in Final Draft, the screenwriting software that contains an amazing 90,000 names in its database.) Apollo comes to Cutter with the chance to take down a heinous villain whom I'll call St. Nick, a guy who betrayed and murdered Frenchy, Cutter and Apollo's closest friend in prison. Frenchy got himself off heroin, turned his life around while in jail, and became a genuinely good person. But when he got out, St. Nick sunk his hooks into Frenchy, using him in the execution of a crime, and then framed and murdered him. Apollo now has a perfect opportunity to get revenge on St. Nick and to make both he and Cutter rich for life. But he needs Cutter's lying and stealing skills, so he blackmails him into helping.

Isolating the Dilemma

This story has a dilemma inherent in it, which not all stories have. Can you see it? How is Cutter damned if he does and damned if he doesn't? Let's isolate this dilemma, articulate its components, and then experiment with maximizing it. At the most basic, it's unacceptable for Cutter to get involved in this revenge scheme because he's sworn off crime and knows it will ruin his life, drawing him back into his addiction to lying and stealing, threatening to destroy his marriage, and pulling him into a deadly game against St. Nick, who is catastrophically dangerous. But it's equally unacceptable not to get involved because he would miss the chance to ruin St. Nick, a horrible monster whom he despises for betraying and killing a beloved friend—plus, Apollo is blackmailing Cutter. If the pull is equal in both directions, then Cutter will short-circuit like Robby the Robot, unable to send a command in either direction.

Building the Magnitude

Remember that the more magnitude built in to a dilemma, the higher the dramatic tension. Clearly, I need to emphasize the importance of Cutter's marriage and his new straight life, as well as his profound need to stay in this world of stability, decency, honesty, sobriety, sanity, and happiness. I also need to make sure that St. Nick is a true monster so that Cutter's need to take him down is absolutely critical. The more Cutter is justified in destroying him, the more the audience will connect with that half of his dilemma—that it's unacceptable not to get in on the revenge scheme. And the more I see how much Cutter's promise to his wife means to him, as well as how dangerous St. Nick is, the more I can substantiate the other half of his dilemma—that it's equally unacceptable to go ahead with it. Cutter's damned if he does and damned if he doesn't. This should be a ferocious tug of war, a high-stakes debate that not only traps our protagonist, but draws in the audience as well.

Exploring One Side of the Dilemma:
It's Unacceptable to Get Involved

Let's start with some reasons why Cutter cannot get involved with his former cellmate's plan. If Cutter used to be a career criminal, then he had some real problems. He's done two prison terms, so with two strikes against him he cannot afford another arrest—that would automatically mean life in prison. Let's say that Margarita is a deeply religious woman who urged him toward the straight and narrow. When he got out of prison and fell in love with her, he made a solemn vow never to lie or steal again and has lived up to his word. He is a decent, hardworking citizen, possibly even a pillar of his community. Do I want to give him children? That would certainly be another reason not to get involved with Apollo. Cutter finally has the solid life he dreamed about while in prison and he senses that, like an alcoholic, if he starts his wicked ways again, it will explode into full-fledged addiction.

What if Cutter has a son (let's call him Mischa) from his first marriage, but he missed most of Mischa's childhood while in prison? Cutter's ex-wife had forbidden Mischa to be around his father, but because Mischa just turned eighteen, he's begun spending a lot of time with Cutter. What if Mischa is a troubled youth, drifting toward criminality, and Cutter has to be a good example in order to steer him right? This can complicate Cutter's dilemma: If he goes to jail again, then Mischa could more easily slip into a life of crime.

It could be that Mischa has heard rumors of the wild things Cutter used to do, but Cutter would downplay all that and tell him it was wrong and destructive. Mischa's future is clearly hanging in the balance, and Cutter is determined to pull him into a good, stable life. This can be compounded by the fact that Mischa possesses Cutter's gift of lying, but Cutter knows that Mischa's energy and brainpower can be channeled into something better. All this would be further complicated when Apollo shows up and starts telling Mischa stories about his father's legendary exploits, like the time Cutter stole the Rolling Stones' limousine—with them in it—and went on a legendary three-day bender in which millions of dollars in damage was done, some people got arrested and others got pregnant, and some were even forced to flee the country, including Keith Richards. The Stones still claim that it was the single wildest party they've ever been to. Apollo can blackmail Cutter with this type of storytelling: "You do this job for me or I'll tell Mischa the *really* crazy stuff."

Another major factor is that the mark, St. Nick, is extremely dangerous and vengeful, so going after him is genuinely suicidal. The word among the criminal element is that years ago St. Nick got caught cheating with a horse he owned at a racetrack in a small Kentucky town and was disqualified. Infuriated, he staged an "accidental" spill of poison chemicals, killing the entire town—on Christmas Eve. Then out of pure vindictiveness he went from house to house robbing the dead, even opening presents and taking things he fancied. He was never caught for it, but this legend in the under-world is how he came by his nickname. Get caught crossing him and every-body you ever knew will get iced. He's a treacherous, twisted monster who is also immensely perceptive and has a genius IQ.

Exploring the Other Side of the Dilemma: It's Equally Unacceptable to Remain Uninvolved

Now let's go deeper into why Cutter cannot walk away from Apollo's job. Cutter should be foaming at the mouth to get even with St. Nick. Why would he? What are some of the worst things St. Nick could have done? He did betray and kill one of Cutter's best friends, but if Frenchy was a crook killed by another crook during the execution of a crime, why would the audience care that deeply? It must be very strongly established that Frenchy had turned his life around in prison, had helped other convicts, and was loved and respected. The more the audience feels the force of Cutter's drive for revenge, the more it will connect to Cutter and his dilemma. What are more reasons why Cutter might loathe St. Nick? The more viewers experience St. Nick as a monster, the more they'll feel that Cutter is absolutely justified in destroying him, just the same as if there were a rabid dog loose in Cutter's neighborhood.

What if Cutter is secretly attracted to Apollo's offer? What if part of him is bored with the straight life and craves action? That opens another level of complication in Cutter's dilemma by making it that much more unacceptable for Cutter to refuse Apollo. Anyone who has sacrificed an adventurous life for a domesticated one will feel that call of the wild, so it's a universal factor that many in the audience can identify with.

Plotting the Revenge

What are some possibilities for a "perfect" crime against St. Nick? As a crim-inal, he probably wouldn't go to the police to report a crime against him, although if what gets robbed is illegal, then he can't report it anyway. He'd still come after Cutter and Apollo though—unless he believes he has seen his stolen material destroyed. What if he thinks the perpetrators are dead? Then he won't pursue them. What if St. Nick has a huge deal brewing and is putting most of his assets on the line, leaving him vulnerable for a short period? Let's say he wants to go legitimate, perhaps buy a bank. He'd have to convert his ill-gotten gains into legitimate assets, which would expose him to the pesky formalities of operating legally. That means St. Nick's hidden illegal assets would come out of hiding, and when he's in this vulnerable state Apollo and Cutter would have a golden opportunity to destroy him.

Presumably, Apollo has found out about this opportunity and needs Cutter for a specialized job—maybe with a false identity as a bank examiner, which gives Cutter access to St. Nick's funds. Now this gives us something specific with which to construct a plot: Cutter would become the inside man and make use of his phenomenal lying abilities, putting him in a position to take down St. Nick—and making for plenty of dramatic tension.

Opening Up Plot Possibilities

As you work with Dilemma, you'll find that by going very deep into it you can discover many story possibilities. You'll come to understand your protagonist's dilemma fully after you've spent a lot of time thinking about it. As mentioned on page 35, it can be very useful to write an essay about the dilemma—try it now for this script. Write about it from Cutter's point of view, and then try it from Apollo's, since he created this dilemma and will be taking advantage of it.

DETOUR: GOING TO THE 36 DRAMATIC SITUATIONS FOR IDEAS

The 36 Dramatic Situations, a remarkable brainstorming tool, are especially useful at this point in the development of a screenplay. I like the raw idea I've got—it's absolutely wide open, which is really fun—but it's still unformed in so many ways, which is also quite daunting. Part of the process at this point is to go through the 36 Dramatic Situations and see what story possibilities they trigger. This step is like pouring gasoline on a fire—it makes everything flare up and explode. The 36 Dramatic Situations offer a complete spectrum of dramatic elements and human emotional conflicts, opening up unexpected avenues and dimensions, especially when a story is brand new. Explosive creativity is naturally a priceless asset for a professional storyteller.

It is almost time to stop reading this chapter and skip ahead to read Chapters 10, 11, and 12 on using the 36 Dramatic Situations, the Enneagram, and Research and Brainstorming in the creation of an original screenplay.

A lot of the heavy lifting of fleshing out this story and constructing the characters is accomplished there. The remainder of this chapter contains ideas that have been developed using the tools in Chapters 10 through 12. As you experienced in Part One, I teach the tools in a certain order, but using them in real time requires bouncing around to use each as needed. It's the difference between learning how to build a house and the actual construction process itself. You study different elements in isolation, such as how to lay the foundation, frame the walls, do the electrical wiring, install the plumbing, and so on. But during the actual building process, you're laying the foundation while you're installing drainage and plumbing. When you're framing up a wall, you're factoring in the wiring, the plumbing, the sheetrock, and the exterior siding as well as windows and doors. Many systems go up simultaneously, and they're all interconnected. This is also true of story creation. In order to get this script up and running, I need to work through the plot possibilities suggested by the 36 Dramatic Situations, develop characters using the Enneagram, and do some basic Research and Brainstorming. So skip ahead to page 207 and read those three chapters before returning here for the rest of the work on Dilemma, Crisis, Decision & Action, and Resolution.

RETURNING FROM DETOUR: CONTINUE FROM HERE

In the first section of this chapter, I started imagining the story and then worked to apply dilemma. It wasn't too hard to see that Cutter is damned if he gets involved with Apollo's plan to destroy St. Nick and damned if he doesn't. Getting involved will ruin Cutter's new life, force him to break his vow to his wife, and open up the way to a life of crime for his son. Cutter knows that once he starts lying and stealing, his old addiction will take over his life like an evil genie gushing out of a lamp. I know how crazy the old Cutter used to be and how dangerous St. Nick is. And yet it's hard to walk away from the chance at revenge on St. Nick, because Cutter *loathes* him, Apollo's plan is solid, and there's an opportunity to make a fortune in the process. Plus, Cutter may be secretly attracted to Apollo's offer to come out of retirement.

To recap, in our detour to Chapter 10, I used the 36 Dramatic Situations to open up our plot by exploring story possibilities; I also invented three new characters. The first, Senator Hutchings, is a crooked politician who needs St. Nick to be the front man and to put up the capital to launch the bank. Senator Hutchings recommends another new character, Shallott, a bank examiner who secretly wants revenge on St. Nick for the death of his brother. The third character introduced is Umbotha, a corrupt African dictator who will be on the receiving end of the government-guaranteed loans that Hutchings and St. Nick will shoot his way in exchange for huge kickbacks.

In Chapter 11, using the Enneagram to explore the characters' identities, I came up with some interesting and unexpected personality traits. The old Cutter would have been a 7, The Enthusiast—adventurous, fearless, and flamboyant—until, trapped in an endless cycle of excess, greed, and hardened insensitivity, he suffered the downside of his lifestyle before he turned his life around. In his new incarnation as a 1, The Reformer, Cutter has become someone with strong personal convictions and a definite sense of moral and religious values. Apollo and St. Nick share some qualities of an 8, The Challenger, and Senator Hutchings seems to be a 3, The Achiever. These types are not set in stone, but are rather an insightful spectrum of possibilities with which to further develop these characters.

Chapter 12 on Research and Brainstorming showed the trail of my research into what it takes to buy a bank. One great find was a book that unexpeectedly turned out to be just what I needed—exactly how the best research often works. I was able to run with it and do a lot of brainstorming in my Writer's Notebook that yielded the core of the mechanics for this story's plot: an agricultural loans scam. I also found an exhilarating movie that triggered a full-blown brainstorming session, exponentially expanding the possibilities for Apollo.

So let's continue from there, using this newly developed Apollo as I get back to working on Cutter's dilemma.

Resuming Work on Cutter's Dilemma

Making Apollo a really tempestuous character—dangerous, but also fun and crazy—will significantly enhance Cutter's dilemma. Because Apollo is so unpredictable and mischievous, Cutter is that much more damned if he gets involved with his scheme. But because Apollo is such a free spirit and adventurer, it makes Cutter that much more damned if he doesn't join in—adding a new layer to the dilemma.

Cutter knows that nothing is what it seems with Apollo; that there's always something going on behind the scenes; that there's always trouble involved. He knows things will spin out of control, insane complications will ensue, and Apollo will stop at nothing to win, seeing it all as some kind of crazy pissing contest with the Fates. Cutter also knows that Apollo will drag him back into dishonesty, and he will soon be stealing, cheating, and lying to cover the lies. And yet he also sees Apollo as fulfilling an irresistible urge, as a breath of fresh air into what's beginning to feel like a stultifying existence bound by the limits he has set for himself. Cutter knows he shouldn't, but he begins to think Apollo really could pull off this perfect crime, a perfect revenge on St. Nick. In fact, he knows it will be an adventure that he wouldn't miss for the world. It will wake him up and bring him back to life, drawing his soul out of the dormant state that he's put it in to survive his self-exile.

Clarifying the Dilemma with a Two-Column Chart

In what ways is it unacceptable for Cutter to go along with Apollo? In what ways is it equally unacceptable if he doesn't? Let's break down Cutter's dilemma using the two-column chart to isolate each half of his internal debate. If necessary, return to Chapter 1 to review this process and recall how this chart facilitates the development of dilemma. Cutter is saying, "Wild horses couldn't drag me into this thing, but on the other hand, I wouldn't miss it for the world. I'm appalled and intrigued. Repelled and fascinated. Panicked and spellbound. Running for my life and spoiling for a fight. Terrified of extinction if I get involved and raging for revenge." Let's continue this line of thinking on the following chart, looking at how Cutter can't go along with Apollo's plan but can't refuse it.

Can't Go Along with the Plan	Can't Refuse the Plan
Must stay on track in new life	Utterly driven to ruin St. Nick
He can't break his vow to his wife	He owes his life to Apollo
His whole family could get killed	St. Nick killed his close friend
He can't go back to his old ways	He's suffocating in his new life
He hates being blackmailed	Apollo will turn him in to the cops
He can't be a bad example to his son	Son sees him as a loser and a wimp
Two strikes, one more is life in prison	Can't let St. Nick get away with it
Apollo is crazy and unpredictable	Apollo is wild and free
He fears his lying addiction	He craves the wide open freedom
He's a domesticated animal	He's a wild animal
It won't be as simple as Apollo claims	It will be unpredictable and fun
It's deadly	It's a call to adventure
He's becoming sane in his new life	He's going crazy with boredom
It's disastrous	It's fascinating
This will destroy him	This will create him
St. Nick is catastrophically dangerous	St. Nick must be taken out
Common sense	Adventurous instinct
Apollo will screw things up	Apollo is a genius
The danger is freaky-scary	The danger is intoxicating
His wife will know he's lying	Apollo will tell her Cutter's secrets
He can't resist his nesting instincts	He can't resist his hunting instincts
Craziest idea he's ever heard	An awe-inspiring plan
He loves his wife and is loyal	He took pride in being the best liar
The community needs him	St. Nick's removal is a public service

His new religion makes his life work	Going after St. Nick is a crusade
He's got enough money to get by	Wealth would help his marriage
Life is nice and predictable	Life is stiflingly predictable
The plan is too free-floating	The challenge is inspiring
Panic and fear of death	Exhilarating adrenaline

You can see how I could keep going with this two-column chart—playing one side of the chart against the other, matching them up. Or you can also just make a long list on each side without trying to connect each statement to its opposite. The chart doesn't have to be neat or exact or clear. I see the dilemma much more clearly once I've done this list, putting all the aspects out there in black and white, and making the obvious apparent. This will come in handy when crisis forces the protagonist to make a choice.

FOCUSING ON CRISIS WHILE CREATING THE STORY

By the time Cutter's dilemma comes to the crisis point, it has been getting tougher and more complex as the story builds until finally it comes to a make-or-break moment. Remember that the Crisis tends to occur at about the two-thirds or three-quarters point in a script, and forces an immediate Decision & Action by the protagonist. In this story, the crisis should cause Cutter to snap and go on a lying spree that lasts much of the rest of the movie. I want this to be flat-out one of the most stunning feats of lying ever seen in a movie.

Testing Possibilities and Extremes for Cutter's Crisis

Let's look at some possibilities for precipitating a crisis. The most obvious is that St. Nick finds out who Cutter is and what he's up to. Generally, in a hidden-identity movie, the point of crisis includes discovery by the opposition. However, I don't think that will work well in *Good Old St. Nick*. If Cutter's cover is blown, then not only would the entire scheme fall apart prematurely, but he'd probably be killed instantaneously. When a spy's cover is blown, the game is over—period. If I want Cutter to be locked in an astonishing liars' contest with St. Nick, then although everything seems to blow up in Cutter's face, his identity should remain intact, at least enough for St. Nick to seriously consider his lies to be valid.

Certainly a *near* discovery could play a role in a good crisis. What about Cutter being betrayed by Apollo? I've been playing with the possibility of Apollo's involvement with counterfeit money; this would be a good time to pull out that option. Even if Apollo just shows up with the money without trying to palm it off at this point, his hidden agenda can then begin to surface or the problems inherent in holding the funny money could begin to catch up with him. What about Mischa showing up? He may see a chance to inject himself into his dad's world in such a way that he can't be ignored. Perhaps he feels that he can make himself valuable or even indispensable. Does Margarita find out where Cutter is, or that he's been having an affair with St. Nick's secretary?

The crisis point is certainly an appropriate time for the murder of Shallott (as suggested on page 242 of the detour). This could be the event leading to the near discovery of Cutter. But how would it happen? Does Shallott snap? Does he slip up? Does he do something that brings suspicion down on Cutter? Why would St. Nick be forced to kill Shallott? How would Cutter distance himself from Shallott, the bank examiner whom he is supposed to be assisting? Is the FBI investigating St. Nick, making him suspicious? Does this screw everything up, or can Senator Hutchings quash the investigation? (All this was developed in Chapters 10 through 12.)

Is Cutter becoming unstable because his medications are missing? Did they get lost? Did Apollo swap them for placebo pills to make Cutter's rampaging side emerge? Does Mischa hide the pills so he can witness the old Cutter in action? Does Cutter lose it altogether, jeopardizing the revenge operation? Does he even realize his meds have worn off? Is he glad they're gone?

Is the window of opportunity vanishing for revenge against St. Nick? Did the situation with the agricultural loans in Africa change so that St. Nick must now act immediately? Does Hutchings find a way to speed up or finalize the bank certification? Does St. Nick move his hidden accounts just when Cutter has finally located them? Does St. Nick suspect something because his instincts are tingling? Look at how many ways I'm considering to complicate the crisis. I may use only a few of them, but I'll know going in what is available to choose from instead of accidentally missing a great possibility.

Compounding Cutter's Crisis

What if the CIA is involved with the bank? That can happen when covert funds are moved overseas to prop up dictators. If the CIA is in the picture, then Cutter is in even deeper water, and it will be all the more difficult to pull off the revenge without being arrested or killed. St. Nick and Hutchings will have powerful allies working behind the scenes to shut down any investigation, citing national security. There could be drugs coming in from Africa, and drug money, money laundering, and so on. An investigation is a nice monkey wrench to drop in at this point; it opens up the unexpected and forces an eruption into pandemonium—especially for our wild liar, Cutter. He could end up lying to spies, senators, dictators, bankers, thieves, FBI agents, drug dealers, customs officials, and lawyers.

What I've just done in this section is to dig up ways to cause a crisis in the script. You can see that many different things could happen, each compounding the next to heighten tension and really hyper-compress the crisis. Remember that in general, crisis is when the worst possible things happen at the most crucial time, and it generally occurs around the two-thirds or three-quarters point of the story and forces immediate decision and action.

FOCUSING ON DECISION & ACTION WHILE CREATING THE STORY

If I've done my job well, Cutter is in a horribly complex situation that's now blowing up in his face. This dilemma has built-in intensity that has now escalated to emergency status; Cutter no longer has time to contemplate it from a distance. Now he must make a crucial decision and take a key action. Everything hangs in the balance. Plus, I've been engineering this script so that at this point the old Cutter bursts out in a fearsome onslaught of lies.

Fight or Flight?

Depending on exactly how he's backed into a corner at the point of crisis, Cutter could explode in varying ways. But I do see him making a conscious choice to embrace his dark gift of lying as a weapon of war. This is his decision. It's the classic story of the gunslinger who has sworn off violence but is now forced to use it. Cutter must come out swinging if he's going to stand a chance of surviving. But this moment should still have a comic edge as well, so the balance between thriller and comedy has to be maintained.

The Judy Garland Transformation

One of the key things I see happening at this point is what I call the "Judy Garland transformation." I read an amazing article about a reporter who was granted backstage access prior to a performance toward the end of Garland's career. She was running late and when she finally showed up, she was so unkempt that the reporter thought she was the cleaning lady. She seemed insecure, worn out, scared, and out of it as her handlers got her ready. Then, because of his special access backstage, the reporter watched as she pulled herself together. This shrunken little run-down woman literally transformed herself right in front of his eyes. She drew herself up and actually grew a foot taller as she seemed to suck power from nowhere, metamorphosing into the mighty Judy Garland as he watched, thunderstruck.

I want Cutter to go through just that—and I want Mischa to be watching from in hiding. Cutter will be on the edge of collapse because of all the things that have gone wrong, and yet he will dramatically pull himself together. It should be a complete and radical transformation of his character—a true transfiguration.

Wrestling with Possibilities

What direction might the script take when Cutter breaks out into a frenzy of fabrications? He's certainly going to be lying to St. Nick as he fights to remain trustworthy, otherwise he risks losing the opportunity to take him down. If the bank certification is on shaky ground, then Cutter would cook up a whopping lie to keep it on track. Does he tell a crazy lie to Umbotha, the African dictator, who's becoming worried about his loan? How would he lie to Senator Hutchings? Does he have to explain who Mischa is and what he's doing there? Has Apollo been around for a while in disguise, or has he shown up just now? Does Cutter have to tell a whopper to cover for him? Can his lies calm a furious Margarita about this deadly caper, about Mischa's involvement, and about an affair with the secretary?

Cutter could be lying to the CIA about some aspects of the bank operation. He could be telling one set of lies to the CIA and another to the FBI. His lies might set things in motion here that would come together spectacularly in the end. He would be stretching and altering bits of information that people know, and capitalizing on what they don't know. This is where studying world-class liars in literature, mythology, history, and film can help me to build on the best—or as many writers say, to "steal from the best." In the film *The Usual Suspects*, Keyser Soze puts on a virtuosic performance as he concocts lies on the spot; based partly on fact, his stories hold water when U.S. Customs agent Dave Kujan checks them out in the adjacent room. That is the most mind-boggling display of lying I've ever seen in a movie—an ideal standard to keep in mind.

Playing with Extremes

A likelihood also exists that once his berserk side resurfaces, Cutter has really returned to being a hardcore criminal. He may have slipped into his deceitful persona so thoroughly that he's now lying to everybody all the time. Perhaps the genie is out of the bottle and nobody's safe. As far as the audience can tell, he's gone completely over to the dark side. Cutter may be convincing St. Nick that he's betraying Shallott or Apollo or Mischa. Mischa may do something stupid in his attempt to thrust himself into his father's life, and Cutter may seem to be sacrificing him. This dark path is tempting to me as a writer, because one of the options I've considered is that Margarita talks him back into telling the whole truth, breaking the spell and resolving things in the end. At this point, then, I can imagine a real demon, a genuine evildoer emerging at the crucial moment. Taking things to this extreme could kick the story into high gear, where things would get scarier, crazier, and hopefully funnier as well.

Technique and Creativity

People often think that structural technique destroys creativity, but I find it liberating. Look at how creative and focused my process is here. The technique suggests certain things, and from experience I know that it tends to make for good screenplays, so I'm working it as hard as I can. And look how much freedom I have—the story is still wide open in so many ways, even though the story logic and probability are steering it toward some kind of point of inevitability on the horizon. I have tremendous leeway to experiment within the corridor in which I've launched this plot. I don't feel as though I'm trapped in some arcane rules, but as though I have guiding principles that help me steer this careening machine. In *The Philosophy of Dramatic Principle and Method*, Price says, "Playwriting is a process of thought, not a matter of rules." Here's David Mamet, again from *On Directing Film*:

> *The purpose of technique is to free the unconscious* [Mamet's emphasis]. If you follow the rules ploddingly, they will allow your unconscious to be free. That's true creativity. If not, you will be fettered by your conscious mind. Because the conscious mind always wants to be liked and wants to be interesting. The conscious mind is going to suggest the obvious, the cliché, because these things offer the security of having succeeded in the past. Only the mind that has been taken off itself and put on a task is allowed true creativity.

Obviously, I believe in technique—this book is all about it. The tool of Decision & Action suggests that my character's reaction to the crisis should kick in here. But I'm bursting with creativity—this certainly isn't paint-by-numbers. Knowing how to use the tools gives me great confidence as a dramatist, and I'm having a blast building this movie.

FOCUSING ON RESOLUTION
WHILE CREATING THE STORY

At the point of Decision & Action it seems as though Cutter's on such a bender that he's gone over to the dark side for good. He seems to have thrown in with St. Nick and Senator Hutchings, but it's hard to tell. Mischa may panic: Who is this monster that used to be his father? Apollo may just ride the tornado that Cutter has become, content for it to serve his purposes if only he can steer it. Margarita probably sees her marriage rapidly falling apart. But the savage Cutter may also be taking steps in terms of lying to the FBI, to the CIA, and to Umbotha—all to create some bizarre opportunities to take down St. Nick and Hutchings. The point of Decision & Action should be such a flurry of contradictory lies that Cutter will seem like a lunatic genius. This wild flurry should lead to the resolution, although in an unexpected and refreshing way.

Pulling Cutter Out of the Fire

If Margarita is able to get through to Cutter and steer him back toward a connection with their stable life, he may begin to "snap to" at the crucial moment. If so, then he can kick events in the right direction just when it looks as though all is lost. What about the old switcheroo: A massive quantity of St. Nick's and Hutchings's money gets burned up in an accidental fire, with them watching. In actuality, it is Apollo's counterfeit money, but believing their missing money to be destroyed, St. Nick and Hutchings won't be looking for it.

Another key action I see on Cutter's part is divulging the whole truth about the plan at a live TV press conference. Before the public eye, this unprecedented honesty about politics would detonate the Senator's career. It could turn out that Apollo knows Umbotha because they played as kids together when their dictator fathers visited each other on business. This acquaintance, when added to Cutter's system of ingenious, interlocking lies, could convince Umbotha that St. Nick is ripping him off. Umbotha would then fly into a murderous rage and punish St. Nick by taking him back to Mambia, where he becomes a highly guarded prison laborer, enduring a fate far worse than death.

The Trickle-Up Effect

The money—it would turn out to be a vast amount—could be mailed out to the taxpayers who make the least money. As Cutter speaks on live TV, this money would already have gone out in the day's mail. He could tell one last little white lie, saying that St. Nick felt such regret for stealing this money from the American taxpayers that he's returning it—directly to them. The TV interviewer would claim that Cutter has caused immense chaos by telling the truth, and Cutter would say that St. Nick should be held accountable—except that he's nowhere to be found. He would say that there will certainly be a lot of happy poor people out there today, and for the wealthy taxpayers who didn't get packages, not to worry because the money will trickle up. Cutter, Margarita, and Mischa can start again with a new life. Mischa has been scared straight by this whole affair; the three are a tight family; and three envelopes of cash will soon be arriving in the mail to help them along.

CHAPTER 9

Using Theme

T he way in which Cutter resolves his dilemma expresses the theme of the script. (Review Chapter 2 to refresh your understanding of the use of Theme.) What Cutter does is to defeat St. Nick and Hutchings, as well as his own internal demons. The way in which he does this is to burst out with an outrageously creative, positive solution that finally uses his gift of lying for good. Burying his problem didn't work; he had to transform it into a force for good in order to be truly liberated. He finds his core of integrity, courage, and wisdom, and from that emerges an ecstatic freedom that changes his whole reality.

The audience experiences the force of Cutter's unstoppable exuberance, his indomitable, transcendent new energy. This is a theme of life, freedom, energy, happiness, health, integrity, and the power of creation. This theme is very much the heart of the story—what the story is really about—and properly done, it can resonate deeply with the audience. In essence it's a creation myth, a shamanic self-transformation; it's the conception of new life, the discovery of an oasis in the midst of a barren desert.

THE VALUE OF KNOWING YOUR THEME

Knowing the theme—having it in my bones—helps to govern the shape, tone, and energy of the script. This begins with Cutter miserably trying to suppress his gift. There's an entire growth process from nothingness to exuberance. The theme reminds me to make him quite stuck emotionally when the audience first meets him, to establish as great a contrast as possible between how he starts out and how he ends up.

However, this screenplay is not a lecture on life, energy, or integrity. It's a rollicking comic thriller about a guy who finally harnesses his troubling natural energy for something good. Do I infuse the script with this by constantly reiterating it and beating the audience over the head with it? No way. That would be the ruin of this movie. Trusting that the theme will emerge organically at the end of the film, I have each part of the plot do its job, using the full arsenal of my craft as a dramatist to tell the story itself as well as possible.

QUOTES EXPLORING THE THEME
OF *GOOD OLD ST. NICK*

I gathered the following quotes to provide insights into the story—to root me more deeply in the theme, the characters, and plot as the script continues to grow.

Character is the governing element of life, and is above genius.
— GEORGE SAUNDERS

Sanity is madness put to good uses. — GEORGE SANTAYANA

The charm of the best courages is that they are inventions, inspirations, flashes of genius. — GEORGE HALIFAX

Fortune is not on the side of the faint-hearted. — SOPHOCLES

Not even hell can lay a hand on the invincible. — PARMENION

In great straits and when hope is small, the boldest counsels are the safest.
— LIVY

The depth and strength of a human character are defined by its moral reserves. People reveal themselves completely only when they are thrown out of the customary conditions of their life, for only then do they have to fall back on their reserves. — LEON TROTSKY

We live in a fantasy world, a world of illusion. The great task in life is to find reality. — IRIS MURDOCH

Lay me on an anvil, O God. Beat me and hammer me into a crowbar. Let me pry loose old walls; let me lift and loosen old foundations.
— CARL SANDBURG

Truth is the cry of all, but the game of few. — GEORGE BERKELEY

Truth is a clumsy servant that breaks the dishes while washing them.
— KARL KRAUS

The truth is a snare: you cannot have it, without being caught. You cannot have the truth in such a way that you catch it, but only in such a way that it catches you. — SØREN KIERKEGAARD

Character consists of what you do on the third and fourth tries.
— JAMES A. MICHENER

Truth-telling frightens me. Lying confuses me. — MASON COOLEY

[Note: If you've followed the detour previously, then you may wish to skip over Chapters 10 through 12, and continue from Chapter 13 on page 249.]

CHAPTER 10

Using the 36 Dramatic Situations

As we develop our original screenplay in Part Two, the 36 Dramatic Situations will be incredibly useful in opening the floodgates of possibility. While this certainly can be as chaotic as it sounds—the fact that it shakes everything up is one of this tool's greatest strengths—this process of trying on all the situations for a fit is also very methodical. A special effort is made to explore all the possibilities, permutations, and ramifications of each situation as it pertains to our rapidly expanding plot. Turning over this new ground exposes dynamic and fresh story options, energizing the entire script development process. Essentially, the 36 Dramatic Situations are a mineral-rich fertilizer feeding our rapidly growing story.

EXPLORING THE 36 DRAMATIC SITUATIONS TO OPEN UP OUR STORY

Let's go through the 36 Dramatic Situations to stir up some ideas. It's important to be wide open to any and all possibilities at this point, because the story is still brand new and unformed. This is a time of rapid, explosive growth—the sky's the limit. Even though some solid ideas are shaping up, anything goes—including the original premise, if something better pops up. Using the suggestive power of this tool in conjunction with imagination and a sense of how to steer this story, the work becomes part intention and part voyage of discovery. Review the list on page 51 while thinking about this unformed story. See which situations jump out at you, bristling with energy and suggesting story possibilities.

1. *Supplication*

Cutter will clearly be asking and begging for help in dealing with both Apollo and St. Nick. Since he's now a churchgoer, he'll be literally praying for guidance from God. If he can talk to his wife about what's going on, he'll also be appealing to her for guidance. For her part, she'll definitely be pleading with him not to get involved, because she knows where it will lead—to all his old addictions ruining their life together. If she doesn't know about the scheme, then she'll beg Cutter to tell her. She will also be praying for him because she knows something's wrong.

Cutter will beseech Apollo to let him off the hook, and he's begging for his life, his marriage and his wife, his son, his happiness, his sanity. He knows that crossing St. Nick could get them all killed, or possibly a fate worse than death. In return, Apollo is also begging Cutter for help: He needs Cutter's skills in this once-in-a-lifetime opportunity to take down St. Nick. What if, in addition, Apollo is in trouble with St. Nick? He will plead his case even harder. Meanwhile, Cutter's son begs for a glimpse of Cutter's old life, which Cutter in turn implores him to forget about. He wants his son to embrace a normal life, and not to get dragged into the criminal world. He's trying hard to influence Mischa positively and to show him by example how to live a good life. Cutter also perceives that much of his son's behavior is a cry for help.

The proposed caper obviously demands that Cutter lie (which is part of the fun of the story), but he'll probably struggle to keep it under control, begging his addiction to stay dormant. Yet at the same time, isn't part of him pleading to be set free? Cutter is somewhat frustrated and bored with his tidy, law-abiding life. A ravenous beast circles his campfire at night, cajoling him to drop this domesticated charade and return to the life of the wild. The part of him that feels trapped, dead-ended, broken down, and claustrophobic secretly desires to break out. Part of Cutter's dilemma is that he's really wants to take St. Nick down. He will be begging for an opportunity to find the chinks in this monster's formidable armor, strip him financially, and get him in trouble with the law—to destroy him, betray him, and ruin his life. Cutter is imploring the gods for a handle on this guy.

On the other hand, St. Nick will be asking for help in entering the lucrative world of legitimate banking in high-level shadow government circles. He's desperate to jettison his stone-age criminal ways for the space-age, street-legal robbery that the government doesn't prosecute and can even covertly be party to. Had he known this all along, he would have started years ago, saving himself trouble with the police and the lowlifes who now populate his world. The way into the VIP club is revealed when one of the crooked senators with whom St. Nick does business clues him into the variety of legal ways to fleece, plunder, and pillage that yield dividends rather than grand jury investigations. St. Nick is desparate to get into this club, making him especially vulnerable at this particular moment. His desire for legal larceny causes him to lower his defenses as he moves his illicit assets into legitimate financial circles.

Let's get a look at the subheadings of *Supplication*:

A. Fugitives imploring the powerful for help against their enemies.
   Assistance implored for the performance of a pious duty, which
      has been forbidden.
   Appeals for a refuge in which to die.
B. Hospitality besought by the shipwrecked.
   Charity entreated by those cast off by their own people,
      whom they have disgraced.
   Expiation: the seeking of pardon, healing, or deliverance.
   The surrender of a corpse, or of a relic, solicited.
C. Supplication of the powerful for those dear to the supplicant.
   Supplication to a relative in behalf of another relative.
   Supplication to a mother's lover in her behalf.

Fugitives imploring the powerful for help against their enemies seems evident in this script. Apollo is asking Cutter for help against St. Nick. Is Apollo a fugitive? It's a possibility that could complicate things in an intriguing way. If he's on the run from St. Nick, then he'd be asking Cutter to pay him back for saving his life. The fact that Cutter is a stand-up guy (which we tend to want of our hero) means he cannot refuse Apollo. Perhaps Apollo is lying about his life being in danger, but Cutter might not know that until later.

Hospitality besought by the shipwrecked is an interesting subheading. Being shipwrecked is a vivid, poetic image suggesting loss, pain, isolation, and desperation. As we said, Apollo could be in big trouble with St. Nick. Cutter, too, would be in a somewhat helpless situation once he infiltrates St. Nick's inner circle and would be seeking help of any kind. Also, in this story both Cutter's wife and his son would harbor feelings of loss and abandonment.

Supplication of the powerful for those dear to the supplicant would be active in this plot if Cutter and Apollo's scheme falls apart and St. Nick catches onto them. He may take Mischa hostage, causing Cutter to beg for his son's life. In such an instance, Cutter would be looking for *Expiation: The seeking of pardon, healing, or deliverance*, another subheading of *Supplication*.

Do you see how looking at many different aspects of the emerging story through the lens of *Supplication* provided new ideas and clarified others? Using the 36 Dramatic Situations helps with exploring, taking inventory, testing ideas, and looking for ways to shake things up. New possibilities could shatter the developing plot and tumble it into a whole new story. Perhaps everything done so far was just a stepping stone. Never be afraid to challenge all your script ideas to the very core. You may end up with two scripts, when by following an odd thread you create an entirely new story. Using this tool without fear can help you become an explosively creative storyteller with substantial craft as a dramatist.

2. Deliverance

When the story starts, Cutter has been rescued by his wife from a life of crime. He is trying to rescue himself from his former criminal habits, which are closing in on him again, and he's also trying to rescue his son from a potential life of crime. Cutter's focus is on deliverance in the same way an alcoholic depends on AA meetings to stay sober. He's trying to preserve his family life by increasing his income, being a good husband, and trying to have a baby. He's also helping his church and being a responsible citizen in his community.

Perhaps Cutter can pull off this caper by delivering himself from Apollo's trap, or by destroying St. Nick. St. Nick is seeking his own deliverance into the lofty world of legal thievery, a kind of heaven where the streets are paved with gold and the CIA helps you fleece the marks. He's right on the edge of having it made—being admitted into this exclusive club by getting the bank certified—and he's jumping through all the flaming hoops to pass the test. Perhaps Apollo has stolen a huge amount of counterfeit money and is seeking a way to pass it or foist it onto someone. His deliverance will depend on how much pressure he's under to get rid of it, which in turn will determine how hard he pushes. Does his life depend on it, or is he just greedy?

Note that at this point in developing the script there is no ending for this story—it is unexplored territory. In the back of my mind there's an ending in which the old Cutter emerges in a full-blown frenzy of phenomenal lying, managing to save the day and destroy the demon, St. Nick. But any ending will obviously be an outgrowth of how the story grows and complicates itself. It depends on what the Crisis, Decision & Action, or Resolution might be. Anything goes at this point, so exploring the 36 Dramatic Situations can open up innumerable possibilities.

Let's look at the subheadings for *Deliverance*:

A. Appearance of a rescuer to the condemned.
B. A parent replaced upon a throne by his children.
   Rescue by friends, or by strangers grateful for benefits or hospitality.

Appearance of a rescuer to the condemned is how Cutter seems to both Apollo and St. Nick, each for different reasons, when he starts his job. Apollo knows that Cutter has the skills to take down St. Nick, while St. Nick sees Cutter (in disguise as a bank examiner) as a key to gaining entrance to the world of banking. This subheading suggests that St. Nick is "condemned"—that he might not get his way unless Cutter helps to certify his bank. Maybe he's struck a roadblock in getting money into the reserve fund that's required to operate a bank. Though this part of the plot is embryonic at this stage, let's speculate on the possibilities. Could St. Nick be having difficulties moving his money from offshore havens into legitimate accounts in the U.S.? Maybe St. Nick's treasure chest is now open to snooping eyes, and the IRS wants to know why this money was never declared before; without making these deposits, he can't complete the certification of his new bank. Perhaps there's an unforeseen complication with law enforcement, or with another criminal stepping on his action. It's all wide open now and can go a hundred different ways.

Rescue by friends, or by strangers grateful for benefits or hospitality suggests that since Cutter owes his life to Apollo, he's willing to rescue him. What if St. Nick finds himself in a sticky situation and Cutter comes up with a fabulous lie that gets St. Nick off the hook? This would get him into St. Nick's good graces and also reveal that Cutter isn't entirely honest—exactly what Cutter needs to get St. Nick to start to trust him.

This brings up questions about the kind of problems St. Nick might have in acquiring his bank. I've decided that St. Nick has gone through the entire application process and now just has to get the reserve fund set up. He could be experiencing other problems, which Cutter could help him circumvent. Clearly, some research will be required to learn what it takes to buy a bank.

3. *Crime Pursued by Vengeance*

The most obvious aspect arising from this situation is that St. Nick has betrayed and murdered Frenchy, Cutter and Apollo's friend from prison. This treachery must be developed to a believable fever pitch in order to motivate Cutter and Apollo so intensely. Frenchy has to be portrayed as one of the best guys they ever knew, someone so high on Cutter's list that he'd consider risking his life to avenge this murder. How would Frenchy be depicted as somebody who turned his life around in prison, got off drugs, and became a truly good guy—one who finally escaped the criminal life. He could be the one who started Cutter thinking about going straight-and-narrow, too. Word on the inside was that Frenchy had a good job out in the world until St. Nick got him back onto heroin, used him for his old breaking-and-entering skills on a huge job, then framed him for the job and murdered him, making it look as though he overdosed. The other convicts swore vengeance on St. Nick, but he was so untouchable and utterly brutal that no one wanted to risk going after him. After that, Cutter, shaken to the core, radically changed his life. He determined to go straight, got released, met Margarita, and turned his life around.

When Cutter learns of the opportunity to take down St. Nick, part of him burns with vengeance. But he's now a more mature man, not the hothead he used to be, and he carefully considers his vow never to do anything illegal or immoral again. His life may be frustrating and he may feel trapped in certain ways, but at least it's healthy and stable. This new life he's built cannot be risked, despite the raging vengeance inside him, driving him like an engine.

I see Apollo not so much as vengeful toward Cutter, but as someone who's willing to use anyone to get what he wants. There's real friendship between them—they were cellmates for eight years—but Cutter knows that Apollo always has something up his sleeve. If Apollo is unstable in any way, then it may not take all that much for him to go off-plan.

From St. Nick's point of view, is there any way a crime has been done to him that deserves vengeance? He's extremely volatile, so he'll perceive any trouble with buying this bank as a crime against him: "How dare they try to exclude me?" If St. Nick didn't have to be on his best behavior now, he might execute every banking official in sight. When they challenge him, they probably have no idea how close they are to sudden, awful death. If Cutter is playing the part of one of these inspectors, for example, then he'll be taking heat from St. Nick as part of his job.

In fact, St. Nick behaves like a dictator who views dissent as a crime—someone used to getting his way on every little thing (Saddam Hussein is an obvious example). A completely offbeat idea occurs to me: I went to school with the son of a dictator and he was a very powerful figure, even as a teenager. He had a real aura of power, and the stories we heard from him and his cousins were astonishing. Thinking about this has made me consider a completely random possibility: What if *Apollo*'s father had been a dictator years ago? That would add a fascinating level to his character, especially since I picture Apollo as a gregarious devil of a fellow—fun, dangerous, mesmerizing, and unpredictable.

A dictator's son is just a spontaneous hit-or-miss idea, an unexpected twist that popped up from the free-association process as part of working with the 36 Dramatic Situations. I was thinking about St. Nick's behavior when it occurred to me, but then I used it for Apollo. It may not amount to anything, but that's what the brainstorming process is like—you generate hundreds of possibilities and toss most of them. You can stumble onto completely unforeseen, stimulating possibilities if you let your brain run wild and free, so really push it—remember, it's the *entertainment* industry.

Bear in mind that all the above ideas came from playing around with *Crime Pursued by Vengeance*. They're not necessarily on target for this particular situation, but that's part of this process. When playing with the 36 Dramatic Situations, don't be afraid to take the train of thought wherever it leads. If a situation catalyzes an idea, no matter how seemingly bizarre the connection, then it's done its job. The situations are only triggers for the writer's mind. Screenwriting is not a rigid process, but a mercurial one. As this chapter shows, the tools can be a portal to seemingly unrelated types of creativity. One script may diverge into two; the ending may be slow in coming; details and the need to research may pop up at inopportune moments; and offbeat free-association ideas may arrive without reason or rhyme.

As various story ideas are examined through the lens of each Dramatic Situation, new options and fresh insights arise on things I've been wrestling with. Especially at this stage of development, the plot is up for grabs—anything goes and the sky's the limit. There's plenty of fun to be had playing with possibilities, which can be the best part of storytelling. With this tool, I work my way through each of the pertinent 36 Dramatic Situations like an inventor wandering through an electronics parts store: "Wow, I could use this. . . . I've got to have that. . . . I'm not sure what this is, but it's really thought-provoking and I'm taking it home with me."

Now let's examine the subheadings for *Crime Pursued by Vengeance*:

A. The avenging of a slain parent or ancestor.
   The avenging of a slain child or descendant.
   Vengeance for a child dishonored.
   The avenging of a slain wife or husband.
   Vengeance for the dishonor, or attempted dishonoring, of a wife.
   Vengeance for a mistress slain.
   Vengeance for a slain or injured friend.
   Vengeance for a sister seduced.
B. Vengeance for intentional injury or spoliation.
   Vengeance for having been despoiled during absence.
   Revenge for an attempted slaying.
   Revenge for a false accusation.
   Vengeance for violation.
   Vengeance for having been robbed of one's own.
   Revenge upon a whole sex for a deception by one.
C. Professional pursuit of criminals.

Vengeance for a slain or injured friend is obviously present in Cutter and Apollo's desire to avenge Frenchy. Once Cutter infiltrates St. Nick's circle, his excluded wife will demonstrate *The avenging of a slain wife* (she feels slain). Cutter's son could act out *Vengeance for a child dishonored* because he's been left out. Both Margarita and Mischa will be seeking *Vengeance for intentional injury or spoliation* and *Vengeance for violation*, as well as *Vengeance for having been robbed of one's own* when each feels that Cutter has turned his back on them.

Revenge for a false accusation is interesting because Cutter is a reformed liar and the truth has become very important to him. Being falsely accused of lying, even while he *is* in fact lying as part of the revenge plan, would be a huge deal to Cutter. He may overreact irrationally, which could complicate things. This possibility would probably never have occurred to me without this subheading triggering it.

If St. Nick has trouble acquiring the bank, he might seek vengeance, feeling as though he's being unfairly "robbed." That brings up *Vengeance for intentional injury or spoliation*, *Vengeance for violation*, and *Vengeance for having been robbed of one's own*. These situations apply to Cutter and Apollo as well, in terms of losing Frenchy. These three situations don't necessarily inspire any new possibilities or insights, but it doesn't hurt to look them over just in case they trigger anything fresh. Often it takes time to notice the hints of relevance, and handling a problem repeatedly from mildly different points of view can shake something loose or make the obvious become apparent.

Professional pursuit of criminals offers abundant possibilities. This can refer not only Sherlock Holmes but even to Michael Corleone—he happens to be a criminal himself, but part of his job is to ride herd on other criminals. The same is true here with Cutter and Apollo pursuing St. Nick; they might also be involved with other criminals, some of whom probably can't be trusted or have agendas of their own. This subheading also suggests the possibility of a lawman who is after either St. Nick, Apollo, or Cutter.

INTERRUPTING THE PROCESS TO BRAINSTORM

Before I take the 36 Dramatic Situations further into this story creation process, I want to stop, regroup, and shake things up. At this point, I've got a good beginning with a strong dilemma. But I feel as though I've applied these first three situations to a story still limited in scope and size, as though I'm stuck in one room of a huge mansion. The work I've done thus far makes me notice that big sections of the story need to be developed much further. I need to get some distance, broaden my point of view, break out the story, shake things up, violate what I've got so far, and go on a creative rampage—nothing's off limits. This tool has given me a good, hard whack in the head, jarring loose some story ideas that just won't wait. (Speaking of which, the book *A Whack on the Side of the Head: How You Can Be More Creative*, by Roger Von Oech, is a great book for expanding and freshening your creative process.)

Stepping Back and Shaking Things Up

In order not to become trapped in my earliest view of the plot, I want to really bang on it and make sure there isn't some other, truly great potential lurking in there that I haven't thought of. This may sound like a wild goose chase, but it reveals the true process of developing a script using all these screenwriting tools. If your story doesn't have some real juice to it, all the structuring in the world won't get the damn thing off the ground.

There are still lots of questions pertaining to the plot that must be laid out and explored. There are big holes in the script's structure as it stands now.

There are doubts about how to make it all work. There are out-to-lunch ideas to experiment with. There are different endings to try on, all of them unformed. There is major research yet to do. What business do I have trying to write a screenplay in the first place? I have a tiger by the tail—what should I do with it? Does any of this sound familiar? Each of you, if you write almost every day, has these questions constantly swirling around in your brain. If you're not exploring them and challenging yourself as much as you can, then your material will be mediocre. When the ideas start knocking at the door, it's best to let them enter. Write them down as they pour in, and worry later about returning to the tools to add structure and fill in the gaps.

So at this point in the process, I'll stop and wrestle with the story—its unformed sections, its rough spots, and all the questions inherent in it. Remember, the writing process is not a linear one; it often requires topsy-turvy methods to be fruitful. The pages below—one of my Writer's Notebook sections (set off in a different font as explained earlier)—are not related to any of the specific tools. They read like a journal entry, and will help me to wrangle the story into shape, to think things through, and to create solutions to the many plot problems that are routine in at this stage of developing a script. I continue working with the 36 Dramatic Situations on page 224.

Beefing Up the Comedy

One of the things I'd like to do is to make this script funnier. Give it a bit of an Elmore Leonard twist—some comic bite. I could make it into a savage thriller, and it may end up there yet, but I'd like to see if I can find a satiric edge. What are some possibilities for this? One of the things I stumbled onto is that Cutter could be much more challenged in his honest life. Perhaps he feels trapped; he's getting old and fat. He may be a hypochondriac or have to stay on mood-altering drugs to deal with reality. What if he needs antipsychotic drugs in order to keep him "normal," or pills in order to sleep?

This leads to the concept of Cutter being run down, defeated, or broken in some ways—the complete opposite of the man about whom we've heard these wild stories, the man who was unstoppable, high-strung, raving mad, indomitable, fearless, feisty, and the life of the party. This new, reformed man is small, broken, boring, pathetic, henpecked, and wasting away, providing a great contrast to the maniac who emerges when he reverts to his deceitful self later in the script. If he's a hypochondriac, he'll feel susceptible to practically everything—colds, flu, migraine headaches, insomnia, allergies—you name it. This has to be handled well if it's to come across as funny. What I'm trying for is to make Cutter pathetic at certain levels, laughable. But how do I maximize this without losing the audience? For this to work they need to be able to see themselves in him.

Basically, Cutter is now unfailingly honest, heroic, determined, realistic, and clear-eyed. But he can also feel trapped, depressed, lifeless, ill, and tired. He's got a nice wife, a good home, and a future free of crime; he is stable, is in love, goes to church, is a good father, and is happy in his own way. However, he's also in debt like much of middle-aged America, is getting old and fat with a bad back and bad teeth, has settled for what he's got, doesn't like his job, and often feels powerless. Once a wild animal, he's now kept in a cage at the zoo. He engages in a certain amount of self-deception to make his life work. All of this can render him a more universal and intriguing character, and can bring more comedy into the mix. You can see how I'm still playing with dilemma because adding this new layer further complicates his dilemma.

Crisis and Decision & Action need to be blazing in a plot like this, which promises catastrophic disaster. When a character who's a ticking time bomb gets dragged into an volatile situation, I rub my hands in glee, thinking, "Wow, I can't wait for it to all go haywire!" What I've seen since the first glimmer of this story is that Cutter would explode back into his wild persona in a desperate attempt to make this impossibly insane situation somehow succeed.

Exploding With Questions

My head is bursting with hundreds of questions about the raw possibilities for this plot. I'll lay some of them out:

1. How zany can this story get? I want it to be off the charts! I want people to be jumping out of their seats. This is hard to do, but it's my intention to blow the audience away with Cutter's virtuosity in lying. He should be stunning, astonishing, and brilliant.

2. It seems inevitable that St. Nick will discover who Cutter is beneath the disguise and what he's up to. Would St. Nick be completely onto him, or would he just discover that Cutter's not who he says he is? What level of desperate trouble would that put Cutter in? What would be the mechanics of this discovery or partial discovery?

3. Will Apollo betray Cutter? I've had it in the back of my mind that Apollo has a batch of counterfeit money he needs to move. Did he steal it? Did he manufacture it? Is it poor quality, so that he needs to palm it off on some sucker? Is the law onto him, so that he can't follow his normal process of circulating it? Is he in huge trouble? How desperate is he? How well-planned is his scheme? Is it a master plan dating way back?

4. If Cutter is on medications to stay "normal," then what happens when the meds are gone? Does Apollo substitute placebos because he needs the old lying Cutter to make an appearance? What's Cutter like without them? Dangerous? Crazy? Fun? This could complicate things immensely and be really funny and wacky.

5. What is involved when Cutter reverts to his old, out-of-control, lying self? How does this manifest itself? What kind of struggle does he put up? Does he consciously choose to go off the deep end in order to deal with the emerging situation? Does he know this could cost him everything? This is a big question and it should be central to the third act.

6. Is St. Nick's bank deal caving in or will it go through? Once St. Nick becomes legit, he'll be home free in the high-flying world of "legal theft" with its behind-the-scenes politics, corrupt corporations, and shady finance. Either way could spell disaster for Cutter. If the deal fails, then St. Nick would be after the "bank examiner" with a meat cleaver.

7. How does Cutter make his disguise as a bank examiner work? What are some possible ways for this cover to unravel? What could cause St. Nick to find out that Cutter isn't what he appears to be? Is there a stupid mistake or an accident? Does Apollo betray him? How much pressure is on Cutter as a bank examiner to certify St. Nick for this bank deal? Is he too obviously ignorant of banking regulations? Does he get caught up in his own complex web of lies? Does an old acquaintance show up out of the blue and blow his cover?

8. What about Cutter's son, Mischa? Does he inject himself into the mix and screw things up? Does he get taken hostage? Is he trying to help his dad? Is he trying to prove that he's got the goods to be a player in his dad's world? How much criminal ambition does he have? Has he been spying on Cutter? Did Apollo put him up to it or encourage him?

9. Does Cutter's wife, Margarita, find out what he's up to? Has he kept her totally in the dark? Does she spy on him? Does she distrust Apollo completely? Does she stumble onto their scheme? Perhaps she even sees Cutter while he's on the job.

10. What about the two strikes against Cutter? Has he committed new crimes that threaten to send him to jail for life? Is somebody onto him? Is Apollo threatening to turn him in for an old crime that's still an open case? Is Cutter falling deeper and deeper into the criminal mindset?

11. What about the law? Are the cops or the feds after St. Nick? Apollo? Cutter? What are the most extreme possibilities? Are the feds trying to entrap St. Nick before he vanishes into this legitimate enterprise? Is a crooked cop in on the deal, threatening to torpedo the whole plan?

12. Does a crook from St. Nick's past barge in on the situation like a bull in a china shop? St. Nick may be clean but he's got a past, and it could be catching up with him. Who else might want to destroy him? How chaotic and bizarre could things get? How dangerous? How funny?

13. What about St. Nick's legitimate connections? Does he have a senator buddy who needs St. Nick's skills to shepherd this through? How much muscle does the senator bring to the table? Does this make St. Nick a shoo-in to get the bank?

14. What outside influences might send everything to hell in a handbasket at precisely the wrong moment? A stock market crash? A corporate scandal? A political scandal? A war? A terrorist attack? A car accident? New laws? Perhaps it rains frogs. Just kidding.

15. In this type of plot, the question of Cutter's access to St. Nick's assets will be important. Does St. Nick's anxiety to become legit give Cutter a way in? What financial resources does St. Nick have? Wouldn't he be intensely suspicious of anyone examining them? How might some of his secrets slip out? How much does St. Nick begin to trust Cutter? Does he bribe Cutter to see things his way? Does Cutter get caught snooping into St. Nick's assets? What does he find? These questions constitute their own separate universe; some research will have to be done regarding banking practices.

16. What about a love interest? Not every movie has one, but most do, and it's a good thing to try out. This type of movie seems to want one. I don't think Cutter's wife will fit the bill because he most likely has to leave her behind to do this job. Perhaps there should be somebody eye-catching that Cutter is in daily contact with. What if St. Nick has a gorgeous secretary? What if she's his daughter? What if Cutter has to pretend to fall in love with her as part of the scam? What if she's really attracted to Cutter, but St. Nick will kill him if he lays a finger on her? What if Cutter is insane with lust for her? How complex could this get? How funny? How erotic? How dangerous?

17. What if this story takes an Inspector Clouseau–style twist? Could Cutter be like Clouseau? Would the script still work if it's that slapstick? Does this undermine the plot's intensity or add to it? It's certainly a sharply different take on the whole thing, and it has enter-taining potential.

18. What about Cutter's wife, Margarita? She's been underdevel-oped so far. Who is she? What's she like? What is her background? What makes her tick? She's rather clichéd now, the poor little pious wife who beats her fists helplessly on Cutter while he gets dragged back into his old life. What are some more multifaceted possibilities for her? Crazy idea: What if she works for Apollo?

19. How old is Apollo? He could be seventy and still look fifty if he takes great care of himself. Maybe he does t'ai chi to stay young. This would make for some dynamic possibilities because his past would be so much more extensive than one would suspect.

20. In what way is this a "perfect" crime? How has Apollo set up a plan that cannot fail? Is it really a perfect crime, or did that concept just serve as a springboard to get the story going? All there is so far is a golden opportunity to ruin St. Nick and maybe disappear with a lot of his money. This aspect has yet to be developed. Building a story out of an initial premise is like mud wrestling: You're in a slippery medium grappling with things that you can feel but not see, and everything's constantly shifting as you try to pull it together.

21. What are some opportunities to make this a perfect crime? Is there a foolproof way to take a huge bite out of St. Nick's hidden assets and get away scot-free? The more perfect the crime appears to be, the harder it is for Cutter to walk away from the job. Presumably Apollo has a reputation for coming up with great plans. Right now this question is absolutely central to the script, but I may come up with a hundred possibilities before finding one that works, or I might even discard altogether the idea of it being a perfect crime.

This last question must be pursued in depth because it's so central to the plot. To pull off the perfect crime, either (1) The victim must be unaware of the crime; (2) The victim must have no idea who did the crime; (3) The victim must believe the person who did the crime is dead and the stolen goods are irretrievable; (4) The victim must believe it was someone else who did the crime and got away clean; (5) The mark himself must get killed, with no suspicion falling on the crook, and therefore no investigation; (6) The mark must end up in jail forever, so there's no recourse, especially if the thief is unknown; (7) For some reason, the thief can never be caught for the crime; (8) The victim must think they foiled the crime, but actually didn't; or (9) Somebody else takes the blame for the crime. There may be dozens, possibly hundreds more ways to pull off the perfect crime, but this gets me started.

Within the current story construct, Cutter is pretending to be a bank examiner, which gives him access to St. Nick's assets. So what kind of perfect crime might be possible? Funds can be transferred electronically, making Cutter and Apollo rich—if they could they get away clean. What if instead Cutter exposes the hidden funds to law enforcement and to the IRS? Then the funds would be confiscated or tied up—disastrous for

St. Nick, which is an acceptable form of revenge (although without prof-it). Another possibility for revenge is to get St. Nick in so much trouble that his superiors (if he has any) will destroy him or even inflict a fate worse than death. In that case, assets could disappear in the confusion. Another option is to have the law storm in, with the ensuing chaos pro-viding a perfect opportunity for Cutter and Apollo to disappear with a large sum. Only St. Nick would ever know the money is gone, but if he's on the run, in jail, or dead, then they'll get away with it.

One of the problems I've been wrestling with is how Cutter would access St. Nick's finances, even if he is acting as a bank examiner. Why would St. Nick even begin to trust an outsider? It keeps sticking in my craw. As I turn the problem over in my mind, it occurs to me that St. Nick would much prefer a crooked bank examiner. Perhaps his books need to be cooked so they'll pass muster. Here's the idea that I came up with: Suppose that St. Nick and the senator (let's call him Senator Hutchings) bring in a crooked bank examiner (let's call him Shallott) who will guide St. Nick through the hurdles of buying a bank. Now suppose that when St. Nick poisoned that Kentucky town years ago over the racehorse cheating incident, Shallott's only family, his severely retarded and wheelchair-bound brother, was killed; he had lived in that town because he had loved horses above all else. This would instill in Shallott a fierce and undying hatred for St. Nick, but he's had to bide his time because St. Nick is too dangerous to mess with. Now this chance has opened up, so Shallott goes to his old friend Apollo and tells him about this once-in-a-lifetime opportunity to crush St. Nick. He needs help, and Apollo thinks Cutter is the best man for the job. Now I can work in Cutter as an assistant—he no longer has to know every-thing about banking, and he has access to St. Nick's books.

Creating Solutions

In answering the quesion above, another question is raised: What makes Cutter the right man for this job? Perhaps he should possess a few more specialized skills, such as being good with numbers and com-puters; perhaps he's a bit of a financial wizard. We know he is fear-less, is good at thinking on his feet, learns fast, can juggle a complex system of lies, is fearless, and makes a good team player—a consum-mate operator. Reminiscent of the vintage *Mission Impossible* TV shows, Cutter and Shallott are working an inside job with access to a corrupt leader's finances, trying to take advantage of a window of opportunity to topple him.

Now that Shallott and Cutter are invited into St. Nick's world to cook his books, the story is easier to develop. Shallott can work things so that St. Nick, eager for the banking commission's approval, will comply, divulging layer after layer of his secret finances. Presumably Shallott and Cutter are finding ways to shift his illegal assets around while putting his money into the reserve fund required by law in order to buy this bank. This must be done properly and with finesse, so as not to attract undesirable attention from the IRS and other predatory government entities.

If Cutter, Shallott, and Apollo trigger a fake investigation right as the bank deal is nearing completion—perhaps by bribing a crooked FBI official—this can help pull off their revenge. If Senator Hutchings is mentioned in connection with St. Nick, then he may have to run for cover, leaving St. Nick exposed. The bogus investigation won't stand up for long, but it doesn't necessarily have to. If St. Nick is distracted temporarily by the threat of the law, then his full attention won't be on what Shallott and Cutter are really up to. It's the basic principle of magic—get the audience watching one hand while the other does the disappearing act—akin to *The Sting*, in which the fake FBI agent was brought in by Paul Newman to get the Chicago cop off Robert Redford's back.

Cutter's Worst Enemy is His Guru

Another story twist that I stumbled onto is this: What if Cutter unexpectedly finds himself in awe of St. Nick when they start working together? St. Nick's skills as a liar and thief could really impress Cutter with their inspired genius. Cutter is unaccustomed to meeting someone who can lie circles around him. The staggering adroitness with which St. Nick and his circle maneuver is dazzling to Cutter. This adds a new wrinkle to his dilemma: It's harder for him to quit this operation, because he's "falling in love" with his worst enemy (*An Enemy Loved* from the 36 Dramatic Situations). Cutter sees a consummate artist at work and realizes he still has a lot to learn. He hates this guy's guts and yet finds himself in awe. His worst enemy has turned out to be a kind of guru to him.

On the flip side, St. Nick could be impressed and invite Cutter to work for him rather than just consult on this project. This would give Cutter deeper access to St. Nick but would also render him more vulnerable. If St. Nick does take him in, then Cutter might stick around and learn about a master plan, not only to destroy it, but also because it's intoxicating. He could be rubbing shoulders with world bankers, senators, corporate CEOs, aristocrats, CIA operatives and drug dealers—a clever mix of legal and illegal business that would make his head spin.

The Research Pays Off

Now we come to something that I hit upon after long hours of thinking, reading, and feeling stumped (see page 244 for the eureka
moment). I want Cutter to be dropped into the world of fat cats, big-
time players with their gigantic banks, corporations, and hidden agendas—the world of legalized theft and manipulation, where masterful
power brokers run things behind the scenes. My research hit on a
mega-scam that Senator Hutchings could set up, in which a government program provides guaranteed agricultural loans to third-world
countries. Hutchings is on the Senate Banking Committee and has
slipped a loophole into a new law at the eleventh hour. This highly
specialized loophole, combined with an obscure tax dodge, affords a
singular opportunity for him to make a vast fortune. Hutchings plans
to offer these loans to countries that are controlled by ruthless dictators and open to all kinds of under-the-table enterprises.

The catch is that Hutchings needs a bank to carry out his plan, but
he has to remain entirely behind the scenes as a silent partner. He seeks
out St. Nick, an old friend who has never even been indicted. He's
worked successfully with St. Nick before and knows St. Nick wants to go
legit. Senator Hutchings recommends Shallott, this crooked bank examiner, as someone who can help St. Nick use his hidden assets to rig the
process of buying a bank.

Creating a New Character

Now I'll add another character to the fold: Joseph Umbotha, an African
dictator from the imaginary country of Mambia who's anxious to do
business. The agricultural loan law allows the export of goods, but not
money, to a third world country struggling with corruption. The bank will
issue a loan for several hundred million dollars, possibly even billions, and
then pay the money to an agricultural corporation for supplies shipped
to Mambia. St. Nick and Hutchings get a kickback from the corporation
for steering business to them—and for the chance to import its genetically modified seed into Mambia. Umbotha uses the seed, agricultural
products, and farming equipment to create an immense modern plantation as his own private business, which will bring in a fortune over the
years. He will sell none of the food in his own country, preferring to
starve his enemies, but will sell and barter it internationally for weapons
and restricted equipment (some in deals set up by Hutchings, who again
gets a kickback). Payments are made for a while until the loan limit is
reached and then Umbotha defaults, causing the U.S. government to
repay St. Nick's bank since the loan is government-guaranteed.

The real kicker is that in exchange for all the lucrative agricultural equipment and goods, Umbotha allows Hutchings and St. Nick to set up a manufacturing plant in Mambia. He provides them with virtually free prison labor and raw materials for a ten-year period, after which this highly profitable operating factory will revert to Umbotha. But by then, Hutchings and St. Nick will use the profits to buy more banks around the world, building a banking empire.

St. Nick and Senator Hutchings work out the details in a secure room that has just been swept for bugs. Any electronic equipment within 100 feet will set off an alarm. But Cutter is hidden behind the wall with two cans and a string stretched taut between them, the primitive children's toy phone, which he uses to eavesdrop. He also hears St. Nick tell Hutchings that he's extremely impressed with Cutter and that he's going to offer him a job in the organization because he needs men with balls and brains like him. Cutter has just fought with St. Nick and thought he'd ruined the revenge operation, but he now learns that St. Nick actually admires him for standing up to him. Hutchings cautions St. Nick not to let Cutter know what's really going on, and St. Nick says he certainly won't for some time yet, but in the meantime they need someone who can think on his feet and who wants to make a ton of money. Plus, St. Nick says that if it all goes wrong, they can pin it on Cutter and, using their connections, get off scot-free. St. Nick stresses that Cutter kicks ass and if they can turn him, he'll be a valuable member of their team.

Catastrophe and Opportunity

Learning of this entire subversive scenario sets Cutter's brain reeling, and when he reports back to Apollo they realize they'll have to alter their plan. But the immensity of Hutchings's master plan also offers greater opportunity to ruin St. Nick, since Cutter will be taken inside the organization and promoted. Now there's a larger crime to derail but there's also higher risk, especially if St. Nick tries to use Cutter as a patsy. The drama is ratcheted up another few notches and Cutter's dilemma is further complicated. There's more money involved now, but there's also a real crime against humanity in Africa with the food scheme and the sweatshop factory. Cutter would also be furious about the American taxpayers being robbed of billions of dollars by the defaulted loans. This might anger Apollo, too, which would make the viewers like him more. In addition, Cutter's addiction is kicking in—he's got the itch to be involved in this type of high-level, high-stakes operation—and he's even more amazed at St. Nick's and Hutchings's brilliance. He knows it's wrong, but he simply must play their game and get involved in this high-wire adventure.

BACK TO EXPLORING
THE 36 DRAMATIC SITUATIONS

With all this new story material, let's return to our investigation of the 36 Dramatic Situations and continue building the plot. Our work with the first three situations (see page 207) showed how deep and wide you can and should go in exploring each situation to jump-start a story from scratch. From here on out I'll work leaner and move faster with this tool, and only list the subheadings particular to this story.

4. *Vengeance Taken for Kindred upon Kindred*

This situation suggests the possibility of infighting between St. Nick and the senator, as well as within their cabal of international bankers, arms merchants, drug smugglers, and CIA operatives. It also turns my attention to Cutter's family—the infighting and its ramifications for the plot. None of the subheadings conjure up anything for me, however.

5. *Pursuit*

Cutter and Apollo are in pursuit of St. Nick (for revenge and wealth), who is himself in pursuit of legitimacy and massive profits. Senator Hutchings is also after big money and power. Cutter is pursued by his demons, by his son, and perhaps by his wife. Cutter could also be pursued by a cop who spots him, remembers him from way back, and wants to punish him for an old crime or insult. Apollo may be pursued by the law, perhaps by someone that he ripped off, perhaps by other criminals who discover what he's up to. Apollo is certainly in pursuit of profits through his hidden agenda with counterfeit money. St. Nick is pursued by Shallott, who wants him dead, but there could also be an untimely and unexpected investigation into his criminal affairs. Two of the subheadings that click are *Fugitives from justice pursued for brigandage* (acts of piracy) *or political offenses, etc.*; and *A hero struggling against a power*.

6. *Disaster*

The reappearance of Apollo in Cutter's life at the beginning of the script is a disaster. Everything goes wrong at the worst possible moment for Cutter, including a betrayal (intentional or not) by Apollo. There's disaster for St. Nick as he sees his dreams of becoming an "aristocrat" fall apart, and for Senator Hutchings as he watches his potential billions disappearing. Margarita sees her family at risk of, or actually, falling apart. Mischa is being drawn into a disastrous life of crime, and gets caught up in St. Nick's terrible grasp at the crucial moment. The most literal disaster of the story is St. Nick's destruction of the horse racing town, including Shallott's brother. Also, Mischa not being able to get his dad to talk about his wild old days is a disaster from Mischa's point of view. Disaster can be physical or psychological, imminent or past. What are the worst disasters that could happen to Cutter at the most crucial moment? What are the craziest? The most unexpected? The funniest? The freakiest? Some relevant subheadings include *Defeat suffered*; *A monarch overthrown*; *A fatherland destroyed* (a good metaphorical image); *The fall of humanity* (St. Nick and Hutchings making money off the suffering of those starving in Africa); *An outrage suffered*; *Abandonment by a lover or a husband*; and *Children lost by their parents*.

7. *Falling Prey to Cruelty or Misfortune*

This situation obviously includes the appearance of Apollo in Cutter and Margarita's life. From St. Nick's point of view, cruelty is anything that impedes his ascension into high society and legalized theft, while Senator Hutchings does not wish to lose his big money and power. Cutter falls prey to Apollo's betrayal. Mischa and Margarita feel left out, forsaken by Cutter. An appearance by the law would be a misfortune for any of the players. Cutter turning out to be a traitor at the crucial moment is falling prey to cruelty from St. Nick and Hutchings's point of view. All the subheadings are useful: *The innocent made the victim of ambitious intrigue*; *The innocent despoiled by those who should protect*; *The powerful dispossessed and wretched*; *A favorite or an intimate finds himself forgotten*; and *The unfortunate robbed of their only hope*.

8. *Revolt*

Shallott and Apollo set a revolt in motion against St. Nick. Cutter rises up against his old life of crime, while his wife is in revolt against his gig with Apollo. Mischa is a troubled teen who rebels against his father. St. Nick and Hutchings are in revolt against their stations in life. Cutter leads a life-or-death mutiny against St. Nick and Hutchings when he's discovered and things fall apart. Some stimulating subheadings include *A conspiracy chiefly of one individual*; *A conspiracy of several*; and *Revolt of one individual, who influences and involves others*.

9. *Daring Enterprise*

Shallott's revenge idea is adventurous, Apollo is a daring and enterprising criminal, and Cutter is famous for his sense of adventure, even though he's inert at the beginning of the story. However, leaving a life of crime can be classified as daring, too. Hutchings and St. Nick are both involved in bold money-making rackets. Cutter's shift to the wild side late in the script is definitely a brash move. Appropriate subheadings include *Preparations for war*; *War*; *Recapture of a desired object*; *Adventurous expeditions*; and *Adventure undertaken for the purpose of obtaining a beloved woman* (Cutter trying to get back to his wife, or maybe being tempted by St. Nick's gorgeous secretary).

10. *Abduction*

Cutter is abducted by Apollo when he is enticed, pressured, blackmailed, and dragged into this plot against St. Nick. *Abduction* also suggests the possibility of a literal kidnapping: Mischa could be taken hostage by St. Nick and Hutchings. Could Cutter or Apollo take someone hostage? What about the law swooping in at a critical moment? Useful subheadings include *Rescue of a captive friend*; *Rescue of a child*; and *Rescue of a soul in captivity to error*.

11. *The Enigma*

Cutter is trying to figure out how to escape this whole affair, and at the same time trying to come to terms with his secret enthusiasm about being dragged into it. Margarita attempts to decipher what's going on with Cutter. Apollo, Cutter, and Shallott are trying to resolve the best way to take down St. Nick. Senator Hutchings and St. Nick are walking a tightrope to pull off their master plan without any glitches. Mischa is looking to crack the riddle of how to get some adventure out of his father. How can Cutter use the element of mystery to trick St. Nick? Is there anything mysterious about Apollo and Cutter's past that is concealed until late in the script? Useful subheadings: *Search for a person who must be found on pain of death*; *A riddle to be solved on pain of death*; *The same case, in which the riddle is proposed by the coveted woman*; and *Tests for the purpose of ascertaining the mental condition*.

12. *Obtaining*

This situation is pretty straightforward, since everybody's trying to obtain various things in this story. Some of them are tangible, such as wealth, and some are intangible—such as respect, integrity, culture, freedom, revenge, love, or power. All the subheadings are valuable: *Efforts to obtain an object by ruse or force*; *Endeavor by means of persuasive eloquence alone*; and *Eloquence with an arbitrator*.

13. *Enmity of Kinsmen*

There is animosity—huge or small, longstanding or momentary—between Cutter and Apollo; between St. Nick, Hutchings, and any of their underlings; between Mischa and Cutter; and between Cutter and Margarita. Constructive subheadings include *Reciprocal hatred*; *Hatred between relatives for reasons of self-interest*; *Hatred of the son for the father*; and *Mutual hatred*.

14. *Rivalry of Kinsmen*

Rivalry exists in the same patterns as above: Cutter–Apollo; St. Nick–Hutchings–underlings; Mischa–Cutter; and maybe Cutter–Margarita. Suggestive subheadings: *Rivalry of father and son, for an unmarried woman* (suggesting that Mischa is also drawn to St. Nick's secretary) and *Rivalry of friends*.

15. *Murderous Adultery*

This solution suggests an intriguing possibility: If Margarita finds out about an affair between Cutter and the secretary, perhaps she'll want to or even attempt to kill her. It also suggests that some kind of adultery creates bad blood in St. Nick and Hutchings's camp. A provocative subheading (probably entirely metaphorical) is *The slaying of a trusting lover*.

16. *Madness*

Cutter has recovered from the "madness" of his former life of lying and stealing, and now Apollo is dragging him back into it. Apollo introduces madness into Cutter's house by infecting Mischa with discontent and bringing discord into Cutter's marriage. The ferocity of Apollo, Cutter, and Shallott's vengeance against St. Nick is a form of madness. St. Nick is essentially a sociopath, and Senator Hutchings may well be, too. The planned revenge sting will get nutty when things fall apart at the crucial moment. Cutter will go crazy in an awe-inspiring way when he's backed into a corner—the crazier the better for the script's purposes. In fact, if he doesn't go off-the-charts wild, then the audience will feel cheated, because that's one of the inherent promises of this movie: seeing Cutter snap back into his old self as a phenomenal liar. There's the possibility that Apollo might have a history of insane behavior. In the end, if Mischa is scared away from a life of crime, then he will escape from that sort of madness. If Cutter ends up divulging what St. Nick and Senator Hutchings are up to, it will overturn the apple cart for many in Washington, D.C. Useful subheadings include *Kinsmen slain in madness*; *Lover slain in madness*; *Slaying or injuring of person not hated*; *Disgrace brought upon oneself through madness*; and *Loss of loved ones brought about by madness*.

17. *Fatal Imprudence*

Cutter knows that throwing his chips back in with Apollo is going to ruin his life. Apollo's effort to enact his hidden agenda with the counterfeit money may sink the whole plan. St. Nick and Hutchings seem to misjudge or underestimate Cutter, Shallott, and Apollo. Does Shallott die in the process of avenging his brother? Do Cutter, Apollo, Mischa, or Margarita recklessly endanger themselves? Does St. Nick die, or suffer a fate worse than death? Does Cutter make a dangerous mistake in the process of the sting? What's the worst mistake that he could possibly make? That St. Nick could make? All the subheadings are valuable: *Imprudence the cause of one's own misfortune*; *Imprudence the cause of one's own dishonor*; *Curiosity the cause of one's own misfortune*; *Loss of the possession of a loved one through curiosity*; and *Curiosity the cause of death or misfortune to others*.

18. *Involuntary Crimes of Love*

Cutter does not intend to hurt or betray his wife or son, nor does Apollo mean to betray Cutter or put him in mortal danger. Cutter may unintentionally mistreat Apollo; St. Nick and Hutchings may do the same to each other. All the subheadings are explicitly sexual in nature (see page 78), so they're not much use to us here.

19. *Slaying of a Kinsman Unrecognized*

Cutter feels as though Apollo, not recognizing who he has become, is "slaying" him with the pressure to join the scheme against St. Nick. Mischa feels left out of his father's life and his confidence, and he also feels excluded when Cutter goes off with Apollo. Margarita feels left out, too—betrayed and abandoned. Are there any potential, partial, or perceived betrayals between St. Nick and Hutchings? Interesting subheadings include *Being upon the point of killing a son unknowingly*; *The same case, strengthened by Machiavellian instigations*; *Being upon the point of slaying a brother unknowingly*; *A father slain unknowingly, through Machiavellian advice*; *Involuntary killing of a loved woman* and *Being upon the point of killing a lover unrecognized* (both metaphorical in this case); and *Failure to rescue an unrecognized son* (perhaps the most potent option of all).

20. *Self-sacrifice for an Ideal*

Cutter has sacrificed to live an honest life, but he also owes his life to Apollo and now feels the need to repay the debt. How much is he willing to risk to ruin St. Nick? Apollo and Shallott both feel very strongly about getting revenge on St. Nick. Does Shallott sacrifice his life to help Cutter pull off the scam? Subheadings that evoke a response include *Sacrifice of life for the sake of one's word*; *Life sacrificed for the success of one's people*; *Life sacrificed in filial piety*; *Life sacrificed for the sake of one's faith* (not literally one's religion, but one's bond or word); *Both love and life sacrificed for one's faith, or a cause*; and *Sacrifice of well-being to duty*.

21. *Self-sacrifice for Kindred*

Cutter and Apollo are willing to put themselves in harm's way to avenge Frenchy. Cutter will do anything for his wife or for his son, who may risk everything to rescue his father in the end. Cutter and Apollo also seem willing to do anything for each other. Is there any of this between St. Nick and Senator Hutchings, or with their underlings for them? Does Shallott risk everything to avenge his brother or to save Cutter so he can complete the revenge? Some useful subheadings are *Life sacrificed for that of a relative or a loved one*; *Life sacrificed for the happiness of a relative or a loved one*; *Ambition sacrificed for the happiness of a parent*; *Ambition sacrificed for the life of a parent*; *Love sacrificed for the sake of a parent's life*; and *Love sacrificed for the happiness of one's child*.

22. *All Sacrificed for a Passion*

This situation is right at the nucleus of the script, driving the Dilemma. Cutter has given up his criminal life out of love for his wife and passion for his freedom. Now Apollo is asking Cutter to sacrifice his new life for the chance to destroy St. Nick, whom they both hate passionately. Shallott is willing to risk everything to avenge his brother. St. Nick's passion to be one of the fat cats and to escape from the world of cops and robbers, drives him to sacrifice his life in the underworld—he has to give up his anonymity and his hidden wealth. But this will enable him to join the big boys' club, where he will have godlike power and be above the law in many ways. Senator Hutchings is willing to risk everything for the chance to become a billionaire and to acquire more power. Mischa will risk everything to break into his father's exciting world; Margarita may do the same in an attempt to rescue Cutter from this same world. When Cutter goes wild at the crisis point of this story, he risks everything in his fervor to take down St. Nick and his operation. In the end, if Cutter tells the whole truth in an attempt to destroy St. Nick, then he will again renounce his underworld life because of his passion for freedom, family, truth, stability, love, and happiness. *All Sacrificed for a Passion* is what the whole movie is about—intense passion, intense sacrifice, intense change. From both sides of the equation, it's about driving, raging, unstoppable willpower. Interesting subheadings include *Religious vows of chastity broken for a passion* (a nice analogy for Cutter breaking his vow never to lie); *Respect for a priest destroyed* (Margarita losing respect for Cutter); *A future ruined by passion*; *Ruin of mind, health, and life*; *Ruin of fortunes, lives, and honors*; and *Temptations destroying the sense of duty, of pity, etc.*

23. *Necessity of Sacrificing Loved Ones*

Cutter is faced with the necessity of sacrificing his loved ones as soon as Apollo shows up: Apollo needs him to leave his family behind for the job. If Apollo's hidden agenda with the counterfeit money is in play, then he may be faced with having to sacrifice Cutter. Does Mischa contemplate putting his father at risk to fulfill his dreams of becoming a high-rolling criminal? This is a dark possibility, but it could add more of that enticing danger to the script. St. Nick may come to truly like Cutter, but he'll face the necessity of getting rid of him if he suspects the truth about Cutter. St. Nick and Senator Hutchings might consider throwing each other to the wolves when things go bad. The following subheadings are suggestive: *Necessity for sacrificing a daughter* (or son) *in the public interest*; *Duty of sacrificing one's child, unknown to others, under the pressure of necessity*; *Duty of sacrificing, under the same circumstances, one's father or husband*; and *Duty of contending with a friend*.

24. *Rivalry of Superior and Inferior*

Rivalry of superior and inferior is always a dynamic situation. Who has the upper hand—where the power lies—is a crucial question. In this script, all the relationships revolve around the struggle over who's the superior operator. This is active between Cutter and Apollo since Cutter never trusts Apollo, even though they're blood brothers. It's active between St. Nick and Hutchings for similar reasons, and in the way Cutter maneuvers to find a way to take St. Nick down. *Rivalry of Superior and Inferior* will especially ring true once St. Nick discovers who Cutter really is and what he's up to. It's evident between Mischa and Cutter in their struggle for dominance, as well as between Cutter and Margarita as she tries to force him to live up to his vow. Intriguing subheadings include *Rivalry of a mortal and an immortal* (various cases can be made for who is the "immortal"); *Rivalry of a magician and an ordinary man* (again, who's the "magician" in any given scene?); *Rivalry of conqueror and conquered*; *Rivalry of a king and a noble*; *Rivalry of a powerful person and an upstart*; *Rivalry of rich and poor*; *Rivalry of an honored man and a suspected one*; and *Rivalry of two who are almost equal*.

25. *Adultery*

Will Cutter have an affair with St. Nick's secretary? This raises lots of story options, including what Margarita is going to do if she finds out. Are there other potential adulterous situations that could complicate the plot? Are there possibilities of metaphoric adultery, like a betrayal of sorts? The subheadings *A wife betrayed for debauchery*; *A good husband betrayed for an inferior rival*; and *Vengeance of a deceived wife* all offer great story possibilities.

26. *Crimes of Love*

Cutter sees himself in a position of betraying his wife, and she certainly feels that she is being betrayed. Apollo betrays his old friend Cutter, and Mischa feels abandoned by his father—both transgressions of love. All the subheadings are entirely sexual in nature (see page 80), and so are not useful here.

27. *Discovery of the Dishonor of a Loved One*

Discovery of the Dishonor of a Loved One would obviously occur when Cutter discovers he's being betrayed by Apollo, or when Margarita and Mischa learn of Cutter's plans with Apollo, or when St. Nick finds out who Cutter really is and what he's up to. This raises the question of a possible betrayal between partners-in-crime St. Nick and Hutchings. Dynamic subheadings include *Discovery of a father's shame*; *Discovery that one's lover is a scoundrel*; and *Duty of punishing a son condemned under law which the father has made*.

28. *Obstacles to Love*

There are obstacles to the love between Cutter and Margarita, possibly to the lust between Cutter and St. Nick's secretary, to the father/son relationship between Cutter and Mischa, and between Cutter and Apollo. One possible relevant applicable subheading is *A free union impeded by the incompatibility of temper of the lovers* (Cutter and Margarita, Cutter and secretary).

29. *An Enemy Loved*

Cutter's relationship with Apollo is an example of *An Enemy Loved*, because as tight as they are, Cutter knows that Apollo is simply not to be trusted. Cutter's relationship with St. Nick shows elements of this situation in terms of fascination with an enemy. If Cutter is astonished by how phenomenally skillful St. Nick is, he must face that his worst enemy is his guru. Cutter's passion for the secretary could be an enemy loved depending on how much of an enemy she really is—and she might be a deadly one. Cutter's respect for Senator Hutchings is also an enemy loved. Does St. Nick still admire Cutter's talent even after he finds out what Cutter is up to? The only significant subheading is *The loved one hated by kinsmen of the lover* (if St. Nick's secretary is related to him).

30. *Ambition*

Each character has lofty ambitions, from Cutter, Apollo, and Shallott wanting to destroy St. Nick, to Hutchings's and St. Nick's ambition to make billions. Cutter also shows his aspiration to tell the truth and follow the straight path. Mischa has the misplaced ambition to be a criminal, and Margarita fosters powerful ambitions for her family. Apollo never quits; his ambition is endless and probably pathological. It's interesting to isolate each person's ambition and look at its origins, how it plays out, how it changes, and how far each character will go to achieve it. All the subheadings are suggestive, including *Ambition watched and guarded against by a kinsman, or by a person under obligation*; *Rebellious ambition*; and *Ambition and covetousness heaping crime upon crime*.

31. *Conflict with a God*

Cutter versus St. Nick is a clear-cut conflict with a "god," but Cutter is a deity in his own right, as St. Nick will discover when their fight to the finish kicks in. Cutter versus Apollo, and Mischa versus Cutter, both play out similarly. Cutter is trying to escape from the godlike, all-powerful pull of his criminal addictions. His conflict with Margarita also falls in this category, because she's up against an unstoppable force of nature, a god of mischief, a wild man. All the subheadings are useful: *Struggle against a deity*; *Strife with the believers in a god*; *Controversy with a deity*; *Punishment for contempt of a god*; and *Punishment for pride before a god*.

32. *Mistaken Jealousy*

Is Cutter really having an affair with St. Nick's gorgeous nymphomaniac secretary, or does Margarita just think he is? Do any of the characters set up a situation intentionally to make someone jealous? Is Mischa envious of Cutter's involvement in this criminal world, while in truth Cutter is having a horrible time? (I've been playing with the possibility that both Mischa and Margarita have separately tracked Cutter, discovered his secret mission, and begun spying on him. This adds significant complications and could be fun.) Among the subheadings that may prove useful are: *The mistake originates in the suspicious mind of the jealous one*; *Baseless jealousy aroused by malicious rumors*; and *Jealousy suggested by a traitor who is moved by hatred or self-interest.*

33. *Erroneous Judgment*

Cutter knows from the beginning that going after St. Nick is a bad idea. Later, he is getting in over his head and knows he's going to make a bad choice or a serious misstep. Cutter is dealing with Mischa's questionable choices in life. Margarita is questioning Cutter's judgment in terms of his loyalty to her and their shared ideals. Apollo is misjudging his enemies, St. Nick misjudges Cutter and the situation, and Nick and Hutchings likewise misjudge each other. Also, I've been figuring that Mischa will make a disastrous choice at a critical moment. Interesting options include *False suspicion where faith is necessary*; *False suspicion aroused by a misunderstood attitude of a loved one*; *False suspicions drawn upon oneself to save a friend* (a particularly intriguing possibility); *They fall upon the innocent*; *The accusation is allowed to fall upon an enemy*; *The error is provoked by an enemy*; *False suspicion thrown by the real culprit upon one of his enemies*; and *False suspicion thrown by the real culprit upon the second victim against whom he has plotted from the beginning* (which could lead to a reversal of fortunes).

34. *Remorse*

Cutter feels remorse for abandoning his straight life. Margarita feels it, too, because she's unable to stop him from following Apollo's influence. Does Apollo feel any remorse? How about Mischa? St. Nick is notorious for his lack of conscience, so he has utterly no remorse. Does Cutter's remorse send him back to the truth at the very end? Appropriate subheadings include *Remorse for a parricide* (if Mischa puts Cutter in harm's way); *Remorse for an assassination* (bear in mind, this isn't necessarily literal); *Remorse for a fault of love*; and *Remorse for an adultery.*

35. *Recovery of a Lost One*

Cutter re-emerges into his old criminal self—falling back into his addictions, a way of life that he loves. Apollo gets his old partner back. In the end, won't

Cutter recover his normal, wonderfully boring life, and a son who has been scared straight? Is St. Nick trying to recover his innocence by escaping the world of crime? Does Senator Hutchings yearn to regain some old family glory? (There are no subheadings for this situation.)

36. *Loss of Loved Ones*

Cutter thinks fondly on his riotous days and misses them; but in returning to those ways, he's torn from his family. Shallott has lost his only family member because of St. Nick. Hutchings and St. Nick lose their gigantic victory at the last minute. Do Apollo and Cutter lose each other in the end? Some useful subheadings are *Witnessing the slaying of kinsmen while powerless to prevent it*; *Helping to bring misfortune upon one's people through professional secrecy*; and *Learning of the death of a kinsman or ally* (various characters could die or be "lost" at the end of this script).

As you can see, I got plenty of mileage out of the 36 Dramatic Situations. In fact, I found much of my plot through this in-depth exploration. These thirty-six elements are the fundamental building blocks of all storytelling, the DNA that story worlds consist of, and you can organize them in any way that suits your needs. I'll make many passes over the 36 Dramatic Situations before I'm done, building the story and revising it (usually looking only at the main thirty-six on subsequent passes), but each time through I find fresh nuance. This tool often suggests subtle ideas, the little differences that can make a story function, make it real, or add that special "magic something." You can see now how useful the subheadings are because they offer so much nuance. I feel as if I've scoured every inch of this story's world with this tool—as if I've left no stone unturned. There's much more work to do on this plot, but the 36 Dramatic Situations have taken it far. I trust that you now feel at home with this process. The more you use it, the more comfortable it will feel. And remember, there are no wrong choices with this tool. If a situation triggers an idea, any idea, then it's done its job.

Using the Enneagram

Let's now explore what the Enneagram has to offer our script in terms of character development. A sophisticated personality-profiling system, this tool is similar in nature to the 36 Dramatic Situations, as it provides an extensive catalog of attributes with which to develop characters. With incisive psychological insights and a broad comprehension of human nature, it's a state-of-the-art tool for any writer. Rereading Chapter 4 on the Enneagram before going through this chapter will help you master its use.

DEVELOPING THE CHARACTER OF CUTTER

The character of Cutter offers up three distinct alternatives. He seems to be a 7, The Enthusiast, when his wild side comes out, and yet when we first meet him he might be a 1, The Reformer, or a 6, The Loyalist. Three entirely different personalities seem like a fun possibility for this particular movie. As described by The Enneagram Institute, a 7 in the Healthy aspect is "highly responsive, excitable, enthusiastic about sensation and experience. [The] most extroverted type: stimuli bring immediate responses—they find everything invigorating. Lively, vivacious, eager, spontaneous, resilient, cheerful." This is what I pictured the former Cutter to be like: excitable, half-cocked, wild-eyed, and devilish.

A 7 in the Average aspect can "become adventurous and 'worldly wise,' but less focused, constantly seeking new things and experiences." Then we strike gold:

> Unable to discriminate what they really need, [7s] become hyperactive, unable to say "no" to themselves, throwing self into constant activity. Uninhibited, doing and saying whatever comes to mind: storytelling, flamboyant exaggerations, witty wisecracking, performing. Fear being bored: in perpetual motion, but do too many things—many ideas but little follow through. Get into conspicuous consumption and all forms of

excess. Self-centered, materialistic, and greedy, never feeling that they have enough. Demanding and pushy, yet unsatisfied and jaded. Addictive, hardened, and insensitive.

This is right on the money for the untamed Cutter. There are so many particular traits to build with, like working with a specialized Lego set that comes with wheels, pulleys, gears, and everything you need to make realistic, functioning constructs. The last two sentences would be an interesting addition to the old Cutter; in fact, the description sounds like a career criminal. I always saw him as addictive, but "demanding," "pushy," "unsatisfied," "jaded," "hardened," and "insensitive" are much more tangible flaws. In addition, these traits would raise tension by helping the audience not to feel safe around him as the movie nears its end.

Now let's look at the Unhealthy aspects of a 7:

> Desperate to quell their anxieties, [7s] can be impulsive and infantile: do not know when to stop. Addictions and excess take their toll: debauched, depraved, dissipated escapists, offensive and abusive. / In flight from self, acting out impulses rather than dealing with anxiety or frustrations: go out of control, into erratic mood swings, and compulsive actions (manias). Finally, their energy and health is completely spent: become claustrophobic and panic-stricken. Often give up on themselves and life: deep depression and despair, self-destructive overdoses, impulsive suicide. Generally corresponds to the Manic-Depressive and Histrionic personality disorders.

This is a fascinating look at the low end or dark side of Cutter. Rich in flaws, it speaks of a broken personality and multiple disorders—all of which I knew I needed for Cutter. Previously, they existed merely in the abstract, if at all, and now here's a missing section of his personality staring me in the face. In this way, the Enneagram is like the 36 Dramatic Situations; an intensely valuable resource to draw on, it can save a lot of brain-wracking and fumbling along blind alleys.

The Enneagram helps to reveal why Cutter went straight. The miserable downside of his persona can be very intense and hard to live with. Words like "desperate," "infantile," "excess," "depraved," "out of control," "erratic mood swings," and "manias" are all so vivid, intense, and suggestive. Then we've got the even darker elements of "deep depression and despair," "self-destructive overdoses," "impulsive suicide." These traits are bad news, and they go to the bottom of a full-spectrum portrait of Cutter. They're a real eye-opener, the traits of a real human being rather than just a limited, two-dimensional take on the character whom I've been seeing in my mind's eye. As I develop him further, I'll be paying careful attention to these promising suggestions.

Now let's explore the other side of Cutter's personality—the sober, honest, and ardent husband, father, churchgoer, and community man. This Cutter jumps out at me as a 1, The Reformer:

> Conscientious with strong personal convictions: They have
> an intense sense of right and wrong, personal religious and
> moral values. Wish to be rational, reasonable, self-disci-
> plined, mature, moderate in all things. Extremely principled,
> always want to be fair, objective, and ethical: truth and justice
> primary values. Sense of responsibility, personal integrity,
> and of having a higher purpose often make them teachers
> and witnesses to the truth.

These traits align with my image of the reformed Cutter, and I want to embed them deeper in him. This is the man I want to open the movie with.

I'm also thinking about the person I want Cutter to be at the end of the movie. I see him being free from hypochondria, medications, claustrophobia, and all his negative baggage. Healthy 1s at their best "become extraordinarily wise and discerning. By accepting what is, they become transcendentally realistic, knowing the best action to take in each moment. Humane, inspiring, and hopeful: The truth will be heard." This Cutter is not just back to where he was before Apollo dragged him into the scheme, but has actually improved quite a lot from this ordeal. He's a real hero.

An Average 1 can "become high-minded idealists, feeling that it is up to them to improve everything: crusaders, advocates, critics. Into 'causes' and explaining to others how things 'ought' to be." I hadn't thought of these aspects for Cutter's reformed personality; they help to flaw him at the film's beginning, keeping him human. There are also comic possibilities in this Cutter as a crusader who can get preachy, "orderly and well-organized, but impersonal, puritanical, emotionally constricted, rigidly keeping their feelings and impulses in check. Often workaholics—'anal-compulsive,' punctual, pedantic, and fastidious." The comedy will be enhanced if Cutter represents the fussy little repressed busybody that people like to laugh at. There should be as much contrast as possible between the Cutter we meet at the beginning and who he becomes when he roars to life late in the story.

There is comic pay dirt as well in Cutter's being "very opinionated about everything: correcting people and badgering them to 'do the right thing'—as [he] see[s] it. Impatient, never satisfied with anything unless it is done according to [his] prescriptions. Moralizing, scolding, abrasive, and indignantly angry." These characteristics are fun because, played properly, this prissy, puritanical anger would be the polar opposite of Cutter's frenzied self. This gives him some real flaws to stress his marriage; it's not all hearts and flowers in Camelot. As I look at the Unhealthy aspects, I don't see too much that I'd want to use: I want him to be in fairly decent shape.

I also see aspects of a 6, The Loyalist, in Cutter. Look at some of this type's Healthy aspects:

> Trust important: bonding with others, forming permanent relationships and alliances. Dedicated to individuals and movements in which they deeply believe. Community builders: responsible, reliable, trustworthy. Hard-working and persevering, sacrificing for others, they create stability and security in their world, bringing a cooperative spirit.

This sums up much of what I'm looking for in Cutter as the story opens—someone who is rooted, or trying to root himself, into his community. There are other intriguing possibilities in the average aspect of a 6 that I'll come back to as I develop the character further, but for now the above attributes provide material that I'll integrate into my portrait of the lawful and earnest Cutter.

DEVELOPING THE CHARACTER OF APOLLO

I see Apollo also as a 7, sharing many of Cutter's attributes. But he also exhibits aspects of a 5, The Investigator: a good planner, the intense cerebral type "possessing good foresight and prediction" as well as "mak[ing] pioneering discoveries and find[ing] entirely new ways of doing and perceiving things," a personality naturally inclined toward "model building, preparing, practicing, and gathering more resources." Traits also interesting for this character are "provocative and abrasive, with intentionally extreme and radical views."

But I'm looking at Apollo as a possible 6, The Loyalist, too: "Able to elicit strong emotional responses from others: very appealing, endearing, lovable, affectionate. Trust important: bonding with others, forming permanent relationships and alliances. Dedicated to individuals and movements in which they deeply believe."

Then again, he has some attributes of an 8, The Challenger:

> Self-assertive, self-confident, and strong: [8s] have learned to stand up for what they need and want. A resourceful, "can do" attitude and passionate inner drive. Decisive, authoritative, and commanding: the natural leader others look up to.

Take initiative, make things happen: champion people, provider, protective, and honorable, carrying others with their strength.

At their best, 8s are "courageous, willing to put [themselves] in serious jeopardy to achieve their vision and have a lasting influence," while the Average aspects of 8s result in

enterprising, pragmatic, "rugged individualists," wheeler-dealers. Risk-taking, hardworking, denying own emotional needs. Begin to dominate their environment, including others: want to feel that others are behind them, supporting their efforts. Swaggering, boastful, forceful, and expansive: the "boss" whose word is law. Proud, egocentric, want to impose their will and vision on everything, not seeing others as equals or treating them with respect.

An Unhealthy 8 is more likely to be "the criminal and outlaw, renegade, and con artist" who "develop[s] delusional ideas about their power, invincibility, and ability to prevail: megalomania, feeling omnipotent, invulnerable." These all offer interesting dimensions for Apollo.

You can see that I'm not just blindly following any one of these types, but rather exploring and drawing from each as needed. While a person tends to be predominantly one of these personalities, he or she will often be a mix of types. Plus, as a screenwriter and not a professional personality specialist, I harbor no special loyalty to the study of the Enneagram. I can borrow from all the nine types for specific character traits to make up one of my characters. For instance, I see Apollo predominantly as a 7, but I keep an open mind and may build him out of as many traits and types as are useful.

DEVELOPING THE CHARACTER OF ST. NICK
I see St. Nick as a straight-up 8, The Challenger: "the powerful, dominating type: self-confident, decisive, willful, and confrontational." His obvious traits include:

Self-assertive, self-confident, and strong: [has] learned to stand up for what [he] need[s] and want[s]. A resourceful, "can do" attitude and passionate inner drive. Decisive, authoritative, and commanding: the natural leader others look up to. Take[s] initiative, make[s] things happen.

One of the things I'm playing with is for Cutter to unexpectedly look up to St. Nick, mainly for his and Senator Hutchings's astronomical ability to deceive.

Some of the attributes above could give St. Nick some good or admirable qualities that make him a multidimensional character and further complicate the plot as well as Cutter's dilemma.

St. Nick should have substantially negative character traits, since he's the central antagonist. As described while developing Apollo, the Average 8 can be "swaggering" and "boastful," "proud" and "egocentric, want[ing] to impose their will and vision on everything, not seeing others as equals or treating them with respect. . . . Confrontational, belligerent, creating adversarial relationships. Everything a test of wills, and they will not back down." On the Unhealthy side, these individuals "develop delusional ideas about their power, invincibility, and ability to prevail: megalomania, feeling omnipotent, invulnerable." They are prone to "recklessly over-extending" themselves. These evocative traits—many of which would not have been solidified without studying the Enneagram for this character—suggest a lot of dynamic possibilities for St. Nick, real flaws that make him more human and give him vulnerabilities that Cutter and Apollo can exploit.

DEVELOPING THE CHARACTER
OF SENATOR HUTCHINGS

It is easy to categorize Senator Hutchings as a 3, The Achiever: "the success-oriented, pragmatic type: adaptable, excelling, driven, and image-conscious." I see him as a highly honored senator, so part of his disguise would be his appearance as "adaptable, desirable, charming, and gracious. Ambitious to improve [himself], to be 'the best [he] can be'—often become outstanding, a human ideal, embodying widely admired cultural qualities. Highly effective: others are motivated to be like [him] in some positive way." Cutter might find himself mesmerized by these attributes. At his best, Hutchings can be "modest and charitable, [with] self-deprecatory humor and a fullness of heart. . . . Gentle and benevolent." The more of these good qualities the Senator displays, the more complex and well-rounded a character he becomes. What great camouflage!

In the Average aspect Hutchings can be

> terrified of failure. . . . Compar[ing him]self with others in
> search for status and success. [3s] become careerists, social
> climbers, invested in exclusivity and being the "best." Become
> image-conscious, highly concerned with how they are per-
> ceived. Begin to package themselves according to the expec-
> tations of others and what they need to do to be successful.

This sounds very much like a career politician. Also consider these traits of an Average 3:

Premeditated, losing touch with their own feelings beneath a smooth facade. Problems with intimacy, credibility, and "phoniness" emerge. Want to impress others with their superiority: constantly promoting themselves, making themselves sound better than they really are. Narcissistic, with grandiose, inflated notions about themselves and their talents. Exhibitionistic and seductive, as if saying "Look at me!" Arrogance and contempt for others.

This connects to the flaws that we just examined in St. Nick—ego problems that could give Cutter and Apollo a handhold they desperately need for the success of their plans.

Looking into the Unhealthy aspect finds that when 3s begin

fearing failure and humiliation, they can be exploitative and opportunistic, covetous of the success of others, and willing to do "whatever it takes" to preserve the illusion of their superiority. Devious and deceptive so that their mistakes and wrongdoings will not be exposed. Untrustworthy, maliciously betraying or sabotaging people to triumph over them . . . relentless, obsessive about destroying whatever reminds them of their own shortcomings and failures. Psychopathic, murder. Generally corresponds to the Narcissistic personality disorder.

This is rich material for developing an extremely ambitious, fiercely intelligent, devious, charming, high-powered, gentlemanly cutthroat. While accustomed to respect, power, and privilege as a United States senator, Hutchings will be a dangerous man when his back is against the wall. Notice that when we look at these personality attributes with a specific character in mind, the Enneagram springs to life and we're able to give our character a full spectrum of dynamic, human qualities.

DEVELOPING THE CHARACTER OF MISCHA

I see Mischa as a 4, The Individualist. Since he is rather unhealthy psychologically, not many of the Healthy aspects look useful. The 4's Average aspects lead them to

heighten reality through fantasy, passionate feelings, and the imagination. / To stay in touch with feelings, they interiorize everything, taking everything personally, but become self-absorbed and introverted, moody and hypersensitive, shy and self-conscious, unable to be spontaneous or to "get out of themselves." Stay withdrawn to protect their self-image and to buy time to sort out feelings. Gradually think that they are different from others, and feel that they are exempt from living as everyone else does. They become melancholy dreamers, disdainful, decadent, and sensual, living in a fantasy world. Self-pity and envy of others leads to self-indulgence, and to becoming increasingly impractical, unproductive, effete, and precious.

All of this depiction is very useful, presenting a good palette of colors with which to paint Mischa. Giving him traits that relate to fantasy and imagination, making him "introverted, moody, and hypersensitive," and allowing him to think that he's different and exempt from normal rules give him depth and flaws.

Let's look at Mischa's potential Unhealthy aspects:

> When dreams fail, become[s] self-inhibiting and angry at self, depressed and alienated from self and others, blocked and emotionally paralyzed. Ashamed of self, fatigued and unable to function. Tormented by delusional self-contempt, self-reproaches, self-hatred, and morbid thoughts: everything is a source of torment. Blaming others, [4s] drive away anyone who tries to help them. Despairing, feel hopeless and become self-destructive, possibly abusing alcohol or drugs to escape. In the extreme: Emotional breakdown or suicide is likely. Generally corresponds to the Avoidant, Depressive, and Narcissistic personality disorders.

This is all good material: If he's "depressed," "alienated," "tormented," "self-destructive," and prone to "abusing alcohol or drugs," I've got a lot to work with to build the character of a troubled teenager who can turn either good or bad.

DEVELOPING THE CHARACTER
OF MARGARITA

I can see Margarita as a 2, The Helper: "the caring, interpersonal type: generous, demonstrative, people-pleasing, and possessive." She would seem to have great qualities:

> Empathetic, compassionate, feeling for others. Caring and concerned about their needs. Thoughtful, warm-hearted, forgiving and sincere. Encouraging and appreciative, able to see the good in others. Service is important, but takes care of self too: They are nurturing, generous, and giving—a truly loving person.

Margarita is a great wife for Cutter, and we see why he hesitates to put his marriage in jeopardy. Naturally, there are some attributes I can use to flaw her a bit:

> [2s] become overly intimate and intrusive: They need to be needed, so they hover, meddle, and control in the name of love. Want others to depend on them: give, but expect a return: send double messages. Enveloping and possessive: the codependent, self-sacrificial person who cannot do enough for others—wearing themselves out for everyone.

So I can see why Cutter might also want to escape from her. If she finds out what Cutter is up to and discovers his affair with St. Nick's secretary, then she's going to flip out and be insanely envious. While this isn't explicit in the description of a 2, I can take the description further and paint my own portrait of an enraged, jealous woman. I don't need to draw everything from this resource; it's a valuable, thought-provoking set of character traits, but there is no need to be limited to it.

DEVELOPING THE CHARACTER OF SHALLOTT

Here's your assignment: Figure out which Enneagram type Shallott is or should be or could be. You've seen enough of him to take a whack at it. Look through the nine types and determine which seem to click for him, or which would make him a rich character for this movie. Which type would be fiercely dedicated to revenge? I'm thinking of having Shallott go to pieces when the going gets tough, leading St. Nick to murder him, so which type would tend to fall apart under pressure? Or more specifically, *how* does each of the various personality types fall apart under pressure? Don't be afraid to go against type and explore the opposite of what is expected of an accountant; don't be afraid to play with who he is. There is no wrong answer, and there are nine right ones.

This has been a tour through the use of the Enneagram in building an actual script. You can see how I used it in various ways, driving on its strengths but not being a servant to it. I'll definitely look to other sources as I continue developing these characters, but I find in the Enneagram a remarkable resource that exposes a fascinating spectrum of possibilities for character development. I can utilize a character type wholesale or make a combination from among several. Remember, in this chaper I've only worked from The Enneagram Institute's Web site descriptions; explore any of the books mentioned in Chapter 4 to delve quite a lot deeper.

CHAPTER 12

Using Research and Brainstorming

Research and Brainstorming can come in handy at any point in constructing a screenplay. As you develop each aspect of the story using the Key Tools, you may find it helpful to stop and seek out relevant material—any information that could unlock greater possibilities and lift your ideas to the next level. Research and Brainstorming can be unavoidable when you don't yet have enough information to continue—or when you're overflowing with ideas that just can't wait.

This chapter shares with you some of my research on this developing screenplay, followed by a brainstorming session. As discussed back in Chapter 5, good research can meet you halfway. You'll see this premise in action here as I score an important find that literally provides me with a major piece of the plot. It wasn't anything that I was looking for or even remotely considering for the story, and if I hadn't stumbled over it in my research I would never have suspected its existence. Let's see what I found and how it can be built into this evolving script.

SOURCES AND RESOURCES

St. Nick is trying to buy a bank, but one of the things I ran up against right away was my unfamiliarity with banking beyond the normal savings and checking accounts, loans, ATMs, and so on. As for the certification process involved in purchasing a bank, I know less than zip.

First, I searched the Internet with the terms *banking, bank examiners, bank fraud,* and *banking regulations.* I spent hours and found much that was interesting, along with plenty that was boring. I knew so little that I didn't even have specific questions yet. I found everything from radical conspiracy theories on the Federal Reserve to rules and regulations tedious enough to put the average reader to sleep in minutes.

Next, I went to the Los Angeles Public Library's Web site and located 2,537 books on banks and banking. Looking through more than half of them in the catalog (typical of the amount of legwork it takes to find quality material), I found an author, Stephen Frey, who specializes in writing banking thrillers the way John Grisham writes legal thrillers. I checked out two of his books on tape, *The Insider* and *The Vulture Fund*, which I listened to in my car (an excellent way to do research in what might otherwise be downtime). Both books were fascinating and useful. I also skimmed a book on bank management and another on how to create your own international bank, both of which had points of interest. I even watched a History Channel show on banks. All these resources helped to deepen my understanding on this topic so crucial to the screenplay.

Additionally, I asked if any friends or acquaintances know any bankers and got two hits. One friend's son-in-law, a bank examiner for the FDIC, directed me to an extremely useful government Web site with information on what a bank must do to get certified. And a client of mine who works in a bank put me in touch with a banker, bank examiners, and government banking officials. So with a little digging I found somebody who knew somebody. Now I was getting some specifics direct from the source—from people in the know.

EUREKA!

My biggest score through researching was a book from the library called *Shell Game: A True Story of Banking, Spies, Lies, Politics—and the Arming of Saddam Hussein*, by Peter Mantius (New York: St. Martin's Press, 1995). A real find, this book is about a banking scandal in the late 1980s. The Atlanta branch of the Italian Banca Nazionale del Lavoro (this was known as "the BNL scandal") used a system of bogus agricultural loans to Iraq through which more than $4 billion was funneled into Saddam Hussein's weapons programs. The evidence indicates the tacit complicity of the CIA and the White House in an end run around the American public to provide support to Iraq in their war against fundamentalist Iran. It was a means of covert foreign policy in the same behind-the-scenes manner as the Iran-Contra scandal. I lifted the agricultural loan concept straight from the book and added my own twists, which gave me part of the core mechanics for the story. This is an excellent example of good research meeting you halfway. In light of this information, I created the character, Umbotha, who you've already met in my Writer's Notebook (see page 222). He sprang directly out of this particular piece of key research.

MORE RESEARCH

As I built this story, I took lots of different forays into research, which is very much part of exploring the possibilities in a good idea. For instance, I checked out great liars in history and in literature; Baron Von Munchausen was one who I looked at with intriguing results because his lies were so colossal. He helped to catapult me out of thinking small and into some unusual prospects that probably wouldn't occur to me on my own. As I'm developing a script, reading and watching things in a similar vein puts me in the zone for that particular type or style of storytelling. I find it useful to expose myself to everything and anything in the genre.

I also investigated a bookstore specializing in mysteries for any books about phenomenal liars or caper stories. The owner led me to *Nobody's Perfect*, by Donald Westlake (New York: Simon & Schuster, 1977)—one of those crime stories in which everything goes wrong. While this book didn't have much to do with liars, it was full of wackiness, stupidity, ineptitude, complications, miscommunications, and double-crosses, which set my brain spinning with comic possibilities.

Then I saw the movie *The In-Laws*, a remake that unexpectedly turned out to be a gold mine of research. In it, a completely crazed and unpredictable spy (played by Michael Douglas) drags a panicky, straight-laced podiatrist (Albert Brooks) into an adrenaline-fueled espionage adventure. This story line opened up a world of electrifying possibilities for me. I had begun to fiddle with Apollo as a really flamboyant character, but it was just an inkling—an attempt to go against type and not make him the grim, thuggish hard-ass you'd expect in that role. As the movie got rolling, it occurred to me that there's a real correlation between *The In-Laws* and Cutter's story. The following section switches to the Writer's Notebook format for a brainstorming session.

A BRAINSTORMING SESSION EMERGING
FROM GOOD RESEARCH

The In-Laws made me realize that I could take Apollo much, much further than I had initially imagined. He was a spark, but Michael Douglas's character in this film was a dazzling sunburst by comparison. It got my imagination reeling. Apollo could be so off-the-hook, so fun to be with that my whole concept of the film got blasted into another dimension. He could be exciting, brilliant, gleeful, fanatical, perceptive, dangerous, unpredictable, free, adventurous, maddening, inspiring, inscrutable, intoxicating, energetic, joyous, deadly, and giddy—which are the types of moods, traits, and emotions I'm looking for to grip the audience. You see this in film characters like Owen Wilson's Dignan in *Bottle Rocket*, Max Bialystock in *The Producers*, Maude in *Harold and Maude*, and Long John Silver in *Treasure Island*, among many others.

The main thing is that these characters are total rascals, rogues, mischief-makers, and scoundrels. Like Loki, the Norse god of mischief, they're troublemakers but can also be bringers of life. If Cutter is intent on his honest, "normal" existence but is secretly bored and frustrated with it all, then the more bored and frustrated he is, the more susceptible he will be to Apollo's infectious energy. Has Cutter lost his spark, his zest for life, his spirit? Won't it add to his dilemma if Apollo isn't just trying to derail his lifestyle, if instead he also represents an irresistible call to adventure and to life, the call of the wild? Knowing this, Cutter would struggle that much more to fend off Apollo, certain that once he takes that first step, it will all be over.

I suddenly saw how much more fun I could have with a story like this, with a character like this, and I started thinking about who this cellmate could really be. Perhaps he's an old con who knows everything and everybody. If Cutter spent years in prison with him, wouldn't he have learned Apollo's entire body of knowledge? What is Apollo's background? What are the craziest possible backgrounds? Was he a dictator's son? A race car driver? A spy? A pool hustler? A karate champion? A safecracker? An aristocrat? A mercenary? Does he have a history of insanity? It's fun to explore the extremities in any genre, but this type of story positively begs for it.

Remember, it's Saturday night at the movies. People are coming for entertainment, so I really want to cut loose. Does Apollo have a hidden agenda with trying to recruit Cutter for this job? If he's a trickster, then how many hidden agendas might he have? Is he actively trying to drag Cutter kicking and screaming back into his former ways? Does Apollo see Cutter as a wild tiger locked in a cage, his soul crying out to be set free? How much can the audience empathize with Apollo's point of view? How much would the audience mistrust him? How much do viewers secretly want him to shake Cutter out of his rut? How much do they truly want Cutter to be able to resist Apollo? Hundreds of questions pour out of me in my heady new enthusiasm for this growing story.

My favorite part of writing a script is the point where there's a premise laid down but everything is utterly wide open. Watching Michael Douglas's character reminded me how over the top you can go. I had begun to form a picture of Apollo, and The In-Laws totally shattered it, then expanded it by a factor of 10,000. The more outlandish Apollo is, the better it will be for this movie. If Apollo sweeps in already caught up in a full-blown adventure, then he's way ahead of where I had pictured him. It's all much less casual if he's being hunted, or in the middle of a crime gone wrong, or in disguise, or in huge trouble, because the movie starts at 100 mph rather than from a standstill. You're supposed to start

a script with a bang. It's called *in medias res*—"in the middle of things."
So, what are some possible reasons for Apollo's sudden appearance in
Cutter's life? Has he stolen something and is now trying to get away
with it? Has he come to hide out? Has he been mowing Cutter's lawn in
disguise for months without Cutter recognizing him? Does he crash a
burning car into Cutter's house? Does he kidnap Cutter from a nice dinner with his family? Did Cutter think Apollo was dead until now, when
he reappears seemingly by magic? Or does he just approach Cutter out
of the blue at the grocery store?

ATTACK AS A STORYTELLER

On page 57, I mentioned science-fiction writer Alfred Bester's idea of attack as
a storyteller: giving the reader the ride of their lives. Do you see in how many
different directions this story can still go? Everything is still wide open and fun.
Any new idea might trigger an explosive brainstorming session. In the paragraph above I talk about starting with a bang. Bester says you should start a story
at white heat and build from there. That is quite a challenge.

How would you handle the opening of this story? What's the craziest opening scene you can possibly invent? What's the most unexpected, the least
clichéd, the most preposterous, the funniest, the scariest, the most ridiculous,
the last thing you'd ever expect? How can you throw a monkey wrench into the
audience's expectations, into your own pattern of storytelling? How do you get
outside your own story, or even outside your own concept of what this story
could be? A big part of the fun of writing is this ride, this joy of creating something that will blow viewers' minds. Think about how *you* go to the movies begging to have *your* mind blown. Tear into your story with that level of attack.
The audience wants the ride of their life, and it's your job to give it to them!

TRYING OUT SOME TITLES
FOR THIS SCRIPT

As I've been developing this story, I've brainstormed and collected some titles.
In *Playwriting for Profit*, Arthur Edwin Krows describes how a London playwright told him that the measure of a good title is if it looks good on a bus.
This may sound funny, but it's actually a great way to gauge a title in a country where plays are advertised on buses. I tend to not get too caught up in the
search when I'm beginning a script because I routinely stumble onto potential
titles as I work through the material. I'll be brainstorming and writing notes
for the story or reviewing my Writer's Notebook and happen on a phrase that
clicks. You'll acquire an ear for it. I find titles all the time in the course of daily
life and keep them in a file. Here is a list of potential titles that I compiled for
this script:

Don't Get Me Started
Good Old St. Nick
Count Your Blessings
Believe You Me
You Don't Want to Know
Straight and True
Laughing All the Way to the Bank
The Slush Fund
It's Only Money
You Bet Your Life
The Whole Truth
The Trickle-Up Effect
Golden Opportunity

There are a few decent ones in there and some regular junk, but I keep coming back to *Good Old St. Nick* because somehow it just works for me. Perhaps I could generate many more, but I liked *Good Old St. Nick* as soon as I hit on it, and while I collected others, none had that particular ring to it—none had the juice. Although it conjures up images of Christmas, it benefits from the irony, as well as a curious sound and a certain playfulness. Could it still be changed? Absolutely, but I think it would look good on a bus.

You should know that a film title cannot be copyrighted. In 1989 there were, in fact, two feature films called *Black Rain* released in theaters. Studios do have agreements not to step on one another's titles, but legally you can put any title on a screenplay.

[Note: If you're following the detour from the Chapter 8, then return now to page196 and resume the book's normal flow.]

CHAPTER 13

Using the Central Proposition

Recall from the information in Chapter 6 that the Central Proposition looks at the core conflict or opposition in a budding plot. The process goes: set up a potential fight, touch off a fight to the finish, and then leave the audience hanging in an unresolved state so you can evaluate how intensely you've got them. The Central Proposition takes you right to the heart of the protagonist-antagonist clash, right to the nucleus of your story, whether it's a goofy comedy or a hard core thriller.

In applying the Central Proposition to *Good Old St. Nick*, focusing on the core conflict between Cutter and St. Nick opens up all kinds of remaining uncertainties in the plot as it stands. There's a difference between knowing roughly what I want to happen and figuring out how to actually enact it. It's like a jigsaw puzzle or an engineering project: If you move this piece or change that piece, how does it impact the whole? As a writer, you learn to hold story possibilities in suspension, often doing much of the work in your head as you wrestle the basic story into shape. However, the Central Proposition requires some of the plot basics to become specific, and certain questions about the protagonist-antagonist relationship to be answered—so you generally don't apply this tool until you're ready to solidify certain aspects of the plot.

DEVELOPING THE CONFLICT

My main question is, If Cutter and St. Nick's conflict builds toward a fight to the finish near the end of the script, then what specifically does their fight consist of? I envisioned that the big showdown between Cutter and St. Nick two-thirds or three-quarters through the story—the touch-off to the fight to the finish—as an outrageous lying contest. But what would that look like? How can I ratchet up that conflict while narrowing in on the specifics? I imagine that Cutter has totally reverted to his old pathological liar self, while St. Nick is still desperately attempting to become a legitimate banker. Cutter's overall intention is to destroy St. Nick, but he can't reveal that or the game is over. If St. Nick discovers that Cutter is not who he's pretending to be, then he'll kill Cutter instantly. In other words, I'm trying to engineer a savage, screwball lying contest, but if Cutter's cover gets blown then nothing he says will regain St. Nick's trust. But if St. Nick *almost* finds him out or suspects something, then Cutter could lie like a wildcat to try to keep his mission of revenge alive. I see the lid finally coming off Cutter's secret with just a few minutes left in the movie, and the two of them begin a real fight to the death.

Much of how the conflict plays out depends on exactly how Cutter comes unhinged. Does he go so far off the deep end that he loses his original focus on revenge? Does he even know what he's doing anymore—who his true self is, why he's involved in this scheme? Does his fascination with St. Nick impact his actions? Has he been steered into a different sense of mission? Also, what's the status of the bank—now a legitimate entity, or just on the edge of being fully certified? Is the first loan to Umbotha hanging in the balance? The conflict or covert conflict between St. Nick and Cutter will have much to do with that.

Wrestling with Plot Problems

Before I get into Cutter touching off the fight to the finish, I need to back-track and figure some things out, incorporating new ideas into the crisis and the decision and action. Shallott is in a state of thinly disguised rage at St. Nick for having murdered his brother and is not a seasoned pro like Cutter. He may slip up and blow his cover but I'm not yet quite sure how—although it will definitely heighten the conflict. I want the FBI to start an investigation of St. Nick and the bank, while Senator Hutchings frantically scrambles to quash it. Umbotha's deal is in trouble somehow, so he has come to America to oversee the first round of agricultural loans released by the bank and has hit it off with Cutter. Perhaps one of St. Nick's old mob friends shows up to black-mail his way into a piece of the action, amplifying the tension even further. Plus, I want the CIA to enter the plot line, along with drug money, arms deal-ers, sheiks, former KGB agents, generals, and billionaires.

Apollo is not in the story enough to suit me—he's too strong a character to lose for a long period—so I'll involve him more, even if he's working in dis-guise as the janitor in the building. I have yet to develop how Mischa finds out where Cutter is and starts spying on him. Finally, I want to keep St. Nick's tan-talizing secretary in the mix, and I need to keep Margarita active. Essentially, I'm trying to increase tension while steering the plot where I want it to go, but I'm also very aware of how the plot is coming together on its own. Remember, screenwriting is part act of creation and part voyage of discovery.

The following section switches over to my Writer's Notebook, as it will take several pages of thinking on paper to figure all these things out.

Creating Some Solutions

Let's say that Shallott's cover is blown during a meeting in St. Nick's office with Umbotha and Cutter present. If Shallott makes a critical mistake and gets badly roughed up by St. Nick, then he could begin to collapse under the pressure. Cutter will immediately come under suspicion since Shallott was the one who brought him in on this job. Cutter must counteract this suspicion or die, and then the mission against St. Nick will be totally lost. I would need to add an earlier scene between Shallott and Cutter, in which they discuss the eventuality that one of their covers will get blown. They agree that each would disavow the other for the good of the mission, and they're deadly serious. So Cutter completely distances himself from Shallott in St. Nick's office, saying that he'd worked with Shallott a few times but didn't know him well before the offer to be his assistant on this job. He'd say, "Hey, I don't give a damn about him. Kill him. What do I care?" The earlier scene between him and Shallott is crucial, otherwise the audience would lose sympathy for Cutter.

So Cutter would cut Shallott loose and Umbotha would be there watching as St. Nick rages at Shallott for being a traitor. He could execute Shallott with an injectable drug that makes it look as though he's had a heart attack. Cutter is on the spot and can show no emotion. Then the phone rings and it's the FBI agent who's investigating St. Nick, wanting new information about an IRS irregularity with the money that's been placed in reserve. St. Nick has Shallott's body on the floor, but he's got to take the call: His whole operation hangs in the balance. He could send Cutter to phone an ambulance, which would buy Cutter a few minutes.

I see Cutter making the call and then going into the bathroom and freaking out, throwing up, looking at himself in the mirror, telling himself that he's going to die—that he's useless and doesn't know how to even begin to pull this off. If he's only getting two hours of sleep a night because he's reading banking books to maintain his cover, then he's primed for a nervous breakdown. I want Mischa, who's spying on his dad, to be hidden in the air vent so he can witness Cutter's meltdown. Then I want Cutter to start to pull himself together with the "Judy Garland transformation" (see page 201). This is the cornered wild animal that comes out fighting, the lump of coal transforming under intense pressure into a diamond. Mischa would see his father completely morph into this legendary wild man he's heard about his whole life but never seen. It should be like watching Dr. Jekyll turning into Mr. Hyde. The Cutter that emerges is ready for absolutely anything.

He goes back into St. Nick's office in attack mode, arguing for his job and for his position of trust. There should be conflict between Cutter and

St. Nick, but it has to be carefully controlled. Umbotha is impressed with Cutter's fearlessness and drive. At that moment, one of St. Nick's old mob buddies barges into the office and demands big money or he'll give the police proof of a murder that St. Nick committed. Cutter turns on this brutal-looking Mafia executioner, cooks up a lie, and threatens to ship him off to work for Umbotha in Mambia, never to be heard from again. Umbotha laughs and picks up on it, desciding a special prison for his political enemies, for whom death is too easy a punishment: tiny cells where you can never lay down, intense prison labor, torture, bad food, and erratic sleep periods. But not to worry because they have excellent health care . . . and it can take decades to die. The mobster turns white and runs out. Cutter and Umbotha smile gleefully and high-five each other. Now Umbotha is even more taken with Cutter and declares to St. Nick that if Cutter does not negotiate his deal, then there won't be a deal. St. Nick is still not convinced, but Cutter pressures him, conjures up lies, and works to earn his respect.

Umbotha's insistence that Cutter do the deal is the strongest thing I can come up with at this point to create overt conflict between St. Nick and Cutter. This catches St. Nick in a tough spot. He has come to like Cutter and wants someone that sharp on his team, but he's no pushover, and Shallott's betrayal has set off his internal alarms. He's got Cutter in his sights.

A CIA agent could show up to get Umbotha out of there after Shallott is killed. But Umbotha brushes him off—he's having fun and besides, an old friend is stopping by for lunch, so he's not going anywhere. The CIA agent could get really aggressive and demand that Umbotha leave, saying too much could be compromised, but Umbotha will not budge and scares the agent off. Cutter could help drive him off, too, with another extravagant lie.

Then one of St. Nick's guys comes in holding Mischa, saying he found him lurking in the hall. Everything grinds to a halt. Our new unleased Cutter turns on Mischa and, without missing a beat, slaps him hard across the face, then kisses him full on the lips and calls him a jealous bitch. Cutter tells St. Nick that Mischa is his boyfriend and he'd heard so much about St. Nick's sexy secretary that he came in to sneak a look at her. Mischa catches on instantly that their survival depends on this, and he drops into character. He's a natural, and he wanted in—he just didn't want in this way. But he's lucky to be alive and so is Cutter. Cutter seems totally unfazed. Umbotha thinks this is hilarious, saying he loves young guys, which throws St. Nick a little. Umbotha sweeps up Cutter and Mischa, insisting that they come out to lunch with him.

They all go out to eat and who should walk in but Apollo! Umbotha leaps up and hugs him, introducing him to Cutter and Mischa as his oldest friend. Cutter is stunned but doesn't show it in the least, and Mischa manages to play it cool. Umbotha explains how they raised hell together as kids when their fathers, both presidents of totalitarian countries, visited each other. Apollo and Umbotha start partying it up, and Cutter matches them drink for drink. Umbotha asks Apollo what he's up to these days, and Apollo says he's into counterfeiting, child pornography, drugs . . . the usual. To Cutter's astonishment, Apollo reaches into his bag and pulls out a stack of counterfeit hundreds. Umbotha is delighted, saying his diplomatic immunity allows him to get away with anything and he loves passing bad money. They end up in a high-stakes poker game at Umbotha's penthouse suite atop a luxury hotel; things degenerate into a raucous party. Cutter is the life of the party, telling lie after outrageous lie to Umbotha, who roars with laughter. Mischa is having the time of his life now and hardly recognizes his father, who is a genuinely changed man—and not in a good way. This is a real adventure and is quite unnerving for Mischa—but it's pure adrenaline all the way.

I need to complicate things here and send everything into a headlong rush toward the ending, so I could see something like St. Nick calling Cutter for an emergency down at the bank. He wants Cutter to cook up some elaborate half-truth for a sheik who won't take no for an answer on some banking business. Meanwhile, Senator Hutchings would be using the White House to help get the FBI off St. Nick's back. Cutter could be eavesdropping with the old can-and-string trick on St. Nick and Hutchings, using what he learns to weave yet more lies. It all remains unformed at this point, but what is certain is that it should get as crazy as possible. I'm just trying to launch the wild Cutter with an element of conflict between him and St. Nick. All of these ideas came from looking at possibilities for creating and cranking up the conflict between them—without Cutter's cover getting blown.

Enough Material to Apply the Central Proposition

I always knew my work would be cut out for me with Cutter and St. Nick's final showdown, but it wasn't until I turned my attention to applying the Central Proposition that I realized just how tricky it would be. Bear in mind that half the musings I just came up with could get tossed out. I'm struggling to find a madcap finale, and at this point I'm only into the first part of the ending. I still need Cutter to build a system of lies that are designed to destroy St. Nick. The ending has to be satisfying, all-inclusive, entertaining, dangerous, and funny. The Central Proposition is helping me shape the material, but it can be an extremely demanding tool. Look at how much I must form, experiment with, turn upside down, throw away, and stretch my concepts in order to utilize it properly. Even after the Writer's Notebook session, I feel that this confrontation still needs more, but being ambitious with a story means feeling stumped regularly. I'm in over my head, but that's where I live as a writer. (If you're not in over your head with your script, then you're probably turning out material that's too simplistic or has already been done to death.) However, this chaotic brainstorming session has produced some necessary raw material, and now I'm ready to return to the Central Proposition.

USING THE FIVE-STEP PROCESS TO CONSTRUCT THE CENTRAL PROPOSITION

Remember, the Central Proposition boils the action down to three sentences—setting up the potential fight, touching off the fight to the finish, and pinpointing the Central Dramatic Question that arises in the minds of the audience. This tool will help us focus on the plot's central and compelling action. The process of building the Proposition consists of five steps. To isolate these five components, we work our way backward through them using deductive reasoning.

Step 1: Visualize the Fight to the Finish

First, we want to *Visualize the fight to the finish*. This will involve Cutter and St. Nick battling to the maximum degree within the limits of this story. Cutter is in the fight of his life, trying to coordinate this whole scheme. To win, he must attack as hard as he can, and not just St. Nick; a big chunk of the conflict that gets touched off is Cutter versus everybody and everything—Senator Hutchings, Umbotha, Apollo, Mischa, the FBI, the CIA, etc. But it's St. Nick he's truly after, and St. Nick who'll be in his face as much as I can arrange it. The Central Proposition keeps the protagonist-versus-antagonist focus strong. From St. Nick's side, he doesn't trust Cutter after Shallott's cover is blown, and that battle isn't over until either St. Nick is finished off or Cutter fails totally.

Step 2: What is the Central Dramatic Question?

Now I need to know *What's the question in the minds of the audience once the fight to the finish has only just started and they don't know how it's going to turn out?* Essentially, the audience will be wondering if Cutter can pull off this revenge against St. Nick. But I should frame the Central Dramatic Question as specifically as possible, because the audience is watching a specific set of events that will give rise to a highly specific question in their mind once the conflict goes beyond the point of no return. If the situation changes and I'm looking at a different or more complex state of affairs, then the question will change, too. Essentially, Cutter is declaring war on St. Nick but also on all those who are conspiring to derail his revenge. The untamed Cutter is like the cavalry that appears at the crucial moment. His old addictions have kicked in and he's in attack mode. I understand this and try to direct it at St. Nick as much as possible. So the question that would arise in the mind of the audience once Cutter launches his attack is, *Can Cutter possibly pull this off and take down St. Nick?*

Now I've isolated the Central Dramatic Question, but how much does the audience *really* care about how the story turns out? I need to know if this question is powerful enough to drive the whole movie. The more trouble Cutter is in and the more we utterly loathe St. Nick, the more powerful the question will be. Merely isolating the question in the minds of the audience is only the first step in evaluating its power. On a scale of 1 to 10, how intensely does the audience care? A weak situation can give rise to a dramatic question with the same wording, but we're not gripped by it. A protagonist about whom we don't care all that much or an antagonist about whom we're not very worried keeps the question weak. Look, for instance, at the plethora of spy movies, many of which would have roughly the same Central Dramatic Question: *Will [our hero] stop [the bad guy] and save the world?* In some instances we'll be in a state of high-intensity suspense, but think about how many other times you couldn't have cared less if the whole damn planet got vaporized. In fact if it did, then the movie would finally get interesting.

In terms of evaluating the power of the Central Dramatic Question for *Good Old St. Nick*, I notice that things could definitely be worse for Cutter. What are various ways to pile on the strain? How can I create a true life-or-death showdown? How can I add to the chaos? How intimidating are St. Nick and Hutchings? How brutally insane, slimy, and darkly humorous is Umbotha? How uncertain is Umbotha's deal? Is the bank on the edge of going under? What about the CIA, the FBI, the IRS, U.S. Customs, the Federal Reserve, the White House, the Senate, the drug runners, and organized crime? These are all possible players in the mix.

Step 3: What Action by the Protagonist Touches Off the Fight to the Finish?

Now we want to put our finger on what sends the conflict beyond the point of no return, so we ask, *What action by the protagonist touches off the fight to the finish, giving rise to the Central Dramatic Question?* The Writer's Notebook session confirmed that Cutter snaps into his old self and explodes into the situation as an out-of-control liar. He's going after St. Nick, Hutchings, the thieves, the hustlers, the billionaire bankers, and the arms dealers who are trying to drag this revenge operation down. I'm still carrying a lot of possibilities as I wrestle this touch-off into shape, but the basic answer to this question is: Cutter snaps and goes on the attack, fighting to keep St. Nick's trust and to keep the deal together so he can complete his revenge.

Step 4: What Earlier Action by the Protagonist Sets Up the Potential Fight?

Moving a giant step backward in the plot, I now want to know *What earlier action by the protagonist sets up the potential fight?* Remember our proportion diagram (see page 126), in which the set-up of the potential fight usually comes much earlier in the plot. I'm trying to integrate the complete action of the script, so I'm looking for a situation earlier in the plot in which Cutter and St. Nick cross swords. This tool reveals that such a scene doesn't exist yet; I'll have to come up with one on the spot. I've been thinking that St. Nick might challenge Cutter on the truth of something Cutter has said. If Cutter—who is struggling to stay honest in this difficult situation (this is, after all, half of his dilemma)— is called a liar, then he might respond fiercely to St. Nick. Being branded a liar, especially by his number one enemy, really pushes his buttons. (This idea comes directly from my brainstorming in Chapter 10 on the 36 Dramatic Situations. The subheading *Revenge for a false accusation* triggered a story possibility: Cutter may overreact irrationally if he is falsely accused of lying, even though he's lying in general with the whole revenge scheme.) Then when Cutter panics, thinking his fight with St. Nick has ruined their plan, he uses the can and string to eavesdrop on St. Nick and Hutchings, and learns that St. Nick is actually impressed by how ballsy Cutter was in standing up to him. I'm not yet sure what this argument between Cutter and St. Nick will be about, but now I've tentatively planned an approximate scene to set up the potential fight at around one-third of the way into the script.

Step 5: Do the Set-up and the Touch-off Have Anything in Common that Can Bind Them Together?

To answer this question and establish this final component of the proposition, I look at both these points and determine if they have anything in common. There isn't really a rule of thumb for the common term except that there should be *some* kind of linkage between the set-up and the touch-off so that there's a valid logical connection between them. The first thing they share is that Cutter gets bent out of shape each time he's called a liar. The second common feature is Cutter's intense dedication to taking down St. Nick. In the set-up, he is freshly undercover in St. Nick's organization and secretly seething with vengeance because of Frenchy's death. In the touch-off, he has just seen Shallott murdered, which would renew this fervor. However, I think the former option feels more like the common element that ties these two plots points together, reinforcing the structural unity of the script.

ASSEMBLING THE PROPOSITION

Now let's assemble the three-sentence Central Proposition from the components we've just ascertained with the five-step process (the common term is underlined):

Set up the potential fight
Cutter, <u>furious at being called a liar by St. Nick</u>, gets into an argument with him.

Touch off the fight to the finish
Cutter, now cornered and in real trouble—and <u>again outraged at being called a liar</u>—snaps and totally reverts to his old lying self, going on the attack against St. Nick

The Central Dramatic Question
Can Cutter pull this off and take St. Nick down?

ADDING A LITTLE MORE DETAIL TO THE PROPOSITION

I'll state the proposition again with a little more information included so that a stranger to the story can make sense of it:

Set up the potential fight
Cutter, a reformed pathological liar who has vowed to his wife never to lie again, is blackmailed into a revenge-oriented "perfect" crime by his former prison cellmate, Apollo, to whom he owes his life. Cutter poses as a bank examiner and reluctantly begins lying again to take down St. Nick, a legendary, savage crime lord who's in the process of going legitimate by buying a bank in collusion with the corrupt Senator Hutchings. When St. Nick falsely accuses Cutter of lying to him, Cutter—refusing to be called a liar—attacks St. Nick and defends his integrity.

Touch off the fight to the finish
Cutter gets drawn deeper into this complicated situation when he

learns of St. Nick and Hutchings's secret plan to make a fortune exploiting government-guaranteed agricultural loans in a crooked deal with a brutal African dictator, Umbotha. The plan changes when Cutter is unexpectedly promoted within St. Nick's organization, and now has a chance both to destroy St. Nick more thoroughly and to derail a deadly criminal conspiracy. Cutter sees one of his partners murdered and, again outraged at being accused of lying to St. Nick, kicks into his old self, going on the offensive against his nemesis and the others in order to pull off the scheme and destroy St. Nick.

The Central Dramatic Question
Can Cutter pull this off and take St. Nick down?

You can see how the proposition tells the core of the story. It actually doubles as a great pitching tool because it forces you right to the nucleus of the plot, which enables you to present it clearly and logically. I've now become focused on the pure drama in this story. This tool also helped by forcing me to pull the story from that diverse collection of possible story elements into a more coherent plot. I often find myself resisting this tool because it forces me to get clear and logical when I'm not ready to give up that expansiveness and chaotic flexibility of another type of creative zone. But then once I've done it, I find that the plot has not only improved, but it is also cleaner and clearer—as is my thinking.

EVALUATING THE PROPOSITION

The next step is to stand back from this proposition and evaluate it. How strong is the Central Dramatic Question? Is it measuring up to my intentions for the film? Are the audience members clinging to the edge of their seats? I've structured the argument, and now I want to step back and see if it's worth a damn.

I've probably got tunnel vision right now—it's easy to get trapped in narrow sets of possibilities when you're deep in the process of developing a story. I've been working it, pounding it, beating it up, shaking it out, violating it, and redirecting it, all to uncover the potential lurking in there. This is the creative process. It takes time to get outside certain types of thinking, and it takes time for the obvious to become apparent. There's just no substitute for time.

So I take some time off from assembling the proposition, and when I return to it, a flood of realizations, ideas, and oversights washes over me. These blind spots are entirely organic to the process. It's very hard to hold everything in your head, and if you direct your thinking to one aspect of the plot, then other aspects can become lost or eclipsed.

As I evaluate what I've constructed, one of the first things that comes to mind is that I want still more conflict. Earlier on I felt the story had been too much of a thriller, so I started developing the comic take on it. Now, I think

I've steered it too much in the direction of comedy. This back-and-forth process is normal. At this point, I want to return to the savagery of the story and make sure that element is properly spun up.

The wacky stuff is entertaining and it does need to be a part of this plot, but it struck me again after I constructed the proposition that St. Nick is a brutal murderer, and the stakes are huge. He and Hutchings are plotting to rob American taxpayers of billions, as well as conspiring with a genocidal dictator to enslave his people in a sweatshop. If Cutter overhears them planning this, then his outrage should be explosive. I want the audience to hate St. Nick with absolute intensity. He must be diabolical, malignant, treacherous, psychotic, demonic, and depraved. All of this will fuel the audience's fiery reaction and upgrade the power of the dramatic question.

As soon as I recognized the need to go darker, a new idea floated up concerning the whole arena of the CIA, arms dealers, money laundering, drug smuggling, covert foreign policy, and government conspiracy. Evaluation often gives rise to more brainstorming—I'll switch to my Writer's Notebook for the following section.

A Dynamic New Plot Possibility Arises

A major new idea has come to me: The situation could change dramatically if Mambia's neighboring country is in the throes of a communist revolution. This may have been brewing for a while, which would have made Umbotha a useful asset to the CIA, but now it's erupted. This would put Umbotha in the catbird seat: He immediately goes from being useful to being absolutely indispensable. All of a sudden the CIA needs to covertly funnel a *lot* of money to Mambia so that Umbotha can arm himself against this threat.

By choosing Communism, I sidestep the whole minefield of using terrorism in a comic way at this point in world history. Terrorism and the various takes on defending ourselves against it is such a politically sensitive hot button that a Hollywood studio might run the other way. I'm paying attention to marketability, which is always a consideration unless you're independently wealthy and are going to make, market, and distribute the movie yourself.

Umbotha is suddenly the toast of the town, and is escorted to high-level meetings with the CIA, the White House, arms merchants, covert operators, high-ranking senators, and so on. I can see the CIA coming to St. Nick and asking to use his bank as a cover for CIA money, because the bank already has a solid relationship with Umbotha and it's new and clean—untouched and unaffiliated. The lid could be taken off the agricultural loan program, with government guarantees being extended from $2 billion to $8 billion, so that "free" money flows like champagne. The loans will be granted, all disguised as agricultural financing, but certain banking regulations will be waived so that a big chunk of the money goes straight to arms purchases from American defense industries. St. Nick, Senator Hutchings, and Umbotha's original plantation and factory deal will still be in place, but it will just be one of many deals, rather than the centerpiece. Plus, all of this will be done through St. Nick and Hutchings's bank, so they'll collect fees on every transaction.

St. Nick and Hutchings would obviously be delighted. Hutchings, who might also be on the Senate Intelligence Committee, could even have steered the CIA to their bank. This arrangement would make any pending investigations of St. Nick or the bank vanish immediately and permanently. Immunities could be issued, subpoenas quashed, and investigators told that it's a matter of national security. St. Nick is now in the VIP club. He's untouchable, and no cop in the world would be looking for him—now or in the future. He's home free!

This is all going to put much, much more pressure on Cutter, who again uses his primitive listening device to eavesdrop on St. Nick and Hutchings in their secure room as they discuss this great turn of events. His window of opportunity to catch and destroy St. Nick is being slammed shut right before his eyes. Now that the stakes are higher, I've just ratcheted up the pressure on the audience as well. There's still a certain tongue-in-cheek aspect to it, but the danger and intensity factors have been cranked way up, and therefore the power of the Central Dramatic Question goes way up, too.

Laying Out the Plot on Note Cards for Clarity

At this point in the process, I'll go back and review all my notes for the script. As usual, this causes certain ideas to pop. To get an overview, I lay out the bare basics of the plot on 3 x 5 index cards, writing on them neatly with a Sharpie marker. Using 3 x 5 cards cut in half (or out-of-date business cards) instead, I can lay out well over a hundred cards on a regular desk—and I can read them from a distance because the Sharpie ink is fat and I've written legibly.

I go to note cards in order to collect my wits before taking the plot to the next level. Having just worked out the Central Proposition for this plot and found that it was missing big chunks of story, I knew it needed lots of work. The cards help me to visualize the whole script, including these gaps. They enable me to see what I already have, lay out the new ideas that come to me, and incorporate them all into the right order. The following list shows what is written on each card. You can recreate them on your own cards if you want to practice with them. Bear in mind that these are my notes to myself, so I don't need to over-explain them. Using note cards that are stripped down to the basics keeps things clear and simple.

1. Cutter is living straight life with wife and son
2. Apollo appears and blackmails Cutter into job
3. Cutter meets Shallott, the crooked bank examiner
4. Senator is setting up bank with St. Nick as front
5. St. Nick's illegal money will go into reserve account
6. Cutter and St. Nick fight—Cutter is called a liar and he's furious
7. Cutter hears plan—government-guaranteed loans to dictator
8. Cutter learns St. Nick and Hutchings are ripping off taxpayers' money
9. Apollo's revenge plan put on hold—Cutter gets promoted
10. Cutter moving crooked money into reserve account
11. Cutter awed by St. Nick's and Hutchings's skills at lying
12. Stock market nosedives—messes things up for St. Nick
13. Complications on moving illegal money
14. FBI and IRS investigate St. Nick—Cutter tells stunning lie, which helps
15. St. Nick goes psycho in private—Hutchings chills him out
16. Hutchings helps get money into reserve account—bank is open for business
17. Old mob pal of St. Nick wants a cut or he spills on St. Nick
18. Umbotha shows up—sees Cutter deal with old mob pal and likes Cutter
19. Umbotha—limos, parties, diplomatic immunity, girls, drugs, and money
20. Umbotha wants St. Nick to launder drug money for him
21. Hutchings nervous about drug money—says no
22. Communist revolution in African country next to Mambia
23. CIA needs Umbotha big-time now
24. Umbotha meets senators, arms dealers, White House, drug smugglers
25. CIA wants St. Nick's bank to be a CIA front
26. All limits taken off agricultural loans—now $8 billion
27. Investigation goes away—immunity—citing National Security
28. St. Nick is now in the VIP club—celebrating with Hutchings— above the law
29. Shallott freaks out and blows his cover
30. St. Nick flips and murders Shallott—turns on Cutter

31. Cutter does Judy Garland transformation and turns wild—Mischa watches
32. Wild Cutter emerges and scares St. Nick's mob pal away
33. Umbotha loves Cutter and won't allow deal to happen without him
34. Mischa gets found and brought in
35. Cutter pretends Mischa is his gay lover to cover for him
36. The wild Cutter goes after St. Nick to keep his trust

This helps me envision the whole plot up to the touch-off of the fight to the finish. It's a very efficient way to lay out the story as it exists thus far. Notice that these cards don't emphasize the beginning of the story, because I have a decent grasp of that; nor do they get into the ending, because that has yet to be invented. I've only just cobbled together a middle, and at this point I'm mighty glad to have that.

ANOTHER TAKE ON THE PROPOSITION

Now that I have evaluated my first attempt at boiling things down to the Central Proposition, I'm going to take another whack at it. This is very much part of using this tool—you set up a proposition, evaluate it, and try again if you're not happy with it. Remember, it's just a *proposal*.

Notice that since my Writer's Notebook session I have changed the common term. With the strengthening of the thriller element, the idea that Cutter would be hung up on being called a liar in a situation of this magnitude no longer worked. I've underscored the new common term in each component.

Set up the potential fight
Cutter, a reformed pathological liar who has vowed to his wife never to lie again, is blackmailed into a revenge-oriented "perfect" crime by his former prison cellmate, Apollo, to whom he owes his life. Cutter finds himself posing as a bank examiner and being forced to start lying again in order to take down St. Nick, a legendary, savage crime lord who's in the process of going legitimate by buying a bank in collusion with the corrupt Senator Hutchings. When St. Nick challenges Cutter for supposedly lying to him, Cutter, refusing to lose this opportunity to take down St. Nick, stands up to him angrily and lies his way out of it.

Touch off the fight to the finish
Cutter eavesdrops and learns of St. Nick and Hutchings's secret plan to legally rob the U.S. taxpayers of billions and to make a fortune by using government-guaranteed agricultural loans in a crooked deal with a brutal African dictator, Umbotha. Cutter is unexpectedly

taken deeper inside St. Nick's organization, and when a communist revolution in Africa puts Umbotha in the driver's seat with the CIA, they offer to make St. Nick's bank a CIA front, with unlimited money flowing and immunity to prosecution. Cutter sees one of his partners murdered and, <u>unwilling to lose his vanishing opportunity at revenge,</u> snaps and kicks into his old lying self, launching a wild attack to stop the plan and destroy St. Nick.

The Central Dramatic Question
Can Cutter stop this plan and take down St. Nick?

You can see how the power of the Central Dramatic Question has altered, because both the stakes and the situation have changed significantly.

A THIRD TAKE ON THE PROPOSITION

As long as the script is in the works, the proposition is always subject to change. One of a trained dramatist's habits of mind is to be wide open to change, always looking for improvement. In fact the more I look at it, the more unsatisfied I am with my second attempt at the Central Proposition. Wrestling with it further, I have come up with something that I think really works.

What's been chewing at me is Cutter's action that touches off the fight to the finish—I'm not happy with it. In general, touching off the fight to the finish is a real declaration of war—like the attack on Pearl Harbor or the destruction of the World Trade Center buildings. My instinct tells me that the touch-off should be an attempt at a killing blow.

Why does Cutter's attack feel so weak to me? Because he's boxed in and can't blow his cover, especially now that Shallott's slip-up has made St. Nick suspicious. Cutter's hands are tied, and yet that's no excuse—the premise is still weak. I've increasingly felt that I had to do better, and I've now spent hours wrestling with this, trying various options. One thing is certain, Cutter and Apollo are very smart and the audience will expect a powerful attack from them. Finally, I hit upon something with some real horsepower to it.

At the point when the old, untamed Cutter surfaces and goes on the attack, he'll arrange for the delivery of a fabricated communiqué to St. Nick's camp, allegedly from the communist group in the country neighboring Mambia. The communists claim to know that through a U.S. bank, the CIA is smuggling weapons disguised as agricultural shipments into Mambia, and they denounce the capitalist dogs for their blatant criminal acts. This is a hard-hitting act by Cutter, touching off a hornet's nest of panic in St. Nick's camp. St. Nick's paranoia would flare up and they would search for a leak. It wouldn't even occur to them that Cutter has anything to do with it, since he couldn't possibly have any knowledge of the inner workings of the bank's secret agenda.

This attack has real clout. It's a true declaration of war within the confines of Cutter's limitations. It still doesn't blow Cutter's cover, and it's infinitely stronger than what I had before. So I'll revise the proposition yet again.

Set up the potential fight
Cutter, a reformed pathological liar who has vowed to his wife never to lie again, is blackmailed into a revenge-oriented "perfect" crime by his former prison cellmate, Apollo, to whom he owes his life. Cutter finds himself posing as a bank examiner and being forced to start lying again in order to take down St. Nick, a legendary, savage crime lord who's in the process of going legitimate by buying a bank in collusion with the corrupt Senator Hutchings. When St. Nick challenges Cutter for supposedly lying to him, Cutter, refusing to lose this opportunity to take down St. Nick, stands up to him angrily and lies his way out of it.

Touch off the fight to the finish
Cutter eavesdrops and learns of St. Nick and Hutchings's secret plan to legally rob U.S. taxpayers of billions and to make a fortune using government-guaranteed agricultural loans in a crooked deal with a brutal African dictator, Umbotha. Cutter is unexpectedly taken deeper inside St. Nick's organization, and when a communist revolution in Africa puts Umbotha in the driver's seat with the CIA, they offer to make St. Nick's bank a CIA front, with unlimited money flowing and immunity to prosecution. Cutter sees one of his partners murdered and, unable to let this evil go unchecked, snaps and kicks into his old lying self, launching into an attack by fabricating a communiqué from communist revolutionaries in which the communists claim to know about the weapons being smuggled into Africa as agricultural shipments, with the money coming from a U.S. bank.

The Central Dramatic Question
Can Cutter destroy this operation and topple St. Nick?

Now the central conflict is hitting pretty hard, and I'm satisfied with it. You can see that it took quite some doing, but I tinkered with the core of the plot and proposed several different takes on it. I found weaknesses in each take and kept banging on it until I came up with something that had much more power than my first take. I hope this example helps you acquire in full a working understanding of the Central Proposition, whose purpose is to tie the plot together and crank up the conflict. Working with the nucleus of the story substantially impacts the entire plot in a very powerful way.

CHAPTER 14

Using Sequence, Proposition, Plot

Now it's time for the actual construction of the script for *Good Old St. Nick* using Sequence, Proposition, Plot. But before I can do this, I need to figure out the script's ending; I certainly can't build the reverse cause and effect without a conclusion. This is daunting, as right now there is truly no ending. I have a few half-baked ideas, but they're simply a set of unconnected concepts that have the luxury of floating free and untethered. I know the basic gist of the ending, because I figured out the story's resolution earlier and the conclusion has been marinating in my brain as I've built the rest of the script. But when I sit down and stare at the empty page in my notebook, I draw a total blank. Now, in order to figure out the ending, I will change over to my Writer's Notebook and do my thinking on paper.

(For a great exercise in screenwriting, stop now and come up with your own ending to this story before you continue reading. Imagine it's your script and you've got to come up with a killer ending. Then come back and read along with the rest of us.)

DEVELOPING AN ENDING FOR *GOOD OLD ST. NICK*

I left off with Cutter fabricating the communiqué from the communist rebels. Now I want to know how St. Nick, Hutchings, Umbotha, and the CIA agents are going to react to the communiqué. It's easy to see them panicking: St. Nick's paranoia would flare up, and the bank office would be swept again for bugs but nothing would be found. Lots of finger-pointing erupts both within St. Nick's group and inside the CIA. Someone had to have leaked this information! Perhaps a patsy is found within the CIA—someone who gets thrown to the wolves.

St. Nick and crew continue to panic and decide to move ahead quickly with the loan operation before anything else goes wrong. They also decide to run as much of it in cash as possible, making it less traceable. Umbotha has had a huge shipment of drugs smuggled into the country, and he launders the resulting mountain of cash through the bank, giving them plenty of ready money. However, some of the weapons manufacturers get greedy for kickbacks and cash up front. Additionally, a U.N. fact-finding commission begins looking into Umbotha's human rights record.

Cutter and Apollo, still raging with hatred for St. Nick, want to stir up more trouble before the bank scam meets with success and they lose their opportunity for revenge. Pretending to be Senator Hutchings, they make some phone calls to arrange for the covert delivery of a weapons system. But the delivery site is actually a food bank where members of the press have been summoned to witness a major donation, and when this Department of Agriculture crate is opened, it's full of stealth missiles. This stirs up a hornet's nest of trouble and in response St. Nick, in a blind rage, burns down an entire block of buildings—he is that vengeful, that evil. Cutter leaks some crucial dirt on St. Nick and Hutchings to a congressional investigative committee; steals some of the cash from St. Nick's stash; and takes great joy in turning several random people into instant millionaires with gifts of cash.

But then Cutter and Apollo's identities are discovered, and Mischa is taken hostage—I'm not yet sure how, but it's probably Mischa's own fault. St. Nick and Hutchings throw someone from the bank to the wolves, enabling the CIA to make the rest of the investigation go away, swept under the rug by citing national security. Cutter is trapped in his web of contradictory lies and sees no way out. Margarita, his wife, convinces him to go back to telling the truth. He agrees, but first he's got to rescue Mischa and take care of a few things. Umbotha, who occupies the top five floors of his luxury hotel, is having a giant bash which has gotten so out of control that it has spilled out onto the street and become a raging block party. Cutter convinces a group of protesters to show up and they wreak havoc, protesting Umbotha's human rights record. In the resulting confusion, Apollo has a band of hired thieves spirit Mischa out of the room where he's being held under guard.

Cutter has learned that St. Nick and crew have the whole bundle of money—$8 billion worth—in trucks, ready to be shipped out as payment to arms manufacturers and agricultural corporations. Cutter and Apollo manage to steal the trucks, and in a riotous chase scene they elude St. Nick and crew by throwing bales of cash into a crowd to create chaos. To confuse things further, they burn a bunch of the counterfeit money. Cutter takes the trucks to an IRS mailing center where they break in, bribe the night watchman, and spend the night using the mailing machines to package, address, and stamp overnight envelopes.

The next day, Cutter arranges a press conference at which he tells the whole truth about the scandalous operation on live national television. In one last deception, he announces that St. Nick had a change of heart and has sent the money stolen from the taxpayers back to them. Packages of $50,000 in cash were sent to America's poorest people. Pandemonium erupts and reporters point out that this will create a lot of chaos. Cutter agrees, but says what can you do? It's all St. Nick's doing and he's nowhere to be found.

Now, I don't know if Cutter and Apollo mailing out the stolen money to the poorest taxpayers is the strongest choice I could have made here, but it was an intriguing option and I kept coming back to it. There is a bit of a Robin Hood element to it, which tickles me, and it seems to go along with the hell-raising spirit of the story. Could I find something stronger for this pivotal point in the plot? Possibly. But I did question it rigorously and it kept working for me, so I retained it.

Senator Hutchings is arrested on a variety of serious criminal charges and sent to prison. St. Nick is grabbed by Umbotha and spirited back to Africa, where he will be a prisoner for the remainder of his days in his own private cell that's too small to lie down in. Cutter goes back to his simple little life, now truly free and happy. Several packages of cash manage to find their way to Cutter's home. Mischa is scared straight, and Apollo runs off to Rio with St. Nick's secretary, accompanied by several bags of cash.

LAYING OUT THE ENDING ON NOTE CARDS

Now there's plenty of material to work with. The ending has some fun elements as well as plenty of danger; it's something I can really begin to shape and fine-tune. Much of it can still be revised or even thrown away. But before we start utilizing this tool by doing reverse cause and effect, I need to lay out the entire story on note cards to get it out of my head and in working order. Review the cards leading up to this point (see page 261) before adding the remaining cards to lay out the ending:

37. Umbotha takes Cutter to party with old friend and it's Apollo!
38. Cutter fabricates false communiqué from communists
39. Communists know about weapons smuggling and U.S. bank
40. St. Nick gets paranoid and suspects everyone
41. "Traitor" found inside the CIA

42. St. Nick and crew panic—move operation at full steam—all cash now
43. Umbotha has sold a big drug shipment—launders tons of cash—in trucks
44. Weapons manufacturer gets greedy, wants kickbacks and cash up front
45. Umbotha is a spoiled brat—can't be told anything
46. U.N. fact-finding crew—human rights violations in Mambia
47. Cutter and Apollo rage in their hatred against St. Nick
48. Cutter has weapons system delivered to food bank
49. St. Nick goes crazy and burns down an entire block
50. Crucial info leaked to Congressional investigation committee
51. Cutter steals money and turns random people into millionaires
52. Cutter and Apollo discovered—Mischa taken captive
53. St. Nick plants evidence against Cutter in plan to frame him
54. CIA quashes new investigation of bank, citing national security
55. Time running out for Cutter
56. Cutter trapped in all his contradictory lies
57. Margarita convinces Cutter to go back to telling the truth
58. Protesters converge on Umbotha's block party—chaos ensues
59. Apollo's band of thieves gets Mischa out of Umbotha's hotel
60. Cutter and Apollo steal $8 billion of St. Nick's money
61. Some money thrown into crowd to create confusion and help escape
62. Cutter and Apollo mail $8 billion in $50,000 chunks to poor people around country
63. Cutter tells truth about operation on live national TV
64. Hutchings gets arrested for banking violations, drugs, and murder
65. Umbotha takes St. Nick back to Africa as his prisoner
66. Cutter goes back to his normal life, happy and now truly free of his demons
67. Mischa is scared straight
68. Apollo and the secretary run off to Rio together

Notice that I've just laid out one possible trail through this story—the one I've developed most thoroughly. Note as well that there's very little detail included. It's hard enough pulling the big picture together, and if the big picture doesn't work, then the details won't matter. I definitely wasn't worrying about the particulars of exactly how Cutter and Apollo get away with the trucks of money, or how St. Nick plants evidence to frame Cutter, or how Mischa gets caught. But now that I've got the big picture nailed down, I can turn my attention to developing these details—as they become necessary. I'll gradually weave them in, working from the general to the particular as I employ Sequence, Proposition, Plot for each part of the screenplay.

SEQUENCE, PROPOSITION, PLOT FOR THE WHOLE SCRIPT

First, I'll use this tool at the overall script level. I'll be working off my note cards as I build the reverse cause and effect for the whole plot. Remember that I'm trying to tie the script together, so I'm working on the big picture (see page 156). I'll skip over details as I work my way backward, each time asking, "What's the cause of that?" rather than, "What comes before it?" In this way, I separate the Necessary from the Unnecessary, only looking at incidents that are connected by cause and effect, so certain cards won't be used on this pass; others will be integrated on successive passes. I'll apply Sequence (reverse cause and effect) first, to isolate the spine of the script in a tight chain of events, and then I'll use Proposition, Plot to lay out the conflict in the whole script.

Reverse Cause and Effect for the Whole Script

What's the Object of the script? Cutter dismantles St. Nick's entire operation and then goes back home to an honest and liberated life, free of his demons.

What's the Final Effect that demonstrates that Object on-screen with real actors? Cutter, now free and truly happy, goes home with Margarita as well as Mischa, who's been scared straight.

What's the Immediate Cause of Cutter going free? The whole operation gets busted, Hutchings goes to jail, and Umbotha secretly takes St. Nick back to Africa as a prisoner.

What's the cause of St. Nick and Hutchings getting taken? Cutter tells the whole truth about the entire operation on live national television.

What's the cause of Cutter spilling the beans? Cutter, Apollo, and Mischa complete their revenge when they steal St. Nick's trucks containing $8 billion and mail the money out to many of America's poorest people.

What's the cause of them stealing the trucks? St. Nick and Apollo create chaos with human rights protesters and rescue Mischa using a band of hired thieves.

What's the cause of them rescuing Mischa? Margarita convinces Cutter to go back to telling the truth instead of trying to lie his way out. He agrees and sets up a plan to accomplish this.

What's the cause of Margarita convincing Cutter to tell the truth? Cutter is trapped in an interlocking set of lies, and with two strikes already against him, it looks as though he's going to prison for life.

What's the cause of Cutter being trapped? St. Nick has framed Cutter to take the fall, and the CIA makes the new investigation against St. Nick go away by citing national security.

What's the cause of St. Nick framing Cutter? Cutter and Apollo's identities are discovered, and Mischa is captured and tortured by St. Nick for key information.

What's the cause of Cutter's and Apollo's covers being blown? Cutter overextends himself by arranging to have a weapons system delivered to a food bank.

What's the cause of Cutter sending the weapons to the food bank? Cutter realizes he's got St. Nick's crew reeling, and knows this is the time to strike. Cutter steals some of St. Nick's hidden cash assets.

What's the cause of Cutter and Apollo needing to strike now? St. Nick and crew panic and lash out in paranoia. They decide to move ahead with the operation, changing it to all cash so nothing's traceable.

What's the cause of St. Nick panicking? Cutter emerges as his old lying, raging self and goes on the attack against St. Nick. Cutter sends him a fabricated communiqué, supposedly from the African communist rebels, claiming to know all about the weapons shipments and the U.S. bank's involvement.

What's the cause of the old, wild Cutter emerging? Shallott's cover is blown and St. Nick murders him, then turns his suspicions on Cutter.

What's the cause of Shallott's cover getting blown? [I don't know yet. What *could* cause Shallott's cover to be blown? Does Shallott do something stupid? Does Shallott get so mad at St. Nick that he flips out? Does something happen that tips off St. Nick? Does Cutter make a mistake? These are all possibilities. One of the handy things about this tool is that I don't need much in the way of detail on the first pass. I can sketch something in and then figure it out in more detail on the next pass—at the act level.] For now, I'll simply say that Shallott slips up because he's so angry.

What's the cause of Shallott betraying his anger? St. Nick and Senator Hutchings are celebrating because they believe they're now above the law. St. Nick seems to be slipping out of Shallott and Cutter's grasp.

What's the cause of St. Nick slipping from Shallott and Cutter's grasp? The investigation against St. Nick is dropped, and the limitation on money loaned to Mambia through the agricultural program is unofficially lifted.

What's the cause of the investigation being dropped? The CIA wants St. Nick's bank, already in business with Umbotha and unencumbered by other clients, to become a purely CIA operation.

What's the cause of the bank becoming a CIA asset? The CIA really needs Umbotha now. He's escorted all over D.C. for meetings with senators, spies, the White House, and arms dealers.

What's the cause of the CIA needing Umbotha so badly? While Umbotha has been in America on banking business, there has been a communist coup in the country next to Mambia.

What's the cause of Umbotha coming to see the bank? Senator Hutchings pulls some strings so the rest of St. Nick's dirty money can slip through the red tape and into the reserves. The bank is now officially open for business.

What's the cause of Hutchings pulling the strings? St. Nick blows his top and tells Hutchings that it's all getting too complicated, that he can't take it—he's going to flip out and blow the deal.

What's the cause of St. Nick freaking out? There are complications in moving St. Nick's illegal assets into the reserves; the FBI starts investigating the bank; and the stock market drops precipitously.

What's the cause of the FBI investigation of the bank? The FBI suspects something when they spot some potential irregularities as Cutter, now trying to get the bank running, helps Shallott start moving St. Nick's hidden assets into the reserve fund.

What's the cause of Cutter now trying to help get the bank running? Cutter tells Apollo about his promotion in the ranks and what he overheard, so they put their original plan on hold to see if working inside St. Nick's system offers a better opportunity to destroy him.

What's the cause of Cutter and Apollo changing their plan? Cutter eavesdrops on St. Nick and Hutchings as they discuss their plan to use government-guaranteed agricultural loans to get filthy rich at the expense of U.S. taxpayers. St. Nick says he really likes Cutter's fighting spirit and decides to promote him.

What's the cause of Cutter eavesdropping on St. Nick and Hutchings? Cutter is afraid that his temper has ruined their revenge operation.

What's the cause of Cutter thinking he's ruined everything? There's a legal glitch with the IRS, and St. Nick's paranoia flares up. He accuses Cutter of being a liar, and Cutter reacts furiously.

What's the cause of Cutter being accused of lying? Hutchings sees a way to exploit the Uruguayan tax shelter, and they start using it to bring in St. Nick's offshore money.

What's the cause of using the Uruguayan tax shelter? Apollo shows up in disguise as a banking client and turns out to be an old acquaintance of the Senator. Cutter is stunned to learn that Apollo is actually a retired ambassador from Uruguay, but doesn't show his surprise. Apollo tells Hutchings that his country is offering some unique tax shelters. [I just made this up. It wasn't in my note cards, but I've been wanting more of Apollo in this story. He's been around for a long time and his father was the dictator of a South American country, so he could have been at least an honorary ambassador at one point.]

What's the cause of Apollo showing up now? Cutter and Shallott begin working to bring St. Nick's illegal assets into the system, and they're fairly stumped on some key issues. Apollo, who is keeping an eye on things from the wings, sees that he needs to act.

What's the cause of starting to bring St. Nick's illegal assets in from hiding? Shallott takes Cutter into the bank as his assistant, convincing St. Nick that Cutter is trustworthy and that he can't bring St. Nick's hidden assets into the system legally without Cutter's help.

What's the cause of Shallott taking Cutter to St. Nick? Cutter reluctantly agrees to help destroy St. Nick when Shallott explains his vulnerability while trying to go legit as part of a crooked senator's banking scam.

What's the cause of Shallott explaining St. Nick's operation to Cutter? Apollo blackmails Cutter into being part of this scheme, and reminds him of their utter loathing for St. Nick. Cutter agrees to talk to Shallott.

What's the cause of Apollo blackmailing Cutter? Cutter refuses when Apollo drops in on his reformed straight life and tries to enlist him in a perfect crime to destroy St. Nick, their archenemy.

Proposition, Plot for the Whole Script

Now let's see how Proposition, Plot lines up for the overall script. (Note that St. Nick killing Frenchy is not the *Initial Act of Aggression* because that doesn't happen in the movie itself but before the movie started—what's known as the *Conditions*

Precedent—events that already happened before the story starts.) Here we're dealing with a very stripped-down conflict map for the overall script. Cutter and St. Nick cross swords fairly early on. Remember that the section we call "Plot" answers the dramatic question and completes the action, wrapping up the story.

Protagonist	**Antagonist**
	Initial Act of Aggression
	St. Nick becomes paranoid when Cutter and Shallott are moving illegal assets and accuses Cutter of being a liar.
Justified Retaliation	
Cutter stands up to St. Nick, saying he did not lie and will not be called a liar.	
	Aggravation of the Issue
	St. Nick murders Shallott and comes after Cutter, certain he's in on Shallott's operation.
Precipitating Act	
Cutter snaps into his old self and goes on the attack, then fabricates a communiqué from communist rebels in Africa declaring they know all about the weapons shipments.	

Central Dramatic Question
Will Cutter and his crew smash the operation and take
down St. Nick, or will St. Nick destroy them?

	St. Nick and crew panic and rush ahead with the operation using only cash, much of it drug money.
Cutter has a weapons system delivered to a food bank, and leaks information to a congressional committee.	
	St. Nick figures out who Cutter is and captures Mischa. He has the CIA stop the congressional investigation, citing national security, and then frames Cutter.
Cutter rescues Mischa, steals $8 billion, and gives it all away. He tells the truth about the operation on live TV, ruining St. Nick and Hutchings.	

DIVIDING THE SCRIPT INTO ACTS

Now I'll divide the script into acts and apply this tool to each one. As I read the reverse cause and effect from the bottom up, putting the story in its correct order, I look for natural breaks in the plot. The best rule of thumb for this division is where one major "chapter" finishes up and another starts. I see Act I ending when, after overhearing St. Nick and Hutchings's scheme, Cutter goes to Apollo and they decide to put their original plan on hold. I see Act II ending with Shallott's murder, and Act III beginning with Cutter's Judy Garland transformation as he clicks into his old untamed persona.

In the following diagram—unreadable but intended only as an overview—you can see the reverse cause and effect that we just did for the whole script. The lines show where I've divided the script into acts; I found three, but there could have easily been four. Act I, on the right, is set off in **bold**.

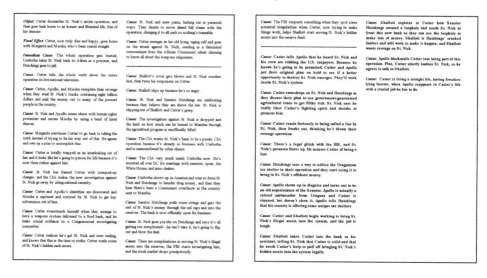

SEQUENCE, PROPOSITION, PLOT FOR ACT I

Next I'll be doing Sequence, Proposition, Plot for Act I, working my way through reverse cause and effect from the the act's ending—the point where Cutter and Apollo put their old plan on hold and decide to go with the flow—to its beginning, which is also the beginning of the entire script. I just worked out the reverse cause and effect at the overall story level; now I have to expand upon it at the act level. I do that by literally going back through the cause and effect I just did, and thinking it through again in more detail for the Act I section. That section is reproduced here as a guide to help me expand upon it below:

Cause: Cutter tells Apollo about his promotion in the ranks and what he overheard, so they put their original plan on hold to see if working inside St. Nick's system offers a better opportunity to destroy him.

Cause: Cutter eavesdrops on St. Nick and Hutchings as they discuss their plan to use government-guaranteed agricultural loans to get filthy rich at the expense of U.S. taxpayers. St. Nick says he really likes Cutter's fighting spirit and decides to promote him.

Cause: Cutter is afraid that his temper has ruined their revenge operation.

Cause: There's a legal glitch with the IRS, and St. Nick's paranoia flares up. He accuses Cutter of being a liar and reacts furiously.

Cause: Hutchings sees a way to exploit the Uruguayan tax shelter, and they start using it to bring in St. Nick's offshore money.

Cause: Apollo shows up in disguise as a banking client and turns out to be an old acquaintance of the Senator. Cutter is stunned to learn that Apollo is actually a retired ambassador from Uruguay, but doesn't show his surprise. Apollo tells Hutchings that his country is offering some unique tax shelters.

Cause: Cutter and Shallott begin working to bring St. Nick's illegal assets into the system; they're stumped on some key issues. Apollo, who's been keeping an eye on things, sees that he needs to act.

Cause: Shallott takes Cutter into the bank as his assistant, convincing St. Nick that Cutter is trustworthy and that he can't bring St. Nick's hidden assets into the system legally without Cutter's help.

Cause: Cutter reluctantly agrees to help destroy St. Nick when Shallott explains St. Nick is vulnerable while trying to go legit as part of a crooked senator's banking scam.

Cause: Apollo blackmails Cutter into being part of this scheme, and reminds him of their utter loathing for St. Nick. Cutter agrees to talk to Shallott.

Cause: Cutter refuses when Apollo drops in on his reformed straight life and tries to enlist him in a perfect crime to destroy St. Nick, their archenemy.

Starting at the top, I'll do reverse cause and effect for Act I, working my way back through what I've already got, using the above as a map and thinking my way through the act, visualizing everything in a little more detail. I also have to check Proposition, Plot for the overall script, specifically the section that pertains to Act I—the initial conflict between Cutter and St. Nick—because there are often actions created in the conflict map that did not exist in the chain of cause and effect.

Reverse Cause and Effect for Act I

What's the Object of Act I? Cutter and Apollo see an expanding opportunity for revenge on St. Nick, as well as a chance to stop a major crime against the American public, so they put their original plan on hold.

What's the Final Effect that demonstrates the Object on-screen with real actors?
Cutter and Apollo realize that a gift may have dropped into their laps:
They know St. Nick's secret plan, and that St. Nick wants to promote
Cutter. This gives them a chance to ruin St. Nick even more spectacularly.

Immediate Cause: Cutter goes to Apollo and tells him what he's just learned.

Cause: Cutter hears St. Nick and Senator Hutchings discussing their plan
to use government-guaranteed agricultural loans to run a scam with an
African dictator: The bank loans him the money, he defaults on the loan,
and the U.S. government repays the bank.

Cause: Cutter eavesdrops on their secure room using two cans and a string.
He hears St. Nick praise Cutter's fighting spirit and suggest promoting him.

Cause: St. Nick gets a grip on himself and cools down. Cutter hides it, but
he's afraid he's ruined the revenge operation.

Cause: St. Nick gets paranoid and accuses Cutter of lying. Cutter, who in
this case actually isn't lying, reacts furiously and lashes out in his own
defense.

Cause: The IRS challenges one of the tax deals through Uruguay. Cutter
says he and Shallott can handle it, that it's not a problem.

Cause: The bank starts using the Uruguayan connection provided by
Apollo, and it's working well.

Cause: Hutchings wants to try the tax shelter and Shallott approves.

Cause: Apollo takes Hutchings aside and tells him about this new tax shelter
that Uruguay has put in place. Hutchings thinks it might work for them.

Cause: Apollo shows up at the office with Hutchings. Cutter, to his surprise, learns that they're old acquaintances: Apollo is a retired ambassador
from Uruguay.

Cause: Cutter and Shallott begin the complex and illegal work of bringing
St. Nick's hidden illicit assets into the system so they can be deposited into
the reserve fund that allows the bank to do business. They're having difficulties doing it.

Cause: Shallott introduces Cutter as his assistant and convinces St. Nick
and Hutchings that he's loyal, reliable, and indispensible.

Cause: Shallott explains to Cutter that St. Nick's part in the deal is to post
the reserve fund required by law to start a bank. To do that, St. Nick has
to bring illegal assets in from hiding, which makes him vulnerable. Cutter
reluctantly agrees to work on it.

Cause: Shallott tells Cutter that Senator Hutchings came to him because he needed a crooked bank examiner to help set up a bank fronted by St. Nick. The bank will take advantage of a banking law loophole that Hutchings slipped into a congressional bill.

Cause: Shallott says he has a once-in-a-lifetime chance to destroy St. Nick. He's waited years for just such an opportunity, because St. Nick killed his only family in the world when he poisoned an entire Kentucky town over a racehorse cheating incident.

Cause: Cutter reluctantly goes with Apollo and is introduced to Shallott.

Cause: Apollo tells Mischa the story about when Cutter stole the Rolling Stones' limo, and Mischa is fascinated and in awe. Cutter caves in and agrees to go with Apollo, because he can't let Mischa learn more of his past, knowing that it will tilt Mischa into a life of crime.

Cause: Cutter won't have anything to do with Apollo, no matter what, even though he utterly despises St. Nick.

Cause: Apollo springs himself on Cutter from out of the blue, pretending to be a sex offender who has just moved into the neighborhood. He threatens Cutter with blackmail if he doesn't join him on a job to destroy St. Nick.

Cause: Cutter has just had a fight with his wife because he's unhappy and she knows he's itching for the old life, even though he swears he isn't.

Cause: Cutter opens the community center he helped organize and reconstruct, and to his surprise he's depressed when the ceremony is over. He takes antidepressants, and Margarita sees him in this slump.

Cause: Cutter is a solid, churchgoing family man, a good husband, and an upright role model to his estranged son. The family heads off to the grand opening of a community center.

The eleven causes in the Act I section of cause and effect for the overall script are expanded here to twenty-three Causes for Act I alone. I thought Act I through further and visualized the next level of detail, inventing some of it on the spot. I'm still free from too much detail—just enough for a little more of the story to come into focus. Notice as well that I am grooming, revising, rethinking, and developing the plot as I go. I'm not a slave to what I already had—that was just a rough map. If it still works, that's fine, but if I stumble onto something new, then I'll run with it.

Proposition, Plot for Act I

The next step is to employ Proposition, Plot for Act I. The *Initial Act of Aggression* for the act will naturally be different from that for the whole script, because we're working with a smaller unit of the script. The proportion, however, is much the same for this Proposition, Plot as it was for the whole script: the set-up about one-quarter to one-third of the way into the act, the touch-off about two-thirds to three-quarters of the way through, and the section called "Plot" constituting the last third or quarter of the act (see diagram on page 160).

Protagonist	**Antagonist**
	Initial Act of Aggression
	Apollo appears, blackmails Cutter into this revenge scam on St. Nick, and takes him to meet Shallott, who explains the job.
Justified Retaliation	
Cutter threatens Apollo and Shallott, saying this has to work or he'll have their heads.	
	Aggravation of the Issue
	St. Nick gets paranoid and accuses Cutter of lying about the handling of the Uruguayan tax shelter.
Precipitating Act	
Cutter stands up fiercely to St. Nick, saying that he is not a liar and will not be called one.	

Central Dramatic Question
Will Cutter make St. Nick back down,
or will St. Nick throw him out or even kill him?

	St. Nick flips out at Cutter and wants to kill him, but manages to cool down a bit.
Cutter panics, sure that he's just ruined his revenge scam, then eavesdrops on St. Nick and Hutchings in their secure room.	
	St. Nick and Hutchings talk about their plan to use government-guaranteed agricultural loans. St. Nick says Cutter has guts and that he's going to promote him.
Cutter and Apollo decide to put their original plan on hold; Cutter's promotion gives them more opportunity to take down St. Nick for good.	

Since St. Nick, the central antagonist, is not in the mix yet, Apollo plays the role of antagonist in the *Initial Act of Aggression*. As for the *Justified Retaliation*, I just invented this one because Cutter didn't have much in the way of retaliation except trying to refuse—not a strong enough action for a protagonist. In other words the tool did its job, suggesting that something stronger was required, and I came up with some conflict on the fly.

DIVIDING THE ACT INTO SEQUENCES

Dividing an act into sequences mirrors the process of dividing a script into acts. Look for natural breaks in the action and determine if they really are acceptable dividing lines. Remember that there are generally two to five sequences in an act (see page 155). A sequence, in turn, usually consists of two to five scenes. Looking at the reverse cause and effect for Act I, I find four sequences, separated by lines in the diagram below:

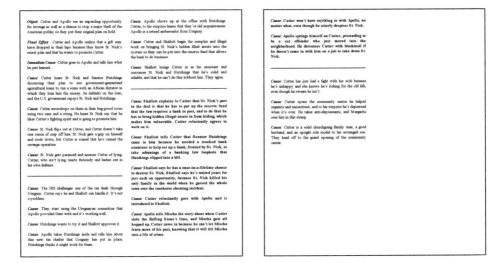

First we have (1) *the opening sequence*, with Cutter doing good works around town and then arguing with his wife. Then we've got (2) *the appearance of Apollo* and the meeting with Shallott. Next is (3) *Cutter going to work at the bank with Shallott*, up through the point where the IRS challenges the Uruguayan tax deal. Finally, there is (4) *the fight between Cutter and St. Nick*, consisting of the overheard plan and Cutter reporting back to Apollo. I'll apply Sequence, Proposition, Plot for the sequence (2) *the appearance of Apollo*, which is set off in bold in the above diagram.

SEQUENCE, PROPOSITION, PLOT
FOR ACT I, SEQUENCE 2

Again I'll be referring to the cause and effect I've just prepared, this time from the Sequence 2 section of the act level (reproduced below). I'll use it as a map as I expand the detail and think through the particulars of the sequence. Remember also to check the section of Proposition, Plot that's pertinent to this sequence (see page 278) for actions that should be included as well. There will tend to be incidents in the cause and effect that aren't in Proposition, Plot, and vice versa. You need to incorporate the full set of actions from the act level into the cause and effect for Sequence 2.

Cause: Shallott explains to Cutter that St. Nick's part in the deal is to post the reserve fund required by law to start a bank. To do that, St. Nick has to bring illegal assets in from hiding, which makes him vulnerable. Cutter reluctantly agrees to work on it.

Cause: Shallott tells Cutter that Senator Hutchings came to him because he needed a crooked bank examiner to help set up a bank fronted by St. Nick. The bank will take advantage of a banking law loophole that Hutchings slipped into a congressional bill.

Cause: Shallott says he has a once-in-a-lifetime chance to destroy St. Nick. He's waited years for just such an opportunity, because St. Nick killed his only family in the world when he poisoned a Kentucky town over a racehorse cheating incident.

Cause: Cutter reluctantly goes with Apollo and is introduced to Shallott.

Cause: Apollo tells Mischa the story about when Cutter stole the Rolling Stones' limo, and Mischa is fascinated and in awe. Cutter caves in and agrees to go with Apollo, because he can't let Mischa learn more of his past, knowing that it will tilt Mischa into a life of crime.

Cause: Cutter won't have anything to do with Apollo, no matter what, even though he utterly despises St. Nick.

Cause: Apollo springs himself on Cutter from out of the blue, pretending to be a sex offender who has just moved into the neighborhood. He threatens Cutter with blackmail if he doesn't join him on a job to destroy St. Nick.

Reverse Cause and Effect for Act I, Sequence 2

Now, constantly referring to the reverse cause and effect above, we'll go back through this sequence section again and develop yet more detail.

What's the Object of this Sequence? Cutter agrees to do the job, but doesn't trust Apollo.

What's the Final Effect that demonstrates this Object on-screen with real actors? Cutter reluctantly agrees, saying he hates St. Nick's guts, but threatens Apollo and Shallott that this better be airtight or he'll come after them— if St. Nick doesn't kill them first.

Immediate Cause: Shallott tells Cutter that Senator Hutchings came to him in need of a crooked bank examiner. Shallott's job is to help St. Nick bring money out of hiding in order to fill a federally required reserve fund. St. Nick is only vulnerable now, but will soon be untouchable. Shallott says that Cutter's special skills are absolutely indispensable in taking down St. Nick.

Cause: Shallott explains that Hutchings slipped a loophole into a law that could make him fabulously wealthy if only he owned a bank. So he got his old friend, St. Nick—who's anxious to go legit—to buy the bank, with the senator as a silent partner. This was Shallott's way in.

Cause: Shallott says St. Nick killed his only family, a severely retarded brother, years ago when he wiped out an entire town in Kentucky over a fixed horse race gone wrong. Shallott had worked with Senator Hutchings, and learned that Hutchings did business with St. Nick, so Shallott stayed tight with Hutchings, hoping for the chance someday to avenge his brother.

Cause: Apollo takes Cutter to meet Shallott, who has a once-in-a-lifetime golden opportunity to wipe out St. Nick and absolutely *must* take this chance.

Cause: Cutter caves in and agrees to listen to Apollo's plan.

Cause: Mischa shows up, and Apollo tells him the story of Cutter hijacking The Rolling Stones in their limousine, and of the legendary rampage the Stones still remember as the single best party they'd ever been to. Mischa is thrilled.

Cause: Cutter says he doesn't trust Apollo and will not help him—period.

Cause: If Cutter doesn't help him, Apollo threatens to tell the police about an unsolved crime Cutter committed. Cutter knows that if Apollo turns him in it'll be his third strike, and he'll go to jail for life.

Cause: Apollo claims he has hit on the perfect way to absolutely devastate St. Nick—a savage criminal who betrayed and murdered Frenchy, their best buddy from prison—and make a fortune in the process. Cutter is moved, but still refuses to have anything to do with the plan.

Cause: Cutter answers the door to find a new neighbor, who says he's a registered sex offender required by law to inform the neighborhood. Cutter tries to be civil, but the guy breaks out laughing—and it turns out to be his old cellmate, Apollo.

Look at how much more detail we're bringing out on this pass. We're getting down to the full particulars of exactly what's happening in this sequence. Notice how I'm actually describing each cause in more detail as I flesh out the specifics, and how I'm *creating* this as I go—it's definitely not script analysis, as it was in Chapter 7. Notice that the *Initial Act of Aggression* for Act I (Cutter threatens Apollo and Shallott) is built into the cause and effect as the *Final Effect* for Sequence 2.

Proposition, Plot for Act I, Sequence 2

One of the things I notice now is that the level of conflict in this sequence could be higher. When starting to use Proposition, I orient myself by asking, "Does this particular sequence build to a fight that erupts two-thirds or three-quarters of the way through? Is there a fight or isn't there? If there is, then what's the fight?" Proposition, Plot is a conflict map, and my job is to set up a conflict and touch it off in order to get the viewers on the edge of their seats. If there isn't any conflict, then I can invent it; any kind of opposition can add Dramatic Action to an act, a sequence, or a scene.

When I look for a possible *Precipitating Act* for this sequence, I find that Cutter doesn't take much of an action that touches off the fight to the finish. He resists Apollo at the beginning and at the end, but there isn't a real confrontation—not enough tension to grip the audience. The reverse cause and effect shows that this sequence was all just Shallott explaining things. They're *interesting* things, but they're only narrative; more conflict would make this sequence much more dramatic. In other words, this sequence is mere Story, not Drama. I need a strong display from Cutter at the point of the *Precipitating Act*. He shouldn't go meekly along, but should be fighting harder for his life. It's fairly routine to use Sequence, Proposition, Plot to up the amperage of an entire sequence—to create conflict where the tool points out that it *could* be.

Now I'll map out Proposition, Plot for Act I, Sequence 2.

Protagonist	**Antagonist**
	Initial Act of Aggression
	Apollo shows up with a way to destroy St. Nick, and blackmails Cutter by telling Mischa about when Cutter stole the Rolling Stones' limo.
Justified Retaliation	
Cutter refuses to have anything to do with Apollo and tries to force him to stop telling Mischa the story.	
	Aggravation of the Issue
	Apollo takes Cutter to Shallott, who explains the opportunity to destroy St. Nick and demands Cutter's help.
Precipitating Act	
Cutter gets furious and tells them St. Nick is so treacherous that they'll get all their families killed.	

Central Dramatic Question

Will Cutter get rid of Shallott and Apollo,
or will they somehow drag him into this job?

	Shallott says that St. Nick already did kill his family, and he wants revenge.
Cutter says he hates St. Nick's guts, too, but he just cannot do the job.	
	Shallott explains that St. Nick is only vulnerable for a limited time and that the scam won't work without Cutter.
Cutter reluctantly agrees, but says he'll kill them both if things go wrong.	

Do you see how Proposition, Plot enhanced this sequence dramatically? This scene now has Dramatic Action; it went from mere Story to actual Drama.

Cutter and Shallott are at each other's throats. They're acting more like desperate criminals than accountants or wimps, and the actors now have so much more to do than merely relay information to the audience. This is a great example of how to dramatize *exposition* (facts that the audience needs to know). It's a gripping, actable scene that will get the audience's attention. This sequence just became stageworthy.

As you work your way down the levels of the structure, from the overall script to each act to each sequence and finally to each scene, doing Sequence, Proposition, Plot for each level, you are constantly grooming each unit. It gives you a chance to keep developing your material as you go—changing, revising, and refining. You're not just robotically using this process; you're an artist who takes the opportunities this tool affords to improve your material on every pass.

DIVIDING THE SEQUENCES INTO SCENES

Next I'll go through Sequence, Proposition, Plot for two scenes in this sequence, which will make them coherent and compelling. These scenes are nested inside the sequence, which is itself tight and dramatic. The sequence is part of the act, which is solid and gripping, and the act is part of the whole script, which has a compelling and coherent structure. Each smaller unit holds up dramatically but is also a mechanical piece of a larger unit so that, presumably, if any of the parts are removed, then the whole will no longer function.

Below is a view of the reverse cause and effect for the sequence, divided by lines into three scenes:

Object: Cutter agrees to do the job, but doesn't trust Apollo.

Final Effect: Cutter reluctantly agrees, saying he hates St. Nick's guts, but threatens Apollo and Shallott, saying that this better be airtight or he'll come after them—if St. Nick doesn't kill them (I took this threat from the Proposition for Act I. It didn't exist in the reverse cause and effect.)

Cause: Shallott tells Cutter that Senator Hutchings came to him because he needed a crooked bank examiner. Shallott's job is to help St. Nick bring money out of hiding in order to buy the bank and fill a required reserve fund. St. Nick is only vulnerable now, but will soon be untouchable. Shallott says that Cutter's special skills are absolutely indispensable in taking down St. Nick.

Cause: Shallott says that Hutchings slipped a loophole into a law that could make him fabulously wealthy if only he owned a bank. He's getting his old friend, St. Nick, who's anxious to go legit, to buy the bank with the Senator as a silent partner. This was Shallott's way in.

Cause: Shallott says he killed Shallott's only family, a retarded brother, years ago when he wiped out an entire town in Kentucky over a crooked horse race. Shallott worked with Senator Hutchings, and then learned that Hutchings did business with St. Nick, so Shallott stayed tight with Hutchings, hoping that he might someday get a chance to avenge his brother.

Cause: Apollo takes Cutter to meet Shallott, who says he has a once-in-a-lifetime golden opportunity to utterly destroy St. Nick, and that he absolutely must take this chance.

Cause: Cutter caves in and agrees to listen to what Apollo wants.

Cause: Mischa shows up and Apollo tells him about how Cutter stole the Rolling Stones' limousine with them in it and went on a legendary rampage that the Stones still remember as the single best party they ever went to. Mischa is thrilled.

Cause: Cutter says he will not help Apollo, period—especially since he doesn't trust him.

Cause: Apollo threatens to tell the police about an unsolved crime Cutter committed if he doesn't help him. Cutter knows that if Apollo turns him in, it'll be his third strike and he'll go to jail for life.

Cause: Apollo says he has the perfect way to absolutely destroy St. Nick, the guy who betrayed and murdered Frenchy, their best buddy from prison. Cutter is moved, but nonetheless refuses to have anything to do with the plan.

Cause: Cutter answers the door and it's a new neighbor saying he's a registered sex offender who's required by law to inform the neighborhood. Cutter tries to be civil, but the guy breaks out laughing and it turns out to be his old cellmate, Apollo.

At first I thought the section that I'm working with might constitute one scene, but it turned out to be two (set in bold in the diagram above). In the first, Apollo is introduced, and in the next, Mischa is learning about his dad's past.

SEQUENCE, PROPOSITION, PLOT
FOR ACT I, SEQUENCE 2, SCENE 1

I'll work my way back through the section below (as well as taking from Proposition, Plot), thinking it through in more detail and using it to build the reverse cause and effect for Scene 1.

Cause: Cutter says he doesn't trust Apollo and will not help him—period.

Cause: If Cutter doesn't help him, Apollo threatens to tell the police about an unsolved crime Cutter committed. Cutter knows that if Apollo turns him in it'll be his third strike, meaning he'll go to jail for life.

Cause: Apollo claims he has hit on the perfect way to absolutely devastate St. Nick—a savage criminal who betrayed and murdered Frenchy, their best buddy from prison—and make a fortune in the process. Cutter is moved, but still refuses to have anything to do with the plan.

Cause: Cutter answers the door to find a new neighbor, who says he's a registered sex offender required by law to inform the neighborhood. Cutter tries to be civil, but the guy breaks out laughing—and it turns out to be his old cellmate, Apollo.

Reverse Cause and Effect for Act I, Sequence 2, Scene 1

I'll develop a little more detail at this stage, but now I'm down to the particulars of exactly who does and says what in this scene. It still has tight cause and effect, and I'm still separating the Necessary from the Unnecessary.

What's the Object of the scene? Cutter is trapped by Apollo.

Final Effect: Apollo has Cutter handcuffed to the wall, and his blackmailing efforts are having some effect.

Immediate Cause: Cutter tries to throw Apollo out, but Apollo clicks handcuffs on him, then threatens to turn him in for an old robbery that's still an open case. He also points out that Cutter owes him—Apollo saved his life in prison.

Cause: Apollo will not go away, and he knows a lot about Cutter's new life.

Cause: Cutter's passion surges at the opportunity to destroy St. Nick, but says he's sworn off that way of life.

Cause: Apollo says he's landed a once-in-a-lifetime chance to destroy St. Nick.

Cause: Apollo takes his disguise off and Cutter panics.

Cause: Cutter is furious, and Apollo's having so much fun that he can't keep up the act and starts laughing.

Cause: Cutter is stunned and doesn't know what to do, and then Apollo starts asking if he has any kids.

Cause: Apollo comes to Cutter's door in disguise, pretending to be a registered sex offender who's just moved into the neighborhood and is required by law to tell each neighbor.

Cause: Apollo has been watching Cutter and decides to make his move now.

Proposition, Plot for Act I, Sequence 2, Scene 1

Protagonist	Antagonist
	Initial Act of Aggression
	A stranger shows up at Cutter's door, saying he's a registered sex offender who's required by law to inform the neighbors. He inquires if Cutter has any kids.
Justified Retaliation	
Cutter becomes furious and tries to get rid of this weirdo.	
	Aggravation of the Issue
	The weirdo turns out to be his old cellmate, Apollo, playing a practical joke.
Precipitating Act	
Cutter flips out and tries to throw Apollo out before he even starts talking.	

Central Dramatic Question
Will Cutter be able to get rid of Apollo, or will Apollo force himself in?

	Apollo says he's found a way to destroy St. Nick—a once-in-a-lifetime opportunity for revenge.
Cutter is moved but refuses, saying he's sworn off all that.	
	Apollo snaps a pair of handcuffs on Cutter and threatens to turn him in for an old crime, which would mean life in jail.
Cutter shouts that he'll kill him, but he's powerless.	

Normally I would write the dialog for each scene right after doing Sequence, Proposition, Plot, but in this case I'll outline the next scene first and then write both scenes together.

SEQUENCE, PROPOSITION PLOT FOR ACT I, SEQUENCE 2, SCENE 2

Again, to build this scene I'm using the relevant cause and effect from the sequence level (below), plus the pertinent section of Proposition, Plot, as a map to help think it through again and expand down to final detail. I'm working from the general to the particular.

Cause: Cutter caves in and agrees to listen to Apollo's plan.

Cause: Mischa shows up, and Apollo tells the story of Cutter hijacking the Rolling Stones in their limousine, and of the legendary rampage the Stones still remember as the single best party they'd ever been to. Mischa is thrilled.

Reverse Cause and Effect for Act I, Sequence 2, Scene 2

Object: Cutter gives in to Apollo's demand.

Final Effect: Cutter is unnerved and says he'll listen to the plan, but that Apollo must shut up now and leave Mischa alone.

Immediate Cause: Mischa is ecstatic and has a million questions.

Cause: Apollo tells Mischa about all the damage they did, the women who got pregnant, and the people who had to leave the country. He brags that the Stones still claim it was the best party they've ever been to.

Cause: Cutter yells at Apollo to shut up. When he won't, Cutter breaks a vase over his head, but this doesn't faze him in the least.

Cause: Apollo offers the joint to Mischa, who wants it but is stared down by his father.

Cause: Apollo is having a blast telling his stories; he lights up a joint.

Cause: Apollo describes how at one point, Cutter was naked on roller skates being pulled down the street by seven naked women also on skates.

Cause: Mischa is stunned that his dad was *that* crazy and asks Apollo to tell him more.

Cause: Apollo tells Mischa that his dad is the world's greatest liar and would steal anything. One time he even stole the Rolling Stones' limo—with them in it—and took them on a legendary three-day bender through five states before the National Guard cornered them at the Canadian border.

Cause: Mischa wants to know about his father's wild side. He says he's heard rumors, but Cutter will never tell him anything.

Cause: Mischa walks in on Apollo and Cutter, and Apollo introduces himself as his father's old friend.

Proposition, Plot for Act I, Sequence 2, Scene 2

Protagonist	Antagonist
	Initial Act of Aggression Apollo tells Mischa about the time time he stole the Rolling Stones' limo took them all on a three-day bender.
Justified Retaliation Cutter tries to force Apollo to shut up and orders Mischa to not listen.	
	Aggravation of the Issue Apollo lights up a joint and offers some to Mischa.
Precipitating Act Cutter orders Mischa not to smoke it, and breaks a vase over Apollo's head to try to stop him.	

Central Dramatic Question
Will Cutter get Apollo to shut up,
or will Apollo tell all to Mischa?

Protagonist	Antagonist
	Apollo says that at one point Cutter was being pulled down the street on roller skates by seven naked girls.
Cutter is screaming, ripping his plumbing apart to get out of the handcuffs.	
	Apollo tells Mischa how Cutter lied his way out of trouble for stealing the limo.
Cutter gives in and says he'll hear Apollo out if he stops talking to Mischa.	

WRITING TWO SCENES BASED ON THE PREVIOUS STRUCTURING

Now I'm able to write the actual scenes based on the structuring I've done with this tool, looking at my blueprint of Sequence, Proposition, Plot for each scene as I write it. I'm not a slave to this structure, but it gives me a shape from which to write that's reliably tight and dramatic. I won't be tempted to introduce anything into this scene that's unnecessary or dramatically flat, but I can also let it breathe. Compare it to jazz—you know the chords you'll be playing, but you can freely improvise on them.

Writing great dialog is such an art form. Probably the best way to learn more about it is to study the masters. Soak yourself in the work of Robert Towne, Billy Wilder, Quentin Tarantino, David Mamet, Preston Sturges, Christopher McQuarrie, Alvin Sargent, Paddy Chayefsky, William Goldman, Ernst Lehman, Howard Koch, Aaron Sorkin, John Huston, the Coen brothers. . . . The list is as long as you and your screenwriting buddies want to make it. Everybody has their favorites.

Remember, this is not the opening scene. Imagine that I've already built the entire opening sequence consisting of several scenes. The scenes I'm inventing here come after the audience has met Cutter, Mischa, and Margarita. Cutter has just had a fight with his wife about her suspicions that he's longing for his old ways, and he's sworn he isn't. He has taken some antidepressants and gone for a bike ride to clear his head. Scene 2 starts when Mischa shows up.

Act I, Sequence 2, Scene 1

EXT. CUTTER'S HOME—DAY
Cutter bikes down the tree-lined street and pulls into his driveway. He waves to the neighbor's Mexican gardener who works among the roses, and goes inside.

The gardener squats down behind a rosebush and, with a furtive look around, strips off his grubby shirt. Underneath is a maroon silk shirt. He steps out of his green work pants and is wearing pleated linen slacks.

He slides off his straw hat and replaces it with a Yankees baseball cap, then slips on a pair of sunglasses and, with another glance around, applies a bushy fake moustache. Crossing the driveway, the gardener rings Cutter's doorbell, holding a rose in his hand.

INT. CUTTER'S LIVING ROOM—DAY
Cutter has just tossed his shirt down the basement stairs when the doorbell rings. He looks down at his tiny biking shorts, then walks over and opens the door.

Standing there is a strange man with a forced smile. He's wearing garish clothes and his posture is terrible. He gazes at Cutter's bare chest uncomfortably, an orange rose held before him like a talisman. Cutter stares at him for a moment too long, then shakes it off.

CUTTER

Can I help you?

MAN

Um, yeah. . . . I. . . . ahh. . . .
(smiling bigger)
I'm new in the neighborhood.

CUTTER
(checking out this weirdo)
That's . . . that's good. Hello, I'm Cutter Haywood.
(holding out his hand)
Pleased to meet you.

MAN

Yes, yes.
(taking his hand)
My name is Jasper Sullivan.

He continues clutching Cutter's hand.

JASPER

I . . . I'm required by law to inform you that I am
a . . . a . . . registered sex offender.

Cutter's eyes go blank, then he looks down, sees he's hardly got anything on and tugs his hand out of Jasper's.

JASPER

I'm so sorry. The police make me do this whenever
I move somewhere new.

Cutter is totally thrown off and stares like a deer caught in headlights.

CUTTER

I . . . that's . . .

JASPER

I know how you must feel. Trying to imagine the
things I must have done, um. . . .
(his smile fading)
Do you mind if I ask you something?

CUTTER

What? Yes . . . okay.

JASPER

Do you have any children?

CUTTER

WHAT?!

JASPER

(his eyes twinkling)
Any teenagers?

Cutter is caught between disbelief and rage.

CUTTER

Who . . . what did you . . . .

He steps up to Jasper, who doesn't pull back, so they stand face to face.
Jasper is intensely aware that Cutter is wearing practically nothing.

CUTTER

Get . . . OUT!

JASPER

I'd just like to speak to your son. Is he here?

Cutter stares in shock.

CUTTER

I don't know who the hell you are, mister, but you
get your ass off my property or I'm calling the cops.
(glaring furiously)
Fact is, I'm calling 'em anyway.

Jasper stares at him dizzily.

JASPER

I . . . just want to play with Mischa.

Cutter is thunderstruck and looks around for something to hurt Jasper with.
He grabs a vase of flowers and turns back to find Jasper giggling.

CUTTER

(hefting the vase)
I'm warning you, buster!

Jasper bursts out laughing and can't stop. Cutter stares warily at him, now
really not knowing what to think.

As Cutter watches, the guy peels off the moustache, removes the glasses, pulls off the baseball cap, and straightens up.

CLOSE ON Cutter's face as his pupils dilate instantly and he draws in a sharp breath.

> JASPER
> You guessed it, buddy boy.

Cutter cannot speak, but a full spectrum of emotions flicker across his face, most of them fear-related.

> JASPER
> Listen, listen. I know what you're gonna say.

> CUTTER
> Apollo. . . .
> *(snapping out of it)*
> NO, NO, NO, NO, NO!! GET OUT!!
> Get out of my house this INSTANT!!
> *(shoving him toward the door)*
> I don't wanna hear it!

> APOLLO
> *(laughing again)*
> Man, the look on your face! It was priceless!

He screams with laughter and Cutter can't help but crack a smile himself. Cutter recovers quickly and glares at Apollo, who turns serious.

> APOLLO
> Listen, man, I got a way to take down St. Nick,
> big-time. Payback for Frenchy.

That gets Cutter's attention and it stops him. He sets the vase down on a shelf, and wrestles with his emotions. Then his eyes harden and he turns coldly on Apollo.

> APOLLO
> Bastard's trying to go straight and buy a bank.
> He's vulnerable right now and we could totally
> finish him off. This kind of opportunity only
> happens in fairy tales.

> CUTTER
> Every word out of your mouth is a friggin' fairy tale!
> Listen, I loved Frenchy as much as anybody . . .

more, but I DO NOT do that stuff anymore. I've
sworn off it . . . straight and true. You don't have the
least idea what my life is like now.

> APOLLO
> (*chuckling*)
> Sure I do . . . you survive on Prozac, sleeping pills, and
> allergy medicine. You're tired, depressed, and feeling
> trapped. You got therapy, you got hives, and . . . hell,
> you used to be Superman himself. Now look at—

> CUTTER
> Goddamn you! I will not—

He goes to raise his hand to make a point, but there's a clicking sound at his
wrist and his arm stops short.

Cutter looks down and finds himself handcuffed to the radiator pipe. He yanks
hard, but he's trapped. Apollo grins happily at him and strides to the mantle,
where he pours himself a tall shot of brandy and gulps it down.

> CUTTER
> I'll kill you! I swear I will!

> APOLLO
> Good. That's great. Then we're in agreement. Now
> maybe we can have ourselves a civilized conversation.

> CUTTER
> Once upon a time you were my best friend, but
> I never trusted you and I sure as hell don't now.
> The answer is no. N-O.

> APOLLO
> (*pouring another brandy*)
> Look, we can do this the hard way where I call
> Detective Henries and remind him about a certain
> missing supercomputer. The statute of limitations
> still ain't run out on that sucker, ya know? Something
> about it being government property and all. Three
> strikes and you're a lifer . . . pally.
> (*smiling expansively*)
> Or we can do it the easy way . . . the good old way,
> ya know? Besides, you still owe me your life.
> Remember that, dickwad?

Cutter's eyes go wide. As he contemplates this, the door opens and Mischa enters.

Act I, Sequence 2, Scene 2

> MISCHA
>
> Who are you?

He spots his dad handcuffed to the wall in tiny red spandex shorts and stares in amazement.

> MISCHA
>
> Dad?

> APOLLO
>
> I'm a buddy of your pop's from back in the day.
> We're just catching up on old times.
>   *(smiling big)*
> You must be Mischa. I'm Apollo Marseilles.
> Damn glad to meet you.
>   *(they shake)*
> Heard a lot about you, sonny.

> MISCHA
>
> Where do you know dad from?

> APOLLO
>
> We were cellmates.

> MISCHA
>   *(cringing; not sure he heard right)*
> Soul mates?

Apollo laughs out loud and shoves Mischa playfully.

> APOLLO
>
> No man . . . CELLmates. In the joint together for
> eight years. Federal prison, ya know?

Cutter cringes as Mischa's eyes go wide and a mischievous grin lights up his face.

> MISCHA
>
> *Really*? Oh my god . . . what was he like back then?
> He'll never tell me *anything*. I've heard rumors and—

> CUTTER
>
> DON'T! Mischa don't! You don't want to know.

Apollo puts an arm around Mischa and they turn to face Cutter.

                    APOLLO
Come on now. I think it's important for a son to
know about his daddy. Especially when you were
in stir for so much of his childhood. This is what
he missed out on.
          (pulling Mischa around)
Now your old man is flat-out the wildest mother . . .
He was CRAY-ZEE! Could lie like a rattlesnake and
steal the stripes off a zebra.
          (laughing)
Hell, man, one time he even stole the Rolling Stones'
limousine . . . with them IN it!

                    CUTTER
Apollo shut UP! Mischa, NO!

                    MISCHA
Dude! The Stones are my favorite band of all time!

                    APOLLO
          (slapping him on the shoulder)
Well they're your dad's, too.
          (winking at Cutter)
See? You two are bonding already.

                    CUTTER
Shut the hell up! You—

                    APOLLO
          (laughing; to Mischa)
They all went off on this legendary three-day bender
through five states before the National Guard finally
cornered them at the Canadian border.

                    MISCHA
I can't believe it. Dad?

Cutter stares daggers at Apollo, whose eyes glitter like sparklers. He pulls out
a fat joint and lights it up, then takes a big hit and offers it to Mischa.

                    APOLLO
          (holding his breath)
It's killer.

NO, NO! DON'T! Goddamn you Apollo!
Mischa don't smoke that!

He frantically searches for anything to murder Apollo with and finds the vase.
He whips it at Apollo and it smashes over his head, but that doesn't faze him
in the least. Apollo turns and shoots him a demented look.

APOLLO

Come on, pardner. Trying to tell a story here, okay?
(taking another toke; to Mischa)
At one point on that trip they found your old man
roller-skating buck naked down Chicago Avenue
being pulled by seven naked girls on roller skates.
Cutter had on a Zorro mask, with a whip in one hand
and a bottle of Jack in the other, singing "Sharp
Dressed Man" at the top of his lungs. Damn police
couldn't catch him—

Cutter screams like a trapped animal. He's ripping the radiator pipe down
through the ceiling but still can't get free. Apollo takes another hit and blows
the smoke at Mischa, who breathes it in, grinning.

APOLLO

When it was all over they'd done $4 million worth
of damage; got nine girls pregnant; six people had
to leave the country, including Keith Richards;
and the Mayor of Cleveland quit his job and ran
off with Keith to be his assistant guitar tech.
(taking another hit)
The Stones still claim it was the single wildest party
they've ever been to.

An expression of criminal glee fills Mischa's face and he looks over at his dad,
awestruck.

MISCHA

WOW! And dad went to jail for that?

APOLLO

Hell no! He lied his way out of it. Weren't you listening? He is *by far* the best liar ever. And that's why I
need him now.

Cutter is bashing his head through the sheetrock.

APOLLO
(*blowing smoke on Mischa*)
But hell, that was a just harmless stunt. You want to
hear about the *really* bad stuff he—

Cutter screams bloody murder, cutting Apollo off.

CUTTER
Okay, okay! I'll do it! I'll listen to your plan,
goddamn you, Apollo! Just stop!

APOLLO
Tell me you love me and I'll take off the handcuffs.

CUTTER
Just get me out of here! I'll do whatever you friggin'
want!

APOLLO
Tell me you love me.

Cutter stands there in his tiny red spandex shorts, his head covered with white
plaster. Tears stream down his face, cutting tracks through the white powder.

CUTTER
Okay . . . I love you.
(*furious*)
Now get me the hell out of here!

Apollo slips the joint to Mischa and grabs a raincoat off a hook behind the
door. He unlocks the cuffs, wraps the raincoat around Cutter, and escorts him
outside as a euphoric Mischa takes a hit.

CUTTER
Mischa, go to church!

So that's the process: I structured everything from the whole script down to
the scene level using Sequence, Proposition, Plot, and then I wrote the scenes
with dialog and stage direction. I had a blast writing those scenes. You can see
they're well written, have good flow, and propel the plot forward. They're lean
yet alive, and they clearly implement the structure that I laid out for them,
without being a merely robotic execution. I discovered all kinds of things and
got to really play around as I wrote the actual scenes, even surprising myself
by how the dialog finally materialized. I didn't feel constricted by the structure I'd put together, but I did feel organized and in control, which is a nice

way to write. In *The Philosophy of Dramatic Principle and Method,* Price sums it up beautifully:

> When you finally arrive at the dialog fresh detail will occur to you as you write. Inspiration accompanies you at every step if you use the proper method of work. If something new did not constantly arise in your mind you would weary of the composition. This same pleasure which you experience is communicated to the audience.

Earlier in the book I mentioned the synchronicity or serendipity that can occur when writing, and an interesting illustration of this happened when I was coming up with dialog for these scenes. As I worked, I was listening to the radio at about 3:00 A.M., and in the section at the end where the handcuffed Cutter finally relents, I heard the DJ on the radio say, "Tell me you love me and I'll take off the handcuffs." I wasn't sure if I was hallucinating—it was so impossibly perfect for the scene, and I was loopy from exhaustion. But then the DJ said it again and I thought, "Wow, that is insane. What perfect dialog for this spot," so I used it. It came out of nowhere and was truly a gift. I couldn't conceivably have made up that line of dialog, but it came to me unexpectedly and it works wonderfully.

DIAGRAMS OF SEQUENCE, PROPOSITION, PLOT FOR *GOOD OLD ST. NICK*

Now let's get an overview of all the Sequence, Proposition, Plot work that we just did for *Good Old St. Nick*, starting on page 269.

Sequence, Proposition, Plot for the overall script of *Good Old St. Nick:*

Sequence, Proposition, Plot for Act I:

Sequence, Proposition, Plot for Act I, Sequence 2:

Sequence, Proposition, Plot for Act I, Sequence 2, Scene 1, followed by the dialog:

EXT. CUTTER'S HOME · DAY

Cutter bikes down the tree-lined street and pulls into his driveway. He waves to the neighbor's Mexican GARDENER, who works amongst the roses and goes inside.

The gardener squats down behind a rose bush, and with a furtive look around, strips off his grubby shirt. Underneath is a maroon silk shirt. He steps out of his green work pants and is wearing pleated linen slacks.

He slides off his straw hat and replaces it with a Yankees baseball cap, then slips on a pair of sunglasses. And with another glance around applies a fake bushy moustache. Crossing the driveway, the gardener rings Cutter's doorbell, holding a rose in his hand.

INT. CUTTER'S LIVING ROOM · DAY

Cutter has just tossed his shirt down the basement stairs when the bell rings. He looks down at his ring biking shorts and then goes over and opens the door.

Standing there is a strange man with a forced smile. He's wearing garish clothes and his posture is terrible. He paces at Cutter's bare chest uncomfortably, an strange rose held before like a talisman.

Cutter stares at him for a moment too long, then shakes it off.

          CUTTER
    Yes. Can I help you?

          MAN
    Um, y'eh... I ah...
    I'm new in the neighborhood.

          CUTTER
    (checking out this weirdo)
    That's... that's good. Hello. I'm Cutter.
    Hey you'd.
    (holding out his hand)

Sequence, Propostion, Plot for Act I, Sequence 2, Scene 2, followed by the dialog:

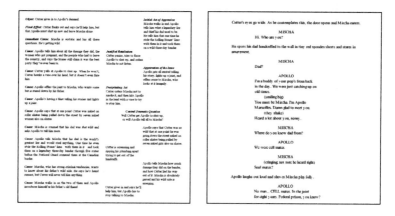

Next let's look at Sequence, Proposition, Plot as a pyramid diagram, an architectural map of the plot's structure (opposite page). It shows the whole script at the top, the acts below that, with the sequences and scenes farther down. Focus on the overlay of what I've just completed for the *Good Old St. Nick* script. I did Sequence, Proposition, Plot for the whole script; for Act I; then for Act I, Sequence 2; and then for the first two scenes in that sequence. You can see that there's a lot more to do in order to work out all the mechanics of the complete script, but I've definitely laid a solid foundation.

To complete the structuring of *Good Old St. Nick*, I would have to apply Sequence, Proposition, Plot to Acts II and III, and then to the remaining sequences. Next I would do the same for the first scene and write the dialog, then for the second scene, writing the dialog after that, and so forth. I would continue on, structuring all the scenes and then writing each one out with dialog and stage directions, until I ended up with a working draft of the screenplay. This would represent a considerable amount of work and is beyond the scope of this book, but the process would be a continuation—and an exact mirror—of what we've already done with Sequence, Proposition, Plot in developing the script, act, sequence, and scene levels.

Notice that we've done exactly what Aristotle was talking about when he said that in constructing a plot, the writer "should first sketch its general outline, and then fill in the episodes and amplify in detail." And Price's quote (see page 162) makes complete sense now: "You saw that each act was about one thing, each scene about one thing, and that each step was a development toward one given end. Following this out, you have seen that a play is a Unit made up of other Units." It really clicks now, hearing Grebanier say, "If we ourselves were asked to whom we were indebted for the basis of our ideas about playwriting, we should have to answer, 'Aristotle and Price.'" That's especially true when you realize that applying Sequence, Proposition, Plot to a script with a powerful dilemma already built into it means you're developing a solid, integrated dramatic structure for a story that's already inherently dramatic. It's crucial to bear in mind that all these advanced structural tools still don't mean anything if your original premise doesn't pass the "So what?" test. It may be the most perfectly structured thing ever, but if the story is lame, then it's going to be . . . BORING!

After reading Price and Krows for almost three years, I finally hit on this key tool. I can still feel the electrifying jolt of that eureka moment. When Price summed up the process of Sequence, Proposition, Plot, I literally saw a light bulb. I had to piece it together with what Krows said about double proposition and then add to it, but this is very much what Price described in 1908. I'm the only person in the world who teaches Sequence, Proposition, Plot, and you won't even find it in Price's books—I had to work like a dog to synthesize it, as though I were tearing gold ore from the ground and extracting the precious metal.

I've worked with this tool non-stop for decades, constantly refining it both through my own writing and by working hands-on with the many thousands of writers I've taught, including story development executives from all the major Hollywood studios. Everybody *loves* this tool, but development executives go bananas over it because they immediately recognize how incredibly

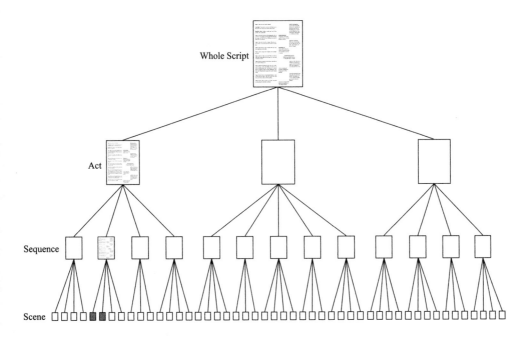

useful it is. They're constantly bombarded with screenplays from the mediocre to the god-awful—the results of poor structure and lack of craft—and these execs consistently say that Sequence, Proposition, Plot is the most advanced development tool in the film industry. It is my genuine pleasure to share it with you.

Post Script

Congratulations on finishing this book. It's a lot of information to wrap your brain around, but I tried to make *Writing a Great Movie* an entertaining read and I hope that sweetens the hard work necessary to acquire a solid working knowledge of these tools. I also tried to make it as truly practical and usable as possible, so that it presents not just theory but highly functional tools and techniques that you can really utilize on a daily basis. Fancy abstract ideas may sound great in a lecture hall, but if you can't go home and build a better screenplay with them, then they're just so much hot air. This book is designed as a practical working manual for the dramatist, and with plenty of hard work, focus, and persistence, you can definitely make these tools your own.

Let's briefly review the Key Tools presented in *Writing a Great Movie*. We started with Dilemma, Crisis, Decision & Action, and Resolution, all of which assist you in both shaping your plot and rendering it dramatic. Theme gets right to the core of what your story's really about—its heart and soul. The 36 Dramatic Situations provide a full spectrum of dynamic elements that can energize your storytelling and trigger fresh ideas. The Enneagram offers a rich resource for creating and developing complex, realistic characters. Good Research can meet you halfway with unexpected story material, and Brainstorming helps you to explore possibilities and open up new story dimensions.

The Central Proposition pulls all your story elements together to form the nucleus of your script, and reinforces the primary conflict. Finally, Sequence, Proposition, Plot is a sophisticated structural tool that guides you through the actual plot construction process. Starting with a master plan, you systematically develop each unit of your script, applying the tool first to the overall story and then to each act, each sequence, and each scene. The result is a structurally unified architectural map of your screenplay, which helps create consistent, coherent, compelling Dramatic Action—the Holy Grail of dramatic writing.

Whether or not *Good Old St. Nick* turns out to be a great movie, I can't tell. At this point it's just the skeleton of a work in progress, but it does give you a comprehensive look at the process in action—a demonstration of how to really use these tools to build your own screenplays. Hearing me think out loud as I developed this story will help instill in you the thought process and habits of a working screenwriter.

MASTER THE CRAFT OF THE DRAMATIST

If you have the burning desire to master the skills in this book, then you should spend at least a year making a professional study of it. When I first started out, I spent three solid years reading Price and Krows before I began writing at all; this gave me a solid foundation in the dramatic craft. Learn the tools inside out, backward and forward. You should be able to disassemble and reassemble all the films in this book the same way a soldier can take his or her rifle apart and put it back together in the dark. My book *Script Analysis: The Godfather, Tootsie, Blade Runner* takes those three screenplays apart in full detail and can help you further substantiate your knowledge of my process. You can buy it on my Web site (www.DevelopmentHeaven.com), or at Amazon (www.amazon.com). You can also get DVDs of my courses through *Creative Screenwriting* magazine's Web site (www.CreativeScreenwriting.com). I'd recommend my 5-DVD set, in which I teach a full-day course and develop an original script on the spot using the Key Tools.

Practice these tools over and over until you become completely comfortable with them and the skills become second nature. Learn to create, develop, and structure a screenplay from a raw premise. Learn to read a script and articulate its strengths and weaknesses, and then build upon its strengths and create solutions for the weaknesses. This is a craft, the same as shoemaking, and the master shoemaker had to study every aspect of his trade, practicing long and hard before he became a master craftsman. In *The Analysis of Play Construction and Dramatic Principle*, Price advises on the process of learning the craft of writing:

> Do not become impatient at going over the same ground a number of times. To him who understands there is constant variety and newness of interest. The deeper you go the more interested you will become. The more facile and correct your work the greater the gratification to you. You will note the gradual acquirement of thinking in drama. A dramatic study requires that you become acquainted first with each principle singly and then in combination with other principles. When you have them firmly fixed in mind and come to apply them to original work you will not be disturbed as to uncertainty as to meaning and application.

Learn the underlying principles behind the tools, as well as the specific application of each particular technique. Practice using each tool diligently until you have a real facility with it. This will pay off in your writing, because your mastery of the process will allow you to exploit the full power of the tool while keeping your focus on your story. Use the tools precisely; don't muddy the distinctions they create if they become inconvenient, because then you lose their power. Dramatic writing is notoriously elusive, and you need every edge you can get. Take all the energy that goes into rewrites and put it into engineering your script properly before you write it. Strive to be one of the very best screenwriters ever. Don't do anything by halves.

Here's another quote from Price (from the same book) about the learning process:

> This period of learning the nature of principle is a necessary
> preparation for actual playwriting. The preliminary work
> required is in effect playwriting itself, for the same processes
> of thought are employed. During this period there should be
> no interruption in the study. One should let it take hold of
> him like a fever that runs its course. One should saturate
> himself with the intelligent analytical reading of plays. In
> every education a point is reached where one can abandon
> his research and can proceed with confidence in applying
> what he has mastered in theory.

Learn the habits of mind of a trained dramatist. Remember, the core of your job is to turn Story into Drama—to turn an interesting narrative into a compelling dramatic plot—whatever the genre. Work from the general to the specific, because if the big picture doesn't work, then the details of the story won't mean anything. Learn to work structurally, so that you train yourself to be able to see architectural blueprint of a plot.

Separate the Necessary from the Unnecessary—it's one of the underlying principles of writing good drama, and it will free you from the profusion of unnecessary detail. It's so easy to get gummed up in material that is not pertinent to your immediate task at hand, which is usually hard enough on its own. Always bear in mind that a movie is a performance medium—actors must be able to act out your story in a way that will grip an audience. Consider studying acting, even if you just audit a class. You're writing for actors, so think about learning that aspect of your craft. It really helps.

Keep a sense of proportion as you work. It will come in handy if you get lost. Think about where you are in the story and where you're headed. Make a quick chart of the script—are you halfway through? Three-quarters of the way? Remember that it's the protagonist's story, so keep making your way back to his or her trajectory. This will give you a compass—a sense of direction. Constantly evaluate and adjust as you go. Stand back from what you're creating and give it a good, hard, objective look. On a scale of 1 to 10, how powerful is it? What works and what doesn't? Your screenwriting tools can help you articulate what the problem is and assist you in creating solutions.

Go back and forth between intuition and logic, between rapture and control, between total fearlessness and meticulous attention to detail. Remember, it's all about the audience. Focus specifically on the mood you want the audience to be in when your movie is over. This will clarify a lot for you. Billy Wilder said, "An audience is never wrong. An individual member of it may be an imbecile, but a thousand imbeciles together in the dark—that is critical genius." Keep this in mind. Christopher McQuarrie, who wrote *The Usual Suspects*, says he has tremendous respect for the intelligence of the audience, which is certainly borne out by that film.

BECOME A GREAT STORYTELLER

Immerse yourself in storytelling—all forms of it. Write every day. Read as much as you can. Listen to books on tape while you drive or exercise. Read the best screenwriters, playwrights, novelists, and other great writers. Study mythology and legend—they're at the core of all storytelling.

Turn off mindless television. Learn to concentrate. When you're writing, turn off the e-mail and Internet on your computer and focus. Be on the lookout for great story ideas. The more you work as a storyteller, the more you'll become sensitive to catchy ideas that swirl about you all the time. Keep a list of story ideas. Always carry pen and paper so that you don't lose fleeting ideas or story fragments. Sometimes a clever observation can lead to an entire screenplay, but it can be lost as quickly as a dream.

Respect your creative instincts. If you've got a hunch, run with it. That's part of the fun of writing. If it turns out to be wrong, you will see that soon enough and will be able to correct it, but if you control everything too rigidly, you'll never stumble into unexpected dimensions. Sometimes your subconscious will produce a left-handed idea that may seem utterly crazy at first, but which turns out to be ingenious, fresh, and dynamic.

Know how to get away from the intensity of your work altogether when you need to. Turn off your brain and take a walk. Give your subconscious a chance to percolate. Go to a coffee shop with a blank notebook, forget everything, and see what pops into your head about the story you're working on. Read a novel just for fun to energize your storytelling. Take the entire day off and go to the movies—you can see five movies in one day. After all, movies are your job. Go to have fun. Go to get away from writing. Go as a kid who wants a great ride. Try sitting in the front row—it's like being *in* the movie. Develop a sense of play. Rekindle that magic and wonder at hearing incredible stories around a campfire when you were a child. Let your imagination run free. You're a screenwriter and it's your *job* to dream. Allow the wild animal in you to charge ahead with your plot and land you in a heap of trouble. If you're not in over your head, then you're just playing it safe.

Explosive creativity is a must for a screenwriter. Always explore the extremes. You can always ratchet it back down to what fits the context of your story, but you might hit on something brilliant that works wonderfully in an unexpected way. Don't be afraid of chaos—you can always use your tools to establish order no matter where you end up. Try to violate your own story-telling patterns. Observe your tendencies and throw a monkey wrench into them once in a while. Always, always start with a great premise; building on a lousy idea is known inside the film industry as "polishing a turd." Notice what you crave when you go out to the movies on a Saturday night, and bring that back to your own writing. Be bold. Get crazy. Remember that the keyword in the entertainment industry is *outrageousness*. Don't let anybody tell you to think small. Cultivate a sense of adventure. It's the movies, damn it!

Think about why you became a writer in the first place. What hunger does it satisfy? How does it tap into your deepest passions? Think about what people are fascinated with in life—what people are drawn to like moths to a flame. The creation and destruction of life, major transitions, control, danger, breaking points, dynamic characters, incredible stories, love, loneliness, energy, and tales with great heart—these are some of the issues that draw people. Write about them—and live them, too! Don't get stuck writing to the exclusion of everything else. Get out there and live a real life with everything you've got, because that's where you'll find the best stories. And if you're getting into the screenwriting business for the money, then do yourself a huge favor and try real estate or something sensible instead. The film industry is a brutal arena, and unless you love movies more than anything, then find another way—any other way—to make a living.

MANAGE YOUR REWRITE PROCESS

When rewriting, let some time elapse before you go back a script—at least a few weeks. You want to forget it as much as possible by the time you return to it. *Always* read a script in one sitting. That's the way you see a movie, and it's the only possible way to evaluate a screenplay properly. I read about a play-wright who, when he was going to read a script, would take a hot bath and dress up in a tuxedo as though he were going out for a night at the theater. He would then read the play in that frame of mind.

Don't give much weight to the opinions of people who *must* tell you that your script is good (your mother, for instance). Get feedback from people who aren't afraid to tell you the truth, because it's very hard to have any objectivity about a script by the time you're done with it. Be brutally tough on yourself, too, because everybody else in the film industry is certainly going to be.

Be willing to slash and burn your own material. Tossing your darlings is notoriously hard to do, but sometimes it can do the trick. Your job as a screenwriter demands that you visualize the story clearly and then work hard to communicate that in writing—but this can lead to overwriting. Know how to prune your script back to the necessities. Continue separating the Necessary from the Unnecessary by stripping out every single word that doesn't absolutely need to be in the script. Keep it simple and clear, and keep it moving forward. Read the best screenwriters and you'll see how minimal most scripts are. Search for "free movie scripts" on Google (www.google.com) or another search engine. You can download thousands of them.

If your screenplay is running long and you don't know what to cut, print an extra copy and do a "throwaway cut." Go through this additional copy and cut like a maniac, tossing anything and everything, telling yourself you can literally throw this copy away when you're done with it. In the throwaway cut, nothing is precious; you can skip the endless internal debate and hairsplitting that accompanies so much of the editing process. If something strikes you as a possible cut, just chuck it overboard and move on. When you get to end, start another pass on the real script. Now you're in the zone and will be more able to cut your own work because the throwaway cut got you loosened up. It's a great trick, and on many occasions I've seen 20 sacrosanct pages vanish from a fat script.

However, be careful about a screenplay getting away from you in the rewrite process. The story can lose its original spark as it gradually morphs into another identity. Check in occasionally with the original idea for your plot, because that's what grabbed you by the throat and made you write this script in the first place. Sometimes that first draft has a raw, living energy—an unbridled freedom—which can easily get lost in the rewrites as it slowly becomes domesticated and homogenized.

SOME HELPFUL HINTS FOR THE PROFESSIONAL SCREENWRITER

Mastering your craft and becoming a great writer is just part of the game in the film industry. In order to make it, you also have to be good at the business end. Learn who's who. Subscribe to the *Hollywood Reporter* or *Variety* and read it every day. Don't write for what you think the market wants, but write the movie that *you* want to see—the movie that you're unstoppably passionate about. This business already has all the standard rehashings of the normal film stories. What it lacks is original, creative storytelling with a distinctive voice.

Make sure that your script submissions are very clean, with excellent spelling and a crisp appearance. You want to come across as a professional writer, and scripts laden with typos send the wrong message right away, even at a subconscious level. If you can't spell (and I know geniuses who can't spell to save their lives), then hire a proofreader to give your script a read. You can get one for $10 an hour, and it's worth it to clean up the typos. Make sure that every aspect of your script is in tip-top shape before you show it to industry professionals, because they won't look at it twice.

There are a number of useful Web sites for screenwriters. The Internet Movie Database (www.imdb.com) is a fantastic database about produced movies and the people involved (actors, directors, producers, writers, crew). ShowBIZ Data (www.showbizdata.com) is a good source of entertainment industry news. MovieBytes (www.moviebytes.com) has the lowdown on scriptwriting contests. Screenwriter's Utopia (www.screenwritersutopia.com) is a good central site and an entrance to a host of other sites. At InkTip (www.inktip.com) you can pay to get your treatment read by producers, agents, and managers who are seeking hot screenplays. ScriptShark (www.scriptshark.com) provides a service in which they evaluate your screenplay for a fee; if they like it, they'll even show it to agents and managers. The Writers Store (www.writersstore.com) offers books on everything you need to navigate your way in the screenwriting business. If you want to study dialog further, Hal Croasmun teaches online classes on subtext in dialog at his Web site ScriptforSale.com (www.scriptforsale.com). David Freeman's seminar has a lot of solid tips about dialog (www.beyondstructure.com), and Karl Iglesias has a good chapter about getting more emotion into dialog in his book *Writing for Emotional Impact.* I do script analysis for a fee and you can contact me through my Web site, www.DevelopmentHeaven.com.

One of the most crucial things to do as a professional writer is to back up your material on several different mediums *every single time* you change anything. People who are new to computers don't know how utterly life and death this is because they haven't yet lost six months of work. The rule of thumb in computers is: Never trust a hard drive, and the bigger they are, the harder they crash. Backing up is not difficult. Zip disks are cheap, data sticks are awesome, and a number of spots provide free memory storage. Google's Gmail gives you 2 gigabytes of free memory, so you can store your screenplays there safely. You have to be invited to Gmail, but anyone can send you an invitation. Yahoo (www.yahoo.com) gives you 30 megabytes of free, password-protected memory in their section called "Briefcase." When I'm done working for the day, I send the current version into Yahoo. Every few days I put my work onto a data stick, too. The rule is to back your stuff up in three different places, and always make sure that one of them is out of the house, in case of a fire. Don't take backing up lightly, and never be lazy about it. You could be cut off at the knees in a flash.

Invest in a proper high-end surge protector ($30–$50) so that your computer doesn't get zapped—a great way to lose everything on your hard drive. Also, *always* print out what you've written. Otherwise it's just electrons stored in silicone, and that ain't much if things get squirrelly—and believe me they can, and they will. A hard copy is real and you can hold it in your hands.

A FINAL ASSIGNMENT

Here's a hardcore assignment for you. Buy the movie *Hostage*, starring Bruce Willis, and take it apart—right down to the last nut and bolt—using everything you've learned in this book. It's a thriller with a brutally intense dilemma. Figure it out and write about it. Write about every aspect of Bruce Willis's dilemma until you have nothing left to say. What's his Crisis? His Decision & Action? His Resolution? What's the Theme? Which of the 36 Dramatic Situations are most active in this film? Define all the characters using the Enneagram. Lay out the Central Proposition. Apply Sequence, Proposition, Plot to the whole script. Divide it into acts, and do Sequence, Proposition, Plot for each act. Then break the acts down into sequences, and the sequences into scenes, doing Sequence, Proposition, Plot for each of them as you go.

This is a professional-level assignment, but even if you're a beginner, go for it. You can absolutely do it. The training you've received in this book will help you through the process. If you're having trouble with a specific tool, then go back and review the chapter on it. You may have to read and digest *Writing a Great Movie* several times to acquire true facility with these tools, but it's doable. Refuse to be intimidated. It's just movie structure, not brain surgery. Taking *Hostage* apart will give you hands-on experience in breaking down a script. All my tools work equally well for both script construction and script analysis, and you use them the same way for each process. If you're stumped, then get together with others who've read this book and figure it out as a team. Don't be afraid to spend several months on it. How long do you think it took me to acquire world-class expertise on the six films that I dissect in this book? It means you're going to have to watch the movie many, many times. Here's a hint: Watch it backward at different speeds to figure out the reverse cause and effect. It will be ferocious hard work, but the film is worthy of repeated viewings and it will give you some practical work with these tools. And have fun—you're in the movie business, baby!

NOW GET OUT THERE
AND WRITE A GREAT MOVIE!

The entire film industry is starving for outstanding screenplays. I was in a major producer's office when she pointed at huge floor-to-ceiling shelves full of screenplays and asked (or more accurately, begged), "Have you seen anything good? *Any* good scripts? None of those are worth a nickel." Being surrounded by bad screenplays is equivalent to being out in a life raft on the ocean, with trillions of gallons of water everywhere but none of it drinkable. If you combine great storytelling with substantial craft as a dramatist, then you have a good shot at becoming a hot screenwriter. So go for it. Take everything you've got and put up there on the big screen. Write a great movie!

Index